REDEEMED!

REDEEMED!

ESCHATOLOGICAL REDEMPTION AND THE KINGDOM OF GOD

BOYD HUNT

BROADMAN
&HOLMAN
PUBLISHERS

Nashville, Tennessee

©Copyright 1993 Broadman & Holman Publishers
All Rights Reserved
4210-46
IBSN:0-8054-1046-5
Dewey Decimal Classification: 234.3
Subject Heading: SALVATION / THEOLOGY
Library of Congress Catalog Number: 92-31878
Printed in the United States of America

Unless otherwise noted, Scripture quotations are taken from the Holy Bible, *New International Version*, copyright © 1973, 1978, 1984 by International Bible Society.

Scripture quotations marked (KJV) are taken from the *King James Version* of the Bible.

Scripture quotations marked (RSV) are taken from the *Revised Standard Version of the Bible*, copyrighted 1946, 1952, © 1971, 1973.

Hunt, Boyd, 1916—
    Redeemed! : eschatological redemption and the kingdom of God / Boyd Hunt.
        p. cm.
    Includes bibliographical references and index.
    ISBN 0-8054-1046-5 :
    1. Holy Spirit. 2. Kingdom of God. 3. Christian life — 1960–
4. Church. 5. Eschatology. I. Title
BT121.2.H83 1993
231.7'2—dc20   92-31878
                                                                      CIP

To Beth, Bill, and Anne

Contents

Redemption & creation are Not synonyms

Foreword

Redemption is the Bible's key concept. The term summarizes in a single word the entire biblical message. Given the standpoint of biblical revelation, the triune Creator God is, above all else, Redeemer. On this basis, the theology of redemption which follows represents the heart of biblical proclamation.

At issue today in defining redemption is the distinction between redemption and creation.[1] The problem is that while some writers stress the difference, others neglect or simply reject it. To disregard the fact that the two terms are not synonyms, however, is to alter significantly how one views a number of *central biblical truths*. It is to ignore the distinctions between:

- The church and the world;

- Special revelation and general revelation;

- What the Bible teaches and what non-Christian secular philosophical, psychological, and sociological authorities teach;

- A creation redeemed through trust in Jesus Christ and a fallen creation in rebellion against Christ;

- Saved sinners and lost sinners;

- Church outreach emphasizing both evangelism and social action and church outreach emphasizing social action without evangelism;

- An eternal heaven and an eternal hell.

Central biblical truths

Before the objection is raised that such distinctions import into Christian theology dualistic notions foreign to biblical monotheism, the fact

---

1. *Redemption* refers to the revelation in Jesus Christ of God's purpose and provision for fallen humankind, including the natural order (John 3:16; Rev. 21–22). *Creation*, as used here and in the Bible generally, refers to humankind and the natural order *since the fall* (Gen. 3). In the biblical worldview, creation includes the reality of superhuman beings, namely angels and demons.

9

should be emphasized that *distinction* is not *dichotomy* or *dualism*. In the biblical worldview, redemption and creation, or spirit and matter, are not simply opposed to one another, as though it were a matter of either-or. Rather, redemption is the redemption of creation!

The biblical distinction between redemption and creation is derivative and contingent, not original and necessary. It is occasioned by the intrusion of sin into the created order. The entrance of sin, and the subsequent acceptance of God's grace in Christ by some and its rejection by others, is the reason that a line is drawn between "creation redeemed" and "creation doomed."

The frequency of universalism in contemporary theology, with its rejection of the redemption/creation, saved/lost, heaven/hell distinctions, contributes to the prevailing confusion regarding the relation between redemption and creation. Writers often speak of the *ultimate compatibility* between redemption and creation, rightfully emphasizing that the same God is both Redeemer and Creator, yet they are prone to disregard the *ultimate incompatibility* between redemption and creation occasioned by sin's invasion of the created order.

On the other hand, however, the relation between redemption and creation is also misunderstood when the ultimate incompatibility between them due to sin is overemphasized to the neglect of their ultimate compatibility *once the sin problem is dealt with.* In Jesus Christ creation is not annihilated; it is redeemed (Rev. 21:26)!

The goal of God's kingdom mission in Christ is nothing less than to bring *all things* into subjection to Christ (Col. 1:20). God's redemptive intent is comprehensive and wholistic. Sin persisted in frustrates the Creator's purpose, so that unredeemed secular culture *as it is* (including government, higher education, and the arts) remains flawed and unfit to enter the New Jerusalem (Rev. 21:27). Redemption, on the other hand, not only fulfills the Creator's cultural intentions, it fulfills these purposes "exceedingly abundantly beyond all that we ask or think" (Eph. 3:20).

Essential to a systematic theology of redemption, given the crucial doctrines of Christ's person and work, are the doctrines of the Holy Spirit, the kingdom present, the Christian life, the church, and the kingdom consummated. Such a study ranges from Pentecost, includes the initial, historical realization of God's kingdom purposes through the Christian life and the church, and continues to the consummation of history at the second coming of Christ.

Inseparable as these themes are in biblical teaching, it is difficult, if not impossible, to find systematic discussions which treat them in their relation to one another. Current systematic theologies tend to move from studies of the person and work of Christ to the Christian life, the church, and the life beyond. Rarely are both the doctrine of the person and work of the Holy Spirit and the doctrine of the kingdom present included as significant separate topics. Because of the omission something of the uniqueness and challenge of the biblical outlook regarding God's purpose for His people is missed.

As long as the world continues, at the heart of God's eternal purposes through Christ and His kingdom, referred to by *The Baptist Faith and Message* as "the great objects of the Kingdom of God" (Art. XIV), stand evangelism and missions, education, and social action. The vast importance of associating the people of God with the determined pursuit of these high goals underscores the enduring significance of the themes dealt with in the present study.

The writing of these pages could not have been accomplished without the help of many. My deepest gratitude is to Connie, my wife, the bright presence in my life. At Broadman Press, thanks is due to John Landers, mover of mountains. At Southwestern Baptist Theological Seminary, appreciation includes a multitude of colleagues, staff, and students, whose generous, ready and willing assistance has known no bounds, especially Bert Dominy, who persisted tenaciously in his encouragement, Debbie Young in computer services, and, in memory, W. T. Conner, my theology mentor and friend.

PART I

The Holy Spirit:

THE EFFECTER OF GOD'S PURPOSE

After the incarnation of God in Christ came Pentecost. Through these two mighty acts, God formally launched His new movement in history, the presence of the kingdom of God. Pentecost, then, is the coming of the Holy Spirit to effect in history the presence and power of God's comprehensive kingdom purposes in Christ.

1. The Spirit and God's Purpose in Christ
2. The Person of the Spirit
3. The Work of the Spirit
4. Spiritual Gifts
5. How the Holy Spirit Effects

1 *The Spirit and God's Purpose in Christ*

The distinctive role of the Holy Spirit in the work of the triune God is to effect, to carry through, and to bring to fruition the purposes of the Father through the Son. The Spirit's role is vastly more comprehensive than is ordinarily understood.

Jesus Christ—Bearer and Imparter of the Holy Spirit
   Jesus Christ—Bearer of the Spirit
   Jesus Christ—Imparter of the Spirit
Two Pivotal Questions
Interpreting Pentecost
The Charismatic Movement
Standard Pneumatology

The New Testament affords no way to speak of the Holy Spirit without also referring to Jesus Christ. Conversely, the New Testament affords no way to speak of Christ without referring to the Spirit. After the incarnation came Pentecost! Through two mighty acts, the incarnation and Pentecost, God inaugurated the presence in history of the promised kingdom and constituted the new covenant with His new people.

Jesus Christ—Bearer and Imparter of the Holy Spirit

In His earthly life and ministry, Christ was both the bearer of the Spirit and the Lord who imparted the Spirit to others.

Jesus Christ—Bearer of the Spirit

The Synoptic Gospels (Matthew, Mark, and Luke) emphasize the role of the Spirit in Jesus' ministry. Over against silence about the Spirit in the literature of the intertestamental period, Jesus' birth signaled a fresh and significant movement of the Spirit of God, beginning even with the birth of His forerunner, John the Baptist (Luke 1-2). In this context of a new moving of the Spirit of God, Jesus was conceived by the Spirit (Matt. 1:18-21; Luke 1:26-38). His birth was accompanied by an outburst of the

14

Spirit's long-silent prophetic ministry (Elizabeth, Luke 1:41; Zechariah, Luke 1:67; and Simeon, Luke 2:25-27). The Spirit descended on Him at His baptism (Matt. 3:13-17) and led Him into, through, and out of temptation (Luke 4:1,14).

Jesus launched His public ministry by announcing that the Holy Spirit was on Him (Luke 4:18-19, cf. Isa. 61:1-2; also Matt. 13:17-21, cf. Isa. 42:1). He sternly warned against blaspheming the Holy Spirit (Matt. 12:37; Luke 12:10; Mark 3:28-29). He cast out demons in the power of the Spirit (Matt. 12:28; cf. Luke 11:20, "the finger of God"). His inner life was inspired by the Spirit (Luke 10:12-22, RSV). He promised the gift of the Spirit to His followers (Luke 11:13; cf. Matt. 7:11, "good things") and the aid of the Spirit when they would be called on to answer opponents in times of persecution (Matt. 10:20; Mark 13:11; Luke 12:11-12; cf. Luke 21:15).

Christ embodied, once for all throughout His life and ministry, what it means for believers to live a Spirit-filled life. Since the incarnation, spirituality and Christlikeness have meant one and the same thing.

Jesus Christ—Imparter of the Spirit

The Fourth Gospel and the rest of the New Testament emphasize that Jesus, following His resurrection as glorified Lord and Savior, bestowed the Spirit on His followers. In His farewell discourse in the upper room (John 14–16), Jesus repeatedly promised that following His death and resurrection He would send the Paraclete, the Holy Spirit[1], who would not speak of Himself but would witness to Christ. After the resurrection Jesus met with the disciples and breathed on them the Holy Spirit (John 20:22). At Pentecost the Spirit was formally bestowed on the new community of believers (Acts 1–2; cf. John 7:39). This event identified the church as the creation of the risen Christ through the Holy Spirit and launched the new community on its universal kingdom mission (Acts 1:8; Matt. 28:19-20).

The Holy Spirit, then, is not a reality in addition to Christ. *The Holy Spirit is the effecter of God's comprehensive kingdom purpose* as revealed through the crucified yet risen Christ. Through the Holy Spirit, Christ Himself is present and at work. Any suggestion that the Holy Spirit came to replace an absent Christ is seriously mistaken. The Spirit did not come to take Christ's place but to make real Christ's presence in the world.

Two Pivotal Questions

The inseparable relation between Christ and the Spirit has a very important bearing on two pivotal questions related to pneumatology (the doctrine of the Holy Spirit).

---

1. See the five Paraclete sayings in John 14:16-17; 14:26; 15:26-27; 16:7-11; 16:12-15.

1. Is the Holy Spirit essentially subordinate or inferior to Christ? This question concerns the Spirit's trinitarian relation to Christ. Those who regard the Spirit's work as merely applying what Christ has already done tend to consider the Spirit subordinate or inferior to Christ. As John Webster says regarding attempts to define the Spirit strictly in terms of what Christ has already done:

What starts as the attempt to protect the identity of the Spirit . . . easily becomes itself a threat to that identity. To tie the Spirit too closely to the person and work of Christ is to underestimate the differentiation within the one divine life and thus to encourage the slow drift into modalism which is so common in western Trinitarian theology.[2]

2. What is the relation of pneumatology to other Christian doctrines? Since the Spirit's role is to effect the purposes of the Father and the Son in all They do in creation and redemption, the Spirit's work is not a completely independent topic in theology. That is, the Spirit does not come with separate programs of His own. The Spirit, together with the Father and the Son, creates and redeems. His redemptive work is to effect the presence and power of God's kingdom in history, primarily through the Christian life and the church. To discuss the doctrine of the Spirit is to speak of these subjects and not the variety of unrelated, mysterious, and arcane topics which nonbiblical mysticism treats.

Interpreting Pentecost

What happened at Pentecost? The answer to this question is basic not only to understanding the Holy Spirit but also to understanding the New Testament. Recognition of the purpose in Christ's coming is at stake. Many throughout the history of Christian thought have considered Pentecost as the birth of the church and the beginning of a new dimension in individual sanctification. Pentecost was all this and much more. *Pentecost was the coming of the Holy Spirit to effect in history the presence and power of God's kingdom purposes in Christ.* The work of the Spirit in the Christian life and the church should be studied in the context of New Testament teaching regarding the kingdom of God. The Christian life and the church are fundamentally kingdom realities, and they must be understood in the light of God's kingdom purpose in Jesus Christ. Pentecost was a kingdom event! It was the inauguration in history of the long-

---

2. John Webster, "The Identity of the Holy Spirit: A Problem in Trinitarian Theology," *Themelios* 9 (Sept. 1983):4-7. Heron makes the same point: "According to the New Testament, Jesus is not only the giver but also the *receiver* of the Spirit. If that is not kept in view, it is all too easy to absorb pneumatology in christology, and so to reduce the very name 'Holy Spirit' to a mere cipher." Alasdair I. C. Heron, *The Holy Spirit* (Philadelphia: Westminster, 1983), 127.

awaited messianic kingdom, the outpouring of spiritual abundance promised throughout the Old Testament for the last days. Yet the inauguration of the kingdom was not its consummation. The kingdom is already present in power, but its consummation awaits the return of Christ.

Neglect of the kingdom context for understanding Pentecost has taken many forms. Traditional Protestantism views Pentecost as the day when the church was brought into existence and gifted with the word and the sacraments. (This reflects the Reformation definition of the church as the place where the word is proclaimed and the sacraments administered.) Older dispensational theology emphasizes the distinction between Israel and the church and views the present age beginning at Pentecost as a parenthesis or intercalation in the divine plan of the ages, something unforeseen in the Old Testament and unrelated to God's great purposes for Israel. Evangelical interpretations of Pentecost emphasize the evangelistic and missionary significance of the event, focusing on Pentecost as the universalizing through Christ of God's redemptive purpose in history (Acts 1:8). Pentecostals view Pentecost as the Spirit's baptism of believers, subsequent to conversion and evidenced by speaking in tongues and by other signs and wonders.[3]

The Charismatic Movement

During the 1960s and the 1970s, the charismatic movement heightened interest in the dramatic gifts of the Holy Spirit. With few exceptions leaders in the charismatic movement arrived at their experience of the Spirit's sign

---

3. For the view of Pentecost as the birth of the church and its gifting with the Word and the sacraments, see Frederick Dale Bruner, *A Theology of the Holy Spirit* (Grand Rapids: Eerdmans, 1970), 170. For a brief, recent criticism of the traditional Reformation view of the church by a Presbyterian, see Shirley C. Guthrie, Jr., *Christian Doctrine* (Atlanta: Knox, 1977), 364-67.For the older dispensational interpretation of Pentecost, see Lewis Sperry Chafer, *Systematic Theology,* 8 vols. (Dallas: Dallas Theological Seminary, 1948), 4:41. More recent dispensational writers such as Craig Blaising, Herman Hoyt, John MacArthur, C. C. Ryrie, Robert Saucy, and others soften the distinction between Israel and the church significantly.

An example of the evangelical approach to Pentecost is J. Terry Young, *The Spirit within You* (Nashville: Broadman, 1977), chap. 9, "The Holy Spirit and the Christian Mission." Young has no direct discussion, however, of the comprehensive scope of God's kingdom purpose.

The Pentecostal stress on signs and wonders finds expression in Steve Durasoff, *Bright Wind of the Spirit* (Englewood Cliffs, NJ: Prentice-Hall, 1972), chap. 1. Durasoff's first sentence in the chapter is: "Pentecostals believe in miracles. They expect the supernatural most anytime, anywhere."

For a charismatic view of signs and wonders, see C. Peter Wagner, *The Third Wave of the Holy Spirit* (Ann Arbor, MI: Vine Books, 1988).

For Pentecost as a kingdom event which includes but goes beyond some of the above emphases, see the next chapter, "Kingdom Present."

gifts through the influence of Pentecostals.[4] Classical Pentecostalism originated in America in the early 1900s and led to the formation of denominations such as the Assemblies of God.

The charismatic movement emerged during the early 1960s when
Dennis Bennett, an Episcopal rector in Van Nuys, California, reported to
his parishioners one Sunday morning that he and some seventy members
of the congregation had been "baptized in the Spirit" and had received
the gift of tongues. What made the incident news was that Bennett did
not join a Pentecostal denominational but remained an Episcopalian.

Soon, tongue-speaking groups of this new, non-separatist variety were
springing up everywhere—at first on campuses such as Harvard, Yale,
Notre Dame, and Duquesne. Then, by the 1970s, the charismatic movement spread among all major denominations, but especially among the
more liturgical bodies such as Roman Catholics, Episcopalians, and
Lutherans. Although charismatics have usually remained within their
parent denominations, they have formed fellowships, rallies, and even
congregations of their own. In other ways as well, the charismatic movement has had a measure of built-in separation or divisiveness, simply
because it claims an experience of the Holy Spirit "beyond" that possessed by "ordinary" Christians.

Charismatics and Pentecostals substantially agree concerning baptism
of the Spirit after conversion. Both charismatics and Pentecostals reflect
weariness with alleged formalism in mainline denominations and hunger
for experiential, participatory, and demonstrative forms of public worship. Both movements reflect preoccupation with the spiritual gifts listed
in 1 Corinthians 12:8-10. Pentecostals and charismatics value the so-
called sign gifts of tongues and healing to the neglect of other gift lists
such as Romans 12:3-8, which never mention sign gifts. Yet lists such as
Romans 12:3-8 are more basic than 1 Corinthians 12:8-10 from the perspective of the New Testament as a whole.

Interest in the Spirit's controversial sign gifts soared with the rapid
spread of the charismatic movement in the 1970s.[5] The movement apparently peaked by the end of the decade. According to Smail, a former leader
of British charismatics who now distances himself from the movement,

---

4. This fact is amply documented by Richard Quebedeaux, *The New Charismatics II*
(San Francisco: Harper & Row, 1983), especially chap. 4, "The Leadership of Charismatic
Renewal."

5. For recent developments in the charismatic signs and wonders movement, see Wagner,
The Third Wave of the Holy Spirit.

For the Fuller Theological Seminary case study of evangelicals and the charismatic signs
and wonders emphasis, see Lewis B. Smedes, ed., *Ministry and the Miraculous* (Pasadena,
CA: Fuller Theological Seminary, 1987). The study concludes: "We distance ourselves from
any intellectualism that could shrink the gospel of Christ to arid formulae, just as we reject
the abuses of power cut adrift from [gospel] truth" (Ibid., 80).

"the charismatic movement as a thing in itself may well be almost over, but the renewal of the Church by the Holy Spirit has only just begun."[6]

Standard Pneumatology

Standard restatements of the doctrine of the Holy Spirit distinguish between the doctrine of the *Person* of the Holy Spirit and the doctrine of the *work* of the Holy Spirit: the Person of the Spirit treats His deity and personality; the work of the Spirit considers His threefold activity in revelation, the Christian life, and the church.[7]

Yet standard pnematology has three weaknesses:

1. Standard pneumatology tends to be too individualistic, majoring on the Spirit's work in sanctification to the neglect of His work in relation to the church.

2. Standard pneumatology tends to be too subjective, commonly viewing the Spirit's work as merely inward or *within* believers, at times even contrasting the Spirit's "subjective" work with Christ's "objective and historical" work.

3. Standard pneumatology often omits explicit recognition of the comprehensive, kingdom-of-God scope of the Spirit's mighty *redemptive* activities.

---

6. Thomas A. Smail, *The Forgotten Father* (Grand Rapids: Eerdmans, 1980), 9-10. See the further reference to Smail below.

Quebedeaux says: "Not unlike other movements of the Spirit before it, charismatic renewal had 'run out of steam' by the late 1970s—but not out of abiding significance." Quebedeaux, *The New Charismatics II,* 239.

Claude Howe has evaluated the influence of the charismatic movement on Southern Baptists. He believes that "the movement has had relatively slight impact upon Southern Baptist life," and that even this impact is declining. Claude L. Howe, *Glimpses of Baptist Heritage* (Nashville: Broadman, 1981), chap. 8, "Southern Baptists and the Charismatic Movement," 121.

7. For three randomly chosen examples of this standard Catholic as well as Protestant approach to pneumatology, see S. C. Guthrie, *Christian Doctrine* (Atlanta: Knox, 1977), chap. 15; Millard J. Erickson, *Christian Theology,* (Grand Rapids: Baker, 1985), 845-83; and Wayne Ward, *The Holy Spirit,* vol. 10, Layman's Library of Christian Doctrine (Nashville: Broadman, 1987), chap. 9.

The standard outline of the doctrine of the Holy Spirit is also clearly evidenced in Article II, Part C, of *The Baptist Faith and Message,* the doctrinal statement of the Southern Baptist Convention, which reads as follows

The Holy Spirit is the Spirit of God. He inspired holy men of old to write the Scriptures. Through illumination He enables men to understand truth. He exalts Christ. He convicts of sin, of righteousness and of judgment. He calls men to the Saviour, and effects regeneration. He cultivates Christian character, comforts believers, and bestows the spiritual gifts by which they serve God through His church. He seals the believer unto the day of final redemption. His presence in the Christian is the assurance of God to bring the believer into the fulness of the stature of Christ. He enlightens and empowers the believer and the church in worship, evangelism, and service.The first sentence deals with the Person of the Spirit, mentioning His deity but only assuming His personality. The second, third, and fourth sentences treat the work of the Spirit in relation to Scripture. The remaining sentences refer primarily to the work of the Spirit in the Christian life. The work of the Spirit in the church is mentioned twice, but only in passing.

See the further reference to the characteristic weaknesses of standard pneumatologies in the discussion below of the 1903 Westminster Confession article on the Holy Spirit.

2 The Person of the Spirit

Although traditional Christian orthodoxy clearly affirms the deity and personality of the Holy Spirit, orthodoxy has no clearly developed understanding of the Spirit's personality.

The clear affirmation of the deity and personality of the Holy Spirit in traditional theology, both Catholic and Protestant, reflects the depth and vitality of trinitarianism. Measured by the New Testament witness, the distinctive dimension of the Christian view of God's personal being is its emphasis on His triune nature. The one God is Father, Son, and Holy Spirit. Christianity is neither unitarian nor binitarian but trinitarian. The Father is God, the Son is God, and the Holy Spirit is God. Christians are baptized "in the name of the Father and the Son and the Holy Spirit" (Matt. 28:19). The trinitarian structure of the Apostles' Creed reflects this New Testament teaching: "I believe in the Father . . . and in the Son . . . and in the Holy Spirit."

Biblical Resources

The following overview of biblical terminology for the Holy Spirit summarizes biblical use of the Hebrew and Greek words for spirit and lists biblical titles and symbols for the Spirit.

Biblical Words for the Holy Spirit

The Old Testament word for spirit (*ruach*) and the New Testament word (*pneuma*) share four levels of meaning: wind (Gen. 8:1; John 3:8), breath (Gen. 6:17; 2 Thess. 2:8), the human spirit (Deut. 2:30; Rom. 8:16), and the Spirit of the Lord or the Holy Spirit (Isa. 61:1; Luke 4:18). In the New Testament *pneuma* also refers to angels (Heb. 1:14), though *pneuma* is not the primary Greek word for either of these realities. In both Hebrew and Greek usage, spirit is associated with evident yet invisible vitality and power, not only at the moral and personal level but also at the natural level.

The New International Version of the Old Testament translates *ruach* as a reference to the Spirit of the Lord at least eighty times.[1] This does not mean, of course, that Old Testament believers understood the full Christian meaning of the Holy Spirit as the third Person of the Trinity. Jews who came to believe in the Trinity in New Testament times were those who had converted to Christianity; these Jews came to confess both the deity of Christ and the personhood of the Holy Spirit, recognizing that they lived after the incarnation and Pentecost events. Old Testament references to the Spirit of the Lord took on additional meaning for New Testament believers. Old Testament references to the Spirit of the Lord prepared the first Christians for fuller revelation about the Holy Spirit and the Trinity (cf. Acts 28:25; Rom. 15:4).

In the New Testament, according to the versions already mentioned, *pneuma* is translated Spirit more than two hundred times, as could be expected given the importance of the doctrine of the Holy Spirit as the third Person of the Trinity in New Testament teaching.[2]

Biblical Titles and Symbols for the Holy Spirit

The customary Old Testament title for the Spirit is "Spirit of the Lord" (or Spirit of God). Although the term *Holy Spirit* is found three times in the Old Testament (Ps. 51:11; Isa. 63:10-11), even these three uses of the title lack the significance of a proper name. The title *Holy Spirit* becomes a proper name in the New Testament because of the full revelation of the Spirit's personhood.

Holy Spirit is the most common New Testament title for the Spirit. (The King James Version, it should be observed, arbitrarily translates the Greek, *hagios pneuma,* either as Holy Spirit or as Holy Ghost. The latter expression, now archaic, has almost disappeared.) Other New Testament

---

1. This compares with some 58 instances in the RSV, and a lesser number in the Cambridge and Oxford editions of the KJV. The Harper edition of the KJV never capitalizes *spirit* in the Old Testament.

2. Two very helpful introductions to the biblical resources for pneumatology are W. T. Conner, *The Work of the Holy Spirit* (Nashville: Broadman, 1949; 1978); and John Koenig, *Charismata: God's Gifts for God's People* (Philadelphia: Westminster, 1978). Both authors review Old Testament as well as New Testament materials.

titles include *Paraclete* (Counselor, John 14:16, NIV) and *Lord* (only in 2 Cor. 3:17-18). The Spirit is also called the Spirit of life, Spirit of truth, Spirit of wisdom, and eternal Spirit. Biblical symbols for the Holy Spirit include water, fire, wind, oil, rain, dew, dove, voice, seal, and cloven tongues.

As this variety of terms readily indicates, resources for the study of biblical pneumatology are rich and challenging.

Historical Perspective

Although traditional orthodoxy, both Catholic and Protestant, affirms the deity and personality of the Holy Spirit in theory, the reality of the Holy Spirit is neglected in practice due to preoccupation with the rituals and structures of the institutional church.[3] The historic creeds and confessions of Christendom, though distinctly trinitarian, tend to limit the Spirit's reality to inward and subjective dimensions, neglecting the New Testament emphasis on the Holy Spirit as the effecter of God's kingdom purposes in history and on Pentecost as an event dramatically altering the course of history. Even the Westminster Confession of 1647 lacked a specific article on the Holy Spirit. In 1903 the General Assembly of the Presbyterian Church U.S.A. added the following article:

> The Holy Spirit, the third person in the Trinity, proceeding from the Father and the Son, of the same substance and equal in power and glory is, together with the Father and the Son, to be believed in, loved, obeyed, and worshiped throughout all ages.
>
> He is the Lord and Giver of life, everywhere present, and is the source of all good thoughts, pure desires, and holy counsels in men. By him the prophets were moved to speak the word of God, and all the writers of the Holy Scriptures inspired to record infallibly the mind and will of God. The dispensation of the gospel is especially committed to him. He prepares the way for it, accompanies it with his persuasive power, and urges its message upon the reason and conscience of men, so that they who reject its merciful offer are not only without excuse, but are also guilty of resisting the Holy Spirit.
>
> The Holy Spirit, whom the Father is ever willing to give to all who ask him, is the only efficient agent in the application of redemption. He regenerates men by his grace, convicts them of sin, moves them to repentance, and persuades and enables them to embrace

---

3. An interesting contemporary example of this subordination of the Spirit to the institutional church can be found in John Macquarrie, *Principles of Christian Theology,* 2nd ed. (New York: Scribner's, 1977). In a volume that exceeds 500 pages, he devotes 10 pages to the Holy Spirit and 139 pages to the church.

Many discussions of the doctrine of the Holy Spirit recognize the neglect of the Spirit in Christian theology and practice.

Jesus Christ by faith. He unites all believers to Christ, dwells in them as their Comforter and Sanctifier, gives to them the spirit of Adoption and Prayer, and performs all those gracious offices by which they are sanctified and sealed unto the day of redemption.

By the indwelling of the Holy Spirit all believers being vitally united to Christ who is the Head, are thus united one to another in the church, which is his body. He calls and anoints ministers for their holy office, qualifies all other officers in the church for their special work, and imparts various gifts and graces to its members. He gives efficacy to the word and to the ordinances of the gospel. By him the church will be preserved, increased, purified, and at last made perfectly holy in the presence of God.[4]

Standard pneumatology discusses the Spirit's subjective work in individual lives but tends to neglect the comprehensive, kingdom scope of the Spirit's activities. Some traditional documents are weaker than others at this point. As one of the more recent and abler statements, the 1903 revision of the Westminster Confession is less vulnerable to this criticism than most older formulations.

Restatement

The Deity of the Holy Spirit

The deity of the Holy Spirit is implicit in the Christian doctrine of the Trinity. Because the Holy Spirit is God, what the Holy Spirit does, God does. In passages such as Matthew 28:19-20, 1 Corinthians 12:4-6, and 2 Corinthians 13:14, the Father is God, the Son is God, and the Holy Spirit is God.

The deity of the Spirit is also implicit in the functions that Scripture ascribes to Him. The Spirit witnesses to Christ (John 15:26), and only God can speak the things of God (1 Cor. 2:10-11). The Spirit is another Paraclete of the same kind as Christ, not of a different kind (John 14:16). The Spirit proceeds from the Father (John 15:26), is sent by the Father in Jesus' name (John 14:26), and is able to make known all that belongs to the Father through the Son (John 16:15). The Spirit is the Holy Spirit, and holy, in its biblical use, is a synonym for deity (Isa. 6:3; Rev. 5:8). The Spirit is the Spirit of God (Rom. 8:9). As the divine Spirit, He gives life, which is the unique prerogative of God (Rom. 8:2). He knows the thoughts of God (1 Cor. 2:11): to lie to the Spirit is to lie to God (Acts 5:3-4). To violate the law of Moses was to die without mercy at the testimony of two or three witnesses, but "how much more severely" does a person

---

4. George S. Hendry, *The Westminster Confession for Today* (Richmond: Knox, 1960), 116-20.

deserve punishment who tramples the Son of God and insults the Spirit of grace (Heb. 10:28-29). The voice of the Spirit (Acts 28:25) is the voice of the Lord (Isa. 6:8-10).

As deity, the Spirit is sovereign. He distributes His gifts as He chooses (1 Cor. 12:11). As sovereign He is as invincible as the wind (John 3:8). Yet, though the Spirit is sovereign and mighty, He is also gentle: He descends as a dove (Mark 1:10). His fruit in the lives of believers is preeminently love, which includes gentleness (Gal. 5:23). Although the God of Scripture is almighty, the Bible insists that He conquers not by might nor by power but by His Spirit (Zech. 4:6).

Since the Spirit is sovereign, believers never "possess" Him, in the sense of taming or controlling him. They can never domesticate the Spirit or manipulate Him according to their own whims. When Simon the sorcerer sought to buy the Spirit's power, Peter answered: "May your silver perish with you, because you thought you could buy the gift of God with money" (Acts 8:20). God's ways are not man's ways! Through His Spirit, God raises up and exalts whom He will. Believers must remain flexible and open to fresh disclosures of the Spirit's guidance.

As deity, the Holy Spirit is the third Person of the Trinity. He is not just any spirit but is always the Spirit of the God we know in Christ. Amid the conflicting voices of many spirits, Christians must "test the spirits to see whether they are from God" (1 John 4:1). The primary means for doing this is through the witness of the Bible. Since the Spirit inspired Scripture (2 Pet. 1:21), the Spirit's message never contradicts the testimony of the Bible.

Finally, since the Spirit is deity He can be invoked in prayer. The usual pattern in Christian prayer is to address the Father in the name of the Son through the energizing of the Spirit. Yet each Person of the Trinity is a proper object of address in prayer and worship. According to the Great Commission, believers are to be baptized "in the name of the Father and the Son and the Holy Spirit." Each Person of the Trinity is invoked. In response to the biblical imperative to "be filled with the Spirit" (Eph. 5:18), Christian hymnody intuitively recognizes the propriety of calling direct on the Holy Spirit for His presence and power. If direct address to the Spirit were contrary to biblical teaching, Christians could not sing familiar hymns such as Edwin Hatch's "Breathe on Me, Breath of God." Yet the Bible is clear: the Spirit is God and therefore worthy to receive the believer's worship, trust, and love.[5]

---

5. The emphasis on invoking the Spirit in prayer as well as the Father and the Son is not at all to suggest that the believer distinguishes between the Persons of the Trinity when he hears God speaking in Christian experience. When the believer opens himself to communion

The Personality of the Holy Spirit

Belief in the deity of the Spirit carries with it belief in the Spirit's personality. Since the biblical view of God is intensely personal and since the Spirit belongs to the Godhead, the Spirit's personal nature is everywhere implicit in the biblical witness. He is no less personal than are the Father and the Son. Biblical indications of this claim are many.

Actions ascribed to the Spirit in Scripture are distinctively personal actions. The most common action is verbal communication, and no action is more personal than intelligible, relation-nurturing speech. Typical pneumatics in both Testaments are the prophets, or those by whom the Spirit speaks, acts out, or writes a message from God. Similarly, Jesus promised the disciples that the Holy Spirit would make them ready and courageous witnesses to the gospel (Acts 1:8). The biblical Spirit, then, is highly articulate. Medieval mystics spoke of "a cloud of unknowing" and an ineffable God to be worshiped in passive silence. The Bible, in contrast, speaks of the Holy Spirit as prone to break the intolerable silence of humanity's alienation from God and loneliness in sin. The supreme role of the biblical Spirit is to bring a living word from God. He speaks!

The Scripture ascribes other personal actions to the Spirit, such as producing Christian character (Gal. 5:22-23, where the fruit of the Spirit is a catalog of supremely personal qualities); guiding believers (Rom. 8:14); creating unity or fellowship among believers (2 Cor. 13:14); richly gifting believers for ministry in diverse ways (1 Cor. 12:7-11); grieving when offended, neglected (Eph. 4:30), lied to (Acts 5:3), or blasphemed

---

with God through Bible study, for instance, he does not hear a voice saying, "This is the Father speaking, not the Son nor the Spirit."

John Peck, however, needlessly complicates the issue of directly addressing the Holy Spirit when he says:

> Normally when we think of a person, we think of someone to whom we can relate and with whom we can converse "over against" ourselves. Now the Spirit is not like that *for us* (although he is within the Trinity). As far as I know, there is only one case in Scripture where the Spirit is addressed directly, and it is in a highly mystical and symbolic passage in Ezekiel, where the prophet is bidden to "prophesy to the wind" (37:9). As John Taylor says, in his controversial book on the Spirit, *The Go-between God* (p. 43): "You cannot commune with the Holy Spirit, for he *is* communion itself." To have dealings with the Spirit always means to have dealings with God in Christ. Any attempt to deal with him as a person on his own, so to speak, would result in a kind of spiritistic religious experience.

John Peck, *What the Bible Teaches about the Holy Spirit* (Wheaton, IL: Tyndale House, 1979), p. 117.

One can agree with Peck regarding his opposition to any effort to relate to the Spirit "as a person on his own," that is, to the exclusion of the Father and the Son, without concluding, as Peck does, that it is improper to address the Holy Spirit directly in prayer. The comment by Taylor which Peck cites, by the way, appears to reflect a modalistic manner of viewing the Trinity.

Redeemed! Eschatological Redemption and the Kingdom of God

—26—

(Matt. 12:32); and—especially characteristic from the standpoint of His key role as effecter—persevering to bring to full fruition the kingdom purposes that He initiates (Eph. 1:13-14). For believers to be filled with the Spirit, then, is to experience the heightening of their personal powers beyond their ordinary limits. This process, however, accentuates the unfolding of personal individuality rather than dramatic displays of the spectacular. Thus, there is a "quaintness of the saints" that markedly distinguishes the Holy Spirit's actions from psychological manipulation, excessive emotionalism, or any kind of stereotyped, depersonalizing experience.

Some writers refer to the Holy Spirit as "It" rather than "He" because the New Testament Greek word for spirit (*pneuma*) is neuter.[6] The writers of the New Testament, however, personalized the concept of spirit when they referred to the Holy Spirit. In effect, they used the neuter noun as a proper name, so that references to the Spirit have the same force as references to the Son or the Father. This is not to ignore the fact that these same writers employ seemingly impersonal expressions when referring to the Spirit. Luke, for instance, speaks of the Spirit as being poured out, as though He were a liquid (Acts 2:17), but Jesus referred to Himself as a door or a gate (John 10:7), and the living God is referred to as a rock (Ps. 18:2). Such accidents of human language must be understood in the light of clear biblical evidence for the Spirit's personality.[7]

According to the Fourth Gospel, Jesus used the masculine noun *parakletos* and a personal pronoun *ekeinos* when He promised the Spirit to His disciples (John 14:26ff.). On the basis of this usage, some writers

---

6. For example, see Koenig, *Charismata,* 74,76. Koenig, however, refuses to reduce the Holy Spirit to an impersonal force.

Heron, on the other hand, goes too far when, seeking to justify his use of "It" rather than "He," he writes:

> There are, however, solid exegetical and theological reasons for seeking to avoid making the impression that the Spirit is "a third he" (or "she") alongside the Father and the Son. This is not to deny that the Spirit is, in the proper sense of the term, the "third person of the Trinity," nor is it to "depersonalize" the Spirit, but it is to underline the Spirit's distinctive identity, character and status as the Spirit *of God,* the Spirit *of Christ.*

Alasdair I. C. Heron, *The Holy Spirit* (Philadelphia: Westminster, 1983), viii. Heron seems to take too lightly the facts that "it" is in English the impersonal pronoun and that references to the Spirit as the Spirit of Christ and the Spirit of God by no means suggests either subordination or modalism.

7. Heron summarizes what is meant by the accidents of language:

> *Ruach* in Hebrew is feminine; *pneuma* in Greek is neuter; *spiritus* in Latin is masculine. To make matters worse, English does not normally use the neuter form for personal subjects. There is no similar difficulty in German, as Mark Twain once illustrated with his literal translation of an everyday conversation: "Where is the girl?" "It is in the kitchen?" "Where is she?" "The *kitchen* is downstairs" (Ibid).

claim that John violates the rules of Greek grammar in order to stress the personal nature of the Spirit. This argument inadequately assumes, however, that the antecedent of the personal pronoun *ekeinos* is the neuter *pneuma* rather than the masculine *parakletos*. Peck, for instance, writes:

> For a neuter word, good Greek would always use a neuter pronoun, "it," leaving the reader to work out whether it might mean "he." But in John 14-16 the personal pronoun "he" is used, and in one text at least this flagrantly breaks the normal rules of grammar (John 16:13).[8]

Yet the distinctive term for the Holy Spirit in John 14-16 is *parakletos*, which explains the use of the masculine pronoun in John 16:13. *Pneuma* is used parenthetically in John 16:13 and in apposition to *parakletos*, so that *parakletos* remains the grammatical antecedent of the pronoun. No rule of Greek grammar is violated.

Most importantly, the Holy Spirit, who is personal, acts personally, not impersonally or magically. Those who view the Holy Spirit as an impersonal power are concerned about how to control or use Him. By viewing the Spirit personally, as the Spirit of the God we know in Christ, our concern should be to let the Spirit control our lives. This points the way to distinctly Christian approaches to spiritual formation and kingdom expansion. Quite to the contrary, however, as Peck recognizes, Satan's methods of work are impersonal, tending to reduce persons to slaves or robots.[9]

The Holy Spirit: Objective and Subjective

Traditional discussions of the doctrine of the Spirit sometimes insist that Christ stands for the objective and historical dimension of the Christian revelation, while the Holy Spirit stands for the inward and subjective aspect. Conner says:

> The work of the Spirit is to make real in us what Christ wrought out for us. Christ wrought out redemption objectively for us; the Holy Spirit works redemption experimentally within us.[10]

What Conner says is important and true as far as it goes, yet there are also subjective dimensions to Christ's work and objective dimensions to the Spirit's work. The Holy Spirit helped those who heard Jesus during His life and ministry. Faith, or inward perception, was necessary to see and

---

8. John Peck, *What the Bible Teaches about the Holy Spirit,* 117.

9. Ibid, 118.

Along the same line, in countering the Pentecostal idea of "appropriating" the Spirit, Bruner writes: "Is a person 'appropriated'? It is the frequently 'thingish' understanding of the Holy Spirit in Pentecostalism which contributes to the offensiveness of the doctrine." Frederick D. Bruner, *A Theology of the Holy Spirit* (Grand Rapids: Eerdmans, 1970), 252, note 40.

10. W. T. Conner, *Revelation and God* (Nashville: Broadman, 1936), 301. Earlier in the same volume, however, Conner recognizes:

hear God at work in Jesus of Nazareth; those who only saw with their eyes or heard with their ears missed His message and meaning. Furthermore, the risen Christ indwells believers subjectively (Gal. 2:20). As the hymn, "He Lives" expresses it, "You ask me how I know he lives: he lives within my heart." Also, this indwelling is corporate as well as individual. Through the Spirit the risen Christ dwells in the midst of His people (Matt. 18:20; 28:20). No serious believer would think of minimizing the great significance for Christian living and kingdom advance of these truths.

The Spirit of the Lord, on the other hand, is objective as well as subjective. He creates historical communities of faith. He inspires the writing of Scripture in known languages which are accessible to all persons. At Pentecost, which was as datable and decisive a happening as any of the great events in the biblical drama of redemption, the Spirit launched a mighty Godmovement, the presence and mission of the kingdom of God in history in power, which keeps altering the course of human events. In a variety of ways the objectivity of the Holy Spirit is to be taken with utmost seriousness.[11]

Nor can we press too far the matter of identifying the objective with Christ and the subjective with the Holy Spirit.... The New Testament not only presents Christ as a character in history; it also represents him as an indwelling power in man.... On the other hand, the Holy Spirit is not to be thought of as a subjective power *only*. He lives in us, but he is not of us. He is other than we are. In this sense, the Spirit is just as objective as Christ. His power is not ours except by his will, not ours [only] (Ibid, 122, italics and brackets added).

The Spirit is objective also in the sense that He is active in history. As John says, we may not be able to *see* the wind with our eyes, but "we hear its sound" (John 3:8). John is speaking of the Spirit at work in the world, and he is saying that the evidence of the Spirit's activity is indisputable *for those who exercise faith* or spiritual vision.

11. A word from Bruner and Hordern is helpful here:

Every Nicene Christian believes that a part of the gospel is the victory that Christ gives over evil spirits. But how this victory is obtained, lived, and evidenced is a subject of disagreement in the churches. There are contemporary "theologies of glory" that do end runs around the suffering of the cross and promise Christians direct access to the power of the resurrection. These theologies take many forms, but they all unite in their focus on power by technique. Against these new triumphalisms, so widespread in the electronic church, but also popular in many Christian churches, movements, and books, the authors propose the Reformation "theology of the cross." ... To sum up, we believe that preaching the gospel is the way of the Spirit's fullness, even in later 20th-century Christendom, against all charismatic spiritisms and new revelations; and bearing the cross is the way Christians live lives of resurrection power, against the many culture-religions of success, prosperity, and easy victories.

Frederick Dale Bruner and William Hordern, *The Holy Spirit—Shy Member of the Trinity* (Minneapolis: Augsburg, 1984), 8-9. Granted the truth these words convey, as the title of the book intimates, Bruner and Hordern overemphasize the Spirit's "shyness" to the neglect of His boldness. Again it is evident that balance in theology is not easily come by.

Since the Spirit is an objective as well as a subjective reality, the Christian experience of the Holy Spirit cannot be reduced to a purely inward experience—a vacuous, ineffable, medieval mysticism. The Holy Spirit is not just any Spirit, but the Spirit of the God revealed in Christ and attested through Scripture. The Bible, therefore, provides definite criteria by which to recognize His presence and activity. The call to Christian ministry, for instance, is more than a mere feeling. The one who is called has good reasons for the sense of call, reasons that can be thought about and tested in experience. A believer led by the Spirit is one thing; a philosophical mystic, adrift in a fog on an uncharted sea of subjectivity, is something else altogether.

The Spirit's identity is at stake here. Webster has recently emphasized that traditional, Christologically oriented doctrines of the Spirit, while protecting the identity of the Spirit from being vaguely suffused throughout creation, tend unduly to subordinate the Spirit to the Son. The Spirit's work comes to be viewed as merely repetitive of the work of Christ; He hardly has a place of His own in the economy of salvation. Over against this weakness, Webster and others insist that Pentecost was a great new event in the biblical series of God's mighty acts of redemption.[12]

---

12. See the statement by John Webster quoted earlier. Berkhof also objects to the undue subjectivizing of the Holy Spirit. He says: "The Spirit is far more than an instrumental entity, the subjective reverse of Christ's work." Hendrikus Berkhof, *The Doctrine of the Holy Spirit* (Richmond: Knox, 1964), 23. Others also speak up. Sweet emphasizes that the Spirit's creative power is invasive from without as well as indwelling. Leonard I. Sweet, *New Life in the Spirit* (Philadelphia: Westminster, 1982), 19. Koenig speaks of the external witness of the Spirit in the world as well as the Spirit's internal witness within believers. John Koenig, *Charismata*, 73. Heron says:

> A weakness of much Protestant theology is that it has commonly inclined to describe [the Spirit] simply as applying the fruits of Christ's work to our souls ... . This effective subordination of the Spirit unobtrusively paves the way for its [*sic*] equation with our experience.

Heron, *The Holy Spirit,* 126.

The Work
of the Spirit

As effecter of God's purpose in history, the Holy Spirit has provided redemption in His historic work and applies it by effecting the kingdom present, the Christian life, and the church.

Biblical writers focus more frequently on the Spirit's work than on His person. This observation is important, not to minimize the significance of the Spirit's person and the doctrine of the Trinity, but to stress the seriousness of the traditional neglect of the Spirit's work. The great creeds and confessions of Christendom have said little about the work of the Spirit.

Biblical Resources

The biblical materials provide rich resources for the study of the Spirit's work, yet at few points in Christian theology is there greater diversity among evangelicals. One central issue, already broached in the first chapter, concerns the place of Pentecost in God's unfolding redemptive purpose. Yet further questions press for answers. What is the relation between the Spirit and Scripture? Is there significant unity between the Old Testament and the New Testament regarding the Spirit's activity? What was the relation of the Spirit before Pentecost to the Spirit after

Pentecost (John 7:38-39)? What is the relation of Pentecost to Jesus' teaching about the kingdom? What is the Spirit's distinctive role in the divine economy? How should the Spirit's work in the conversion and sanctification of believers be interpreted?

The Unity of the Old and New Testaments

In response to these questions, the present discussion is predicated on the following convictions:

• Old and New Testament teachings regarding the Spirit are a unity.

• The unifying theme of the Bible is redemption from sin to newness of life in the Spirit.

• The incarnation and Pentecost are the decisive events in the biblical drama of redemption.

• The wholistic nature of God's redemptive purpose in Christ is best summarized by the concept of the kingdom of God as both a present and future reality. Christ inaugurated the kingdom at His first coming and will consummate it at His second coming. The kingdom comprehensively embraces God's new covenant purpose for the entire creation.

• The work of Christ and the work of the Holy Spirit are inseparable in history and experience, though distinguishable for purposes of doctrinal analysis.

Guided by these principles, the tendency to multiply artificial distinctions between the work of the Spirit in the Old Testament and the work of the Spirit in the New Testament, even though it is commonplace, is to be strongly resisted.

An example of this tendency is a rejection of the cosmic aspect of the Spirit's work in the Old Testament on the basis that it is not taught in the New Testament. The distinguished evangelical writer Griffith Thomas goes even further. He rejects any idea of a cosmic dimension to the Spirit's activity in either Testament, insisting that general revelation is the work of the eternal Logos, or second Person of the Trinity, not the work of the Holy Spirit. Griffith Thomas writes, "Christ, as God's wisdom and Word, has cosmic functions, but not the Spirit."[1]

---

1. W. H. Griffith Thomas, *The Holy Spirit of God,* 3d ed. (Grand Rapids: Eerdmans, 1955), 187.

More recently, George Hendry, *The Holy Spirit in Christian Theology,* 2d ed. (Philadelphia: Westminster, 1966), 26, and C. F. D. Moule, *The Holy Spirit* (Grand Rapids: Eerdmans, 1978), 20, take similar positions.

Another example of exaggerating the distinctions between Old Testament and New Testament teaching about the Spirit's activity is the claim that the Spirit indwelled Old Testament saints temporarily but now indwells Christians permanently. Psalm 51:11 ("Do not . . . take your Holy Spirit from me") is often cited to support a temporary indwelling in Old Testament times. This sharp distinction between the Spirit's indwelling in the two Testaments is more speculative than substantial. One has only to recall the profound spirituality of the Psalms to recognize the surpassing quality of Old Testament sainthood.

This contrasting of the Spirit's work in the two Testaments is particularly objectionable when it reflects an inadequate understanding of God's triune nature. Sometimes the two Testaments are interpreted as though God did not become triune until the events of New Testament revelation. Although God's triune nature is clearly revealed only in the incarnation and Pentecost events,[2] God is essentially and eternally triune. Father, Son, and Holy Spirit are each involved in all that God does, in both creation (or general revelation) and redemption (or special revelation). The work of each is as extensive as the work of God. Compartmentalizing is artificial and should be avoided. We must compromise neither the unity of God nor His threeness.

The Old Testament

Given this recognition of the essential unity of Old and New Testament teaching regarding the work of the Spirit, it is important to begin with Old Testament insights.

1. The Old Testament stresses the Spirit's role in the natural creation. In the Old Testament the Spirit stands for God's purposive and controlling presence in creation as well as in redemption. The New Testament assumes this insight and builds on it. The essence of biblical monotheism is that the same God is both Creator and Redeemer, and that, as Creator, the triune God is the Author, Sustainer, and Controller of the universe.

Genesis 1:2 ("the Spirit of God was hovering over the water," NIV) implies that order and design in creation are the work of the Spirit (Gen. 1:32:3). Just as the Spirit works in redemption to create wholeness, He also works in creation to create order and beauty (Ps. 33:6; Isa. 40:12-14). The Spirit causes the hidden beauty in God's creation to express itself (see Job 26:13, where breath translates *ruach*). God's Spirit continues to work creatively in the natural order (Ps. 104:30), especially at the human level (Job 27:3; 33:4; 34:14-15; Ps. 139:7), since in the biblical view the

---

2. This is the most obvious explanation to the enigmatic statement in John 7:39 that the Spirit had not yet been given before Jesus' resurrection.

Spirit is radically personal, in contrast to the impersonalism of pagan and animistic views of spirit.

2. The Old Testament teaches that the Spirit's most important work is redemption (Neh. 9:20; Ps. 51:11; Isa. 63:10-11; Ezek. 36:27). According to George Johnston, "Israel was constituted God's holy nation no less by the presence of his Spirit than by the covenant of Sinai."[3] Yet the Spirit's redemptive work builds on His creative work. Creation and redemption are neither to be contrasted, as in dualistic views of the relation between the material and the spiritual orders, nor simply identified, as in monistic and universalistic teachings, which deny the reality of sin and the need for redemption.

Here again, the New Testament assumes the teaching of the Old Testament, namely that the Spirit renews and heightens the God-given natural powers of His people (see Ex. 31:3; Num. 27:18; Judg. 3:10; 1 Sam. 16:13), especially in their intellectual life (Gen. 41:38; Num. 11:17).[4] The prophet was the characteristic Old Testament pneumatic (Num. 11:16-17,25, 29; 1 Kings 18:12; Mic. 3:8; cf. 1 Cor. 14:11), and at the heart of the predictive form of prophecy was the messianic hope with its anticipation of the coming One on whom the Spirit would rest uniquely (Isa. 11:2; 42:1; 61:1). The Messiah was to usher in a new age of unparalleled spiritual abundance (Joel 2:28-29; cf. Jer. 31:31; Ezek. 11:19).

The New Testament

With the coming of Christ, the long-awaited messianic age, with its promised spiritual abundance, broke decisively into history.

1. New Testament pneumatology builds on Old Testament foundations. The Spirit poured out on Pentecost is the Spirit who worked in the Old Testament. The New Testament presupposes rather than rejects the Old Testament view of the cosmic activity of the Spirit. It cannot be said too often that the New Testament writers took their Old Testament seriously.

2. Yet, there is a dimension of radical newness to the New Testament teaching regarding the Spirit. In the Old Testament the new age of the Spirit is promise; in the New Testament the arrival of this new age through the incarnation and Pentecost events is heralded everywhere. Newness is evident in the opening chapters of the Gospels. The Spirit is the *Holy Spirit,* a term that acquires the force of a personal name. From the outset of the New Testament era, the Spirit was recognized as a distinct personality. He was more clearly named in the New Testament than in the Old. As early as the first chapter of Luke, even before Luke's

---

3. George Johnston, "Spirit," in Alan Richardson, ed., *Theological Word Book of the Bible* (London: SCM, 1950), 237.
4. See below, the fourth guideline for the use of spiritual gifts, 42.

account of Jesus' birth, there are four references to the Spirit and each refers to the Spirit as the Holy Spirit. The change in terminology from the Spirit of the Lord in the Old Testament to Holy Spirit is abrupt and startling. (References to the Holy Spirit in Psalm 51:11 and Isaiah 63:10-11 are too exceptional to be regarded as clear references to the doctrine of the Trinity.)

3. The Synoptic Gospels, the Fourth Gospel, Acts, and the rest of the New Testament summarizes four perspectives in the New Testament approach to the work of the Spirit. The *Synoptic Gospels* relate the Spirit to Jesus' life and ministry. The Holy Spirit energized the life of Jesus from His birth to His resurrection. The life of Jesus showed what it means for the Spirit to be at work in fullness in a life. Jesus alone had the Spirit without measure (cf. John 3:31-34). He was the unique and exemplary pneumatic. He was a prophet, but more than a prophet! All that the New Testament has to say regarding the fruit and gifts of the Spirit in the lives of believers simply draws out the meaning of Jesus' character and ministry.

References to the Spirit in the *Gospel of John* center on five Paraclete sayings in Jesus' farewell discourse in the upper room (14:16-17; 14:26; 15:26; 16:7-11; 16:12-15). In these passages Jesus repeatedly promised to bestow the Spirit on believers after His death and resurrection. The incarnation and Pentecost events were indissolubly related. Christ was at once the unique Bearer of the Holy Spirit and the indispensable Bestower of the Spirit.

The Book of Acts records the Pentecost event and the launching in history of the world-wide God-movement that the incarnation, atoning death, and resurrection of Jesus Christ made possible. Attempts to view Pentecost as merely the birthday of the church or as the experience of a new dimension of individual sanctification or even as the inauguration of the church's worldwide mission (Matt. 28:19-20) miss the wholistic kingdom significance of the Spirit's work. Pentecost, as primarily a kingdom reality, includes each of these emphases *and more.*

The rest of the New Testament develops a theology of the Spirit's God-movement in history. What is initiatory and undeveloped in early Acts unfolds and blossoms in the remainder of the New Testament, as the Spirit *effects* the writing of the New Testament and a growing understanding of the new experiential realities of the Christian life and the church. These three—Scripture, Christian life, and church—are the chief instruments of the Spirit's mighty God-movement in history, the kingdom of God as a present reality awaiting consummation with the return of Christ. Always, of course, the initiative in redemption, as well as in creation, remains with the Spirit. Humanity's first need is for what only God in Christ by the Holy Spirit can accomplish.

Historical Perspective

Catholic and Protestant orthodoxy, though acknowledging the Spirit's work in principle, tends to neglect the subject in theological formulations. If the weakness in Catholic pneumatology is a subordination of the Holy Spirit to the institutional church,[5] Protestant pneumatology emphasizes the work of the Spirit in individual sanctification but neglects the Spirit's work in the church.[6]

In the eighteenth-century Evangelical Revival and the Great Awakening, theological interest in the work of the Holy Spirit received fresh impetus through the ministry of John Wesley, Jonathan Edwards, and others. Beginning in 1792, the modern missions movement emphasized the Spirit's activity in world missions. Especially in nineteenth-century Britain and America, revivalism and the holiness movement contributed to a rediscovery of the biblical stress on the work of the Holy Spirit, as have the Pentecostal and charismatic movements in the twentieth century. Wesleyan and holiness teaching, however, tends to focus on the Spirit's work in believers to the neglect of other aspects of His work; Pentecostals and charismatics give exaggerated emphasis to signs and wonders, such as tongues and healing.

Restatement

How should we distinguish the work of the Father from the work of the Son and the work of the Holy Spirit? The Father is often referred to as the Creator, the Son as the Savior, and the Spirit as the Sanctifier.[7] Again, to refer to the Spirit as the Sanctifier is to limit His role unduly to the individual, and thus to merely inward and subjective dimensions.

---

5. Under the heading of "The Church the appointed teacher of revealed truth," Smith says:

This, then, is the way of approach to God's truth which Christ himself has ordained: a visible Church with a living teaching authority (*the magisterium of the Church*), infallible because the Holy Ghost is with her, preserving her from error.

George D. Smith, *The Teaching of the Catholic Church* (London: Burns and Oates, 1948), 27-28.

6. The new emphasis on the laity, or the recovery of the doctrine of the priesthood of all believers, at the time of the Protestant reformation was effectively stopped short of undercutting the catholic preoccupation with the institutional church by the reformers' retention of such practices as infant baptism and the union of church and state.

Only with the Anabaptists and the radical Reformation was there a significant recovery of the close relation between the church and the Holy Spirit. As primarily the Spirit's creation of the new people of God, the church in the biblical view is first of all a spiritual organism and secondarily an institution.

7. See, for example, Thomas A. Smail, *The Forgotten Father* (Grand Rapids: Eerdmans, 1980), 24.

What, then, is the most adequate way of conceiving the Spirit's distinctive role?

What the Holy Spirit's Role Is: The Effecter

The Spirit's distinctive role.—The key biblical idea to distinguish the Spirit's role from those of the Father and the Son is the idea of *effecting*. The Spirit is the effecter of God's purposes, whether in creation or redemption!

Effectiveness, of course, is to be distinguished from efficiency. Efficiency is not necessarily concerned with qualitative values; efficiency easily becomes an end in itself, justifying whatever means it finds expedient. Effectiveness, however, is concerned with the quality of its methods and results. As the Effecter of God's creative and redemptive purposes in history and experience, the Spirit actualizes God's purposes in a manner that promotes the long-range growth of persons. The Spirit, then, is the *effective* actualizer of God's intentions.

This way of conceiving the Spirit's role has two distinct advantages. First, it includes the Spirit's role in creation as well as in redemption, avoiding the traditional tendency to limit the Spirit's work to subjective, individual sanctification. Second, it points to costly patience and effective endurance, rather than spectacular signs and wonders, as the biblical characteristic of the Holy Spirit's work. Signs and wonders are not excluded, but they are not major indicators of the Spirit's activities.

The first fruit of the Spirit is love, the strong *agape* revealed in Christ, the quality of love that perseveres despite obstacles (John 13:1; Heb. 12:2). The Spirit's best gift is the love that "always protects, always trusts, always hopes, always perseveres" (1 Cor. 13:7, NIV). Such love is no momentary flash. It is the quality of moral power (*dunamis*) raised to its zenith, not to overwhelm but to overcome evil with good. The power of Christ is power in weakness, the power to endure hardship as a good soldier of the cross (2 Cor. 12:10).[8]

The unity of the work of the trinitarian Persons.—Although the Bible distinguishes the Persons of the Trinity, each of the Persons is involved in the work of the others. While the Father is regarded as Creator, the Son as Savior, and the Spirit as Effecter, each person is involved in each of

---

8. Frederick Dale Bruner, *A Theology of the Holy Spirit* (Grand Rapids: Eerdmans, 1970), "The Sphere of the Spirit as the Believer's Weakness," 303-19.

See also John Koenig, *Charismata: God's Gifts for God's People* (Philadelphia: Westminster, 1978), "Warning against Shallow Celebration," 67-70. Koenig distinguishes giftedness from giddiness. Life in the Spirit does not escape suffering and death, as the excessively "enthusiastic" Corinthians seemed to believe.

these activities. Christians should carefully avoid compartmentalizing the work of the trinitarian Persons.

The Spirit at Pentecost did not come with a wholly new and discrete program of His own. Instead, Pentecost built on and was one with the work of God in creation, in the history of Israel, and in the life and ministry of Jesus Christ. This was true because the Spirit was involved, no less than the Son, in all of the divine work before Pentecost. His work is always, at one and the same time, the work of the Father and the Son, even as Their work is always the work of the Holy Spirit!

Instead of the Spirit taking the place of an absent Father or Son, as is sometimes said, the Spirit effects Their presence and activity. Every filling of the Spirit is at the same time a renewed commitment to God's redemptive purpose in Christ. No New Testament principle is more essential than this to understanding of the Spirit's work.

When the Gospels are said to focus on the kingdom as earthly and Jewish while Acts and the Epistles focus on the church as heavenly and spiritual, the unity of the Bible is brought into question as is the unity of the work of the Son and the Spirit. The same is true when Christ's work is said to be objective and historical, while the Spirit's work is limited to subjective and inward dimensions, or when it is said that the object of the believer's faith in the experience of justification is Christ, while the object of faith in the experience of sanctification is the Holy Spirit.

In popular Christianity many such artificial distinctions find expression. In the Bible, however, the unity of the Persons of the Trinity in all they do is never compromised. To magnifiy one Person of the Trinity at the expense of the Others finds no biblical support whatever. To magnify one is to magnify all.

What the Holy Spirit Effects

Since the Spirit does not come with an independent program of His own apart from the Father and the Son, His role is best defined as *effecting* the purposes of the Father through the Son. The New Testament points in this direction by defining the Spirit as the Spirit of truth (John 15:26; 16:13). The Spirit is not sent to speak of Himself, but to witness to God's truth as revealed in Christ. This is not to reduce the Spirit to a subordinate status, inferior to that of the Father or the Son, as though the Spirit were a mere influence or subjective impression.

What does the Holy Spirit effect? Traditional discussions of the Spirit's work speak of the Spirit's threefold activity (in relation to biblical revelation, to the Christian life, and to the church). In the present discussion, however, this standard approach is broadened (1) in order to underscore the Spirit's role as the Effecter of God's purposes in creation as well as in redemption and (2) in order to show that the Spirit's threefold redemptive role can only be adequately understood when rooted in the *comprehensive kingdom scope* of God's redemptive purpose in Christ (Col. 1:20).

The work of the Spirit in creation.—Although the Bible does not dwell on the fact, it leaves no doubt regarding the Spirit's role in creating and sustaining the world. The Bible everywhere assumes that creation and sustenance are the work of the one triune God. If God "is not far from each of us" (Acts 17:27) and if God is triune, then the Father, Son, and Holy Spirit are as near as breath itself.

God's Spirit is the power that brings to fulfillment God's purpose and design in creation (Gen. 1:2; Job 26:13; Ps. 33:6; Isa. 40:13), but He is also the power that *sustains* creation from moment to moment (Ps. 104:27-30). This is especially true of human life (Num. 16:22; Job 27:3; 33:4; Ezek. 37:1-14). What kind of power is behind the universe? The Bible answers that it is the power of the God who is personal, spiritual, good, and almighty. Because of the Spirit's effecting work, the universe is orderly, life has meaning, and history presses toward its God-intended goal.

On the basis of this biblical worldview, the Holy Spirit Himself is seen to be the Effecter of general revelation; thus the triune God mediates *all* truth, goodness, and beauty in human experience through the Holy Spirit. Every time a person adds two and two and gets four, the Spirit is at work. The same is true whenever morality is practiced or beauty is perceived.

Of course, this work of the Spirit in relation to the material and human orders generally is not adequate to fulfill God's redemptive purpose; nor does it in any sense minimize the awful reality of sin and evil. As the ultimate source of all that is true, good, and beautiful, the Spirit constantly wages war against falsehood, immorality, and ugliness, superhuman as well as human, ultimately triumphing over all such intruders and usurpers.

The work of the Spirit in redemption.—Since God's first purpose for a fallen world is redemption, the Spirit's primary work is redeeming us from sin. This redemption is first provided, then it is applied.

1. Providing redemption.—The Spirit's work in originally providing redemption can best be understood as involving all that God accomplished in redemptive history beginning with His pursuit of Adam and Eve after the fall to the end of the New Testament period. This is the special or redemptive revelation of God to which the Bible bears witness. The Spirit's indispensable role in this redemptive activity is evident in His inspiration of the writers of the biblical accounts and in His relation to the life and worship of the people of Israel, to prophecy, to the life and

ministry of Jesus Christ, and to the creation, empowering, and leadership of the church as the people of God of the new covenant.

Today, God redeems primarily through the Spirit's quickening of the biblical witness to these mighty saving acts of God. Secondarily, however, the Spirit also works redemptively today through Christian tradition. Today's believers are not the only ones who have had the Holy Spirit. Other Christians throughout the long history of the church have also experienced the Spirit's redeeming work, so that the Spirit can now speak through tradition as well as through Scripture. Scripture, though, remains the primary and final authority.

The Spirit's speaking is spiritually discerned. Since "no man has ever seen God" (John 1:18), all of God's self-revealing activity has a spiritual quality (1Cor. 2:11-13); faith, or spiritual perception, which is the Spirit's enablement, is essential to the receive revelation (1 Cor. 2:14). Jesus' enemies, lacking spiritual perception, explained away all evidence of God's presence in His Son (Matt. 12:24). Nor did unbelievers recognize the Holy Spirit's activity on the day of Pentecost (Acts 2:13).

Only the Spirit enables believers today to understand and apply the teaching of God's word to each new situation. The Bible, the living Christ, and the Holy Spirit are all involved when God speaks a redeeming word today. It is futile to argue that one of these factors *apart from* the others is the final authority. Each is indispensable. Just as Christ is the living Christ and the Spirit is preeminently the Giver of life, so the words of the Bible through Christ and the Spirit are living words, always bursting to say more than printed words can say, never serving the purpose they were intended to serve until they are interpreted, proclaimed, and lived.

Finally, the Spirit *abundantly* provides redemption. "The New Testament," says Koenig, "was written by and for people who felt themselves extraordinarily gifted."[9] The church's present spiritual poverty cannot be traced to any lack of spiritual resources. The Holy Spirit readily offers spiritual abundance, making the church's failures ever sadder and less excusable.

2. Applying redemption.—Three aspects of the Spirit's work in the application of redemption are treated in the following discussion. The Spirit applies redemption by effecting:

• The kingdom present,
• Christian life and the church, and
• Fullness of the Spirit and bestowing spiritual gifts.

First, *the Spirit applies redemption by effecting the kingdom present.* Through the Spirit, the kingdom of God, as inaugurated by Christ

---

9. John Koenig, *Charismata*, 48.

through His life and ministry, begins to break into history in power, dramatically altering the course of human events. Traditional discussions of the Spirit's redemptive work tend to omit reference to its significant kingdom dimensions. Theologians have usually spoken only of the Spirit's work in relation to biblical inspiration and illumination, to the Christian life, and to the church.

Yet, in the biblical view, Jesus' promise of the kingdom (for example, "Thy kingdom come," Matt. 6:10; "seek first His kingdom and his righteousness," Matt. 6:33) was initially fulfilled on Pentecost. Peter clearly explained Pentecost: "Exalted to the right hand of God, and having received from the Father the promise of the Holy Spirit, He has poured forth this which you both see and hear" (Acts 2:33). Peter went on to insist that God raised Christ to reign over His enemies: "Let all the house of Israel know for certain that God has made Him both Lord and Christ—this Jesus whom you crucified" (Acts 2:36). Pentecost, then, is the living Christ pouring out His Spirit in resurrection power in order that the Spirit might effect or actualize the inauguration of the kingdom in history, anticipating the consummation of the kingdom at the second coming of Christ.

Traditional pneumatology often neglects the Spirit's work in effecting the presence of the kingdom of God in history, which should take logical precedence over the Spirit's work in effecting the Christian life and the church. The Christian life and the church are essentially kingdom realities. These outcroppings or manifestations of the kingdom of God are *signs* of its presence and *agents* of its advance. They are intended to fulfill kingdom purposes. Consequently, the Spirit's work in the Christian life and the church can be adequately understood only in the context of what God designs to accomplish through His kingdom.

The Spirit-kingdom association says a great deal about the scope of the Spirit's redemptive work. Rather than limit the Spirit's work to the subjective, the kingdom emphasis also views the Spirit's work as objective, comprehensive with reference to the needs of whole persons. Ultimately, God's kingdom goal through the Spirit is to subject all things to Jesus Christ (Col. 1:20).

This insight is indispensable to any evangelical today who endeavors to work through the evangelism/social action controversy. The New Testament thinks boldly of the scope of God's purpose through Christ and His kingdom. According to *The Baptist Faith and Message,* Christ's people should cooperate toward "the great objects of the Kingdom of God" (Art. XIV). Where the Spirit works to effect God's kingdom, the young see visions and the old dream dreams (Acts 2:17).

The Spirit-kingdom association also says a great deal about the nature of the kingdom. The kingdom of God is a Holy Spirit reality, and kingdom power is spiritual power. The power of the kingdom is redemptive, not merely political, national, or military. In a variety of ways Jesus emphasizes that His kingdom is not of this world (John 18:36). As the Sermon on the Mount makes clear, kingdom law is radically new (Matt. 5:3-12). For Paul, "the kingdom of God does not consist in words, but in power" (1 Cor. 4:20), and Christians are to witness "not in words taught by human wisdom, but in those taught by the Spirit" (1 Cor. 2:13). Since Jesus reigns in history from a cross, the Spirit's mightiest weapon for kingdom advance is the gospel of Jesus Christ, crucified and risen.

Second, *the Spirit applies redemption by effecting the Christian life and the church as the signs and agents of the kingdom of God in history.*

The New Testament views Christian experience as the Spirit's work from beginning to end. The Spirit convicts of sin, of righteousness, and of judgment (John 16:7-11); points persons to the Savior (1 Cor. 12:3); regenerates (John 3:1-8); nurtures Christlike character (Gal. 5:22-23); strengthens in weakness (Rom. 8:26; 2 Cor. 12:7-10); bestows gifts (1 Cor. 12:11); seals to the day of final redemption (Eph. 1:13); gives assurance of adoption (Rom. 8:16); guides (Rom. 8:14); gives victory over sin (Rom. 8:9); intercedes (Rom. 8:26); teaches (1 Cor. 2:14); illumines Scripture (Heb. 10:15); gives liberty (2 Cor. 3:17); infills (Eph. 5:18); sanctifies (2 Thess. 2:13); renews (Titus 3:5); unites believers in fellowship in Christ (2 Cor. 13:14); gives boldness in time of persecution (Luke 12:12; Acts 4:13); and empowers in Christian witness to the ends of the earth (Acts 1:8). Scripture attributes primarily to the Holy Spirit all that believers are and can become.

Since the Spirit's work in the Christian life is kingdom work, the Spirit's work can never be reduced to regeneration and sanctification as merely inward and individual concerns. Instead, the Spirit's work in believers must always be viewed in relation to the comprehensive, wholistic scope of God's kingdom purpose in Christ.

Since the Spirit's work in believers is always kingdom work, and since the kingdom of God is a corporate as well as an individual reality, *effecting the Christian life inescapably involves effecting the church.* The Holy Spirit binds believers to one another in a oneness in Christ which finds expression both generally in the unity of all believers in the one body of Christ and locally in congregations or fellowships of believers. Such congregations are not only *signs* of the kingdom's presence but also *agents* of the kingdom's comprehensive mission.

As the creation of the Holy Spirit, these congregations are essentially spiritual fellowships or organisms, not primarily institutions or organizations. Only the Spirit can create a church, and only the Spirit can make churches effective in fulfilling the limitless goals of their kingdom mission.

Redeemed! Eschatological Redemption and the Kingdom of God

—42—

That churches are supremely the creation of the Spirit as He effects His kingdom purposes is the main point of Pentecost (Acts 2). "All believers were together and had everything in common. . . . Every day they continued to meet together . . . and ate together" (Acts 2:44,46, NIV). Then Luke adds: "And the Lord was adding to their number day by day those who were being saved" (2:47; since "to their number" is a circumlocution for the church, the KJV understandably translates the phrase "church," though the word church is not in the original). Furthermore, as the New Testament story of the missionary expansion of the early church unfolded, wherever believers were won to Christ, there the Spirit kept on creating similar congregations of God's people.

As creations of the Holy Spirit, New Testament churches are infinitely more than voluntary associations, such as civic clubs and parent-teacher associations. Various Baptist confessions, including *The Baptist Faith and Message,* define churches as voluntary associations of believers in Jesus Christ; this definition needs to be qualified by an understanding that churches are first of all creations of the Spirit and not of human beings. Churches are God's idea before they are ever thought of by persons. Believers voluntarily associate in congregations because the Holy Spirit draws them together.

Such *voluntary* togetherness by the Spirit should not surprise us, for the first fruit of the Spirit in believers is love, including the love of believers for one another. Always, though, "we love, because He first loved us" (1 John 4:19). We are taught love and oneness by the Spirit.

The Spirit creates churches, but He also makes their worship and work effective. Through the abundance of His gifts He constantly seeks to renew God's people. He gives gifts of ministry (1 Cor. 12:1-11; Rom. 12:6-8) and gifts of leadership (1 Cor. 12:27-31; Eph. 4:11-13). He guides (Acts 13:2-4; 15:28; 16:6-7; 21:4). He produces community-building character (Gal. 5:22-23). A biblical understanding of the church must recognize the essential relation between pneumatology and ecclesiology.

Third, *the Spirit's work in applying redemption especially involves His effecting the New Testament experience of the fullness of the Spirit and His bestowing of spiritual gifts.* Reference to these issues is not to be viewed as the introduction of a different topic from the two already treated, but rather as a recognition of the large amount of attention they have received in recent years due to Pentecostal, charismatic, deeper life, and church renewal influences. The matter of spiritual gifts has received sufficient notice to justify devoting an entire chapter to its consideration (see the following chapter).

"Baptism of the Spirit" is not a New Testament expression.[10] Although the New Testament uses the verb *baptize* in the expression "baptize with the Spirit," the noun *baptism* is never so used. In Pentecostal theology "baptism in the Spirit" is defined as a wonderful experience "distinct from and subsequent to the experience of the new birth," the initial evidence of which is speaking in tongues.[11]

Outside Pentecostal circles, evangelical theology usually makes no distinction between being baptized with the Spirit (Mark 1:8; Acts 1:5; 11:16; 1 Cor. 12:13) and receiving the Spirit in initial conversion (Acts 2:38; Gal. 3:2). Regarding the latter, Paul is clear: "If anyone does not have the Spirit of Christ, he does not belong to Him" (Rom. 8:9). Believers, therefore, need not seek the Spirit as a second, subsequent blessing, in addition to receiving the Spirit in conversion.

The New Testament emphasizes that the full range of the Spirit's activity is available to every believer from the beginning of the Christian life. The Samaritans received the Spirit only after Peter and John arrived from Jerusalem (Acts 8:12-17); the Spirit fell on Cornelius and his household before they were baptized (Acts 10:44-48); and certain Ephesian disciples, who had been baptized with John's baptism only, had not received the Spirit when they believed (Acts 19:2-6). A consistent pattern of initial conversion had not yet established itself in this earliest phase of Christian history. By seeking to make these exceptional passages normative for New Testament Christianity, Pentecostals elevate the early narrative portions of Acts above later doctrinal portions of the New Testament, which traditional writings sadly neglect.

Pentecostals and many charismatics seem to confuse being baptized in the Spirit with being filled with the Spirit. Scripture never exhorts believers to be baptized in or with the Spirit, for they have already received the Spirit in conversion. Paul exhorts believers to be filled with the Spirit (Eph. 5:18). The expressions "full of the Spirit" and "filled with the Spirit" are Lukan (Luke 1:15,41,67; 4:1; Acts 2:4; 4:8,31; 6:3,5; 7:55; 9:17; 11:24; 13:9,52), but the idea is implicit in all New Testament teaching about sanctification.

The New Testament teaches that to be filled with the Spirit is to be like Christ. Beyond this emphasis, the New Testament is flexible. To be filled with the Spirit can refer either to the general character of one's life (Acts 11:24) or to filling for a special occasion (Acts 4:8; 13:9); it can refer not only to individuals but also to an assembly of Christians (Acts 2:4).

---

10. For a thoughtful recent discussion of the work of the Holy Spirit in the life of the believer, see Earl C. Davis, *Life in the Spirit,* vol. 11, Layman's Library of Christian Doctrine (Nashville: Broadman, 1986).

11. This is the formal definition used by the Assemblies of God, according to Bruner, *A Theology of the Holy Spirit,* 60-61.

Does spiritual maturity (or Christlikeness) come gradually but never finally in this life, or does it come suddenly in a once-for-all crisis experience? Many Christians, perhaps most, become seriously committed to Christ only after a crisis experience following initial conversion, whether the subsequent experience comes quickly or belatedly. Scripture itself recognizes that some Christians do not grow in grace. Paul distinguishes sharply between worldly and spiritual Christians (1 Cor 3:1; see also Rom. 6:3; 8:4-13; 12:1-2; Gal. 3:2-5; Heb. 6:1). In such cases "something more" happens to transform nominal Christians into committed Christians. This subject is so important that it will be dealt with more specifically in the chapter on the Christian life.

Yet there is no uniform way to achieve the Spirit-filled life. Christian pilgrimages vary considerably. Both the long, hard struggle and the sudden, crisis transformation play important roles. Either way, Christian maturity is neither easy nor automatic. Believers always need daily renewal. Many experience longer or shorter periods of burnout and backsliding, yet mountain peak experiences of spiritual ecstasy are often accompanied by new temptations to trust in self rather than in the Holy Spirit. Consequently, Christians should resist the temptation to canonize one type of spiritual experience as normative for all Christians, and they should recognize that their need for daily renewal is never finally outgrown in this life.

4 *Spiritual Gifts*

*God has richly gifted His people, empowering them
for kingdom service and enabling them in attitude
and action to minister in Jesus' name.*

The Fact of Spiritual Gifts in the Bible
The Special Interest in Gifts in American Christianity since
    World War II
Two Types of Approaches to Spiritual Gifts
Defining a Spiritual Gift
Guidelines for Using Spiritual Gifts Today

This chapter continues the discussion of the work of the Holy Spirit in the application of redemption which was begun in the preceding chapter. As noted there, the work of the Spirit in creating the Christian life and the church involves especially His work in filling believers and bestowing spiritual gifts.

The Fact of Spiritual Gifts in the Bible

That spiritual gifts are a reality according to the Bible is readily apparent from the different gift lists in the New Testament.[1] In 1 Corinthians 12-14, the classic passage on spiritual gifts, Paul speaks of "varieties of gifts, but the same Spirit." The Greek word translated "gifts" is the familiar *charismata* (the plural of *charisma*), from *charis* (grace). This means that gifts of the Spirit are gifts of God's grace in Jesus Christ. In addition to the gifts listed in 1 Corinthians 12:7-11 and 27-31, other lists are found in Romans 12:6-8, Ephesians 4:11, and 1 Peter 4:10.

---

1. For a general survey of biblical teaching about giftedness, see John Koenig, *Charismata: God's Gifts for God's People* (Philadelphia: Westminster, 1978). Koenig sees beyond gift lists to giftedness. Readers who disagrees with Koenig on details will still appreciate his contribution.

For a valuable exegetical study of New Testament teaching about gifts in 1 Thess. 5, 1 Cor. 12–14, Rom. 12, and Eph. 4, as these passages are viewed in their contexts, see Kenneth S. Hemphill, *Spiritual Gifts: Empowering the New Testament Church* (Nashville: Broadman, 1988).

The Special Interest in Gifts
in American Christianity
Since World War II

No discussion of spiritual gifts in American Christianity today can ignore the special interest in the topic since World War II. Two quite different developments contributed especially to this new attention. One influence was the church renewal movement.[2] Another has been the charismatic movement. The literature regarding these movements is vast, and, unfortunately, no adequate overview of the topic has yet appeared in print.[3]

A major outcome of the charismatic movement has been a new openness to the validity of the so-called Pentecostal "sign gifts" in mainline denominations. In fact, Quebedeaux contends that the charismatic movement had this wider legitimizing of Pentecostal sign gifts as its primary purpose. Consequently, he argues that by the late 1970s, when this goal was accomplished, the movement peaked, having lost its distinctive purpose for existence and much of its media visibility.[4]

Along with the new accommodation of Pentecostal sign gifts in mainline denominations is a change in theological perspective among evangelicals regarding sign gifts. The older Warfield conservatism, which dominated much non-Pentecostal, evangelical thinking on the subject before World War II, taught that sign gifts had *ceased* with the death of the apostles and

---

2. Following are two randomly selected examples of concern with spiritual gifts in the church renewal movement antecedent to or independent of the charismatic movement. For an introduction to church renewal literature, see Bob E. Patterson, ed., *The Stirring Giant: Renewal Forces at Work in the Modern Church* (Waco, TX: Word, 1971).

The Church of the Saviour, Washington, D. C., established by Gordon Cosby in 1947 as an experiment in church renewal, has given significant attention to spiritual gifts. See Elizabeth O'Connor, *Call to Commitment: The Story of the Church of the Saviour, Washington, D.C.* (New York: Harper & Row, 1963); *Journey Inward, Journey Outward* (New York: Harper & Row, 1968); and *Eighth Day of Creation: Gifts and Creativity* (Waco, TX: Word, 1971).

Independent of the charismatic movement, Ayres included a chapter on spiritual gifts in his book on recovery of the laity in the life of ecumenical Protestant churches in America. See Francis O. Ayres, *The Ministry of the Laity* (Philadelphia: Westminster, 1962), chap. 5.

Confessional materials mention spiritual gifts in passing. *The Baptist Faith and Message* says that the Holy Spirit "bestows the spiritual gifts by which [believers] serve God through His church" (Art II).

3. McDonnell's collection of ecclesiastical documents on the charismatic movement is invaluable but makes no attempt to discuss the many books on spiritual gifts. Kilian McDonnell, ed., *Presence, Power, and Praise* (Collegeville, MN: Liturgical Press, 1980).

Quebedeaux thoroughly analyzes the charismatic movement but has few references to spiritual gifts. Richard Quebedeaux, *The New Charismatics II* (San Francisco: Harper & Row, 1983).

4. Quebedeaux, *The New Charismatics II*, 83, 236. See also the discussion of the charismatic movement in the introductory section of this study.

the writing of the New Testament.[5] This outlook now finds diminishing support among evangelicals. MacGorman, for example, concedes that "speaking in tongues is a valid charismatic gift."[6]

Despite this new evangelical openness to Pentecostal sign gifts, the difference between non-Pentecostal and Pentecostal evangelicals remains clear. Evangelicals generally prize the Spirit's fruit above modern displays of "sign gifts," eschewing overemphasis on signs and wonders as evidences of the Holy Spirit's work.

Two Types of Approaches to Spiritual Gifts

Despite their new openness to spiritual gifts, however, non-Pentecostal evangelicals are not altogether agreed on the subject. Broadly speaking, they follow one or the other of two approaches. Some enumerate and precisely define New Testament gifts, often elaborating gift inventories and developing programs of gift discovery. Others avoid precisely defining the gifts, understanding rather that gifts and giftedness are intended to show how abundantly the Holy Spirit endows believers for kingdom service and growth.[7]

---

5. Warfield argues that the miraculous working which is but the sign of God's revealing power, cannot be expected to continue, and in point of fact does not continue, after the revelation of which it is the accompaniment has been completed. B. B. Warfield, *Counterfeit Miracles* (New York: Scribner's, 1918), 26-27.

To cite a more recent example, Carnell goes beyond Warfield: "Few realize it, but the doctrine that miracles no longer occur is one of those fundamental canons which separate Protestantism from Roman Catholicism." E. J. Carnell, *An Introduction to Christian Apologetics* (Grand Rapids: Eerdmans, 1948), 272. Carnell could have referred to fundamental canons that separate Protestantism from Roman Catholicism *and Pentecostalism*.

It should be noted that in the revised edition of his *An Introduction to Christian Apologetics*, after a storm of protest from evangelicals, Carnell modified his position in order to acknowledge the miraculous character of regeneration, answers to prayer, and the like. Current writers who deny the validity of sign gifts today are cautious not to deny the occurrence of miracles altogether. See, for example, John F. MacArthur, *The Charismatics* (Grand Rapids: Zondervan, 1978), 84.

6. Jack W. MacGorman, *The Gifts of the Spirit* (Nashville: Broadman, 1974), 83. MacGorman comments on "how grievous it is to read where a church excludes members for claiming a New Testament experience" (Ibid., 120). Even so, MacGorman says little about healing and exorcism and devalues tongues: "Had glossolalists . . . become central, the book of Acts would never have been written. You can make a meal out of evangelism as meat and ecstasy as salt, but you'll die of starvation with ecstasy as meat and evangelism as salt (Ibid., 122)."

7. For an example of spiritual gift lists and programs, see C. Peter Wagner, *Your Spiritual Gifts: How to Find Your Gift and Use It* (Glendale, CA: Regal, 1974). Wagner refers to the Modified Houts Questionnaire used by Fuller Evangelistic Association, to the "Spiritual Gift Inventory," by Gordon McMinn, used at Western Baptist Seminary, and to "Nexus," a table game for discovering gifts produced by the Sunday School Board of the Southern Baptist Convention. Ibid., 255.

For an approach emphasizing spiritual gifts as God's provision for the believer's spiritual well-being and kingdom service, see: Hemphill, *Spiritual Gifts;* John Koenig, *Charismata: God's Gifts for God's People* (Philadelphia: Westminster, 1978); and J. Terry Young, *The Spirit within You: Straight Talk about God's Gift to All Believers* (Nashville: Broadman, 1977), 77-101.

Two reasons prompt the adoption of the broader of the two approaches:

- nothing indicates that New Testament gift lists were meant to be exhaustive or final;

- the New Testament never clearly defines many of the gifts. What are "helps" and "administrations" (1 Cor. 12:28)? How should we apply them today? What is the gift of tongues or the gift of healing? We know little about the relation of the Holy Spirit to tongues or where to draw the line between alleged miraculous healing in public services and healing through doctors, hospitals, and medicines.

Evangelicals agree that God works miracles, but there is still much to learn about tongues, prophecy, healing, exorcism, and the like. There is no evangelical consensus, for instance, about the relation of tongues at Pentecost (Acts 2) to tongues at Corinth (1 Cor. 12–14), to say nothing of the exegesis of passages on which Pentecostals and charismatics base their distinctive teaching about baptism in the Spirit as a distinct experience after initial conversion. Non-Pentecostal evangelicals believe the Pentecostal and charismatic signs-and-wonders approach to spiritual gifts assumes to know more than is really known.[8]

Defining a Spiritual Gift

Spiritual gifts are God empowering His people through the Holy Spirit for kingdom life and service, enabling them in attitude and action to live

---

8. Unlike the Pentecostal claim that the tongues phenomenon is clearly "supernatural" and "remarkable," Heron says:

> Speaking in tongues was treated (in classical Pentecostalism) as *the* biblical evidence for "baptism in the Spirit." Recent studies, however, suggest that the phenomenon is essentially a *natural* one, though there is as yet no entirely satisfactory description of the mechanism by which it is brought into operation or the pattern of its working.

Alasdair I. C. Heron, *The Holy Spirit* (Philadelphia: Westminster, 1983), 134. Classical Pentecostals strove for the gift of tongues, some for a lifetime without success. Today's charismatics turn tongues on and off at will, but not all charismatics give "signs and wonders" the same prominence that characterize classical Pentecostals.

See Richard Quebedeaux's comment about *faster* ways to receive the Spirit among charismatics in *The New Charismatics II*. One of the most penetrating exegetical critiques of classical Pentecostal claims is Frederick Dale Bruner, *A Theology of the Holy Spirit: The Pentecostal Experience and the New Testament Witness* (Grand Rapids: Eerdmans, 1970); see especially 213-214.

Classical Pentecostalism is changing. See Paul B. Tinlin and Edith L. Blumhofer, "Decade of Decline or Harvest? Dilemmas of the Assemblies of God," in *The Christian Century*, July 10-17, 1991, 684-87. The article concludes:

> Theological issues, too, cannot be ignored much longer. Dissatisfaction with the traditional answers that have validated tongues speech as uniform initial physical evidence of Spirit baptism comes at a time when Pentecostal scholarship offers theological alternatives (Ibid., 687).

and to minister in a manner which glorifies Christ.[9] On this basis, it is evident that biblical teaching about spiritual gifts is richer, broader, and more flexible than some have suggested.

Guidelines for Using Spiritual Gifts Today

The following guidelines are meant to apply to the use of spiritual gifts the understanding of the Holy Spirit and the manner in which He works which is developed in the present study. Their number and scope witness to the richness of the subject.

1. The Giver is more important than the gifts.—The best gift is the giver Himself![10] Without His empowering there are no spiritual gifts, just as using gifts without His blessing is fruitless (1 Cor. 3:6). He sovereignly distributes His gifts (1 Cor. 12:11), and He establishes controls for using them (1 Cor. 14). He is to be the Master, not the ministry to which He calls. Let God be God! All is to be done to His glory.

---

9. Hemphill acknowledges the difficulty in formulating a definition of a spiritual gift: "Perhaps you are somewhat disappointed that after all this study we have not been able to give a simple definition of spiritual gifts. Believe me, I have struggled with this dilemma for many hours." He continues with the suggestion that it is probably better to "give greater effort to discovering and fully utilizing the multiplicity of gifts that are available for the church on mission." Despite this demurer, it is difficult to sense anything in Hemphill's discussion contrary to the working definition suggested above.

In fact, earlier in his discussion he says that "gifts and *behavior* were closely interwoven in 1 Corinthians," in that gifts provided a means for expressing love. He adds that in 1 Cor. 12:28 "Paul intentionally broadens the 'gift' concept to include leadership and routine service abilities (such as church parking lot duties today!)." Hemphill continues: "The suggestions that *charismata* are only 'activities of the moment' or that they are [only] heightened natural abilities are both too narrow. On the other hand the idea that anything done for the good of the body becomes *charismata* is too broad. Paul had in mind abilities, both transitory and permanent, miraculous and routine, which enable one to function as a member of the body." Kenneth S. Hemphill, *Spiritual Gifts: Empowering the New Testament Church* (Nashville: Broadman, 1988), 72,125-26,206.

Young says: "A gift of the Holy Spirit is best considered a calling to perform some function of service for the church. . . . It could be any practical expression of the Christian life. . . . It does involve the leadership and power of the Holy Spirit working through us, most often in quite ordinary ways." J. Terry Young, *The Spirit within You* (Nashville: Broadman, 1977), 94-95.

The definition of a spiritual gift should avoid claiming too much. Writers sometimes say that God has given every saved person a special gift to excel in a specific ministry in the name and power of Christ. Young's suggestion that the Spirit most often works through believers in ordinary ways is better.

10. In his chapter on "Common and Special Gifts in the Old Testament," Koenig has a section on God's special gifts to Israel (including the Aaronic benediction in Num. 6:24-26). He says:

> Israel finds its identity and its task in its many gifts. But, as always, the fundamental gift is the presence of God himself. "With thee is the fountain of life" (Ps. 36:9). . . . Above all, God walks "with" Israel. . . . The Lord has a passion to dwell among his people. That is the finest gift of all.

Koenig, *Charismata*, 28-29.

While the New Testament speaks of the Spirit as the Giver of gifts (1 Cor. 12:11), it also refers to God as the Giver (Rom. 12:3) and to the exalted Christ as the Giver (Eph. 4:8). Ultimately the Giver of gifts is the triune God.[11]

2. *Timeless biblical commands take precedence over the gifts.*—These commands include the first and greatest commandment (Matt. 22:37-38), the Great Commission, (28:18-20), and New Testament teaching about the Spirit's fruit in the lives of believers (Gal. 5:22-23). We can never legitimately excuse disobedience to God's commands by pleading that we lack the resources necessary for obedience. God's commands are His enablements! When the King says "Go," he also says, "I am with you always" (Matt. 28:19-20). Believers are not free to ignore the Great Commission on the ground that they lack the gift of evangelism! Nor can they excuse lovelessness, as though character were secondary to gift display. As 1 Corinthians 12–14 makes clear, gifts without love create jealousy, rivalry, division, and many other problems, but gifts exercised in love build up the body of Christ.[12]

3. *Every believer is richly gifted.*—"To each one," Paul said, "is given the manifestation of the Spirit for the common good" (1 Cor. 12:7). There are no second-class Christians.[13] All have unique and important gifts for building up the body.

In Christ every believer is a qualified priest and minister, though some have learned more than others. Each should reflect a keen sense of abundance through the Spirit and a profound awareness of Christian identity, of worth to God, and of a mission and purpose in life, however deprived

---

11. Regarding the action of the triune God in spiritual gifting, Koenig says:
> The Spirit's residence within believers creates a hospitable heart that allows them to welcome Jesus and the Father, to be at home with God. . . . In the Spirit, the Father of Jesus Christ and Giver of every good and perfect gift (Jas. 1:17) draws near to become our Father (Ibid., 91-92).

Smail, a former leader in the charismatic movement in Britain, compartmentalizes trinitarian activities, stressing the role of the Father. The dust cover of the book summarizes Smail's position:
> In recent years there has been a Jesus movement and a charismatic movement with its emphasis on the Holy Spirit. The basic thesis of this book is that the Christian gospel itself is a Father movement. Smail says: "I believe that in the Spirit and through Christ we are being called back from all charismatic onesidedness to the forgotten Father to find something of the wholeness of our life in him." Thomas A. Smail, *The Forgotten Father* (Grand Rapids: Eerdmans, 1980), 19-20,186.

Surely it is better to God's saving action is a movement of the triune God rather than a Jesus movement, a charismatic movement, or a Father movement!

12. Hemphill says that in 1 Corinthians 13 Paul "was not contrasting love with the gifts as if the Corinthians should seek love instead of the gifts. . . . Spiritual gifts are essential to the life of the church and thus cannot be put aside even for love." Hemphill, *Spiritual Gifts,* 74.

13. Lynn P. Clayton, *No Second-Class Christians* (Nashville: Broadman, 1976).

and oppressive daily circumstances might be. Christ could do the Father's will even when nailed to the cross. This truth is one with the doctrine of the priesthood of every believer and with the emphasis on the ministry of the laity and the shared ministry.

4. Gifts are closely related to talents.—According to biblical monotheism, talents are God's gifts too (Gen. 1:26-27; 1 Cor. 4:7; Jas. 1:17). Scripture is clear: all credit for anything good in a person's life is ultimately God's. Since the Redeemer is also the Creator, there is no good in a person's life that is not God's good gift.

At the same time, God must empower a person's talents if they are to serve as spiritual gifts (1 Cor. 15:10).[14] Believers may be extraordinarily talented yet ineffective in Christian service, or they may be limited in talent yet unusually effective in ministry.

Talents and gifts, then, are neither antithetical nor simply identical. Some say that a spiritual gift is a God-given ability that has caught fire. Others suggest that the difference between a gift and a talent is that believers have a Christlike character and attitude. Yet, though talents and gifts are closely related, there is no necessary relationship between them. A talented junior high school teacher found that his gift at Sunday School was in driving a church bus rather than in teaching junior high students![15]

Without question, since believers are new creatures in Christ (2 Cor. 5:17), the Spirit often releases abilities and graces that surprise even the persons themselves. When a person's talents are surrendered to Christ, they become gifts of the Holy Spirit in a special way. The Holy Spirit multiplies the fruitfulness of talents committed to Christ's service.

When the Holy Spirit gifts a believer for ministry, He works with that person's God-given individuality and identity. He enhances rather than annihilates the person's individuality. He works *through* persons, not instead of them. A spirit who compels, who takes impersonal, mechanical control of persons is the spirit at work in pagan ecstasies, not the Holy Spirit of the New Testament. The Spirit furthers personal self-realization and self-fulfillment through a trusting, personal relation to Christ. For this reason, the Spirit customarily works through ordinary means.

---

14. See the Scripture references cited above for the Spirit's Old Testament work in heightening a person's natural powers for doing God's work. According to Hemphill:

> Most Christians I have talked to have not given testimony to receiving new abilities for service at the point of their conversion. I have, however, been involved in the discipling process when an individual made the discovery that all ability comes from God (1 Cor. 4:7). This knowledge has led [the] believer to a humble commitment to use personal abilities in service to the Lord in the fellowship of the church.

Hemphill, *Spiritual Gifts*, 206.

15. Clayton, *No Second-Class Christians*, 11-12.

Christ's followers often hunger for "miracles"—for the sudden, the showy, or the spectacular, even as they often find it difficult to recognize and appreciate how God so frequently accomplishes His redemptive purposes through ordinary events.[16] No theology of spiritual gifts based on the New Testament can justify preoccupation with the spectacular as the primary evidence of the Spirit's activity in Christian experience.

5. *New Testament gift lists are not exhaustive.*—Lists in 1 Corinthians 12:4,11,28-30, Romans 12:6-8, and Ephesians 4:7-16, vary significantly. The apostle selected the gifts in each list to address a specific situation.[17] Situations, persons, and ministries change constantly. There is nothing static or wooden about God's gifting His people. New ministries supersede old ones, so that former gifts may no longer be needed. New situations develop, presenting unprecedented opportunities for ministry. God grants fresh gifts, empowering His people for new challenges.

6. *Gifts and gifted persons are intimately related.*[18]—This is clear in the gift lists that include both abilities and persons. Paul speaks of the gift of prophecy (1 Cor. 12:10) but also speaks of prophets (1 Cor. 12:28). He moves freely between abilities and persons:

> And since we have gifts that differ according to the grace given to us, let each exercise them accordingly: if prophecy, according to the proportion of his faith; if service, in his serving; or he who teaches, in his teaching; or he who exhorts, in his exhortation; he who gives, with liberality; he who leads, with diligence; he who shows mercy, with cheerfulness. (Romans 12:6-8.)

In Ephesians 4:11 there is no question: the gifts are gifted persons—apostles, prophets, evangelists, pastors, teachers!

The inseparable relation between spiritual gifts and persons is to be expected, for the Spirit is intensely related to persons. He is never impersonal, for neither the Spirit nor the believer is a mere "it." Yet persons are complicated entities, and the relationship between spiritual gifts and persons is necessarily complicated.

---

16. Bruner refers to carnal Corinthians as "miracle-hungry." He is careful to explain, however, that a part of their problem was limiting miracles to the "only visibly miraculous." Frederick Dale Bruner, *A Theology of the Holy Spirit* (Grand Rapids: Eerdmans, 1970), 302,312.

17. A strength of Hemphill's discussion is his attention to the historical background of the spiritual gift passages. Hemphill, *Spiritual Gifts.*

18. Hemphill says:
> Now it is clear that the person was not the gift, but the relationship between the individual and the gift possessed was so integral that an individual could be referred to in terms of the gift. . . . The fact that [the] gifts mentioned [in Eph. 4:11] are gifted persons [apostles, prophets, evangelists, pastors, teachers] should not surprise us. It simply illustrates the close relationship between the individual and the gift one possessed (Ibid., 146, 180).

Flynn argues that gifts are not offices. He has a point, for a person could have the gift associated with an "office" without formally having the office; someone could be gifted to teach but have no opportunity to teach. Yet the New Testament sometimes relates gift to office (1 Cor. 12:29). Flynn even contrasts persons and gifts: "Offices pertain more to the person, whereas gifts relate to endowments given the person by the Spirit." This appears to regard gifts as impersonal endowments.[19] To emphasize the close relation between gifts and persons, then, is simply to underscore the personal manner in which the Holy Spirit operates.

7. *Gifts function in the body.*—Paul developed his most extensive teaching on spiritual gifts in order to confront abuses in the Corinthian congregation (1 Cor. 12-14). Faced with excessive individualism at Corinth, he broadened the teaching on gifts to stress their corporate dimension. Paul argued that the Holy Spirit enriches the unity of the church through the diversity of gifts operating in the body of Christ. This body imagery enriches our understanding of spiritual gifts. He writes:

> There are different kinds of gifts, but the same Spirit . . . Now to each one the manifestation of the Spirit is given for the common good... All of these [manifestations] are the work of one and the same Spirit, and he gives them to each one, just as he determines. The body is a unit, though it is made up of many parts; and though all its parts are many, they form one body . . . God has arranged the parts in the body, every one of them, just as he wanted them to be . . . God has combined the members of the body and has given greater honor to the parts that lacked it, so that there should be no division in the body, but that its parts should have equal concern for each other. . . Now you are the body of Christ, and each one of you is a part of it (1 Cor. 12:4,7,11,12,18,24-25,27, NIV).

This variety of members and their gifts insures limitless possibilities for multiple ministries. Humphreys and Wise explain:

> Some ministries are large (such as the operation of a great hospital), and some are small (the giving of a cup of cold water). Again,

---

19. Leslie B. Flynn, *Nineteen Gifts of the Spirit* (Wheaton, IL: Victor, 1974, 1981), 24-25.
After insisting that gifts are not offices, Flynn argues that gifts are not even ministries. Here again he seems to oversimplify: "Though a Christian's gifts remain the same, his ministries may change" (Ibid., 25). On what basis, other than a "thingish" view of gifts, could it be said that they remain the same if they need to be discovered, understood, developed, and, at times, even superseded?
Bruner uses "thingish" to describe the overemphasis in classical Pentecostalism, appropriating the Holy Spirit as a prelude or condition to what Pentecostals describe as baptism *in* the Holy Spirit. Bruner says: "In connection with 'appropriation' it can fairly be asked: Is a person 'appropriated'? It is the frequently 'thingish' understanding of the Holy Spirit in Pentecostalism which contributes to the offensiveness of the doctrine." Bruner, *A Theology of the Holy Spirit,* 252, note 40.

> some are named in the New Testament ("the word of wisdom," 1 Cor.
> 12:8, KJV) and others are not (the ministry of pastoral counseling, for
> example). Some are public and visible, such as the ministry of mass
> evangelism; others are private and inconspicuous, such gifts of charity
> to the needy [often are].[20]

Ministries vary as do the members of the body and their gifts. Nor is this
the end of the matter. The living God *continues* to supply fresh gifts for
new ministry needs as His people rise to the new opportunities occasioned by rapidly changing social, cultural, and historical circumstances.

God designs this diversity within the unity of the body of Christ. The
Spirit distributes His gifts "just as He wills" (1 Cor. 12:11), and God
placed each member in the body "just as He desired" (1 Cor. 12:18). God
has "composed the body" and it is He who "appointed" its gifted members (1 Cor. 12:24,28).

God bestows gifts "for the common good" of the body (1 Cor. 12:7).
At the heart of 1 Corinthians 14 is the stress on edification: "Since you
are zealous of spiritual gifts, seek to abound for the edification of the
church" (v. 12). Paul would rather have spoken five words in the church
with his mind "than ten thousand words in a tongue" (v. 19).

This stress on the common good emphasizes the corporate dimension
of spiritual gifts. Congregations, too, are gifted! Like believers, no two
congregations are gifted exactly alike. Recognizing the importance of the
corporate aspect of gifts, Ken Hemphill says that "even the most abundantly possessed gift has no meaning when taken out of the context of the
church."[21]

The corporate nature of the gifts means that members of the body
need one another. No room is left for rivalry, contention, jealousy, or
envy to divide Christians. Since no member has every gift, the eye cannot
say to the hand, "I have no need of you" (1 Cor. 12:21), for members of
the body are interdependent. The corporate nature of the gifts also suggests that Christians should do things "properly and in an orderly manner" (1 Cor. 14:40). "God is not a God of confusion but of peace" (1 Cor.
14:33).

Instead of capitalizing on spiritual gifts for selfish use or arrogant display, believers should use gifts to extend the church's ministry to all of life
and to all the world.

8. *Both gifted leaders and gifted members are necessary for gifts to
function properly in the body.*—Leaders include apostles (1 Cor. 12:28;
Eph. 4:11), pastors (Eph. 4:11), teachers (1 Cor. 12:28; Rom. 12:7; Eph.

---

20. Fisher Humphreys and Philip Wise, *Dictionary of Doctrinal Terms* (Nashville: Broadman, 1983), 72.
21. Hemphill, *Spiritual Gifts,* 208.

4:11), prophets (1 Cor. 12:28; Eph. 4:11), and evangelists (Eph. 4:11). Regarding the emphasis on gifts of leadership in Eph. 4:11, Hemphill says:

> All of the gifts mentioned here are specifically related to leadership functions.... This does not suggest that the church in [the book of] Ephesians had a more structured leadership than other churches such as those in Thessalonica, Corinth, or Rome. . . . For Paul, a [gifted] community did not mean a community without clearly recognizable and responsible leadership.[22]

Does gifted leadership suggest an unstructured church life?[23] According to Ephesians 4:12, gifted leaders equip gifted saints "for the work of service, to the building up of the body of Christ." This is a central New Testament passage regarding the ministry of all believers. Even though every believer is gifted, God's people still need leaders to help equip them for their God-given calling. Gifts require discovery, understanding, and development, and they prosper only as they are continually refreshed and renewed.

9. Spiritual gifts and ministry tasks work hand in hand.—Neither gifts without tasks nor tasks without gifts is a tolerable situation.[24] God's call

---

22. Ibid., 180, 196.

Hemphill correctly emphasizes leadership structures in the early Christian communities. The title of his chapter on 1 Thess. 5:12-22 is, "An Early Look at Ministry Structure." Even though there is no specific reference in this early passage to leaders equipping members or to every member ministry, the foundation for these developments is already present (Ibid., 18-39). Referring to the mention of apostles, prophets, and teachers in 1 Cor. 12:28, Hemphill says that these leaders were involved in leadership functions from the very beginning of the Christian community (Ibid., 71).

Discussing Rom. 12:6-8, he says that the second gift in the list, ministry or service, may point to a "regularized" ministry existing in some, if not all, early congregations: "There exist side by side in the charismatic community 'leaders' who are empowered for service by God and 'members' who have their own unique service roles. Paul apparently saw no conflict between these two principles" (Ibid., 147). Eph. 4:7-16 emphasizes that gifted leaders must equip gifted followers (Ibid., 185).

23. Young makes a strong case for pastoral supervision in today's churches while advocating minimal congregational structures. Doyle L. Young, *New Life for Your Church* (Grand Rapids: Baker, 1989), 94-100.

24. Koenig has a chapter entitled "From Gift to Task to Giver" addressing those who suffer from a long absence of God's discernible power in their lives. Many are stuck between giftedness without tasks and tasks without giftedness (or burnout), so that God Himself may seem far away. Koenig, *Charismata*, 146-48.

Many writers deplore contemporary church life as task-oriented, not gift-oriented; but gifts and tasks must not be juxtaposed. Gifts are sometimes discovered when ministries are undertaken. At other times a person recognizes a gift, then seeks a way to use it. Frequently it is necessary to experiment with different ministries.

In Acts 6:3, task and gifts worked together: "But select from among you, brethren, seven men of good reputation, full of the Spirit and of wisdom, whom we may put in charge of this task."

is not merely to privilege, but also to responsibility. There is work to do, and God bestows gifts for kingdom tasks. Gifts renew established ministries and raise up new ministries to take advantage of new opportunities.

God gifts His people with gifts necessary to fulfill the church's four basic functions: worship, nurture, evangelism, and service. Properly understood, these functions are wholistic in scope: they speak to the whole of life and reach out to the whole world. Small wonder that their pursuit calls continually for the creation of new structures to cope with new cultural circumstances.

Different congregations inevitably reflect varying emphases with reference to the four functions. Large churches sometimes stress a dynamic Sunday morning worship service focusing celebration. Other congregations involve their members in various ministries to the needy. Still others emphasize evangelism and/or missions. Some churches stress discipleship. Although congregations vary, balance between the four functions remains the ideal.

10. Spiritual gifts must be discovered, developed, used, renewed, and even at times superseded.—Although short-term programs of gift inventory and discovery can be eminently worthwhile, there is no substitute for developing God's people through the long-term pursuit of the church's basic functions. Here again, gifts are best discovered and developed while worshiping and working in the congregation. The Bible admonishes believers to discover and possess the gifts Christ has already given them (1 Cor. 12—14; 1 Tim. 4:14; 2 Tim. 1:6; Heb. 10:24-25; 1 Pet. 4:10).

Together with a zeal for gifts, Christians must also be aware of how easily gifts can be abused and misused. The Corinthians and many believers today have failed to understand this.

11. Discovering and using gifts is often costly in terms of suffering and sacrifice (Luke 9:23; 2 Cor. 12:10).[25]—This is not to deny the sheer joy of fulfilled ministry! Jesus endured the cross "for the joy set before Him" (Heb. 12:2). Paul was imprisoned facing a death-threatening crisis when he wrote, "Rejoice in the Lord always; again I will say, rejoice" (Phil. 4:4). Next to love, the fruit of the Spirit is joy (Gal. 5:22). Seeking an easy way

---

25. O'Connor says: "When one really becomes practical about gifts, they spell out responsibility and sacrifice." Howard A. Snyder, "Misunderstanding Spiritual Gifts," *Christianity Today*, October 12, 1973, 18, quoting Elizabeth O'Connor, *Eighth Day of Creation* (Waco, TX: Word, 1971), 42. Snyder adds: "Spiritual gifts come to their full biblical legitimacy and meaning only in the rhythm of incarnation-crucifixion-resurrection" (Ibid.).

See also Bruner's discussion of Paul's "weakness theology" ("when I am weak, then am I strong," 2 Cor. 12:10) in 2 Corinthians, the epistle that Bruner regards as Paul's most concentrated writing on spiritual formation. Bruner, *A Theology of the Holy Spirit,* 303-19. The discussion is continued in Frederick Dale Bruner and William Hordern, *The Holy Spirit— Shy Member of the Trinity* (Minneapolis: Augsburg, 1984), 8-9.

out is shameful, but enduring hardness as a good soldier of the cross is ennobling.

In conclusion to this study of spiritual gifts, the question arises: What would a gifted congregation look like?[26] Two New Testament descriptions come to mind:

- The Spirit works freely in a church enmeshed in Bible study, sharing, worshiping, and witnessing (Acts 2:42-47). The Jerusalem church continued in the apostles' doctrine, shared, and cared; and the Lord added to their number daily.

- The Spirit works freely in a church committed to God's purpose in Christ regardless of cost (Rom. 12:9-18). Here again, the spectacular signs are not so important as Christlike character.

---

26. Koenig, *Charismata*, 165-66.

5 *How the Holy Spirit Effects*

The Holy Spirit effects the great purposes of the Kingdom of God through the human personalities of Christians.

Ordinarily the Holy Spirit Works Gently
The Holy Spirit's Work Is a Mediated Immediacy
The Necessity for Spiritual Renewal Is Never Left Behind
Uppermost Is the Holy Spirit's Amazing Vitality

How does the Holy Spirit relate to the human spirit as He effects the application of redemption?[1]

Ordinarily the Holy Spirit Works Gently

The Spirit's characteristic way of working with persons is to nudge gently. When the Lord passed by Elijah, He was not in the wind, the earthquake, or the fire, but in the gentle whisper (1 Kings 19:11-12). God seeks to enable persons to realize their highest potential voluntarily and from within, rather than by coercion. In this way the Spirit touches individuals at the core of their moral and spiritual being. Any other kind of redemption would leave persons essentially unchanged.

The Spirit's characteristically gentle way of working distinguishes the Holy Spirit from other spirits. Koenig cites examples from ancient Hellenistic culture to show that, in pagan practice, spirit-possessed individuals experienced a loss of ordinary selfhood. Pagan spirits tended to take over, to compel, and to drive the possessed. Koenig concludes that the

---

1. See especially W. T. Conner, *The Work of the Holy Spirit* (Nashville: Broadman, 1949, 1970), chap. 10.

For additional treatments see: Frederick Dale Bruner and William Hordern, *The Holy Spirit—Shy Member of the Trinity* (Minneapolis: Augsburg, 1984), 7-10; Arnold B. Come, *Human Spirit and Holy Spirit* (Philadelphia: Westminster, 1959); George S. Hendry, *The Holy Spirit in Christian Theology,* rev. ed. (Philadelphia: Westminster, 1965), chap. 5; John Koenig.

Charismata: God's Gifts for God's People (Philadelphia: Westminster, 1978), 79,100; and J. I. Packer, *Keep in Step with the Spirit* (Old Tappan, NJ: Revell, 1984), especially 38-45.

The suggestion that the Spirit's characteristic way of working with persons is to nudge gently is Koenig's (79-80,100).

distinctiveness of the biblical Spirit is that (1) the Holy Spirit witnesses not to Himself but to Christ, and (2) Spirit-filled believers and Spirit-led congregations "are allowed a larger measure of conscious control over their behavior than the possessing spirits of the Hellenistic age permit."[2]

In view of the many spirits clamoring for our attention, as witnessed in the proliferation of cults, the question of criteria for determining when the Holy Spirit, and not just any spirit, is speaking assumes a new importance. "Test the spirits," John says (1 John 4:1). But how is this to be done?

The spirits are tested as any alleged revelation from God is tested—by the Christian's fourfold authority, namely, by Scripture, tradition, reason, and individual opinion. These are the tests, not only for doctrine, but for the validity of any alleged Christian experience.

The primary test, of course, is Scripture. Since Scripture points to Christ, the test of Scripture is one with the test of conformity to Christ's teaching and character. John says: "By this know the Spirit of God: every spirit that confesses that Jesus Christ has come in the flesh is from God; but every spirit that does not confess Jesus is not from God" (1 John 4:2-3; cf. Gal. 1:6-9). Consequently, when a voice which claims to be the Spirit's contradicts what is known of Christ as witnessed by the four authorities, it is not the voice of the biblical Holy Spirit.

The Holy Spirit's Work Is a Mediated Immediacy

The Holy Spirit works gently, respecting human personality and freedom. He works *through* the human spirit, not against it or apart from it. It is best to say that the Holy Spirit *interpenetrates* the human spirit, rejecting such terms as eradication (Warfield) and counteraction (Keswick). Operations of the Spirit are direct and immediate, yet ever mediated through the four authorities. The Spirit's interpenetration of the human spirit is thus *a mediated immediacy.*

This gentle operation of God's Spirit toward the human spirit bears significantly on the evangelical evaluation of Pentecostal claims concerning the priority of the sign gifts of tongues and healing. Sometimes Pentecostals even speak of the gift of prophecy (1 Cor. 14:1) as sudden, "direct" communication from God, in contrast, for instance, to prepared sermons.

Pentecostals are not alone in claiming a *direct* experience of God. Most Evangelicals insist on the crucial importance of "direct, intensely personal religious experience."[3] The problem with the classical Pente-

---

2. Koenig, *Charismata*, 90.
3. Hill, from whom this quote is taken, also cites Donald G. Matthews' "standard" definition of evangelicalism. Matthews says: "The Christian life is essentially a personal relationship with God in Christ, established through the direct action of the Holy Spirit." Samuel S. Hill, Jr., "The Shape and Shapes of Popular Southern Piety," in *Varieties of Southern Evangelicalism,* David Edwin Harrell, Jr., ed. (Macon, GA: Mercer University Press, 1981), 90,93.

costal approach is the claim that the directness is *unmediated,* an emphasis that circumvents the evangelical use of the fourfold authority for testing alleged revelations and activities of the Holy Spirit.[4]

Classical Pentecostals tend to think of the four authorities as barriers to the Spirit's direct actions. Instead of acting as barriers, the authorities, *when properly subordinated to the Holy Spirit,* are the very means the Spirit uses to mediate directly His presence and leadership in Christian experience.

The Spirit's approach is a mediated approach because persons are free, rational beings. Through the authorities the Holy Spirit seeks to elicit from persons a free and rational response. Otherwise the Spirit's action is reduced to something merely mystical, magical, or non-moral. In other words, the Spirit's use of mediation undercuts the medieval mystic's tendency to identify the Holy Spirit with the human spirit. The use of mediation safeguards the Spirit's objectivity by providing external means for verifying whether the Spirit is or is not speaking.

Pentecostal preoccupation with the dramatic sign gifts undercuts the Spirit's preference for the gentle and the enduring. The Holy Spirit points to the Jesus who washed the feet of His disciples; who mounted a cross and died; whose main concern was the spiritual and the redemptive, not the sensational and the sudden. The fruit of the Spirit is more fundamental than the sign gifts. *Agape*, the suffering and preserving love, rules the Spirit's gifts.

Viewing the Spirit's work as a mediated immediacy not only points up a basic difference between non-Pentecostal and Pentecostal evangelicals, it also guards against false views of the relationship between the Spirit's activity and the believer's activity. Since the Spirit's characteristic way of working is to *interpenetrate* the human spirit, then neither the idea of the believer's sufficiency without the Spirit, nor the notion of the Spirit's sufficiency apart from responding human efforts, is adequate. The Bible gives no support to the view that since God works there is therefore nothing for persons to do! Rather, the Bible says that God's work enables the believer's work (Phil. 2:12,13). God's grace is never intended as a substitute for human responsibility.

---

4. Packer has some curious things to say regarding the immediacy of the Spirit's actions. He helpfully suggests that:

> *Experience* is a slippery word, and *experiences* (that is, specific states of thought and feeling) coming to imperfectly sanctified sinners cannot but have dross mixed with their gold. No *experience* just by happening can authenticate itself as sent by God to further his work of grace.

At the same time, his sympathies for what he thinks of as a Puritan type of spiritual contemplation lead him to make a strange and ambiguous comment about affirming alleged direct perceptions of God that go *beyond* the text of Scripture. Packer, *Keep in Step with the Spirit*, 201-75.

The Necessity for Spiritual Renewal Is Never Left Behind

The Spirit's method of relating to the human spirit, then, does not eliminate the inescapable ongoing struggle and fierce spiritual warfare of Christian experience. The fact that some theologies of the Christian life promise too little victory in Christ is no license for theologies which promise too much victory, thus ignoring the struggle and warfare of Christian experience.[5] Promises of a life of unbroken fellowship with God overlook such crucial realities as the following:

- The unpredictability of tomorrow's trials and temptations, resulting in the believer's inability always to be prepared adequately to trust and obey the Lord.

- Burnout, reflecting as it often does the failure to pay the high price for daily renewal in Christ.

- The possible intensification of the struggle with evil as good matures. (For instance, which was more fierce in Jesus' experience, the wilderness temptation at the beginning of His public ministry, or the Gethsemane experience on the eve of His crucifixion?)

- The limitless propensity of the human ego to deny its shortcomings and to excuse them as justifiable exceptions, not only to what it knows very well that God expects, but also to what it unquestionably condemns in others.

---

5. Following are three examples of evangelical theologians who promise too much victory in the Christian life. The theologians are Lindsell, Leavell, and Conner.

Lindsell, who is neither Pentecostal nor charismatic, but who does have some affinity with a Keswick deeper Christian life kind of spirituality, speaks of the Spirit-filled life as a "steady state" of *unbroken fellowship with God.* He says that "it *is* possible for any believer to remain filled with the Holy Spirit without interruption."

While he rejects Warfield's idea of the eventual eradication of the believer's sinful nature, he nevertheless opts for the Keswick notion that moment by moment the believer can be kept from deliberate sin.

His stress, though, is not on holiness but on blamelessness. That is, when the believer's performance is less than perfect, God accepts his/her *intention* to live blamelessly in lieu of his/her failure to do so. In this sense, he recognizes that no one loves God perfectly.

Harold Lindsell, *The Holy Spirit in the Latter Days* (Nashville: Nelson, 1983), 146,162. Similarly, Leavell says: "Over a period of time as Christians win their continuing struggle with ingrained sin, they become more and more able to contain the fullness of the Holy Spirit." Landrum P. Leavell, II, *The Doctrine of the Holy Spirit* (Nashville: Convention Press, 1983), 68.

Finally, Conner may have come closer to a steady-state view of the Spirit-filled life than he intended when he says that "the condition of the Christian ought to be one, in which as a regular and permanent characteristic, he is full of the Spirit." W. T. Conner, *Revelation and God* (Nashville: Broadman, 1936), 312.

- The never-superseded necessity of humbly beginning over again and again in the Christian life.

There is, to be sure, something better for the Christian than complacency in deliberate sinning and minimized imperfection, but the believer who expects always to live on the mountaintop of perfection looks for something the Bible never promises on this side of heaven.

The Christian's ongoing struggle and warfare means that the Spirit customarily relates to our spirit by an unending process of spiritual renewal. Fresh submission to God's leadership in the believer's life is necessary every day (Luke 9:23). No set of pre-determined conditions to the Spirit-filled life, however arduous and demanding, guarantee the fullness of the Holy Spirit.[6] Christianity, unlike gnosticism, teaches no secrets for persons to master in order to lead infallibly to lives of unbroken, unclouded fellowship with God.

Uppermost Is the Holy Spirit's Amazing Vitality

Here we return to what was said earlier regarding the Spirit's distinctive trinitarian role. The key biblical way of characterizing the Spirit's role is to think of the Spirit as the *Effecter* of all that the Father purposes through the Son. To effect is *to carry through to fruition*. The Spirit completes the Father's creative and redemptive purposes through the Son, however costly and extended the process. He does this in a manner which always promotes rather than undercuts the well-being, fulfillment, and abounding fruitfulness of the redeemed.

This means that the Holy Spirit perseveres in His pursuit of God's kingdom purposes. His prevailing persistence takes *agape* seriously— God's love, the durable love manifested at the cross, the love which never lets go, which always considers first the well-being of its object, and which is invincible as it keeps on and on overcoming evil with good.

There are depths of meaning here which defy complete analysis. The Spirit is as mighty as the rushing wind, yet He is as gentle as the dove descending on Jesus, the suffering Servant, at His baptism.

Consequently, the church's understanding of the Holy Spirit and His ways remains a vital polarity embracing both mystery and reality. The mystery is never fully probed ("the wind blows wherever it pleases"), yet the church knows the Spirit's working as walls of stubborn resistance to

---

6. Torrey, for instance, goes too far when, with reference to his seven steps to the baptism with the Holy Spirit, he says: "There is a very plain path laid down in God's Word, consisting of a few simple steps that anyone can take, and *it is absolutely certain that any one who takes these steps will be "baptized with the Holy Spirit."*

R. A. Torrey, *The Holy Spirit* (New York: Revell, 1927), 155.

God's reconciling grace tumble time after time ("you hear its sound," John 3:8).

Referring, then, to the amazing dynamic of the Holy Spirit in the history of the early church, Laeuchli says:

> We do not know why [the early church] arose. That is exactly the secret of its nature.... The charisma had no patterns.... [It] just came—this is the miracle of it. And it is even more of an enigma because many attempts to anathematize it, or at least to domesticate it, were frustrated.... The cult of the Vesta in the [Roman] forum... did not know the turmoil of the Christian history with one schism after another.... But Vesta was dead and the church was not![7]

---

7. Samuel Laeuchli, *The Serpent and the Dove* (New York: Abingdon, 1966), 244-46.

PART II

The Kingdom Present:

GOD'S PURPOSE IN HISTORY

The kingdom present is the new redemptive order established by the Christ and Pentecost events that inaugurated the last days promised in the Old Testament.

6. Jesus' Master-Thought
7. A Theology of the Kingdom Present
8. The Kingdom Present and Election

Jesus'
Master-Thought

The central message of Jesus was the presence of the kingdom of God. The comprehensiveness of God's purpose in Christ becomes apparent only by viewing the Christian life and the church in kingdom perspective.

The Kingdom Present Defined
The Kingdom Present and the Christ-Pentecost Events
Eighteenth- and Nineteenth-Century Evangelical Kingdom Vision
The Loss and Recovery of Evangelical Kingdom Vision
The Aim of This Discussion

According to James S. Stewart, the kingdom of God was the master-thought of Jesus. Stewart writes:

> Every great leader who has ever arisen among the sons of men has been possessed by one master-thought. . . . And Jesus, like all [other great leaders], came with *His* master-thought, glorious and thrilling, world-shaking and world-transforming, and Christ's master-thought was "the Kingdom of God."[1]

Yet summaries of Christian doctrine have neglected the kingdom of God. This results in a loss of kingdom vision. No other term so well expresses the comprehensiveness of God's redemptive purpose in Christ. Consequently, no item on the evangelical theological agenda is more urgent than a return of the kingdom to the center of Christian thought.

The Kingdom Present Defined

The kingdom present is one of four primary biblical uses of the term "kingdom." These four uses are

- God's universal kingdom,

---

1. James S. Stewart, *The Life and Teaching of Jesus Christ* (London: SCM, 1933), 53.

66

- The kingdom of Israel,

- The kingdom present,

- The kingdom consummated.

God's *universal kingdom* is grounded in His role as Creator and Judge of creation. His kingdom rules over all (Ps. 103:19). He is sovereign over all nations (Ps. 22:8).

The *kingdom of Israel* is the customary Old Testament use of the kingdom concept (1 Sam. 24:20). Israel, to be sure, was God's earthly kingdom, but the specific phrase "the kingdom of God" is not in the Old Testament. The idea of the kingdom of God is there (as in Ps. 103:19) but the phrase itself is not.

Kingdom present is a New Testament concept that refers to the kingdom of God between Christ's first and second comings (Mark 1:15).

The *kingdom consummated* is the perfection of the kingdom present after Christ returns.[2]

The kingdom is God's reign.[3] God is the living God who controls His creation, actively working in His world; He is working out His redemptive purpose in history; and history is meaningful.

God's rule in creation is to be distinguished from His redemptive rule. Redemption is always creative, but creation and redemption are not synonyms. *The distinction between creation and redemption is one of the most sensitive areas in contemporary theology.* Many modern theologians, charging that the distinction is difficult to maintain, simply identify God's work as Creator with His work as Redeemer. On this basis, no personal trust in Christ is necessary for salvation. For evangelical theology, however, the distinction between creation and redemption is important, since

---

2. Although Ladd's prolific writings concerning kingdom themes are invaluable, his thinking regarding the distinction between the kingdom present and the kingdom consummated remains ambiguous, primarily because of his sharp distinction between history and eschatology.

His constant references to "both the historical present and the eschatological future" betray a basic resistance to the fact that all of God's redemptive action–Old Testament, present, and future–is in some sense eschatological.

He recognizes the kingdom present as a dynamic power in history, yet he describes its presence as hidden and insignificant and reserves the kingdom in an eschatological sense for the future following Christ's return. He seems to have little sense of the wholistic nature of the mission of the kingdom present.

See George Eldon Ladd, *The Presence of the Future* (Grand Rapids: Eerdmans, 1974), 130–38,147,149,235,etc.

3. Ladd says, "The kingdom of God as the dynamic rule or reign of God has become the most widely accepted definition [of the kingdom as a present New Testament reality]. . . . In its dynamic meaning, the Kingdom of God is God himself, not merely ruling in the universe but actively establishing his rule."

Ibid., 126-27,145.

Redeemed! Eschatological Redemption and the Kingdom of God

—68—

it is one with the crucial differences between the world and the kingdom, nature and grace, general revelation and special revelation, and lost and saved persons.

God is realizing His redemptive rule in three main stages: (1) the Old Testament promise of the kingdom of God, (2) Christ's coming to initiate the presence of the kingdom, and (3) Christ's return to consummate the kingdom. The kingdom present, then, is the form of the kingdom of God between the first and second comings of Christ.

On the basis of these considerations, the kingdom present can be defined as *the new redemptive order established by the Christ and Pentecost events that inaugurated the eschatological last days promised in the Old Testament and consummated when Christ returns.* As God's pursuit of His redemptive purpose between the two advents of Christ, its central focus is the Great Commission.

So understood, the kingdom present stresses four biblical themes that have often been separated in the history of Christian thought:

- redemption,

- the kingdom of God,

- mission, and

- eschatology.

The Kingdom Present
and the Christ-Pentecost Events

God made the decisive provision for achieving His redemptive purpose in history in the Christ and Pentecost events. H. Wheeler Robinson describes the unfolding of God's mighty acts in history this way:

> If we recur to the figure of the Bible as a divine drama, then we may say that there are five acts in it—the first when God gathered a nation out of Bedouin tribes, the second when He raised up prophetic teachers with their fragments of truth, the third when exile purged and disciplined the religious consciousness of Israel, the fourth when the tragedy of the Cross of Christ brought man's sin face to face with God's grace, the fifth, when the Holy Spirit began the creation of a fellowship not yet achieved, the inauguration of the kingly rule of God.[4]

---

4. H. Wheeler Robinson, *The Christian Experience of the Holy Spirit* (London: Nisbet, 1928), 183.

More recently Dyrness has developed a biblical theology of wholistic mission using the dramatic action of the kingdom of God as his primary metaphor. See William A. Dyrness, *Let the Earth Rejoice!* (Westchester, IL: Crossway, 1983), 12.

Surely the claim that the Christ-Pentecost events inaugurated the kingly rule of God accords with Scripture, yet traditional discussions of the kingdom of God have all but ignored the kingdom present, referring only to the kingdom consummated. Doctrinal summaries have often moved from presentations of the person and work of Christ to discussions of the Christian life and the church, omitting the Holy Spirit and rarely mentioning the kingdom present.[5]

In biblical perspective, however, the *primary* focus of the Christ-Pentecost events is the kingdom of God, the foremost theme in the teaching of Jesus. The Christian life and the church are essentially kingdom realities and can be understood adequately only in the context of the God's redemptive, kingdom mission.

Eighteenth- and Nineteenth-Century Evangelical Kingdom Vision

The most significant exception to the generalization regarding the traditional neglect of the concept of the kingdom present is the kingdom consciousness associated with John Wesley (1703-91) and the Evangelical Revival in England, with Jonathan Edwards (1703-58) and the Great Awakening in America, and with William Carey (1761-1834) and the modern mission movement.

Richard Niebuhr argues that the "Great Awakening and the revivals were ushered in by a new awareness of the coming kingdom." Referring to Edwards, Niebuhr says that this new awareness represented a shift in Edwards' thought "from the eternal kingdom into which souls enter one by one to the kingdom coming upon earth."

> [This] expectation of the coming kingdom upon earth . . . became the dominant idea in [early nineteenth-century] American Christianity. If the seventeenth was the century of the sovereignty and the eighteenth the time of the kingdom of Christ, the nineteenth may be called the period of the coming kingdom. The great hopefulness which prevailed in all areas of life in the time from the Revolution to the World War was due to many factors besides the experience of the Christian movement, but it is likely that the latter was one of its major sources. Among the Christians of America, at least, the opti-

---

5. It is to the credit of *The Baptist Faith and Message* that it has an article on the kingdom *prior to the article on the last things.* Unfortunately the relation of the kingdom to the purpose of the Christian life and the church is not referred to explicitly. Arts. XI-XVII, which deal with the church in the world, appear to be attached as a sort of addendum, with no clear relation to the great doctrines of the Christian faith summarized in the first ten articles. See below, note 14.

mism of the nineteenth century was intimately connected with the experience of the anticipated Christian revolution.[6]

This older kingdom consciousness neglected the radical persistence and power of sin in human experience, socially as well as individually, but it contributed to great missionary, evangelistic, cultural, and social achievements. Isaac Watts' hymn, "Jesus Shall Reign," written half a century before the modern mission movement, still speaks to the challenge of the comprehensive scope of biblical kingdom vision.

The Loss and Recovery
of Evangelical Kingdom Vision

Snyder laments the fact that after 1890, "social gospelers secularized this kingdom vision and conservatives spiritualized it."[7] Webber recognizes the complexity of accounting for this loss of evangelical kingdom vision but suggests three factors that were involved: (1) the difficulty of sustaining any movement for a long period of time; (2) the impact of the Civil War, which dashed dreams for the betterment of society; and (3) the rapid rise of the older dispensationalism, with its stress on the worsening of conditions in the present age and the postponement of the kingdom until the return of Christ.[8]

- Evangelicals have recovered some of this kingdom vision since World War II. Snyder traces three stages in the recovery: From 1947 until the early 1960s, an uneasy evangelical social conscience, documented by Henry's 1947 book, *The Uneasy Conscience of Modern Fundamentalism;*

- From the latter 1960s until the 1970s, the new social conscience, marked by Wirt's 1968 volume, *The Social Conscience of the Evangelical*, and by such developments as the 1973 Chicago Declaration and the organization of Evangelicals for Social Change;

- In the later 1970s and following, the new kingdom consciousness indicated by volumes such as Snyder's *The Community of the King.*[9]

---

6. H. Richard Niebuhr, *The Kingdom of God in America,* Torchbook ed. (New York: Harper, 1959), 135,143,150-51.

7. Howard A. Snyder, *The Community of the King* (Downers Grove, IL: InterVarsity, 1977), 28.
Moberg provides a description of this loss and recovery of evangelical kingdom vision. See David O. Moberg, *The Great Reversal* (Philadelphia: Lippincott, 1972).

8. Robert E. Webber, *The Secular Saint* (Grand Rapids: Zondervan, 1979), 174-75.

9. Carl F. H. Henry, *The Uneasy Conscience of Modern Fundamentalism* (Grand Rapids: Eerdmans, 1947); Sherwood Wirt, *The Social Conscience of the Evangelical* (New York: Harper & Row, 1968); and Howard A. Snyder, *The Community of the King* (Downers Grove, IL: InterVarsity, 1977).

Snyder explains the new evangelical kingdom consciousness as follows:

> The question is not one of adding a social dimension to an evangelistic gospel. Rather evangelism, conversion, social justice and other gospel emphases must be seen as part of God's cosmic/historical redemptive plan. . . . [This] goes beyond what most evangelicals—even those emphasizing social conscience—have been saying. Here is a global, cosmic perspective that sees God's plan in its space-time totality and focuses on what God is doing through the Church here and now. This represents a move, at least, in the direction of a new consciousness of the Kingdom of God.[10]

In the light of the variety of kingdom views bequeathed by history, it is evident that an adequate and balanced theology of the kingdom present is not easily achieved.

---

10. Howard A. Snyder, *The Community of the King* (Downers Grove, IL: InterVarsity, 1977), 22–27. Snyder sees five ingredients as crucial for an evangelical kingdom consciousness today: an emphasis on the cosmic dimension of the gospel; a recovery of the dynamic breadth of the Word of God; a recovery of a sense of history; a new emphasis on the ethics of the kingdom; and a Christian view of culture (Ibid., 29-31).

Other discussions signaling the rise of a new evangelical kingdom consciousness include Lesslie Newbigin, *Sign of the Kingdom* (Grand Rapids: Eerdmans, 1980); Peter Toon, *God's Kingdom for Today* (Westchester, IL: Cornerstone, 1980); C. Peter Wagner, *Church Growth and the Whole Gospel* (San Francisco: Harper, 1981).

An example of the current evangelical rediscovery of the wholistic kingdom emphasis is the "Mission beyond the Mission" theme developed by the Fuller Theological Seminary faculty in an attempt to restate their vision of the seminary's task. This reads: "Simply stated, the commands to which we respond are these: Go and make disciples; Call the church of Christ to renewal; Work for the moral health of society; Seek peace and justice in the world; Uphold the truth of God's revelation." See the sixteen-page insert, *Christianity Today* (October 7, 1983).

Self-designated fundamentalists also reflect a heightened social conscience. Truman Dollar is quoted as saying at the Baptist Fundamentalism 1984 Convention in Washington, D.C., that:

> When petty dictators violate the rights of our poor brothers in South and Central America, it is [we] who should care. . . . It ought not be the ACLU who opposes the violence of the KKK in our towns. It ought to be fundamental Baptists. It ought not be liberal public school teachers who fight for quality education. It ought to be fundamental Baptists. . . . We must not let our zeal for evangelism make us ignore hunger, illness, or starvation.

See Cal Thomas, "Lord, Send Us More 'Dollars,'" *Fundamentalist Journal,* July/August 1984, 12.

In the light of the renewed conservative interest in the kingdom theme, Pinnock's criticism of Erickson for neglecting the emphasis is understandable. Referring to Erickson's preoccupation with the individual aspects of salvation, Pinnock says:

> Is this perhaps the reason why the kingdom of God as a topic is not treated? . . . Having blamed Erickson for being too Calvinistic in theology proper, I now object to his not being Calvinistic enough when it comes to the holistic scope of salvation.

See Clark H. Pinnock, "Erickson's Three-Volume Magnum Opus," *Themelios* 9 [Jan.-Feb.]: 3. Pinnock is reviewing Millard J. Erickson, *Christian Theology,* 3 vols. (Grand Rapids: Baker, 1983-85).

The Aim of This Discussion

The aim of this discussion is to speak to the importance of the priority of the kingdom of God for an understanding of the nature and wholistic scope of God's redemptive purpose in Christ. The comprehensiveness of God's purpose becomes apparent only when it is viewed in the perspective of "the great objects of the Kingdom of God" (*The Baptist Faith and Message*, art. XIV). A biblical view of the vast sweep of God's redemptive purpose is at stake. Believers are called to costly discipleship, not merely to privilege. The mission of the church includes every aspect of the Great Commission—nothing less than the extension of Christ's influence to all of life. "Even now, before the return of Christ," Snyder says, "man in Christ has responsibility for all of culture."[11]

This is not to make a shibboleth of the word "kingdom." In another context, Hoskyns asks, "Can we rescue a word, and discover a universe? Can we study a language, and awake to Truth? Can we bury ourselves in a lexicon, and arise in the presence of God?"[12] Hoskyns is aware that biblical words cannot be divorced from their context. As Stott says, "The fullness of the gospel depends not on our use of particular words but on the substance" of what the gospel is saying.[13]

---

11. Ibid., 26.
12. E. C. Hoskyns, *Cambridge Sermons*, paperback ed. (London: SPCK, 1970), 70.
13. Ronald J. Sider and John R. W. Stott, *Evangelism, Salvation, and Social Justice*, Grove Booklets on Ethics, no. 16 (Auburn, MA: Grove, U.S.A., 1977), 27.

The Baptist Faith and Message (Articles XI-XVII) has the essence but not the specific concept of the kingdom present. This statement does not explicitly recognize that the church's involvement in culture is a kingdom necessity.

This necessity can be stated in different ways. The Redeemer and the Creator are one. The kingdom of God inescapably includes the redemption of creation. The great commission and the great commandment each involves the creation or cultural mandate of Gen. 1:26-28. Humankind's social and cultural responsibilities have not been abrogated. When Christ is Lord, His people seek nothing less than His reign in all of life. This requires, along with the priority of evangelism, the pursuit of excellence in every area of life. See above, note 6.

7 A Theology of the Kingdom Present

The kingdom present is the redemptive reality of God's rule in history and is expressed in the wholistic mission of God's people.

Biblical Resources
Historical Perspective
Restatement: Characteristics of the Kingdom Present
The Kingdom Present Is God's Kingdom
The Kingdom Present Is a Redemptive Order
The Kingdom Present Is an Eschatological Reality
The Kingdom Present Is a Vital Force in World History
The Kingdom Present Is Mission
The Kingdom Present Is Wholistic Mission
The Kingdom Present Creates the Christian Life and the Church
The Kingdom Present Calls for Radical Obedience
The Kingdom Present Wages Warfare against Sin and Satan
The Kingdom Present Inspires both Realism and Optimism

This chapter develops implications of the kingdom present for contemporary Christianity by surveying ten characteristics of the kingdom present.

Biblical Resources

Four biblical uses of the kingdom idea.—As noted above the kingdom present is one of four biblical uses of the kingdom concept. In one sense, the four uses reduce to two: God's rule in creation and His rule in redemption. Yet, since God's redemptive reign is realized in three stages, namely, the kingdom promised (Old Testament), the kingdom present (inaugurated through the Christ-Pentecost events), and the kingdom consummated (following Christ's return), the two uses are best understood as expanding to four.

Two of the four biblical uses, God's rule in creation and the kingdom consummated, are treated elsewhere in summaries of Christian doctrine.

73

It remains in this chapter to take note of the kingdom present as promised in the Old Testament and as inaugurated through the Christ-Pentecost events.

The kingdom present as Old Testament promise.—The Old Testament idea of the kingdom is important for the kingdom present because of the underlying unity between the people of God of the Old Testament and the people of God of the New Testament. The old and new covenants should be distinguished, but there is an overarching continuity between Israel and the church.

Three important characteristics of the kingdom of Israel no longer apply to the kingdom present: Jesus' kingdom transcends (1) race, (2) nation, and (3) temple ritual. Despite these important differences, however, *God's redemptive purpose unites the two testaments.* Jesus did not come to abolish Old Testament promises but to fulfill them in a far grander way than any Old Testament saint could have imagined (Matt. 5:17). The church, then, is the full heir to the promises of God to Israel (Rom. 4:16). The Old Testament itself promised a *new* Israel, an inward and spiritual covenant (Jer. 31:31), so that already in Jeremiah's day some Old Testament saints viewed the old covenant as obsolete.[1]

The kingdom present as inaugurated through the Christ-Pentecost events.—Turning to the New Testament, it is impossible to overemphasize the importance of the fact that the kingdom was Jesus' main theme. He came preaching the kingdom of God (Mark 1:15). His parables were the parables of the kingdom. His gospel was the gospel of the kingdom (Matt. 24:14): except a person be born again he cannot enter the kingdom (John 3:3). Jesus' works were the works of the kingdom (Matt. 12:28). His all-consuming passion was for the coming of the kingdom (Matt. 5:33). The kingdom was like a treasure hid in a field; whoever finds it, sells all in order to buy it (Matt. 13:44).

Following His death and resurrection, Jesus claimed all authority (kingship) in heaven and on earth and commissioned His followers to take the gospel into all the world. Exalted at the right hand of the Father,

---

1. See John Bright, *The Kingdom of God* (New York: Abingdon-Cokesbury, 1953), 125-26. Earlier Bright speaks forcefully regarding the unity of the two testaments:

> There nevertheless runs through [the Bible] a unifying theme which is not artificially imposed. It is a theme of redemption, of salvation; and it is caught up particularly in those concepts which revolve about the idea of a people of God, called to live under his rule, and the concomitant hope of the coming Kingdom of God. . . . The concept of the Kingdom of God involved, in a real sense, the total message of the Bible. . . . To grasp what is meant by the Kingdom of God is to come very close to the heart of the Bible's gospel of salvation.

Ibid., 7,10. In the last sentence, Bright could have said that to grasp what is meant by the kingdom of God in the New Testament is far more than "to come very close to" the heart of the Bible's gospel of salvation. It is, in fact, the heart of the gospel.

He sent the Holy Spirit to effect His kingdom purpose in history. He promised to return to consummate His kingdom (John 14:3).

In establishing this new redemptive order, Jesus forthrightly rejected the political notions of the kingdom, which many Jews associated with the coming of the messianic age. The power of Jesus' kingdom was the power of the cross-centered Holy Spirit (Acts 1:8); the law of His kingdom was the law of *agape* (John 13:34); and the ethic of His kingdom was a self-forgetting ethic (Matt. 5:1-12).

The apostles continued Jesus' teaching about the kingdom, but terminology shifted after Pentecost from references to the kingdom to references to Christ as Lord. Because Jesus not only proclaimed the kingdom but also embodied the kingdom in His person, to proclaim Jesus Christ as Savior and Lord was to proclaim the kingdom. The kingdom is Christ! Since Christ sent the Holy Spirit to effect the presence and power of the kingdom in history, direct references to the kingdom decreased after Pentecost and references to the Holy Spirit rapidly increased.

Terminology changed, but the message remained the same. By making real Christ's presence as Savior and Lord, the Holy Spirit effects the kingdom in history. Newbigin says that in Jesus Christ the kingdom received a name and a face!

> In the New Testament it is clear that the only sign of the kingdom is Jesus himself.... When we separate the cause from the person, when we separate the kingdom from the king, we fall into ideology and we become the victims of the law instead of bearers of the gospel.[2]

Historical Perspective

The traditional neglect of the kingdom present is reflected in the Augustinian tendency to confuse the kingdom with the institutional church. This confusion dominated theology during the Middle Ages. Even the Lutheran and Calvinistic reformations retained the union of church and state, which, coupled with infant baptism, tended to sanctify unduly the role of the institutional church. In traditional theology generally, the institutional church takes the place of the kingdom present; any reference to the kingdom is, for the most part, to the kingdom consummated.

Reference was made earlier to the fresh interest in the kingdom present in eighteenth- and nineteenth-century evangelical theology. It was also noted that this development was flawed by an unrealistic hope

---

2. Lesslie Newbigin, *Sign of the Kingdom* (Grand Rapids: Eerdmans, 1980), 69. Newbigin emphasizes that to separate Christ and the call to discipleship is to substitute cheap grace for costly service.

for the improvement of the human situation prior to Christ's second coming.

Other inadequate theologies of the kingdom present have appeared more recently. Reference to three of these will illustrate the continuing confusion regarding the kingdom concept.

First, the nineteenth-century social gospel view of the kingdom reflected the belief in inevitable human progress that still characterized American culture at the beginning of the twentieth century. Assuming a secular, evolutionary viewpoint, this version of the social gospel naively expected humanity to bring in the kingdom by means of educational programs and social improvement, a perspective still widely influential in liberal circles despite two dehumanizing World Wars and the like.[3]

Second, the futuristic or apocalyptic view of the kingdom takes different forms. Albert Schweitzer, in *The Quest of the Historical Jesus,* attributed an exclusively futuristic view of the kingdom to Jesus.[4] Reacting against the social gospel of his mentor, Adolf Harnack, Schweitzer struck a blow that eventually demolished some aspects of the older liberal view of Jesus as a mere teacher of a social gospel. His study of the Gospels led him to the conclusion that Jesus was a fanatical, eschatological prophet of an imminent, apocalyptic day of doom. Schweitzer, however, with his humanitarian Christology, believed that Jesus was mistaken in this eschatological outlook. Nonetheless, his partial rediscovery of the eschatological dimensions of the Gospels helped to usher in an exciting new era in New Testament studies.

A quite different form of the futuristic or apocalyptic view of the kingdom is advocated by the older, Scofield Bible, form of dispensational

---

3. For the older liberal view of the kingdom, see Adolf Harnack, *What Is Christianity?*, trans. Thomas Barley Saunders, 2nd ed. (Oxford: Williams & Norgate, 1901), and Shailer Mathews, *The Social Teaching of Jesus* (New York: Macmillan, 1897). For a more evangelical view of the social gospel see Walter Rauschenbusch, *A Theology for the Social Gospel* (New York: Macmillan, 1917).

Regarding an evaluation of the naive, evolutionary type of the social gospel, Niebuhr's familiar dictum stands: "A God without wrath brought men without sin into a kingdom without judgment through the ministration of a Christ without a Cross." See H. Richard Niebuhr, *The Kingdom of God in America* (New York: Harper, 1937), 193. With only slight modification, this dictum still describes the secular emphasis in current theological discussion.

Contemporary liberation theology has much in common with the social gospel view of the kingdom present, but with the difference that some forms of liberation theology are more oriented toward a Marxist view of class conflict than the idea of inevitable progress through human perfectibility by means of education. See Arthur F. Glasser, "Liberation Theology Bursts on the Scene," in Arthur F. Glasser and Donald A. McGavran, *Contemporary Theologies of Mission* (Grand Rapids: Baker, 1983), 150-66.

4. Albert Schweitzer, *The Quest of the Historical Jesus*, trans. W. Montgomery, 2d . ed. (London: Black, 1911), 238. Schweitzer termed Jesus' eschatology a "consistent" eschatology, because he believed that it must be consistently applied in order to understand the teaching of Jesus.

premillennialism, with its emphasis on the kingdom offered by Jesus as essentially a future, earthly, national, Jewish millennial age following the return of Christ.[5]

Third, another recent, inadequate kingdom concept is represented by the realized eschatology of C. H. Dodd.[6] In essence Dodd's view is a modified version of the older, secularized social gospel. Dodd all but denies the second coming of Christ, speaking only of the historical Jesus and the presence already of an imminent social kingdom hidden within history.

Finally, in addition to these three inadequate views of the kingdom in relation to history, reference must also be made to the varying kingdom ideas in the different millennial theologies, even though the fuller discussion of the millennial question belongs to a treatment of the doctrine of the kingdom consummated. The millennial options considered represent the four more familiar views in contemporary American theology—historical premillennialism, dispensational premillennialism, amillennialism, and postmillennialism.

The two premillennialisms tend to neglect the reality and importance of the kingdom present in order to stress the necessity of the second coming as a prelude to the fuller earthly rule of Christ. Amillennialism stresses the present rule of the risen Christ, but it is of a divided mind regarding the kingdom present as a vital force in world history. Often the kingdom is viewed by amillennialists in such inward, hidden, and spiritualized terms that its redemptive potential to change the course of history is neglected. Postmillennialism, on the other hand, tends to be overly optimistic regarding what the preaching of the gospel can be expected to accomplish in the transformation of humankind and society before Christ returns.

In the light of this variety of kingdom views bequeathed by history, it is apparent that an adequate, balanced, biblical theology of the kingdom present is not easily achieved.

Restatement:
Characteristics of the Kingdom Present

In formulating a restatement of the doctrine of the kingdom present, the following discussion surveys ten key characteristics of the kingdom present in biblical teaching.

---

5. More will be said of this view in discussing millennial options.

6. See C. H. Dodd, *The Parable of the Kingdom,* rev. ed. (London: Collins-Fontana, 1961), 41, and also *The Coming of Christ* (Cambridge: University Press, 1951), 17, 27.

For a more radical version of realized eschatology, see John A. T. Robinson, *Jesus and His Coming* (London: SCM, 1957).

The Kingdom Present Is God's Kingdom

Nothing is more important to the idea of the kingdom than its emphasis on God's sovereign might and initiative. "Unless the Lord builds the house, its builders labor in vain" (Ps. 127:1). The word of the Lord to Zerubbabel was, "'Not by might not by power, but by my Spirit,' says the Lord Almighty" (Zech. 4:6). More than once and in varied ways Jesus said, "'Abba, Father, everything is possible for you'" (Mark 14:36). Several truths are implicit in the fact that the kingdom present is first of all God's kingdom.

The kingdom focuses on prayer and worship.—It directs our attention away from our limitations to God's infinite resources. Newbigin says that the model prayer, "Thy kingdom come" (Matt. 6:10), is important for two reasons: it centers everything in the living God Himself; and it protects us from converting the gospel into a mere ideology, a program, or a law—that is, from putting our trust in anything other than God.[7]

The kingdom is God's gift before it is human achievement.—Membership in the kingdom is a matter of grace, not of works. Since we love because He first loved, kingdom service is willing service, service rendered freely, gladly, and spontaneously. Grace impels but never compels.

The kingdom as God's stands in judgment over human agendas.—It can never be merely identified with earthly or human structures, whether social, political, or even religious. Since humans as sinners corrupt whatever they touch, the presence of the kingdom always calls for repentance. Consequently, Jesus inaugurated His kingdom ministry with the call to repentance: "The kingdom of God is near. Repent and believe the good news" (Mark 1:15). Rather than trust in human perfectibility, the kingdom perspective recognizes our sinfulness and inclination to self-worship.

The kingdom is the kingdom of the triune God.—The kingdom of Father, Son, and Holy Spirit. The kingdom is the God movement, the reign of Christ, and the sway of the Holy Spirit!

The Kingdom Present Is a Redemptive Order

The kingdom and redemption are inseparable, so that the kingdom present is God's pursuit of His redemptive purpose in Christ. *Redemption* is the key characteristic of the kingdom; other characteristics must be understood in a redemptive sense. This makes it even more remarkable that the relationship between the kingdom and redemption is seldom emphasized in theological discussions.

---

7. Lesslie Newbigin, *Sign of the Kingdom* (Grand Rapids: Eerdmans, 1980), 19. Newbigin is commenting on the importance of the petition as the theme for the 1980 conference of the World Council of Churches in Melbourne, Australia.

What, then, is redemption? One might expect wide agreement on a subject so central to the biblical witness, but there are, broadly speaking, two views of redemption in contemporary theology—the evangelical view and the ecumenical view.[8]

The evangelical view stresses that the redemptive, Christ-Pentecost events are the heart of the biblical message. Evangelicals understand these events as God's once-for-all, basic provision to save humanity from sin.[9] This approach recognizes both continuity and discontinuity between God's work in creation and redemption. There is continuity for a variety of reasons:

- In biblical monotheism Redeemer and Creator are one and the same God. They are not two gods, an evil creator and a righteous redeemer. The one God both creates and redeems.

- The material order is essentially God's good creation. Matter is not inherently evil. Redemption is the redemption of creation, not an entirely new creation *de novo*. The wonder of wonders is that God redeems His fallen creation! He steadfastly refuses to abandon it.

- God created humans in His own image and made them lord of creation under the Lord (Gen. 1:26-30). This creation mandate is crucial to any understanding of the wholistic nature of God's kingdom purpose through Christ.

- Common grace is real because of the continuity between creation and redemption. As Creator and Provider the Father is infinitely good to all persons (Matt. 5:45).

- The eternal Word of God "became flesh, and dwelt among us" (John 1:14). God in human flesh! There must be some kind of continuity between creation and redemption.

- Christ died for every person. Persons in sin are unworthy of God's love. Yet as creatures made in God's own image, He counts them worth redeeming, even at infinite cost to Himself.

- The consummation of the kingdom involves the resurrection of the body and the transformation of the present material creation. The

---

8. The discussion between the evangelical and ecumenical views of redemption is widely reviewed and evaluated in contemporary theological literature, especially in missiology.

For an introduction to the discussion see: Richard J. Coleman, *Issues of Theological Conflict* (Grand Rapids: Eerdmans, 1980), especially chap. 6; Norman A. Horner, ed., *Protestant Crosscurrents in Mission* (Nashville: Abingdon, 1968); Newbigin, *Sign of the Kingdom;* Arthur F. Glasser and Donald A. McGavran, *Contemporary Theologies of Mission* (Grand Rapids: Baker, 1983); and Stephen Neill, "Ecumenical and Evangelical Missiology: An Historical Understanding," *Foundations* 25 [January-March]: 9-21.

9. John R. W. Stott, *Basic Christianity* (Grand Rapids: Eerdmans, 1958). This is probably the most widely used brief summary of the evangelical view of redemption.

See John R. W. Stott, ed., *Evangelism and Social Responsibility,* Lausanne Occasional Paper, no. 21 (Wheaton, IL: Lausanne Committee for World Evangelization, 1982), for an update of Stott's views regarding evangelical social involvement.

Christian hope is the anticipation of consummation, not of total discontinuity. This recognizes the wholistic character of biblical redemption, a truth to which we will return in discussing the New Testament teaching about the kingdom.

In the evangelical view, however, there is *discontinuity* as well as continuity between creation and redemption.

First, there is discontinuity primarily because this is a fallen world; it is God's good creation gone wrong. Humanity has no direct access to the kingdom. Persons can enter the kingdom only by way of the cross, the way of redemption, the way of new birth. Without the Savior, sinners are eternally lost. Stott says, "For myself, I still want to insist that the kingdom of God in the New Testament is fundamentally a Christological concept, and that it may be said to exist only where Jesus Christ is consistently preached" as Savior and Lord.[10]

Additional indications of discontinuity between creation and redemption include the fact that while the material creation is temporal, the redemptive order is everlasting (Matt. 6:19; 16:26; 2 Cor. 4:18), and the fact that redemption is not merely a quantitative but a qualitative extension of creation. Redemption is more than creation because more is gained in Christ that was lost in Adam. The new heavens and the new earth are infinitely more than Eden restored.

While evangelicals insist on both continuity and discontinuity in kingdom/world relations, recent *ecumenical* theologians tend to emphasize the continuity and minimize the discontinuity due to sin and Satan. Coleman summarizes the difference between the two viewpoints as follows:

> The liberal is willing to overlook any final distinction between physical and spiritual, secular and sacred, while the evangelical is not. The lib-

---

10. Ronald J. Sider and John R. W. Stott, *Evangelism, Salvation, and Social Action,* Grove Booklets on Ethics, no. 16 (Auburn, MA: Grove, U.S.A., 1977), 23.

In distinguishing between God's rule in creation and His rule in redemption, a Lausanne occasional paper says:

Perhaps we should reserve the expression "the kingdom of God" for the acknowledged rule of Christ, since this is the new thing he inaugurated at his coming, while referring to the more general "sovereignty" of God over all things [in terms which make the distinction clear].

The paper is quick to recognize God's work in providence and common grace, but clearly distinguishes such activity from God's redemptive work. See Stott, *Evangelism and Social Responsibility,* 33.

Newbigin expresses a similar viewpoint:

An entity can be defined either in terms of its boundaries or in terms of its centre. The Church is an entity which is properly described by its centre. It is impossible to define exactly the boundaries of the Church, and the attempt to do so always ends in an unevangelical legalism. But it is always possible and necessary to define the centre. The Church is its proper self, and is a sign of the Kingdom, only insofar as it continually points men and women beyond itself to Jesus and invites them to personal conversion and commitment to him. Newbigin, *Sign of the Kingdom,* 68.

eral perceives God as already present in the world; one has only to discover, develop, and cooperate with the divine spark already there. Because Jesus is located in the other person, the liberal finds His faith tied into society—not accidentally but inherently. For the evangelical certain priorities must be kept in order to insure that we do not lose the distinction between the natural and supernatural, worldly and divine, body and soul. Redemption is a gift of God won by Jesus Christ, not a human achievement or the evolution of man's goodness.[11]

---

11. Richard J. Coleman, *Issues of Theological Conflict* (Grand Rapids: Eerdmans, 1980), 222-23. Coleman's entire chapter speaks to the difference between the two viewpoints; see chap. 6, "The Church and Social Involvement," 205-51.
Neill says:
> One wing of the church will say unhesitatingly: Yes, without Christ men and women are lost; by coming to know him they will be saved. Another wing will say, We do not go to take Christ to the non-Christian world, we go to find him already there. We go to help our non-Christian friend to realize the Christ who already dwells within him; we may find in the process that our non-Christian is able to show us much more of Christ than we shall be able to show him. When all the chips are down, this really is the heart of the argument between conservative and liberal.

Neill, "Ecumenical and Evangelical Missiology," 15.
Referring to ecumenical theologians, Dayton and Fraser say:
> They have stressed a more this-worldly interpretation of Christianity with emphasis on the servant role of the Church in relating to the dire social and political needs of millions of people. Salvation is seen as essentially the humanization of humanity and its world.

Edward R. Dayton and David A. Fraser, *Planning Strategies for Evangelization* (Grand Rapids: Eerdmans, 1980), 62.
Barth's position with reference to universalism continues to be debated. Rising to Barth's defense, Ramm says:
> From the standpoint of *de jure* (legal reckoning), all the world is reconciled to God in Christ. But *de facto* (as things actually are), only Christians know this and confess it. But in that all people are *de jure* Christians, the Christian is to treat all people as brothers and sisters.

Ramm sees Barth's approach as a new and radical basis for Christian social ethics. He continues:
> The traditional manner of treating this problem was to make a distinction between creation and redemption. All people have significance before God in the order of creation. . . . Barth approached the meaningfulness of the non-Christian person from another direction. . . . Christ died for all. . . . This means that Christ is related to all people. . . . However, this relationship is secret. . . . Non-Christians do not know it, but the fact remains unchanged.

Ramm finds this approach exciting and commendable. He makes no attempt, however, to ground it in New Testament teaching. Bernard Ramm, *After Fundamentalism* (San Francisco: Harper, 1983), 169-71. Evangelicals see Christ's death for all persons as highly significant motivation for evangelism and compassionate Christian social action, but not as an excuse for blurring the distinction between lost and saved persons.
Finally, Towner affirms a universalism which frankly denies redemptive discontinuity between the kingdom and the world. He says: "The world was created good and the people in it are already redeemed and are now awaiting the glad word of their redemption." The zeal for mission today lies in sharing this good news, accompanied with "deeds that are modern analogies to Jesus' healing miracles, prefigurations of life as it is lived in the Kingdom of heaven," not in spending time "consigning the unevangelized to hell." W. Sibley Towner, *How God Deals with Evil* (Philadelphia: Westminster, 1976), 152-53.

The difference between the evangelical and ecumenical views of redemption/creation relations comes to a focus in the ongoing evangelism/social action discussion. While distinguishing between evangelism and social action and insisting on the *logical* priority of evangelism (the priority of the eternal over the temporal, Matt. 16:26), evangelicals insist on the crucial importance of both evangelism and social action in God's kingdom mission. Ecumenical theologians, on the other hand, tend to major on social action. This issue will be discussed in the treatment of the *wholistic* nature of the kingdom mission.

In summary, the kingdom present as a redemptive order clearly distinguishes it from the kingdom as God's general rule in creation, despite the fact that redemption and creation are closely related in many significant ways.

The kingdom present as a redemptive order also emphasizes that *the power of the kingdom is the power of the Holy Spirit, not primarily military might, political expertise, intellectual genius, or cultural achievement* (Zech. 4:6; Rom. 14:17).[12] Although New Testament Christians felt themselves richly gifted through the work of the Holy Spirit, they also knew that the way of the kingdom was the way of the cross, not the way of a shallow triumphalism. This may explain why Paul counseled his new converts concerning the kingdom (Acts 14:22). Although Jesus promised His followers the sufficiency of the Holy Spirit and assured them that He had overcome the world, He nonetheless told them frankly that in the world they would have trouble (John 16:33).

Finally, it should be pointed out that as a redemptive order *the kingdom has both positive and negative effects.* The kingdom means salvation

---

12. The renunciation of military force as a means to further the kingdom distinguishes the evangelical view of the kingdom from those liberation theologies which under some circumstances seek to make a Christian virtue of revolutionary violence, in the sense of a bold concession to Marxist philosophy.

Discussing such theologies, Henry says: "The New Testament assault on social injustice is not 'revolutionary' in the sense of reliance on physical violence to promote structural change." Carl F. H. Henry, *God, Revelation, and Authority,* vol. 4, *God Who Speaks and Shows* (Waco, TX: Word, 1979), 592.

Yet, note also White's comment:

> Many evangelicals recoil from liberation theologies because of the use of Marxist analysis. But others believe that the affirmation that God is on the side of the poor is a starting place for yet more faithful understandings of the meaning of discipleship. Although the Third World liberation theologians state that their programs cannot be directly translated to North America, at the same time there has been fruitful interchange with . . . theologians working out the meaning of justice.

R. C. White, Jr., "Gospel, Social Implications of." Walter A. Elwell, ed., *Evangelical Dictionary of Theology* (Grand Rapids: Baker, 1984), 476.

for those who believe but it also means judgment on unrighteousness and injustice and God's condemnation for all who reject salvation in Christ. Divine judgment is both present and future, both individual and corporate. As present and corporate, Jesus said to unbelievers, "I say to you, the kingdom of God will be taken away from you, and be given to a nation producing the fruit of it" (Matt. 21:43). Edge calls this verse "one of the most pivotal, important, and significant verses in all the Bible." His point is that judgment begins at the house of God. God's people are called to mission, and their failure to bring forth the fruit of redemption is serious.[13]

The Kingdom Present Is an Eschatological Reality

According to the three-stage redemptive eschatology of the Bible, the following concepts are inseparable: (1) the kingdom of God, (2) redemption, and (3) eschatology. All redemption is eschatological, so that the *kingdom*, as the Bible's most *comprehensive* term for God's pursuit of His redemptive purpose, is inescapably an eschatological concept.

Interpreters such as Ladd stop short of this conclusion, distinguishing between the kingdom present as historical and the kingdom consummated as eschatological, whether during the millennium or in the final consummation: "This new covenant," he observes, "is now established not in the eschatological kingdom but in history; it nevertheless looks forward to the coming of the eschatological kingdom."[14]

To say that the kingdom present is an eschatological reality emphasizes two truths. First, it stresses that the last things, or the redemptive order promised in the Old Testament, breaks into history decisively through the Christ-Pentecost events. Or, in the terms of the biblical idea of the two ages (e.g., Matt. 12:32), the future, glorious age is already invading the present, evil age (Rom. 12:2; Gal. 1:4; 2 Tim. 1:10; Heb. 6:5). Believers do not wait for the second coming of Christ to experience the last things. Instead they have been living in the last days since the inau-

---

13. Findley B. Edge, *The Greening of the Church* (Waco, TX: Word, 1971), 36.

14. George Eldon Ladd, "The Kingdom of God," in *Dreams, Visions, and Oracles,* eds. Carl E. Armerding and W. Ward Gasque (Grand Rapids: Baker, 1977), 141.

See also Ladd's volumes, *The Presence of the Future* (Grand Rapids: Eerdmans, 1974), and *A Theology of the New Testament* (Grand Rapids: Eerdmans, 1974).

In a similar manner, a chapter in a Lausanne Occasional Paper is entitled, "History and Eschatology." See Stott, *Evangelism and Social Responsibility.*

Ridderbos, to cite a further example, distinguishes between holy (salvation, biblical) history and eschatology. See the *Illustrated Bible Dictionary,* s.v. "Kingdom of God" by H. N. Ridderbos.

Redeemed! Eschatological Redemption and the Kingdom of God

—84—

guration[15] of the kingdom present through the Christ-Pentecost events (Acts 2:17; Heb. 1:2).

Second, because the kingdom present is an eschatological reality, those who live in the kingdom experience the tension between what is already achieved and what is yet to be completed. The decisive events of the gospel (the Christ-Pentecost events) have taken place, but the devil and his forces fight on, refusing to concede defeat.[16] The final victory in the battle with evil is yet to be won.

Oscar Cullmann compares Christ's two comings with the "D-Day" and "V-Day" battles of World War II. Cullmann's analogy helps us conceptualize the tension between the decisive turn in the warfare against evil *already* won and the *not yet* of the final triumph that remains future.[17]

In summary, Christian existence in the kingdom present is an eschatological polarity between the new spiritual abundance made available through the Christ-Pentecost events and the ongoing warfare between the powers of light and the powers of darkness. God's new people are transformed, yet sin persists. Life in the kingdom present remains an uneasy tension between the already and the not yet. Neither of the poles can be neglected without distorting the biblical view of the kingdom present. When the not yet is emphasized to the neglect of the already, the church becomes discouraged about kingdom possibilities. Stressing the already while neglecting the not yet results in unrealistic optimism. Theology must maintain a creative tension between both poles in order to assess adequately the present role of God's people.

---

15. Many writers today employ the term "inaugurated eschatology" to describe the emphasis that through the Christ-Pentecost events the kingdom of God has already broken into history. The term is interpreted in such a wide variety of ways, however, that it is practically meaningless. Some use it to describe a realized form of eschatology. Others use it to describe eschatologies such as Ladd's, where the eschatological kingdom remains a future reality. Others use it as practically synonymous with amillennialism.

16. "In a profound new way God's presence and power are a *now* reality to accomplish His will on earth." C. Norman Kraus, *The Community of the Spirit* (Grand Rapids: Eerdmans, 1974), 11. See the later reference to Kraus in the discussion of the kingdom present as mission.

17. Oscar Cullmann, *Christ and Time*, trans. Floyd V. Filson (Philadelphia: Westminster, 1950), 84.

Hoekema devotes a chapter to "The Tension between the Already and the Not Yet," reflecting the emphasis he gives to the concept. Anthony A. Hoekema, *The Bible and the Future* (Grand Rapids: Eerdmans, 1979), 68-75.

The difficulty in articulating the tension between the already and the not yet aspects of the kingdom present is illustrated by the following remark from a Lausanne Occasional Paper:

How can Christ claim universal authority if the whole world still lies in Satan's power? The answer is that over his redeemed people Jesus is King *de facto,* while it is only *de jure* that he is presently King over the world, his right being still challenged by the usurper.

Surely the sense in which Jesus is already king over his people itself has both a *de facto* and a *de jure* sense. See Stott, *Evangelism and Social Responsibility,* 33.

The Kingdom Present Is a Vital Force in World History

One of the most important elements in a recovery of an evangelical kingdom consciousness is the nurturing of a sense of history![18] Two schools of thought are prevalent. Many evangelicals support the idea that Christian events have a significant impact on human history while others feel that the evidence that supports this concept can be disputed. In support of the former point of view, the following discussion notices: first, that the Christian sense of history grows out of the decisiveness for all history of the Christ-Pentecost events; second, that the outward evidence for the kingdom as a historical force is disputable; and third, that the danger of reducing the kingdom to a merely inward and subjective dimension is to be avoided.

First, the Christian sense of history roots in the conviction that something decisive happened in the Christ-Pentecost events. Hoekema says:

> The coming of Christ [is] the single most important event of human history. . . . Christ has indeed brought in the new age, the age of the kingdom of God. The world is therefore not the same since Christ came; an electrifying change has taken place. . . . The fact that not all men are by faith participating in the blessings of the new age does not nullify the existence of the age.[19]

In a similar vein Lightfoot says:

> The life of the Church was to fill something more than a brief pause between the penultimate and the final scene . . . . The growth and experience of the Church had shown that the Lord's life was not only an event in Jewish history, but in world history . . . . It was itself the manifestation in history of the spiritual Power through which the worlds were made.[20]

This sense of a new spiritual abundance through the Christ-Pentecost events pervades the thinking of New Testament writers.[21] The redemp-

---

18. Snyder lists a recovery of a sense of history as one of five essential ingredients in an evangelical kingdom consciousness. See note 11 above.
Henry concurs:
> Although very different in nature from ancient (and not so ancient) Constantinian projections or modern revolutionary alternatives, the church of Christ Jesus is an actual structure and indestructible power in history ruled even now from the heavenlies by its eternal King.

Henry, *God Revelation, and Authority,* 4;530.
19. Hoekema, *The Bible and the Future,* 29,31.
20. R. H. Lightfoot, *St. John's Gospel,* ed. C. F. Evans (Oxford: Clarendon, 1956), 49.
21. Koenig says: "The New Testament was written by and for people who felt themselves extraordinarily gifted by God through the events surrounding the ministry of Jesus." For a luminous discussion of this claim, see John Koenig, *Charismata: God's Gifts for God's People* (Philadelphia: Westminster, 1978), 48-70.

Redeemed! Eschatological Redemption and the Kingdom of God

—86—

tion promised throughout the Old Testament is breaking into history. The last days have arrived. The Lamb reigns! Deadly warfare between God and Satan still rages, but Christ has already won the decisive victory over the powers of evil, and His final triumph is sure.

Rottenberg refers over and again to the history-making aspect of the kingdom:

> The proclamation of the gospel of the kingdom is a historical force of the first order (18,90). . . . We must learn to see *conversion* in terms of the kingdom. When the power of God's future breaks into the present and radically renews a human heart, this is a revolutionary happening. It certainly is a central manifestation and sign of the power of the new age (21). . . . The kingdom of God is the power of the new age entering into our world and transforming it according to God's plan for the fullness of time (22). . . . The Holy Spirit is operative, not only in the hearts of people, but in the history of the world. The end of the ways of God is still corporeality (57). . . . In a very special way the power of the new age is manifested in the Church. . . . The signs of the kingdom are indeed in our midst. They are not empty signs, for in them the power of the new age is manifested. In that sense the kingdom of God is realized on earth (67). . . . The gospel of the kingdom has an impact upon the nations where it is preached. We ought not dismiss the impact of the gospel too quickly by saying that it is only a thin veneer covering the surface of societies (69). . . . As Christians we can never again view the world as if the incarnation had never happened, and as if the Holy Spirit is not present in history (17). . . . Christian mission does more, however, than filling the historical interim; it creates history in the power of the Holy Spirit (88). . . . Through the proclamation of the Word and the power of the Holy Spirit, the gospel of the kingdom *happens* (90). . . . The proclamation of the gospel of the kingdom. . . . has influenced societal structures and legislation. The world is different because prophets of the Lord have spoken (91).[22]

He suggestively relates the kingdom's history-shaping power to the New Testament's use of such terms as "guarantee," "first fruits," and "signs." Regarding these he says:

> It would be a mistake to place the emphasis here on the "smallness" of the "beginning" of the presence of God's renewing power. In the Old Testament the first fruits are *representative* of the whole harvest, and this is also the idea conveyed by the New Testament.[23]

---

22. Isaac C. Rottenberg, *The Promise and the Presence* (Grand Rapids: Eerdmans, 1980). It is this sense of the history-shaping power of the kingdom present which is missing in writers such as Ladd, with their stress on the kingdom present as a small, insignificant force in history. See note 2 above.

23. Ibid., 57.

This emphasis on the kingdom present as a vital force in history is no naive triumphalism that assumes Christians have automatic solutions to individual and world problems. Christian history witnesses triumphalism in many forms:

- the imperial claims of the medieval papacy,

- the sometimes partial confusion of the gospel with western cultural forms in nineteenth-century missionary presence,

- Cox's celebration of the secular city as a triumph of God's kingdom,

- the recent Prosperity Gospel with its "God wants you rich" and similar themes.

Triumphalism takes many forms, but it easily forgets the humiliation, suffering, and ongoing warfare against evil at the center of the gospel of Christ.

There is, to be sure, a triumphant, resurrection note in Christian proclamation, but Smedes explains how it is best sounded:

> Jesus is Lord. He is Lord of the present time, in charge, on top of things . . . . This is the optimistic, triumphant note of the Christian faith. It is best sung, though, by people hiding in catacombs, by disciples on the run. It comes off nobly as a victory cry from people crushed by the lords of this world. From sleepy people in cushioned pews, it comes too cheap to be a desperate victory of faith. . . . I still want to say that Jesus is Lord. . . . [But] the right way is to confess that it is Jesus who is Lord. For Jesus is the servant of men, and His lordship is a lordship of service. When we look for a sign of His triumph, we have to look, not for a Caesar riding home with captives on His line, but for a workingman riding home after a day's labor. He is always the Lord *Jesus*, and this means Lord Servant.[24]

Second, the resistance by many evangelicals to any form of the idea of the kingdom present as a vital force in world history points to the fact that

---

24. Lewis B. Smedes, "The Christ of the Present Time II," *The Reformed Journal,* December 1966, 5-6. Smedes' insistence that Jesus means Servant should not be taken as a denial that in its biblical use the name Jesus is associated primarily with His role as Savior.
Speaking of suffering as an element in the strategy of missions, Kerr says:
> Christ the Lord expects His church to manifest a faithfulness in its task commensurate with His own. This demands a discipline in suffering which gears the church to its mission. . . . A miracle occurs if in truth the Christian suffers for his Lord: the miracle of personal transformation, the miracle of church unity, and the miracle of evangelistic victory.

William M. Kerr as quoted by Arthur F. Glasser, "Confession, Church Growth, and Authentic Unity in Missionary Strategy," in Norman A. Horner, ed., *Protestant Crosscurrents in Mission* (Nashville: Abingdon, 1968), 221. Kerr's article appeared originally in *The Gordon Review,* Fall 1965, 15.

the outward evidence for the claim can be disputed. Evil often seems the victor in the warfare between good and evil, so that 2,000 years of Christian history give no final indication to most evangelical observers that society generally is gradually becoming more and more Christian. This problem is confronted more directly later in the text, when the question regarding the progress of the kingdom in history is faced, but the point concerning the disputability of the external evidence for the kingdom as a historical force requires an immediate response here.

The contestability of the claim that the kingdom present is a shaping force in world history is to be explained by the fact that it is the form which the kingdom takes between the times, between the first and second comings of Christ. The kingdom is already present in power, but its ultimate triumph awaits the return of Christ. Prior to the second coming of Christ the warfare between good and evil continues to rage. While the decisive victory has been won and the final outcome is sure, for the time being Satan fights on furiously. The kingdom present, then, is the earthly form of the kingdom, not the final and heavenly form. There are victories, glorious victories, but no final victories until earth gives way to heaven.[25]

This means that though there are signs of the kingdom's presence, for the time being they are veiled. They must be discerned. They require interpreting. They are perceived by faith, not merely by sight, so that those without faith are inclined to explain kingdom phenomena in naturalistic terms, without any reference to the reality of God's mighty redemptive presence and activity in history.

That signs of the kingdom's presence exist is evident in Jesus' response to John's disciples when they asked Him for signs which they could report

---

25. Regarding New Testament references to the binding of Satan in the Christ-Pentecost events, see Ladd, *The Presence of the Future,* 149-54. Ladd cites Cullmann: "As Oscar Cullmann has so quaintly put it, we may think of Satan as bound with a rope which can be lengthened or shortened" (Ibid., 152).

In the light of the Christ-Pentecost events, faith is confident that the kingdom triumphs ultimately, however ambiguous the present signs of triumph might be. Faith perceives the resurrection of Christ as a manifestation that He, and not the political, religious, and demonic forces which raged against Him, is the mightiest force in history. Rutenber says:

The grain of the universe ran in Christ's direction, not Herod's or Caiaphas'. The things for which Christ stood, the truths of which he spoke, the love which he demonstrated—these were the enduring, living, powerful realities of the world; not the lust, the power-drive, the hate, the selfishness, the sin of men and nations. God's guarantee stood back of Christ's kind of life. He was right, forever right.

Culbert Rutenber, *The Reconciling Gospel* (Philadelphia: Judson Press, 1960), 135. Rutenber is aware that in a sense the vindication for the moment was incomplete: "The risen Christ came only to the disciples. His enemies neither saw his resurrection nor did they believe the apostolic witness to it" (Ibid).

to John that Jesus was in truth the messiah which was to come. Jesus' response was that they should report that the blind receive sight, the lame walk, lepers are cured, the deaf hear, the dead are raised, and good news is preached to the poor (Luke 7:22). That these signs retained a certain indefiniteness is evident in Jesus' warning concerning false messiahs and false prophets who perform signs which are capable of deceiving even the elect (Matt. 24:24).

Discerning signs of the transforming power of the presence of the kingdom in history, then, requires spiritual perception and involves the risk of error. Signs are often best understood in hindsight. Glasser illustrates this fact with reference to the expulsion of missionaries from China at the time of the rise of the People's Republic. At the time, many of the missionaries felt that they had dismally failed both God and the Chinese people, but what they did not realize, says Glasser,

> was that the Chinese church had reached the level of "critical mass." Western missionaries were no longer needed. Despite the persecution and suffering that lay ahead, the Lord knew that in His way the Chinese church would explode with growth and greatly accelerate the evangelization of the Chinese people. Each new day provides us with fresh evidence of this.[26]

Third, since the signs of the kingdom present as a world-shaping force are not readily discernible outwardly, precautions must be taken against the danger of reducing the idea of the kingdom to merely inward and subjective dimensions. Because the evidence of its power can be disputed (cf. Acts 2:13 and many similar passages), theologians of various kinds too easily conclude that the kingdom present is merely a small, inward, and insignificant historical force. Their temptation is to remove the effects of the kingdom from any meaningful relation to the course of daily events and the shaping of world history.

This tendency is particularly strong in much modern theology, as Smart recognizes:

> Reality is reduced to two dimensions: the material world without, which is the realm of the natural sciences and which man progressively masters by His science, and the experiential world within, conscious and unconscious, which the psychologists and the psychiatrists explore and seek to bring under control. Banned from the outer

---

26. Arthur F. Glasser, "A Review and a Revision: Lessons from the Protestant Mission to China," *Theology, News and Notes,* December 1984, 8. Glasser's next sentence, "God will indeed win in history," raises the issue to be dealt with below, in the discussion of the reality of the ongoing warfare between the forces of light and the forces of darkness, with reference to the extent of kingdom progress which is to be expected in history prior to Christ's return.

world, God retreats into the inner world.... History is the all-compre-
hensive reality and God is just one of the elements in history.[27]

Some evangelicals have not proved any more successful than other
Christians in escaping the tendency to deny that the kingdom present is
a vital force in history. Dispensational theology tends to minimize the
kingdom as a present historical force by postponing it for the most part
until a millennium following Christ's return. As was noted above, even
Ladd, as a historical premillennialist, and despite his strong reaction to
older dispensational theology, speaks of the smallness of the kingdom
present, contrasting it with the greatness of a millennial kingdom after
Christ's return (see note 2).

The tendency among some conservatives to reduce the historical significance of the kingdom present, however, has deeper roots than the postponing of the kingdom's historical vitality until a future, post-second
coming millennial age. Speaking of the divorce between evangelism and
social responsibility, which is closely related to the reductionist tendency
with reference to the kingdom present, a Lausanne Occasional Paper says:

> We tend to set over against one another in an unhealthy way soul
> and body, the individual and society, redemption and creation, grace
> and nature, heaven and earth, justification and justice, faith and
> works. The Bible certainly distinguishes between these, but it also
> relates them to each other, and it instructs us to hold each pair in a
> dynamic and creative tension. It is as wrong to disengage them, as in
> "dualism," as it is to confuse them, as in "monism." It was for this
> reason that the Lausanne Covenant, speaking of evangelism and
> socio-political involvement, affirmed that they "are both part of our
> Christian duty" (Paragraph 5).[28]

In conclusion, over against either the error of triumphalism or the
error of reductionism, the kingdom present, though it is essentially a
veiled, spiritual, and redemptive force, is nonetheless a powerful and
vital historical force.

From the perspective of biblical faith, Stephen's dying prayer for the
forgiveness of his murderers was a far more potent historical force than
the brute power of the rocks which crushed the life from his body (Acts
7:59-60). Prayer may seem a lesser historical power than evil's weapons
of destruction, but Jesus distinctly linked the coming of the kingdom with

---

27. James D. Smart, *The Strange Silence of the Bible in the Church* (Philadelphia: Westminster, 1970), 131.

Kolden has recently written of the Barthian variation of the same theme. He indicates
that the eschatological insights of the New Testament were "transformed by neoorthodoxy
into nontemporal notions of transcendence (Barth) or existential urgency (Bultmann)."
Marc Kolden, "On Speaking of the Kingdom Today," *Word and World* 2 [Spring 1982]: 150-51.

28. Stott, *Evangelism and Social Responsibility*, 20.

prayer and taught us to pray, "Thy kingdom come, Thy will be done, on earth as it is in heaven" (Matt. 6:10).

The Kingdom Present Is Mission

As the kingdom in history, the kingdom present is God's pursuit of His redemptive purpose in Christ. It is God's primary mission in the world. The following discussion defines mission, underscores the fact that as mission the kingdom is a dynamic and not a static reality, and indicates that the kingdom is task as well as gift.

Defining mission.—There are both broad and narrow definitions of the Christian mission. Some writers understand the mission of the kingdom in terms of the church's outreach only, as though mission had no reference to other functions of the people of God, such as worship and nurture. McGavran, for example, quotes Richard Niebuhr's definition that mission is "everything done outside our four walls, . . . everything the church does for nonmembers."[29]

This, however, will hardly do. Mission should be understood more broadly in terms of all that God *purposes* His people to be and to do in the realization of His kingdom goals. On this basis worship and nurture are as much the mission of God's people as evangelism and social action. This is the sense in which mission is broader than missions. "Missions" commonly refers to world missions and home missions, while "mission" embraces the whole response of the whole of God's people to the whole of God's redemptive purpose. Only when mission is understood in this comprehensive manner does it make sense to say that the church *is* mission.[30] Those who object to this slogan usually do so because they limit their understanding of mission to the church's outreach only.[31]

---

29. Glasser and McGavran, *Contemporary Theologies of Mission*, 17.

McGavran narrows mission further than Niebuhr, limiting mission primarily to evangelism. The truth in McGavran's view is the *logical* priority of evangelism in the church's outreach.

30. Antedating the cliches of the 1960s, Brunner says: "The Church exists by mission, just as a fire exists by burning. Where there is no mission, there is no Church." Emil Brunner, *The Word and the World* (New York: Scribner's, 1931), 108.

Hoekendijk, reflecting "the church in the world" emphasis in ecumenical missiology during the 1960s, says that the church "does not engage in missions, but she herself *becomes* mission." J. C. Hoekendijk, *The Church Inside Out*, ed. L. A. Hoedemaker and Pieter Tijmes, trans. Isaac C. Rottenberg (Philadelphia: Westminster, 1966), 43.

Guthrie faults the classical Protestant definition of the church in terms of the pure preaching of the Word of God and the right administration of the sacraments for its omission of an emphasis on mission. Shirley C. Guthrie, Jr., *Christian Doctrine* (Atlanta: Knox, 1977), 364-65.

Moody represents the widespread current acceptability of the idea that the church is mission: "Indeed, the church is mission, and where there is no mission there is no church." Dale Moody, *The Word of Truth* (Grand Rapids: Eerdmans, 1981), 427.

31. Both Stott, an evangelical, and Gilkey, an ecumenical theologian, object to saying that the church is mission, on the ground that mission excludes worship and nurture. See John R. W. Stott, *Christian Mission* (Downers Grove, IL: InterVarsity, 1975), 19,30,35, and Langdon Gilkey, *How the Church Can Minister to the World without Losing Itself* (New York: Harper, 1964), 63–65, note 6.

Jeffery sees more clearly than many the integral relation between the functions of the church as gathered and scattered, though he stops short of actually saying that the church's mission includes the functions of worship and nurture. He says:

> If mission is central to the life of the Church, then Christian congregations need to be missionary congregations and not be merely concerned with the pastoral care of the faithful. Since the apostolate is part of the whole life of the Church, it is important that mission and worship should be related to each other. The God we worship is a sending God, and therefore we need to relate worship to the missionary movement of God to man. The inward emphasis of worship as building up the Body of Christ needs to be supplemented by an equally essential outward emphasis in worship. Baptism is not simply incorporation into the life of Christ; it is a commitment to the missionary life which is Christ's. . . . All the elements of Christian worship have a mission-dimension.[32]

In a similar manner it should be said, to his credit, that McGavran sees the integral relation of mission to all of theology. He speaks forcefully of the central *redemptive* concern of the Bible when he writes concerning "Making Doctrines Missionarily Effective and Biblically Correct."[33]

The emphasis on the kingdom as mission roots in the missionary nature of God Himself. Jeffery says:

> The God of the Bible is a sending God; he sends messengers, prophets, and leaders to His people. Finally, he sends His Son to bring in the *malkuth* (Kingdom), the active reign of God, to man and to the world.[34]

As mission the kingdom present is a dynamic and not a static reality.— The kingdom present is not merely a realm but a mighty *God movement* in history. It works aggressively to establish itself despite the rebellion and opposition of the enemy.

Notice, however, that to speak of the kingdom as a dynamic movement is not to deny that it is also a realm, the realm of salvation in its vertical, Godhuman dimension. Salvation is a relational status as well as an experience and a movement in history. The believer is a child of God; in Christ

---

32. R. M. C. Jeffery, "Mission, Theology of," in Alan Richardson, ed., *Dictionary of Christian Theology* (Philadelphia: Westminster, 1969), 219.

In a noteworthy article, Brown argues for a comprehensive view of the church's mission. He contends that mission includes the call both to be and to do. Ronald K. Brown, "The Church's Mission in Two Dimensions," *Search* [Summer 1985]: 21-24.

33. Glasser and McGavran, *Contemporary Theologies of Mission,* chap. 8.

34. Jeffery, "Mission, Theology of," 217.

Newbigin relates God's missionary nature to his trinitarian nature. Lesslie Newbigin, *Trinitarian Faith and Today's Mission* (Richmond: Knox, 1964). A summary of this argument is given in Lesslie Newbigin, *The Open Secret* (Grand Rapids: Eerdmans, 1978), 20-72.

For a stimulating, systematic study of the concept of the sending God, see Francis M. DuBose, *God Who Sends: A Fresh Quest for Biblical Mission* (Nashville: Broadman, 1983).

he or she has eternal life. In this sense, the kingdom is a condition of existence, a harbor, a sheepfold, an arriving, a homecoming, but the kingdom is also a movement. It is not only an arriving; it is also a warfare, a task, a race, a pilgrimage, a goal. In other words, the kingdom is a realm, but never in any merely static sense.

In the Cotton Patch Version of the Gospels, Clarence Jordan felicitously translates the kingdom of God as "the God movement" (Matt. 6:33), or as "God's new order of the Spirit" (Matt. 3:2). Referring to Jordan's translation, Kraus distinguishes a movement from a mere society. While a society is an organizationally defined association, a movement is less structured, more heterogeneous and flexible. It gains its character and structure from the purpose for which it exists—its mission. What is probably more significant is its relation to the whole group within which it operates. A movement aims to effect changes in the larger social order. It does not exist to perpetuate itself as a movement but to bring its purposes to realization within the whole social order of which it is a part.[35]

The kingdom present is task as well as gift.—God's people are quick to stress the gift aspect of the kingdom, while the kingdom as task is a much less popular notion. Yet biblical redemption is always a call to service as well as to privilege. God saves and gifts His people for mission. This truth is stated with matchless simplicity in the words of James: "Faith without works is dead" (2:26).

The order here, however, is all-important. The kingdom is gift before it is task. Since humankind's response roots in God's grace, all that God's people are and all they achieve is by the grace of God. The practical significance of this truth is its insistence that what believers do in kingdom service they are to do spontaneously and voluntarily, not in order to earn salvation but because of God's free and unmerited favor. No room is left for any kind of salvation by works. Believers obey God because they want to. They forego comforts, endure hardships, and overcome obstacles out of a sense of gratitude. They do willingly what they could never be forced or paid to do (Acts 5:41). They are impelled not compelled. They serve not only because the King commands but also because the Spirit energizes.[36]

---

35. Kraus, *The Community of the Spirit*, 27, note 1. Kraus later amplifies these statements (37-44). He says: "A movement forms as a consequence of powerful convictions or events which call for action and change in response. Mission rather than organizational structure gives cohesiveness and form to a movement" (38).

Similarly, as early as 1968, Duthie said: "The Christian mission to the world may aptly be described in many of its aspects by the word 'movement," a word which suggests life, activity, purpose." Charles S. Duthie, *Outline of Christian Belief* (Nashville: Abingdon, 1968), 85.

36. This is Boer's point. He grounds the vitality of the early Pentecostal community, not first in its obedience to the great commission as a command, but in the continuing renewal wrought by the Holy Spirit. Harry R. Boer, *Pentecost and Missions* (Grand Rapids: Eerdmans, 1961), 217.

Yet, though the kingdom is gift before it is task, it is never realized in history easily or automatically. The lives of Christians are not usually significantly changed without sustained Christian discipline, nor do Christians readily effect long-range changes in their societies. Peace on earth is more than a dream; it is an arduous, never-ending task. These matters will be encountered again in the discussion of the kingdom present as a warfare and a goal.

The Kingdom Present Is Wholistic Mission[37]

One of the more significant characteristics of the kingdom present idea is its *comprehensive* nature. It has the awesome power to gather into a single, overarching unity the total sweep—individual, socio-cultural, and cosmic—of God's redemptive purpose, which is nothing less that ultimately to bring *all things* into subjection under Christ (Col. 1:20).[38] Verkuyl says:

> The kingdom to which the Bible testifies involves a proclamation and a realization of a total salvation, one which covers the whole range of human needs and destroys every pocket of evil and grief affecting mankind. Kingdom in New Testament has a breadth and scope which is unsurpassed; it embraces heaven as well as earth, world history as well as the entire cosmos.[39]

---

37. In current practice "wholistic" is sometimes spelled "holistic." The wholistic spelling is used here in order to emphasize the relation of the term to "whole" and its distinction from "hole" and "holy." Precedent for this spelling is found in "wholeness" and "wholly." Furthermore, "holistic" and "holism" are sometimes technical terms referring to specialized perspectives in contemporary psychology or to holistic health cults related to the human potential movement.

Stott's disclaimer that though he uses the term wholistic he has "always found the term harsh in sound and ugly in aspect" is difficult to justify. See Stott, "The Biblical Scope of the Christian Mission," *Christianity Today*, January 4, 1980, 34. In his article Stott views the Christian mission in terms of the whole world, the whole gospel, the whole mission, and the whole church. He might also have spoken of whole persons.

For presentations of the wholistic emphasis, see David O. Moberg, *Wholistic Christianity: An Appeal for a Dynamic, Balanced Faith* (Elgin, IL: Brethren, 1985), and C. Peter Wagner, *Church Growth and the Whole Gospel* (San Francisco: Harper, 1981).

38. The ultimate intent of God's redemptive purpose in Christ is not to be confused with universalism. It is not God's will that any perish (2 Pet. 3:9), but the New Testament speaks of the eternal lostness of those who persist in their sin (Matt. 25:46).

39. Johannes Verkuyl, *Contemporary Missiology*, trans. and ed. Dale Cooper (Grand Rapids: Eerdmans, 1978), 197-98.

Henry says:
> Evangelical commitment to the new birth involves also commitment to the new society—to preservation of human justice and order, and to fuller humanization of man's fallen life through divine renewal and reorientation.

Henry, *God, Revelation and Authority*, 4:591.

In the hymn, "Joy to the World! The Lord Is Come," Isaac Watts says that Christ "comes to make His blessings flow / Far as the curse is found." On this basis, no one should take the wholistic dimension of the kingdom mission more seriously than those who name the name of Christ!

Yet, important as the wholistic emphasis is, it has often been neglected in Christian history, and in recent times has also been the occasion of considerable controversy. Concerning the neglect of the emphasis, Glasser says of evangelicals prior to the recent renewal of interest in the kingdom present theme:

> We tend to interpret the victory of Jesus Christ almost exclusively in individualistic terms. Our theology fails to grapple with culture. Our ethic does not embrace the totality of human endeavor, particularly the cultural pursuit. We are preoccupied with noncultural activities (prayer meetings, Bible studies, personal witness) and imply that God finds in them alone His will being done "on earth as it is in heaven."[40]

Concerning the post-World War II controversy over Christianity and social issues, particularly from the standpoint of world evangelization, see the discussions by Glasser and McGavran, Newbigin, and Padilla.[41]

Because of the comprehensiveness of the theme as well as because of the neglect and controversy associated with it, developing a theology of the wholistic emphasis is no simple matter. In order to give shape to the topic, the following matters will be discussed: the wholistic claim; the biblical basis for the claim; the basic problem—the logical priority of redemption over creation in God's purpose through Christ; the focal issue—the logical priority of evangelism over social action in the mission of the church; and the wholistic emphasis as limitless challenge.

The wholistic claim.—Simply stated the wholistic claim is the biblical emphasis that the concerns of the kingdom present are as wide as creation. The claim thus represents a firm rejection of any false dichotomies between the realms of redemption and creation. Instead of only negating the fallen aspect of creation, redemption seeks to fulfill God's intentions

---

40. Glasser, "Confession, Church Growth, and Authentic Unity," 181-182.

Regarding evangelical neglect of the wholistic emphasis, see Carl F. H. Henry, *The Uneasy Conscience of Modern Fundamentalism* (Grand Rapids: Eerdmans, 1947), and David O. Moberg, *The Great Reversal: Evangelism versus Social Concern* (Philadelphia: Lippincott, 1972).

Regarding evangelical rediscovery of the wholistic emphasis, in addition to note 48, see Robert K. Johnston, *Evangelicals at an Impasse* (Atlanta: Knox, 1979), especially chap. 4, "Evangelical Social Ethics."

41. Glasser and McGavran, *Contemporary Theologies of Mission;* Newbigin, *Sign of the Kingdom;* and Rene Padilla, ed., *The New Face of Evangelicalism: An International Symposium on the Lausanne Covenant* (Downers Grove, IL: InterVarsity, 1976).

for creation. *Only in redemption are the purposes of creation, which the entrance of sin has frustrated, fulfilled.* Left to itself creation destroys itself. Redeemed it learns to sing again!

The emphasis on the applicability of the gospel to all of life received special notice in the secular theology of the 1960s. This was not all gain, however. Shibboleths such as "the world sets the agenda for the church," "the secular city," "religionless Christianity," and "honest to God" tended to substitute the world for the kingdom and creation for redemption. MacLeod's observation that "Jesus was not crucified in a cathedral between two candles, but on a cross between two thieves,"[42] was a needed corrective for a post-World War II western Christianity overly concerned with institutional self-preservation, but it overlooked the fact that the opposition to Jesus was led by religious forces.

The wholistic emphasis is vital, but it is biblical only so long as the priority of redemption to creation is respected. God is involved in the six days of work as well as the one day of worship, but the right use of the day of worship is the key to the significant use of the six days of work. The emphasis of the 1960s that church work includes daily duties at home or office, as well as activity on the church ground on Sunday, proved an exciting recovery of neglected biblical perspectives, as was the fresh stress on the need for believers to involve themselves in the affairs of community, government, and world.

A Christian experience which is merely individual and private, or which seeks to escape from the world, finds no biblical sanction. Such emphases avail little if the stress on the six days is made at the expense of the centrality of the one day! Worship remains primary in the biblical outlook regarding the godly man's life in the world.

As difficult to achieve as a balanced wholistic emphasis is, the challenge is worth the effort. No insight so transfigures the daily life of the believer, powerfully counteracting the forces of burnout, as the realization that one's daily work is God's work and that the daily walk is the arena of obedience to God. Even a cup of cold water given in Jesus' name has eternal significance.

The biblical basis for the wholistic emphasis.—The biblical foundation for the wholistic emphasis is both implicit and explicit.

First, the wholistic emphasis is implicit both in the virile monotheism of the biblical world view and in the doctrines of the incarnation and atonement. According to biblical monotheism, the Redeemer and the

---

42. George F. MacLeod, *Only One Way Left* (Glasgow: Iona, 1956), 38. One cannot help wondering if the double meaning of MacLeod's title was intentional.

Creator are not two different gods but one and same Lord God almighty, Maker of heaven and earth. This is my Father's world! There could be no redemption if there were no creation, preservation, providence, and common grace. The God who redeems is the God who controls the universe, sends the sunshine and the rain, notes the sparrow when it falls, and numbers the hairs of our heads. He who saves our souls teaches us to trust Him for our daily bread.

Contrary to the false dichotomies between the kingdom present and the world, the spiritual and the material realms, the eternal and the temporal, the soul and the body, redemption and creation, and evangelism and social action, the Bible forthrightly affirms the ultimate compatibility in principle between kingdom concerns and the common life of humankind in all of its God-created dimensions—religious, individual, social, economic, political, cultural, and cosmic.

This is a stupendous claim! It is the ground for the amazing confidence of biblically based faith that the common life of humanity has been created good and is redeemable in Christ.

It should also be noted that since there is only one God, there is therefore only one human race under God! This means that the ability of humankind to live together is a divine concern, a concern which the gospel not only affirms but intensifies.[43] "Red and yellow, black, and white, / They are precious in His sight. / Jesus loves the little children of the world."

Both of these wholistic emphases, the ultimate compatibility of redemption and creation and the oneness of all humankind under God as Creator, are also implicit in the doctrines of the incarnation and the atonement. The incarnation was possible because human beings are God's creatures made in God's image. It stands as the final demonstration of the ultimate compatibility between the Creator and the Redeemer, between the divine and the human, and between Creator and the creature.

In a like manner, since Christ died for all humankind, not for just one race but for all races, the atonement also teaches the oneness under God of all persons. Paul grounded his appeal to the Gentile Corinthians for a generous offering for the Jewish poor in Jerusalem on the facts of the incarnation and the atonement (2 Cor. 8:8-15). As Christ freely gave

---

43. Borthwick's recent study reflects the current evangelical concern for global Christianity and multiculturalism. Paul Borthwick, *How to Be a World Class Christian* (Wheaton, IL: Victor, 1991).

Redeemed! Eschatological Redemption and the Kingdom of God

—98—

Himself on behalf of people everywhere, Gentiles as well as Jews, His followers are to do the same.

Second, the wholistic emphasis is explicit in the biblical teaching regarding the two kingdom mandates. These are, first, the *redemption mandate*, as summarized in the two greatest commandments (Matt. 22:37-40), the great commission (Matt. 28:19-20), and all of the redemption imperatives of the Bible, and, second, the *creation* or *cultural mandate*, expressed initially in Genesis 1:26-30, renewed and expanded in Genesis 9:1-7, repeated in Psalm 8:6-8 and Hebrews 2:6-8, and continually developed and applied in the extensive individual-social-cultural-cosmic teachings of the Bible.[44]

The wholistic view of the kingdom mission focuses attention on the fact that the redemption mandate opens the way to creation's fulfillment. As originally recorded in Genesis 1:26-30, the creation mandate roots in God's creating persons in His own image, and charging them as lords of creation under the Lord to be fruitful, to increase in number, to fill the earth, and to subdue it. Essentially, the image of God in humans is a relational matter. To be persons in God's image is to be persons in relation, in relation primarily to God, but also to others, to self, and to things.

Persons are not only discrete individuals; they are also social and cultural beings. In creating persons, God created society, including the possibility for individual growth, marriage and the home, religious institutions, and economic and political orders. This comprehensiveness is overwhelming![45]

---

44. Regarding the origin of the expression "cultural mandate," Wagner, who uses the evangelistic/cultural terminology for the mandates, indicates that he first came across the term in Glasser, "Confession, Church Growth, and Authentic Unity," 178.

Wagner says: "Glasser denies that he originated the term 'cultural mandate'; nevertheless it is he who has popularized the slogan as a rallying point for evangelical social ministry." In his chapter in the Horner volume, Glasser refers to an earlier article which included a reference to the cultural mandate: Edwin Walhout, "The Liberal-Fundamentalist Debate," *Christianity Today*, March 1, 1963, 520. Did Glasser get the term from Walhout? Was the term original with Walhout?

Wagner, *Church Growth and the Whole Gospel*, 12,26 (notes 33-34). Wagner's volume is indispensable for the study of the recent evangelical recovery of the wholistic emphasis.

Stott has something else than the two mandates in mind when he speaks of "the great commission" and "the great commandment (love your neighbor)," insisting that both require both evangelism and social service. Stott, *Christian Mission in the Modern World*, 22,28.

45. Few writers who speak of the creation mandate adequately view its comprehensiveness. Individual emphases vary. For instance, Holmes stresses education, Webber the socio-cultural dimension, and Wagner the importance of social action as well as evangelism.

See Arthur F. Holmes, *All Truth is God's Truth* (Grand Rapids: Eerdmans, 1977); Robert E. Webber, *Secular Saint* (Grand Rapids: Zondervan, 1979); and Wagner, *Church Growth and the Whole Gospel.*

Unbelievable as it is, God created *persons* and charged *them* with their part of the responsibility for the course of civilization![46]

The following section further emphasizes that the redemption mandate reinforces and enhances the creation mandate rather than minimizing it.

The basic problem: the logical priority of redemption.—The basic issue at stake in the wholistic emphasis is the question of an adequate theological foundation for Christian social and cultural responsibility. The answer to the question is that, given sin and the fallenness of creation, the only adequate foundation for the wholistic emphasis is found in the redemption that is in Jesus Christ.

This assertion of the logical priority of redemption to creation, however, is one of the most controversial issues in contemporary theology. A significant part of the controversy, as was noted in the above section on the kingdom as a redemptive order, centers in the difference between evangelical and ecumenical understandings of redemption. Assuming a conservative view of redemption, two key principles can be suggested to guide in the effort to conceptualize the relation between redemption and creation.

The first principle to guide in the effort to understand the relation of the redemption and creation mandates is the insistence that the spheres of redemption and creation, though distinct, are nonetheless inseparable. In the above discussion of the kingdom as redemptive, it was noted that, while evangelical writers clearly distinguish between redemption and creation, ecumenical theologians tend to minimize the distinction, thus blurring the difference between grace and nature, as well as between special revelation and general revelation.

According to the ecumenical view, God in Christ is already at work redemptively in the world apart from biblical or special revelation. Hence, Christ is regarded as redemptively present in the experience of other persons regardless of whether they know Him personally as Savior

---

46. Regarding the reach of the cultural mandate, Wagner says:
>   The specific content of the cultural mandate is awesome. God expects a great deal of those to whom he has entrusted the earth and all of its goodness. Distribution of wealth, the balance of nature, marriage and the family, human government, keeping the peace, cultural integrity, liberation of the oppressed–these and other global responsibilities rightly fall within the cultural mandate. Since it is God's will that the human race live in *shalom*, those among them who have been born again into the kingdom and who purport to live under the Lordship of Jesus Christ are required to live lives that will promote *shalom* to the greatest extent possible.

Vitally important in the cultural mandate, of course, is also the pursuit of knowledge and wisdom. Wagner, *Church Growth and the Whole Gospel*, 13.

and Lord. According to the evangelical view, however, persons without Christ are lost in sin and are in need of the Savior.[47]

This distinction between God's work in redemption and His work in creation, however, is complemented by a stress on the inseparability of God's two works. As already noted, the discontinuity between redemption and creation, occasioned both by the essential distinction between the Creator and the created and by the intrusion of sin into the created order, is complemented by the continuity between them, due both to the fact that the Redeemer and Creator are one and the same God, and to the fact that the very essence of redemption is that it is the redemption of creation. Since creation is redeemable, all false dichotomies between the two are ruled out, a truth which ecumenical theologians choose to ignore when they charge evangelicals with teaching the heresy of dichotomy or dualism.

The second principle for understanding the relation of the redemption and creation mandates is the assertion of the logical priority of redemption over creation in the fulfillment of kingdom purposes. As will be evident in the following discussion of the evangelism/social action controversy, this claim concerning the logical priority of redemption is widely disputed, not only by ecumenical writers but also by some evangelicals. Some of the dispute, to be sure, is due simply to a failure to understand what is meant here by a *logical* priority.

Essentially the logical priority of redemption over creation is the biblical insistence on the priority of the first and greatest commandment, to love God supremely, over the second greatest commandment which is like it, to love one's neighbor as one's self. The vertical or God/human relation takes logical precedence in the biblical worldview over the horizontal or human/human-self-world relations. Worship takes logical precedence over ethics. The eternal needs of the soul take logical precedence over the temporal needs of the body (Matt. 16:26). Note that the reference here is to a logical priority. The distinction between a logical priority and a chronological priority will be indicated in the next section.

The logical priority of redemption emphasizes that the only way to fulfillment for a fallen creation is the way of redemption. Consequently, instead of negating or deprecating creation, the insistence on the logical priority of redemption enhances the possibilities for fallen creation. This is not to rule out the fact that Christ as Judge condemns impenitent cre-

---

47. For an introduction to these two views, see Glasser and McGavran, *Contemporary Theologies of Mission*, chap. 1, or Newbigin, *Sign of the Kingdom*, chap. 1.

For brief, frank, individual statements of the ecumenical position, see John Macquarrie, *Principles of Christian Theology,* 2d ed. (New York: Scribners, 1977), 327, or W. Sibley Towner, *How God Deals with Evil* (Philadelphia: Westminster, 1976), 151-52.

ation. It is, however, to insist that, where persons are responsive to the powers of redemption, the relation between redemption and creation can be illustrated with two concentric circles, with the larger circle representing creation redeemed. It is also to remember that the initiative in redemption remains with God. Sin blocks creation's way to entrance into the kingdom. A fallen world does not first seek God; rather, God in redeeming grace first seeks His fallen creation.[48]

In the history of Christian thought special credit is due to the Reformed tradition for its undergirding of the wholistic emphasis. The Calvinistic stress on the sovereignty of God in Christ inevitably tends to expose the inadequacy of any false dichotomy between religion and culture. When God in Christ is seen as sovereign in all of life, then every aspect of life takes on a religious character. The callings of everyday life become God's callings. Menial tasks in the daily routine acquire a new dignity and meaning. Nor is this a merely arbitrary arrangement on God's part. For what glorifies the holy and righteous triune God is in reality that which magnifies and serves the well-being of His creatures and creation.[49]

---

48. To illustrate how redemption enhances creation consider these words of Henry concerning Paul's Philemon epistle:

If any letter of the New Testament might profitably be priority reading for evangelical Christians today, it is Paul's letter to Philemon. . . . The gospel did not come to this member of the enslaved class through Philemon, for slaves were considered less than human and beneath any merit of instruction. But Paul did not withhold Christ's gospel from this pilfering runaway who had no legal rights and toward whom no one acknowledged any responsibilities. Paul knew that Christ's gospel is the Magna Charta of mankind, and that to transform this representative of the lowest race into a son of God's kingdom declared to all the world the reality and assurance of a divine regenerative power, equality and brotherhood that supersede all human ideologies and determinations. . . . The New Testament assault on social injustice is not "revolutionary" in the sense of a reliance on physical violence to promote structural change. But as F. W. Farrar says, the Epistle to Philemon was nonetheless "the practical manifesto of Christianity against the horrors and inequities of ancient and modern slavery" (*The Life and Work of St. Paul*, 625). It was "a revelation of eternal principles" that motivated the Christian community to work among its ranks in an age when rabbis declared it "forbidden to teach a slave the Law" and when pagans regarded slaves as "living chattel" without rights and to whom no one owed any duties. A blow was struck against slavery by three words simple enough for any schoolboy to grasp: "a brother beloved." Henry, *God, Revelation and Authority*, 4:591-92.

49. For a recent summary of Calvin's views on kingdom-world relations, see Webber, *The Secular Saint*, 144-53. For the contribution of Dutch Calvinism, especially that of Abraham Kuyper, to American evangelicalism, see James D. Bratt, *Dutch Calvinism in Modern America* (Grand Rapids: Eerdmans, 1984). Bratt stresses that for Kuyper Calvinism embraced every sphere of life-politics, economics, science, and art. Rottenberg, however, faults Kuyper for his emphasis on the formation of separate magazines, labor unions, school systems, and the like for Christians. Isaac C. Rottenberg, *Redemption and Historical Reality* (Philadelphia: Westminster, 1964), 176. For a recent study by a Calvinistic writer of the ultimate compatibility of redemption and creation in the biblical worldview, see Richard J. Mouw, *When the Kings Come Marching In: Isaiah and the New Jerusalem* (Grand Rapids: Eerdmans, 1983). Mouw quotes Kuyper: "There is not one inch in the entire area of our human life about which Christ, who is Sovereign of all, does not cry out, 'Mine!'" (Ibid., 67).

The focal issue: the logical priority of evangelism.—The importance of the principles which guide in conceptualizing the redemption/creation relation becomes apparent when one seeks a way through the recent, vexing, evangelism/social action discussion. Here the "distinct yet inseparable" and the "logical priority" principles are invaluable aids in presenting the evangelical viewpoint.

Before considering these principles, familiarity with Wagner's analysis of five typical ways of handling the evangelism/social action issue is helpful. Wagner lists the following groups and their approach to the problem: *secular humanists*—all social action, no evangelism; *ecumenical missiologists*—both social action and evangelism, but social action receives the emphasis; *some evangelicals*—both evangelism and social action, but neither has priority over the other; *evangelicals*—both evangelism and social action, but evangelism has a logical priority; and *older, early twentieth-century conservatives*—Christian mission refers to evangelism only.[50]

Notice how the application of the two guiding principles already established leads to the position held by the majority of evangelicals, that is, that while both evangelism and social action are essential, evangelism takes a logical priority over social action.

First, regarding the distinct yet inseparable principle, the Lausanne Covenant is emphatic. Referring to the *distinction* between evangelism and social action, the Covenant says: "Reconciliation with man is not reconciliation with God, nor is social action evangelism, nor is political liberation salvation" (art. 5).[51]

---

50. Wagner, *Church Growth and the Whole Gospel,* 101-4.

Also suggestive is Johnston's discussion of the varying editorial positions of four leading evangelical periodicals regarding the evangelism/social action issue. Johnston, *Evangelicals at an Impasse,* 81-94.

Discussing the priority given to social action in ecumenical missiology, Rottenberg refers to the shibboleth that the world sets the agenda for the church. He objects to the slogan, saying that when the world sets the agenda we become worldly in the wrong way:

> The burning issue is not so much whether the churches should be concerned about mundane matters, but rather how they should be worldly in the right way and maintain a theological perspective that does justice to all the dimensions of the biblical witness.

He considers the recent proclamation-versus-presence debates as nothing short of tragic, as if proclamation has nothing to do with presence, and as if Christian presence could ever be severed from the Word and the Spirit and still remain redemptive presence.
Rottenberg, *The Promise and the Presence,* 71,77,91.

51. A Lausanne Occasional Paper raises the question as to whether it is "right to refer to the emergence of justice and peace in the wider community as 'salvation,' and to attribute to the grace of Christ every beneficial social transformation?" The paper reports: "Most of us . . . consider that it is more prudent and biblical to reserve the vocabulary of salvation for the experience of reconciliation with God through Christ and its direct consequences. None of us would dream of following those who have portrayed Hitler's Germany or Mao's China or Castro's Cuba as having experienced 'salvation.'"
Stott, ed., *Evangelism and Social Responsibility,* 29.

The distinction between evangelism and social action is necessary because the Bible clearly differentiates between a person's eternal, spiritual needs and his/her temporal, material needs (Matt. 10:28; 16:26). The basic human problem is the sin problem, not the problems associated with finiteness, such as hunger or mortality. In the biblical view, a person's dilemma is not that he/she is a creature, for God created persons as creatures! A person's basic problem is his/her rebellion against God. Without Christ as Savior, a person is "without hope and without God in the world" (Eph. 2:12, NIV). As poignant and hurtful as the material and social needs of fellow human beings are, the New Testament emphatically refuses to reduce the gospel of eternal salvation to a merely social message. No person lives by bread alone (Matt. 4:4).

Yet, though evangelism and social action are distinct, they are also *inseparable*! Although the Lausanne Covenant is quick to distinguish between the two, at the same time it also expresses "penitence both for our neglect [of social action] and for having sometimes regarded evangelism and social concern as mutually exclusive." The Covenant affirms that both are part of our Christian duty, for "both are necessary expressions of our doctrines of God and man, our love for our neighbor, and our obedience to Jesus Christ" (art. 5).

Evangelism and social action are inseparable because in biblical monotheism the God who saves us from our sin is the same God who made our bodies and our world in the first place. Consequently, the gospel addresses the whole person. No basis is left for any false dichotomy between the spiritual and the material, between justification and justice, or between revelation and reason. Again, in the words of the Lausanne Covenant: "The salvation we claim should be transforming us in the totality of our personal and social responsibilities. Faith without works is dead" (art. 5).

If evangelism and social action are inseparable, what about the claim of Sider and others that inseparability involves equality? The question anticipates the discussion of the second principle, the priority-of-evangelism principle. Let it be said here that if evangelism and social action are equal partners in kingdom mission, then it would seem that Pentecostals are right when they insist that bodily healing is included in Christ's atonement for our sins on the cross and that physical health and temporal blessings are as essential to kingdom effectiveness as the forgiveness of sins and a walk with God.

Sider says: "The Gospels provide no indication . . . that Jesus considered preaching the Good News more important than healing sick peo-

Redeemed! Eschatological Redemption and the Kingdom of God

—104—

ple." He recognizes that evangelism and social action are inseparable, but he insists on their equal importance to the kingdom mission.[52]

Second, regarding the logical priority principle, the Lausanne Covenant is also clear with respect to the logical priority of evangelism over social action. The Covenant says: "In the church's mission of sacrificial service evangelism is primary" (art. 6). To expect initial, individual decisions for Christ radically and permanently to change society instantly and automatically can be presumptuous, but to expect to change society for the better in any significant Christian sense without responsible evangelism is even more naive!

Since the matter of the logical priority of evangelism over social action seems forever settled by Jesus' clear teaching in Matthew 16:26 and similar passages, on what ground can some evangelicals object, at times quite vehemently, to the idea?

One reason is that evangelicals work with varying definitions of evangelism and social action. For the purposes of the present discussion, Wagner's update of the definitions used by the Lausanne Covenant will suffice. His definition of evangelism includes the nature, purpose, and goal of evangelism:

> The *nature* of evangelism is the communication of the Good News. The *purpose* of evangelism is to give individuals and groups valid opportunity to accept Jesus Christ [as Savior and Lord]. The *goal* of evangelism is to persuade men and women to become disciples of Jesus Christ and to serve him in the fellowship of His Church.

Note that this definition of the goal of evangelism includes the necessity for social service. Wagner's definition of what is involved in Christian social responsibility distinguishes between social service and social action. The former is viewed in terms of direct ways of seeking to meet individual and group social needs, for instance, through relief and devel-

---

52. Ronald J. Sider and John R. W. Stott, *Evangelism, Salvation and Social Justice,* Grove Booklet on Ethics, no. 16 (Auburn, MA: Grove, U.S.A., 1977), 17-20.

Instead of equal importance, it appears that Sider is primarily interested in insisting that neither evangelism nor social action can be left undone if discipleship is to be judged by kingdom standards.

Spain severely criticizes Southern Baptists for their emphasis on the priority of evangelism. Again, however, the problem seems to be Spain's refusal to recognize a difference between a legitimate biblical emphasis on the logical priority of evangelism in the kingdom mission, and a false, unbiblical dichotomy which sets evangelism and social action over against one another.

While faulting Southern Baptist theology, Spain says that in practice Southern Baptists recognize the legitimacy of social service. In the end, then, Spain's quarrel with Southern Baptists is with their failure to believe that giving a cup of cold water in the name of their Founder is "an end within itself." On this basis, Spain seems to be the one who *unduly separates* evangelism and social action by his insistence on the legitimacy of social action without evangelism as a fulfillment of the Christian mission. Rufus B. Spain, *At Ease in Zion* (Nashville: Vanderbilt, 1967), 213.

opment programs, while the latter is viewed in terms of slower, long-range efforts to change socio-political structures, changes which might or might not involve revolution, violence, or civil disobedience.[53]

Given these definitions of evangelism and social service, as well as evangelical presuppositions regarding the logical priority of the eternal over the temporal, it becomes difficult to justify any evangelical objection to the logical priority of evangelism over social service. Of course, the significance of the term *logical* must not be overlooked. The qualification is necessary because in practice social service often precedes evangelism chronologically. In the situation of a person starving to death, for instance, extended verbal presentations of the gospel await prior ministry to bodily needs. As the African proverb says, "An empty stomach has no ears."[54]

---

53. Wagner, *Church Growth and the Whole Gospel*, 56-57,35-36.
Over against Wagner's sharp distinction between social service and social action, the present discussion, while recognizing the validity of the two kinds of social work, nevertheless uses social service and social action interchangeably.
Wagner's definition of evangelism presupposes the distinction between evangelism in general and missions evangelism, or the distinction between witnessing and ministering to others within the usual traffic patterns of daily living, and witnessing and ministering to others outside of normal traffic patterns. Missions, in other words, typically calls for crossing geographical, linguistic, and cultural barriers in order to present the gospel of Christ. The tragedy occurs when evangelism is lost in a view of mission which allows social service to overwhelm evangelism.
Unfortunately, Stott and other evangelicals seem to think of evangelism in terms of words and social action in terms of actions, a view which distorts the New Testament meaning of evangelism. If Stott's intent is simply to insist that "we must exhibit what we proclaim," then his objection is not to responsible, New Testament evangelism, but to shallow perversions of evangelism. Stott, *Christian Mission in the Modern World*, 24,28,108.
Kirk's sharp attack on the idea of the priority of evangelism over social action is based on this inadequate view of evangelism as words and not deeds. He accuses those who speak of the logical priority of evangelism over social action as having a two-tiered cake model of evangelism and social action. He views the bottom tier as representing the corrupted material order and to the top tier as referring to a pure spiritual world, the place of God's existence. According to such a model the kingdom ideal becomes the escape from material existence to a spiritual realm which remains mainly future and suspended somehow above the mundane world. For Kirk, then, to speak of the priority of evangelism is to inject a dichotomy into our understanding of the gospel between the spiritual and the material orders. He says:
> Until both the verbal and the visual . . . are fully emphasized as equal parts of the one evangelistic enterprise, until the whole notion of priorities is abandoned, both evangelical and non-evangelical Christians will be guilty of misunderstanding God's intention for his people.
Apparently Kirk is unaware of the distinct yet inseparable and the logical priority principles which are developed here. J. Andrew Kirk, *The Good News of the Kingdom Coming* (Downers Grove, IL: InterVarsity, 1983), 103.
54. Quoted by Stott. Stott proceeds to speak of social action as not only at times a *bridge* to evangelism but also as at other times a *consequence* of evangelism and always as a *partner* of evangelism. Viewed in this way the insistence on the logical priority of evangelism leaves room for a variety of ways in which evangelism and social action relate to one another. Stott, *Evangelism and Social Responsibility*, 20-24.
Elsewhere Stott says: "The good Samaritan's ministry to the brigands' victim was not to stuff tracts into his pockets but to pour oil into his wounds. For this was what the situation demanded." Sider and Stott, *Evangelism, Salvation and Social Justice*, 22.

Another sense in which in practice evangelism does not always precede social service is the fact that while in some situations the stress is on evangelism, in other situations the emphasis falls on social action. One reason for this diversity is that spiritual gifts vary. Some Christians are more effective in evangelism; others are more gifted in social service ministries. Consequently, though both evangelism and social service are the responsibility of each and every Christian, without specialists in each of the functions kingdom progress is seriously hampered.

In summary, the reference to the logical priority of evangelism emphasizes the logical, not necessarily the chronological, priority of evangelism over social action. The stress is especially crucial at the point of an adequate motivation for serious social service. How quickly the well springs of social action altruism dry up unless they are constantly fed and refreshed by the fountains of the Spirit's energizing through God's redeeming grace in Christ. *The only sure road to humanization leads by the way of the cross.*[55]

The wholistic emphasis as challenge.—This discussion of the wholistic dimension of the kingdom mission cannot be concluded without a final underscoring of the importance of the comprehensive dimensions of kingdom vision. Reference to three quotations will help to summarize the wholistic challenge.

First, *The Baptist Faith and Message* employs a fine phrase rooted in nineteenth-century usage, notably the reference to "the great objects of the Kingdom of God" (Art. XIV). "Objects," here, means goals or ends. Articles XI-XVII of the statement summarize the great objects of the kingdom: evangelism and missions, education, stewardship, cooperation, the Christian and the social order, peace and war, and religious liberty.

Concerning the challenge of education the statement says: "The cause of education in the Kingdom of Christ is co-ordinate with the causes of missions and general benevolence." That is, since in biblical monotheism

---

55. What is meant here by the logical priority of evangelism is illustrated by an incident which Edge recounts in order to stress the inadequacy of social action without evangelism.

While Edge was interviewing an underprivileged woman living in an American, inner-city ghetto, she suddenly exploded: "The church has lied to us!" The church, she explained, was saying that the ghetto problem is poor housing, inadequate wages, lack of education, and the like, when the real problem is sin. Persons need a great deal more than a little education if they are to love God supremely and their neighbor as themselves. Edge concludes: "The reality of sin in human experience is of such radical nature that man, in his own strength, is inadequate to deal with it. The remedy must come from God." Edge, *The Greening of the Church* 71.

In the context, Edge is faulting the tendency in ecumenical social action to substitute social action for evangelism. His points are well taken, but the emphasis on the logical priority of evangelism goes a step further than the insistence that the kingdom mission involves *both* evangelism and social action.

the Creator and the Redeemer are the same God, revelation and reason are *ultimately compatible*. All truth is God's truth! The creation mandate of Genesis 1:26-30 provides, among other challenges, the charter for sacrificial Christian involvement in responsible academic pursuits. God uses legitimate educational enterprises to help overcome and dispel the *incompatibility* between revelation and reason *occasioned by sin*.

Christ's lordship demands the believer's best, so that the call to excellence is built into the Christian faith. Christian education should be the best education available, for a school lesson well prepared in a spirit of Christian commitment is a prayer sincerely offered.

A second graphic reminder of the importance of the wholistic emphasis is provided by Walhout, who says: "The routine of participation in human civilization is the very arena of obedience to God."[56]

A third quotation comes from Trueblood. Commenting on Christ's commission to go "into all the world," Trueblood says:

> Too often, we have understood these great words in a merely geographical or extensive sense. It is equally reasonable to understand them in an intensive sense. Christ's ambassadors, then, are required to go *into* politics, *into* business, *into* homes, *into* education. The purpose of the gospel is to penetrate the whole of common life, making confrontation with Christ a universal and potentially redemptive experience.[57]

Statements such as these speak powerfully to the inescapable importance of Christian social and cultural responsibility. In fact, for Christians the creation mandate is actually enhanced and reinforced by the redemption mandate. This means that Christians know, as non-believers do not, that when the ordinances of creation, such as true religion, conscience, home, government, education, and culture are flaunted, the foundations of society itself are threatened. No legitimate way remains, therefore, for believers to escape responsibility for full participation in the public debate concerning social and cultural issues. The great commission relentlessly mandates both evangelism and social service.

The Kingdom Present Creates the Christian Life and the Church

No theology of the kingdom present can afford to overlook the question of the relation between the kingdom and the people of God, in both their individual dimension, or the Christian life, and their corporate dimension, or the church. A kingdom without subjects would not be a

---

56. Walhout, "The Liberal-Fundamentalist Debate," 520. The statement is quoted in Glasser, "Confession, Church Growth, and Authentic Unity," 180.

57. D. Elton Trueblood, *Confronting Christ* (New York: Harper, 1960), 180.

kingdom. At the same time, since the focus for the present is on the doctrine of the kingdom present, this is not the place for a full development of the doctrines of the Christian life and the church as such.

What requires discussion here is the claim that the Christian life and the church are the signs and agents of the kingdom present. The Christian life and the church are best understood as primarily kingdom realities. If, as already stressed, the kingdom present is a vital force in history, the question is inescapable as to where in history the kingdom is at work. What, then, does it mean to say that the Christian life and the church are to be understood as kingdom realities?

First, viewing the Christian life and the church in this manner stresses that their existence presupposes the reality of the kingdom present. God's comprehensive kingdom purpose precedes and provides the rationale for the creation of God's people. The emphasis is on the divine initiative, as well as on the scope of God's purpose in Christ. The Christian life and the church are God's creations, not humankind's. All is of grace. This means that neither the Christian life nor the church can be reduced to mere psychological or social dimensions. They are instead redemptive realities, so that wherever redemption from sin through Christ is muted, there the Christian life and the church are emptied of their essential biblical meaning.

Second, since the kingdom is a redemptive order it creates a new people of God, not a merely national or political entity. The kingdom is a dynamic God movement in history, not a static, fixed institution. Under the old covenant God's people formed a nation; they were a people of promise looking forward to a "better" covenant. Under the new covenant, sealed by Christ's blood, God's people are a spiritual people, a new humanity, gathered into voluntary communities which are the creations of God's Spirit through the Word of God and scattered in daily life in the world as witnesses and servants of Christ.

These new communities of God's people fulfill the Old Testament promises, transcending the racial, national, and ceremonial limitations which characterized God's people of the old covenant. They are God's instruments in His strategy for world transformation: "His intent was that now, through the church, the manifold wisdom of God should be made known" (Eph. 3:10, NIV).

Third, to say that the Christian life and the church are kingdom realities is to recognize that the kingdom has both individual and corporate dimensions. One important strength of the kingdom present emphasis is that it keeps these dimensions together, when in the history of Christian thought and experience, with their neglect of the kingdom theme, they are forever drifting apart.

Some theologies are preoccupied with the church or the corporate dimension of Christian experience, viewing the church as the realm where the redemption of individuals is taking place. Other theologies tend to place all of their stress on the Christian life or the individual dimension of Christian experience, viewing the church as a voluntary fellowship of believers. Finally, some forms of recent liberation theology give too little thought to sin as individual and personal, and tend instead to equate sin with corporate evil, reflecting a moral human/immoral society emphasis.

The kingdom emphasis, however, stresses both the individual and the corporate dimensions of the life of God's people. On the one hand, kingdom existence is crucially personal and individual. Persons enter the kingdom one by one, through the experience of individual conversion: "Unless one is born again, he cannot see the kingdom of God" (John 3:3). This is basic. On the other hand, kingdom existence is inescapably corporate. Believers are bound to one another by the Holy Spirit in a common loyalty to Jesus Christ. Drawn together by God's Spirit as fellow members of Christ's body, they are led to unite in congregations, better to pursue God's purposes in history.

Fourth, the recognition that the Christian life and the church are kingdom realities underscores the double truth that while the kingdom and the church are inseparable, they are nonetheless distinguishable and are not to be confused. The kingdom creates and works through the Christian life and the church, but the kingdom is not to be directly identified with any historical manifestation of God's people. The importance of both of these truths requires underscoring.

The kingdom and the church are inseparable in the sense that God's people are both the sign of the kingdom's presence and the agents of the kingdom mission. The sign of the kingdom's presence is the Christian movement in history. Though the church can be driven underground and its institutions destroyed, God's people persevere. In addition, they are not only the sign of the kingdom's presence, they are also the agents of the kingdom's mission. God works through His people as the salt and light of the world in order to advance His kingdom purpose in history.

Yet, though the kingdom and the church are inseparable realities, they are not to be confused. In the first place, the kingdom is a broader concept than the church. The kingdom includes Old Testament as well as New Testament saints, while the church usually points to the latter. Furthermore, the kingdom, in its fullest sense, is both a temporal and an eternal reality; the church, on the other hand, is a temporal entity—the shape of God's people in the interim period between Christ's first and second comings.

In the second place, the church, as God's present pilgrim people, always remains under the judgment of the kingdom of God. To identify any expression of God's people on earth directly with the kingdom of God is idolatry. The kingdom remains the ideal and the goal, forever beckoning God's people onward and upward. This means that the Christian life and the church are never ends in themselves, but exist for the sake of the kingdom (Matt. 6:33).

The Kingdom Present Calls for Radical Obedience

Jesus' radical kingdom ethic, with its call for uncompromising obedience, is variously interpreted today, even among evangelicals. To place the issue in perspective, we will review the biblical record and then seek to list the chief characteristics of Jesus' ethic in order to determine how it relates to Christian living today.

The biblical record and Jesus' demands.—Concerning the biblical witness to the radical nature of Jesus' demands, note that Jesus consistently gives kingdom concerns unchallenged priority in the lives of His followers (Matt. 6:33). The first and greatest obligation is to love God supremely (Matt. 22:37-40). No one can serve two masters (Matt. 5:24). Small is the gate and narrow the road that leads to life (Matt. 7:13). If the eye causes one to sin, it is to be gouged out; if the right hand causes one to sin, it is to be cut off (Matt. 6:29-30; 18:9).

If anyone seeks to follow Jesus and does not hate his father and mother, his wife and children, his brothers and sisters—yet, even his own life—he cannot be Jesus' disciple (Luke 14:26; cf. Matt. 19:29). The kingdom is like a treasure hid in a field; when a person finds it he sells all he has to buy the field (Matt. 13:44). Treasures on earth do not last, but investments in the kingdom are forever (Matt. 6:19-20). A do-nothing servant is to be cast outside where there is weeping and gnashing of teeth (Matt. 25:30). Anyone who follows Jesus must deny himself and take up his cross; for whoever seeks to save his life loses it (Matt. 16:24-25).

What good is it for a person to gain the whole world, yet forfeit his/her soul (Matt. 16:26)? The demand for undivided loyalty takes precedence over personal comforts, over burying the dead, and over delays for family reasons (Luke 9:57-62). Not everyone who says "Lord, Lord" will enter the kingdom (Matt. 7:21). If one is struck on one cheek, he is to turn the other; if a challenger wants one's tunic, he is to be given one's cloak as well; if one is imposed upon to go one mile, he is to be willing to go two miles (Matt. 6:38-41).

One is to love his/her enemies (Matt. 6:44). Jesus' followers are to reflect the spiritual qualities highlighted in the beatitudes (Matt. 5:3-12). The law condemned murder and adultery, but Jesus went beyond outward acts to inner attitudes, condemning anger and lust (Matt. 5:21-22). Hypocrites give to be seen and applauded, but Jesus' followers are to seek no acclaim for well doing (Matt. 6:2-4). Jesus' law is the boundless law of loving as He Himself loved (John 13:34).

Such is the evidence that Jesus called for radical obedience on the part of the subjects of His kingdom. The question today is, how is an ethic so radical as this to be interpreted? What are the characteristics of Jesus' kingdom ethic and how do these characteristics relate to Christian living today?

Characterics of Jesus' Ethic.—First, Jesus' ethic can be characterized as a qualified perfectionist ethic. On the one hand, He calls for nothing less than perfection itself (Matt. 5:48). In this sense His ethic represents the ideal, not a goal which is fully attainable now, but a finality realizable more fully only in the age to come. On the other hand, Jesus teaches His disciples that kingdom participants are never done praying the prayer of the penitent, "God, be merciful to me, the sinner" (Luke 18:13).

Jesus' perfectionist ethic, then, is a qualified perfectionism when it comes to the life of God's people in the present interim prior to the kingdom consummated. His ethic is characterized by a tension between His call to perfection and His recognition of the failure of His followers to achieve perfection in daily life. Consequently, the repeated falling short of perfection on the part of believers, when confessed in penitence, meets not only with the Father's loving forgiveness, but also with Jesus' renewed call to strive earnestly for something better.

Because of the difficulty of relating in Christian practice the two poles of this tension, Jesus' call for radical obedience is interpreted today in a variety of ways.[58] Some interpreters emphasize the perfectionist aspect of Jesus' call and stress the distinction between the church and the world. Mouw, who speaks of this approach to Jesus' ethic as "culturalism," that is, as living in opposition to the cultural status quo, views it as a spectrum embracing a variety of options. For instance, referring only to the mainstream of twentieth-century American Protestantism, he says:

> Rauschenbusch's understanding of "the social gospel" is one such manifestation. More recently Liberation Theology, with its emphasis on the primacy of structural change, seems to be a straightforward culturalism. The same holds for a variety of "radical Christian" communities and programs which have emerged in the last decade or so;

---

58. In presenting four typical evangelical approaches to the application of Jesus' ethic, Johnston reviews the editorial stances of four different evangelical journals: the conservative approach of the *Moody Monthly*; the moderate approach of *Christianity Today*; the reformist approach of *The Reformed Journal*; and the radical approach of *Sojourners*. Johnston, *Evangelicals at an Impasse*, 81-94.

their "countercultural" posture points toward an entire reconstruction of life, and thus belongs with the culturalism described here.[59]

Typical of some of the more recent versions of radical Christianity is Bonhoeffer's stress on costly discipleship. The emphasis here is on the quality of Christian commitment to the disparagement of almost any concern for the reaching of new converts to Christianity. Consequently, the church growth movement and the attention given to large churches are favorite targets of criticism. Servanthood is contrasted with celebrityhood, often in a manner that seems to prize social action and to minimize the necessity for evangelism. Deeds are readily contrasted with mere words, and practice with doctrine. An advocate of this approach might be imagined as saying:

> With my whole mind and heart, I believe in radical Christianity. Absolutely repugnant to me are baptism for unbelievers, hocuspocus religion, any hierarchy, and all the mass of paganism which has leaked into institutional religious practice through the centuries. Radical Christianity insists on holiness without which "on one will see the Lord" (Heb. 12:14). Radical Christianity is biblical Christianity as opposed to creedal Christianity.[60]

While some interpreters stress the perfectionist aspect of Jesus' ethic, others, focusing on the failure of believers to achieve perfection, settle too quickly for Christian imperfection and succumb to a sadly superficial view of Christian commitment.

Obviously, however, neither a perfectionist nor a superficial view of Jesus' call for radical obedience is adequate. Both the call to perfection and the failure of Christians to achieve perfection must be taken seriously. Neither elitist communities of the super-committed nor undisciplined communities of the half-committed is radical enough.

The obedience to which Jesus calls is not merely human obedience. It is rather the spontaneous, glad, wholehearted obedience which freely grows out of a vital personal walk with Christ as Savior and Lord. It is enthusiastic, sacrificial Christian discipleship. Though God is forever gra-

---

59. Richard J. Mouw, "The Bible in Twentieth-Century Protestantism," in Nathan O. Hatch and Mark A. Noll, eds., *The Bible in America* (New York: Oxford, 1982), 149.

60. Two examples of radical Christianity in this sense are the Sojourners movement (which takes the name of the *Sojourners* magazine) and the Church of the Savior in Washington, D. C. For a brief description of the Sojourners approach, see Johnston, *Evangelicals at an Impasse,* 91-94. For a description of the Church of the Savior approach, see Elizabeth O'Connor, *Call to Commitment* (New York: Harper, 1963). O'Connor's subsequent books update the story.

Webber's treatment of the separation model of kingdom-world relations is valuable. He discusses pre-Constantinian views, the Anabaptists, and the more recent Christian community movements. Webber, *The Secular Saint,* 75-103.

cious and forgiving in relation to His failing but penitent children, Jesus' call to perfection is never relaxed. The glory of God's way with His kingdom subjects is that He deigns to work through human instruments, and not only that, but through His weaker as well as through His stronger children. How else are the weak to grow stronger?

Second, Jesus' ethic is an ethic, not a gospel. It is not a way to earn one's salvation. Becoming a Christian is conditional on a faith-relation to Jesus Christ. Jesus' invitation is, "Come, follow me" (Matt. 16:24). Ethical performance, or the living out of the Christian life which the Holy Spirit plants within, grows out of this Christ-relation, it does not establish the relation in the first place. Participation in the kingdom is primarily a gift (Luke 12:32), not a reward for ethical performance.

Third, Jesus' radical ethic is corporate as well as individual. It is social as well as personal. It is an ethic for the whole Christian community. When Jesus says, "You are the light of the world," His reference is corporate as well as individual. In the same passage He refers to a city, a corporate reality, that is set on a hill and cannot be hid (Matt. 5:14). Socially, as well as individually, Christians can be the salt "of the earth" or the light "of the world"!

Fourth, as essentially personal and attitudinal Jesus' ethic is never directly convertible into the law of the land or into rules to govern Christian conduct mechanically. Laws can relate to the attempt to curb murder, and rules can attempt to check adultery, but hate and lust are matters of the heart and as such cannot be fully controlled by merely outward means. Jesus' ethic always stands in judgment over the ethical pronouncements of humans.

Fifth, as primarily a matter of abiding principles rather than inflexible laws or rules, Jesus' ethic remains applicable to Christians of every era. That it relates to life in this world, and not merely to some future age beyond history, is evident from the fact that it assumes the existence of the evils which mark the present age, such as pride, hypocrisy, lust, anger, envy, murder, war, and materialism, evils which have no place in the kingdom consummated which is yet to be. It is a basic ethic which challenges believers individually and corporately in every area of daily living.

Yet the answer as to how Jesus' ethic relates to specific issues, especially to the complex social problems of modern life, is by no means immediately apparent. Such practical application requires the discerning use of all of the resources available to the Christian community, including the Bible, tradition, reason, and opinion. Furthermore, since the kingdom is a redemptive order, the church cannot be true to itself and act as though its primary purpose were political. Grounds says:

Christian political ethics cannot say what should or must be done but only what may be done. . . . In politics the church is only a *theoretician*. The religious communities as such should be concerned with *perspectives* upon politics, with political doctrine, with the direction and structures of the common life, not with specific directives. . . . Their special orientation upon politics is, in a sense, an exceedingly limited one; yet an exceedingly important one.[61]

This means, for one thing, that Christian ethical actions which are highly controversial may well be undertaken by special interest groups, rather than by congregations or denominations as such.[62]

In conclusion, the present discussion should make clear the fact that Jesus' call for radical obedience leads readily to the two following topics: the kingdom present is an ongoing, costly struggle and warfare, and it is the basis for an undefeatable but realistic optimism. Jesus obviously expected His kingdom to make a difference, not only in the lives of His disciples, but in the world.

The Kingdom Present Wages Warfare against Sin and Satan

Since redemption in Christ involves confronting and defeating sin and Satan, from the moment it was indicated above that the kingdom is a redemptive order, the discussion has been moving toward the recognition that the kingdom present wages a fierce, ongoing warfare against evil. This fact exposes afresh the deeply polar nature of redemptive truth.

Consider, for instance, the following tensions: the kingdom is present, yet it is still to come; the present interim between Christ's two comings, while it is a time of great spiritual abundance through the reality and work of Christ and the Holy Spirit, is also a time of intense conflict, struggle, and suffering; the kingdom is a vital force in history, yet it often appears small and ineffective; and, since the Redeemer and Creator are one, while there is ultimate compatibility between the kingdom and the world, at the same time, given sin, there is utter incompatibility between God's kingdom and a world gone wrong. The conclusion is inescapable: the reality of the kingdom present involves a basic polarity between the kingdom in a state of warfare and in a state of abundance.

Two matters especially concern us regarding the ongoing warfare which the forces of the kingdom present wage against sin and Satan: the nature of the warfare, and the kingdom/world relations in the light of the warfare.

---

61. Vernon C. Grounds, *Evangelicalism and Social Responsibility* (Scottdale, PA: Herald, 1969), 34-35. Grounds is quoting Paul Ramsey, *Who Speaks for the Church?* (Nashville: Abingdon, 1967), 152.

62. Wagner, *Church Growth and the Whole Gospel,* 191-92. Wagner says that the more clearly a particular social issue can be justified by the Bible, the more appropriate is congregational involvement.

The nature of the warfare.—With reference to the nature of the warfare, two observations require mention. The first observation concerns the superhuman dimensions of the evil principalities and powers against whom the warfare is waged.[63] While Ephesians 6:12 would seem to settle the matter, the tendency has been strong in recent discussions of kingdom/world conflict, even among evangelicals, to reduce the principalities and powers to the level of the merely sociological.

On this basis the principalities and powers are understood to refer merely to the injustice and oppressiveness of impersonal socio-political-economic structures when these are controlled and used by evil persons. Against such reduction, Padilla says:

> Those who limit the workings of the evil powers to the occult, demon possession, and astrology, as well as those who consider the New Testament references to those powers as a sort of mythological shell from which the biblical message must be extracted, reduce the evil in the world to a personal problem, and Christian redemption to merely a personal experience. A better alternative is to accept the realism of the biblical description.[64]

The second observation with reference to the nature of kingdom warfare with evil relates to its corporate dimension, over against a merely individual emphasis. The corporate aspect is readily understandable in the light of the social nature of human existence. Since persons inescapably create social structures, evil persons inevitably create evil social structures. And, since evil has superhuman dimensions, human social structures readily become demonic in their oppressiveness and cruelty. One need only mention evils such as racism, nationalism, totalitarianism, terrorism, torture, war, scientism, depersonalizing technocracy, waste, and pollution to be reminded that individuals are caught up in a conflict

---

63. What is said here about the demonic powers assumes their personal nature. Piggin, summarizing the biblical teaching concerning the demonic principalities and powers, suggests that the biblical drama of the powers has six acts: creation (Col. 1:16), fall (2 Pet. 2:4), defeat by Christ (Col. 2:14-15), learning the wisdom of God by witnessing the experience of the church (Eph. 3:10), continuing warfare (Eph. 6:12; Rom. 8:38-39), and total defeat (1 Cor. 15:24). F. S. Piggin, "Principalities and Powers," in *Evangelical Dictionary of Theology*, ed. Walter A. Elwell (Grand Rapids: Baker, 1984), 878.

64. Rene Padilla, "Spiritual Conflict," in Rene Padilla, ed., *The New Face of Evangelicalism* (Downers Grove, IL: InterVarsity, 1976), 208-13.

With reference to the sociological view of the powers, Stott refers to the writings of Gordon Rupp, Hendrikus Berkhof, G. B. Caird, Ronald Sider, Jim Wallis, and John Howard Yoder. See Sider and Stott, *Evangelism, Salvation, and Social Justice,* 24.

On the other hand, while not clearly positioning himself with reference to the personal or impersonal nature of the powers, Lutheran Knutson takes the position that evil social structures, rather than the problem of personal sin and guilt, are *the basic human problem*. He argues for the *Christus victor* theory of the atonement, over against a substitutionary view. Kent S. Knutson, *His Only Son, Our Lord* (Minneapolis: Augsburg, 1966), 78.

not only against flesh and blood but against superhuman principalities and powers.

The four horsemen of Revelation 6:1-8 ride roughshod through history: the white horse of deception, counterfeit religions, and myriads of cults; the red horse of war, with the modern threat of nuclear extinction; the black horse of hunger, famine, and pestilence; and the pale horse of death and hades. Kingdom warfare is intense, and it is real.[65]

The warfare and kingdom-world relations.—The second matter regarding kingdom warfare pertains to its influence on kingdom/world relations. The problem of an adequate concept of kingdom/world relations is compounded not only by the complexity of the kingdom and world realities themselves, but also by the polarity between the potential, ultimate compatibility of kingdom/world relations due to the oneness of the Redeemer and the Creator, and the utter incompatibility of their relation given the entrance of sin. Ultimate compatibility affirms the world as God's good creation. Utter incompatibility recognizes the reality of humankind's fall and the more-than-human, as well as the human, dimensions of evil.

The difficulty of conceptualizing kingdom/world relations is reflected in the variety of models which have been proposed to express the relation. Niebuhr's classical analysis distinguished five types of models: Christ against culture, the Christ of culture, Christ above culture, Christ and culture in paradox, and Christ the transformer of culture.[66]

More recently, Webber first distinguishes three traditional models, namely the separational, identificational, and transformational models, and, then, recognizing the inadequacy of any one of these models by itself, proceeds to argue for an incarnational model embracing in one overarching perspective the truths minus the weaknesses in the basic models.

Contending that no one of the traditional models does justice to the fact that the kingdom both affirms and condemns the world, he proceeds to point out the particular shortcomings of each of the models. The sep-

---

65. Regarding a partial shift in emphasis in the work of the Commission on World Mission and Evangelism of the World Council of Churches, evident at the Melbourne conference in 1980, Rottenberg says:

> One senses an implicit confession that some of the statements issued in recent years were overly optimistic about the prospects of the human condition and the impact the churches could have in bringing about major changes in society. The principalities and powers of this world, the forces of social-economic and political self-interest, and the stubborn resistance to change proved to be far more powerful than some ecumenical pronouncements had intimated.

Rottenberg, *The Promise and the Presence,* 51.

66. H. Richard Niebuhr, *Christ and Culture* (New York: Harper Torchbook, 1956), 39-43. Niebuhr, of course, regards the first two types as basic either/or options. The last three are median models.

arational model excuses Christian withdrawal from the world, the identificational model seeks to justify compromise with evil as the
characteristic stance of the kingdom in relation to the world, and the
transformational model fails to take sin with biblical seriousness.

In addition to these weaknesses, Webber observes that none of the
basic models is sufficiently flexible by itself to respond to the constantly
changing situation of God's people in history, such as the difference
between the church in a free society and the church under repression, or
the difference between churches in an affluent society and those trapped
in abject poverty through grossly unjust economic circumstances.[67]

Webber's argument is that while one situation in history might call for
one of the traditional models, a different situation might call for one of
the others. The pre-Constantinian period of Christian history, for
instance, which was a time of fierce persecution at the hands of an idola-
trous culture, called for implementing the separational model. The post-
Constantinian period, however, found the church identifying with a culture which looked on the Christian movement with favor and encouraged
participation by Christians in government-related vocations.

He believes that the incarnational model preserves the essential truths
in each of the basic models without the weakness of their inflexibility. In
the incarnation, he observes, Christ "identified with the world; was separate from the ideologies that rule it; and by His death, resurrection, and
second coming assured its transformation."[68]

Webber's discussion has much to commend it. He appears, however, to
give undue weight to a triumphalist-type of emphasis, thus neglecting the
seriousness of the ongoing warfare between the kingdom and the forces
of evil. He is so concerned to stress that there is only one culture and one
history that the ongoing antagonism between the kingdom and the world
is pushed into the background. An example of his too facile optimism is
his glowing estimate of the gradual Christianization of society in the Middle Ages.[69]

---

67. Regarding churches in these contrasting political and economic circumstances, see
also Stott, *Evangelism and Social Responsibility,* 48-61.

68. Webber, *The Secular Saint,* 188-200.

69. Ibid., 187-88. Throughout his study he seems more aware of the victory won by Christ
through the incarnation than he is of the continuing warfare between the kingdom and the
fallen world order. He says:

The kingdom of God is in our midst. This means that the rule of Christ is also everywhere
present. Christ has already destroyed the power of sin and overcome death. Therefore those
who are "in Christ" have the power to overcome sin (Ibid., 181).

To give Webber the benefit of the doubt, it is easy to believe that he did not intend for
these statements to stand with such finality.

This brings the discussion of the key characteristics of the kingdom present to the final, crucial question of the goal of the kingdom in history. Can we, or can we not, speak of the progress of the kingdom present in history?

The Kingdom Present Inspires Both Realism and Optimism

Hoekema insists that the Christian is "basically an optimist" with reference to his expectations of the triumph of the kingdom of God. He says:

> Though the Christian is realistic enough to recognize the presence of evil in the world and the presence of sin in the hearts of men, he is yet basically an optimist. He believes that God is on the throne, and that God is working out His purposes in history. Just as the Christian must firmly believe that all things are working together for good in his life, despite appearances to the contrary, so he must also believes that history is moving toward God's goal, even though world events often seem to go contrary to God's will.[70]

What Hoekema appears to have in mind, however, is not an optimism with reference to the effects of the kingdom present in history, but rather an optimism in the sense of a confidence in the power of God to effect His purposes ultimately. This is the kind of optimism Paul expresses in Romans 8:35-39, where he is sure that nothing will ever separate him finally from the love of God in Christ Jesus the Lord.

When the focus is shifted from the ultimate to the present, however, instead of suggesting that optimism is more basic to the Christian outlook than realism, it is better to emphasize the importance of both realism and optimism. The later discussion of the kingdom consummated will consider the believer's hope of ultimate victory. Here the concern is with faith's proximate hope, or the hope for a measure of present victory for the kingdom in history.

After 1900 years of Christian history, is the world getting better, or is it getting worse? This is the question concerning present kingdom progress. In the quest for a response to the dilemma, the following pages first recognize the necessity to avoid two extremes; next they develop the case for a realistic optimism; and finally they seek to identify the goal of the kingdom in history.

The necessity to avoid two extremes.—Any attempt to answer the question regarding kingdom progress with biblical seriousness seeks to avoid two extremes. At one extreme is the excessive optimism which thinks of kingdom progress in terms of the world growing better and better. In the

---

70. Hoekema, *The Bible and the Future,* 38.

nineteenth century and the early part of the twentieth century such optimism was frequently voiced by staunch conservatives whose kingdom outlook was essentially postmillennial. Writing in 1924, after World War I but prior to World War II, Conner spoke of the uplifting power of Christianity in the world:

> New ideals of righteousness have been introduced into human society. Some great social evils have been eradicated and others are being attacked. Slavery is practically a thing of the past. The whiskey traffic is going. Other great evils will follow. The recent great war has made some people pessimistic with reference to the power of the gospel to transform human society. But war will go.[71]

At the other extreme is the pessimism which views kingdom influence on the decline and world conditions as worsening. An example of pessimism is the older dispensational notion of the world as a sinking vessel. Referring to Scofield's early twentieth-century view, Weber says:

> C. I. Scofield found an ideal setting for the sinking ship/lifeboat metaphor in 1912, when he addressed a memorial service in Belfast, Ireland, for the victims of the *Titanic* disaster. Obviously aiming close to home, Scofield warned that "the ship upon which humanity is crossing the sea of time is doomed," but he added that God had provided a lifeboat that was large enough to hold all who wanted to climb aboard.[72]

---

71. W. T. Conner, *A System of Christian Doctrine* (Nashville: Sunday School Board, Southern Baptist Convention, 1924), 52.

The passage is repeated in *Revelation and God* (Nashville: Broadman, 1936), 137. In *The Gospel of Redemption* (Nashville: Broadman, 1945), however, after World War II, Conner's optimism is qualified. He speaks, for instance, of periods of retrogression in history as well as periods of progress (Ibid., 300).

Conner's earlier postmillennial optimism was shared, of course with other staunch conservatives. In 1835, for instance, Finney wrote: "If the church will do her duty, the millenium [sic] may come in this country in three years." Quoted by William G. McLoughlin, Jr., *Modern Revivalism* (New York: Ronald, 1959), 105.

Such conservative postmillennialism is to be distinguished from liberal, evolutionary optimism. Conner's reference to "the power of the gospel" stands in contrast to the secularized notion of inevitable, evolutionary progress. To illustrate the latter, Case says:

> The course of history exhibits one long process of evolving struggle by which humanity as a whole rises constantly higher in the scale of civilization and attainment, bettering its condition from time to time through its greater skill and industry. Viewed in the long perspective of the ages, man's career has been one of actual ascent. Instead of growing worse, the world is found to be growing constantly better.

Shirley Jackson Case, *The Millennial Hope* (Chicago: University of Chicago, 1918), 238.

72. Timothy P. Weber, *Living in the Shadow of the Second Coming* (Grand Rapids: Eerdmans, 1983), 71. Earlier Weber, who is irenic in his attitude toward the dispensational viewpoint, and who clearly demonstrates that its pessimism is not an unrelieved pessimism, cites D. L. Moody's use of the same metaphor (Ibid., 53).

Either of these extremes oversimplifies the dynamic of the biblical outlook. Denney says:

> The question is sometimes asked whether the world gets better or worse as it grows older, and optimists and pessimists take opposite sides upon it. Both . . . are wrong. Its progress is not simply a progress in good, evil being gradually driven from the field; nor is it simply a progress in evil before which the good continually disappears: it is a progress in which good and evil alike come to maturity, bearing their ripest fruit, showing all that they can do, proving their strength to the utmost against each other; the progress is not in good itself, not in evil itself, but in the antagonism of the one to the other.[73]

The case for both realism and optimism.—In the biblical view, the kingdom hope for history is a realistic optimism which seeks to keep in balance the twin realities of kingdom abundance through the ChristPentecost events and the ongoing kingdom warfare against sin and Satan. Unrelieved pessimism neglects the former, while unbridled optimism neglects the latter.

First, regarding the case for a realistic optimism, what are the reasons for insisting that expectations of building utopia on earth before Christ returns are vain?[74]

Unredeemed humanity.—The first and basic reason for realism is the inescapable and seminal fact of the unredeemed nature of each new generation of human beings! Since Christian parents cannot pass their Christian experience automatically to their children, the astonishing truth is that, in principle, at any given point in history, humankind is only one generation away from paganism.

Radical sinfulness.—A second reason for sober realism regarding human progress is a serious regard for the radical nature of human sinfulness. In his criticism of Wesley's definition of sin, which limited sin to a voluntary transgression of a known law, fellow Methodist Flew recognizes that "our worst sins are often those of which we are unconscious."[75] Sin, then, is not a thing which can be removed from a person as a cancerous tumor is removed. Rather it is a disposition, one of the worst forms of which is the

---

73. W. Robertson Nicoll, ed., *The Expositor's Bible* (New York: Funk and Wagnalls, 1900), *The Epistles to the Thessalonians,* by James Denney, 313-14.

74. The Lausanne Covenant, art. 15, says: "We reject as a proud, self-confident dream the notion that man can ever build utopia on earth."

75. R. Newton Flew, *The Idea of Perfection in Christian Theology* (London: Oxford, 1934), 233.

unconscious hypocrisy of Pharisaism, which is most likely to find expression in those who are too sure of their virtue and righteousness.[76]

Christian growth never automatic.—A third reason for realism is the recognition that kingdom growth comes slowly in history because Christian growth and maturity are never automatic or final. That their price tag is high is evident from the fact that failure to grow is epidemic in Christendom. That they are never final is due, for one thing, to the relational nature of Christian experience. It is the nature of personal relationships that they cannot be taken for granted, but must instead be renewed and reestablished again and again. There are no graduates in God's school; all are beginners.

Kingdom growth never automatic.—Another reason for realism is that influence of the kingdom on society is never automatic. Changed persons, persons who have become Christians, do not necessarily move out to change society. Christian social change takes doing; in fact, it takes a great deal of doing. The more complex the issue the more involved the process of change.

Tares also grow.—Christians must never forget that as the wheat is growing the tares are also growing (Matt. 13:24-30). Niebuhr charges liberalism with a neglect of this truth. He says: "In its one-sided view of progress which saw the growth of the wheat but not of the tares, the gathering of the grain but not the burning of the chaff, . . . liberalism was indeed naively optimistic."[77] Furthermore, since the evil grows with the good, kingdom warfare, instead of lessening, can even intensify. Christ for instance, who was without sin, nonetheless wrestled against the onslaughts of temptation more intensely than any of us ever do (Matt. 27:46).

---

76. Ibid., 333-34.
One need not agree with all of Braaten's theology to appreciate the important truth in his critique of some liberation theology:
Liberation theology is right in broadening the concept of sin to include the social dimension, but its view nevertheless remains rather shallow. Sin is basically a lack of original righteousness (*carentia iustitiae originalis*), a classical definition that points to a false relationship with God. Sin is concupiscence, the driving tendency of the human heart to curve in on itself manifested as rebellion against God. Some of the richest pictures of sin in the Bible and the classical tradition are blurred in liberation theology. Sin provokes the wrath of God; it is slavery to Satan; it is a state of spiritual death; it is a disease of the whole person-a sickness unto death. It is a state of corruption so profound that the elimination of poverty, oppression, disease, racism, sexism, classism, capitalism, etc., does not alter the human condition of sinfulness in any fundamental way.
Carl E. Braaten, *The Flaming Center* (Philadelphia: Fortress, 1977), 154-55.
77. H. R. Niebuhr, *The Kingdom of God in America* (New York: Harper, 1937), 193.

Christians also sin.—Clear-cut kingdom victories in history are hard to come by because Christians themselves are easily involved in the very evils they oppose. Though they condemn pollution and the wanton waste of natural resources, for example, at the same time they continue to drive air polluting automobiles and to needlessly waste resources.[78]

Ambiguous progress.—Even to raise the question of kingdom progress involves difficulty, simply because the evidence for progress is marked by an element of ambiguity. How is kingdom progress to be discerned? Since it is never fully visible to physical sight, human judgment as to where it is taking place can easily reflect a misreading of the evidence. In addition, what seems a setback for the kingdom today may be regarded as a victory tomorrow, and vice versa. The signs of kingdom gains, therefore, are susceptible to varied interpretations, as was noted above in the discussion of the kingdom as a vital though veiled force in history.

Fleeting victories.—It is vain to expect a utopia before Christ returns because kingdom victories are never permanent. Kingdom victories must be constantly re-won. Where renewal forces are not at work, past gains can be quickly wiped out. This explains in part why so often in history seasons of seeming great advance are followed by what appear to be eras of tragic decline: following Reformation vitality and renewal came a sterile period of dull scholasticism. First loves can be soon abandoned (Gal. 1:6; Rev. 2:4).For reasons such as these Christians are realistic in their expectations of kingdom victories in history.

Second, since believers are not only realistic but also optimistic, what is the case for a Christian optimism? On what grounds, for instance, is *The Baptist Faith and Message* justified in speaking expansively of "the great objects of the Kingdom of God" (Art. XIV)? Or, on what basis can it be said that the challenge of Carey, the father of modern missions, "to expect great things from God and to attempt great things for God," reflects a biblical outlook? Following are some of the reasons for Christian optimism.

God's power.—Christians are optimistic regarding kingdom achievements in history because of their monotheistic faith in God's supremacy and omnipotence. They believe in God the Father almighty, Maker of heaven and earth! From the biblical perspective, God was not only at

---

78. Webber says that believers "may be against white supremacy but many of their communities are exclusively white; male domination, but many are male; hunger, but many overeat; pollution, but most drive cars that pollute; poverty, but they live, if they are Americans, in the richest nation in the world." Webber, *The Secular Saint,* 198.

work as Creator in the beginning, but He is also mightily at work in the world today as Preserver, Ruler, and Provider, as daily He blesses all of His creatures in manifold ways. He is also at work as Redeemer, regenerating, gathering into congregations, sanctifying, equipping, sending, guiding, and keeping the people of God. Out of such faith springs the confidence that with God all things are possible (Matt. 19:26).

The decisive victory has already been won.—Christians are optimistic because they know that, through the Christ and Pentecost events, the decisive victory for the kingdom of God in history has already been won. Because of this once-for-all victory believers know, not only that the final victory is certain, but that in Christ there is always a way ahead (1 Cor. 10:13), whatever the present obstacles. *No temptation has overtaken you but such is common to man.*

Significant victories are being won.—Believers are optimistic because, despite the failures and the appearances to the contrary, faith says that significant Christian victories are constantly being won. Not only major events which signal monumental kingdom advance take place, like the Protestant Reformation, but also individual lives by the multitude are transformed.[79]

Kingdom overspill in society.—Believers have occasion for optimism because of the overspill of kingdom effects in society in general. Stott says:

> As the world lives alongside the Kingdom community, some of the values of the Kingdom spill over into society as a whole, so that its industry, commerce, legislation and institutions become to some degree imbued with Kingdom values. So-called "Kingdomized" or "Christianized" society is not the Kingdom of God, but it owes a debt to the Kingdom which often is unrecognized.[80]

After attributing the now popular "one world" concept to the fruits of the Christian mission, which is a startling insight indeed, Jeffery says: "Certainly the influence of Western Christianity on the rest of the world,

---

79. Boice cites Gallup poll evidence that committed Christians are happier, have stronger families, are more tolerant of people who differ from them, and are more involved in social programs than non-Christians. James M. Boice, *Eternity*, April 1984, 22-25.

80. Stott, *Evangelism and Social Responsibility,* 34.

Krass quotes Kuyper: "The stream of particular grace breaks all the dykes and spills out over all the world." Alfred C. Krass, *Five Lanterns at Sundown* (Grand Rapids: Eerdmans, 1987), 157.

Berkhof says: "Wherever the missionary endeavor has gone, the curious situation arises that a whole nation gratefully eats of the fruit, but only a minority desires the tree which produces the fruit." Hendrikus Berkhof, *The Meaning of History,* trans. Lambertus Buurman (Atlanta: Knox, 1966), 91.

Redeemed! Eschatological Redemption and the Kingdom of God

—124—

through exploration, colonization, education and technological advance, has been considerable."[81]

What, then, is the purpose of the kingdom present in history? Since the Christian hope for history is a realistic optimism, the first purpose of God's people is not to Christianize society but to be God's new community in history, exhibiting to the world the reconciliation to God and to others which Christ and the Holy Spirit make possible. They are to recognize that God builds His kingdom in His way and by His time (John 3:8), and that they remain pilgrims, resident-aliens in search of a "city which has foundations, whose architect and builder is God" (Heb. 11:10).

Their role in relation to the world is the prophetic role. As witnesses to Christ and His Word, their mission is to penetrate society as salt and light, not to take it over by force. In this manner they are destined to be the world's greatest reformers, unless, forgetting their role as witnesses, they seek only to reform the world. In Reinhold Niebuhr's words:

> Man's task is not that of building utopias, but that of eliminating weeds and tilling the soil so that the Kingdom of God can grow. His method is not one of striving for perfection or of acting perfectly, but of clearing the road by repentance and forgiveness.[82]

One of the boldest things that God's people can do is to pray publicly for the coming of the kingdom. Glasser says:

> Many non-Christians have been reached not so much by the irresistible arguments of gospel preachers as by the Christian love apparent in the prayers overheard on their behalf. What I suggest here goes beyond asking God to draw His own to himself through the gospel. I refer to public prayer that embraces all the concerns of those being evangelized, asking that their sick be healed and their harvest be abundant, interceding for the state and for its local and national leaders. People today are keenly aware of social and political issues, but their mood is one of despair. They wonder why more is not being done to alleviate human suffering and establish justice among men. Their frustration should be expressed to God in public prayer. He is concerned about these matters, and he has made personal and social transformation possible by the gospel of His Son. . . . The newest Christian congregation in an area still being opened to the gospel should early adopt the pattern of regular prayer against such evils as racial discrimination, social injustice, economic exploitation, and political corruption. From the very beginning of their corporate

---

81. Jeffery, "Mission, Theology of," 220.
82. Cited in *The Christian Century,* July 4-11, 1984, 662.

life Christians should be known as the people in the community who are particularly concerned about truth, love, and righteousness. Social concern need not divert them from praying that the proclamation of the gospel will also lead their neighbors to individual repentance, belief, and submission to the lordship of Jesus Christ.[83]

Jesus said, when you pray, pray "Thy kingdom come."

---

83. Glasser, "Confession, Church Growth, and Authentic Unity," 210-14.

The Kingdom Present and Election

> *God pursues His kingdom purposes through free agents whom He chooses to salvation and service. Election is a missionary doctrine.*

The doctrine of election has been disputed for centuries. What is election? Where should election be discussed in an orderly presentation of Christian beliefs? These questions evoke various responses. Theological systems viewing God's sovereignty as His predetermination of all that happens in creation and history often discuss election in relation to creation.[1] Systems that define election primarily as God's choice of individuals for salvation usually relate election to the doctrine of the Christian life.[2] The present study, however, focuses on God's pursuit of His kingdom's purpose in history and relates election to the kingdom present. In this perspective, election is essentially a missionary doctrine.

---

1. Guthrie, for instance, refers to predestination rather than election in his chapter heading. He discusses election before humanity presenting the doctrines of the world and humanity before his study of redemption. S. C. Guthrie, *Christian Doctrine* (Atlanta: Knox, 1968), 125-47.

2. Clark H. Pinnock, ed., *The Grace of God; The Will of Man* (Grand Rapids: Zondervan, 1989). The essays seek to relate God's sovereignty to human freedom and responsibility.

Defining Election

Election is God's use of free agents, whether individuals or groups, to pursue His redemptive purposes. In the Old Testament, as H. H. Rowley observes, God elected even pagan nations as instruments to judge rebellious Israel (Amos 6:14; Isa. 10:5-6; Jer. 1:15-16).[3] God more frequently used agents for redemption than for judgment.[4] In any case, election is to kingdom responsibility and service as well as to personal salvation. Election is to salvation, but it is not merely to salvation. In the biblical view, to forfeit one's election is not necessarily to forfeit one's salvation but rather to lose one's opportunity in kingdom service (Matt. 21:43; Heb. 6:6).

Biblical Resources

The Variety of the Biblical Vocabulary for Election

The biblical vocabulary for the idea of election includes a variety of terms such as call, call by name, choose, covenant, elect, foreknow, foreordain, keep, know, love, promise, purpose, save, seek, and send. Election roots in the central concepts of biblical monotheism—God's sovereignty and free grace. Election also emphasizes that God uses whom He will to pursue His purposes. We do not first choose Him. He first chooses us (John 15:16; 1 John 4:19). Such ideas are ubiquitous in Scripture! *omnipresent: existing or being everywhere at the same time.*

The Bible and Election as a Missionary Doctrine

Consider the following passages for their emphasis on election as a missionary doctrine:

- God chose Abraham to make him a great nation through which to bless all peoples of the earth (Gen. 12:1-3).

- God redeemed Israel from Egyptian bondage, entered into covenant with her, and established her as a kingdom of priests and a holy nation among the nations of the earth (Ex. 19:5-9).

- Jesus told His disciples, "I chose you, and appointed you, that you should go and bear fruit" (John 15:16).

- The Holy Spirit raised up the church as God's new covenant people to enlighten a sin-darkened world (1 Pet. 2:4-12).

Admittedly the Bible also includes verses that, when isolated from their context, appear to emphasize only God's unconditional sovereignty,

---

3. H. H. Rowley, *The Biblical Doctrine of Election* (London: Lutterworth, 1950), 122.
4. Ibid., 45.

leaving no room for the elect to exercise God-given freedom of choice or to assume significant responsibility as agents of God's missionary purpose.

- What does it mean to be clay in the potter's hand? Some interpreters isolate passages from the wider biblical teaching and understand them to mean that persons are passive in God's hands (Isa. 29:16; 45:9; 64:8; Jer. 18:6; Rom. 9:21).[5]

- Who hardens a sinner's heart? Though Exodus 4:21 and similar verses say that God hardened a person's heart, other passages such as Exodus 8:32 indicate that persons harden their own hearts.

The Bible teaches both God's sovereignty and human freedom—and in that order. Human freedom is the gift of the sovereign God! Citing 2 Corinthians 5:19-20 and similar passages, Conner says:

> It is not a surprising thing that God the Creator should command man his creature. But it is surprising that God should entreat man. It shows distinctly the respect that God has for man's will.[6]

Historical Perspective

The Augustinian-Calvinistic Misunderstanding

The Augustinian-Calvinistic tradition has said more than any other theological tradition about election. Yet this tradition has neglected the Bible's missionary stress on election, emphasizing only God's sovereignty in selecting individuals for salvation and privilege. F. H. Klooster, after noting varied aspects of the biblical idea of election, nonetheless focuses exclusively on election as choosing individuals to salvation.[7]

An adequate discussion of election must stress God's sovereignty in redemption. Scripture is plain: "As many as had been appointed to eternal life believed" (Acts 13:48; cf. 2 Thess. 2:13). Salvation is only by God's grace. Before we seek God, He relentlessly pursues us. How sad, though, when an emphasis on election to status and favor overshadows election as God's call to mission and service!

---

5. Rowley shows that nothing arbitrary is implied in the use of such imagery. Ibid., 40.

6. W. T. Conner, *The Gospel of Redemption* (Nashville: Broadman, 1945), 11.

7. F. H. Klooster, "Elect, Election," in *Evangelical Dictionary of Theology,* ed. Walter A. Elwell (Grand Rapids: Baker, 1984), 348-49. See also Loraine Boettner, *The Reformed Doctrine of Predestination* (Nutley, NJ: Presbyterian and Reformed, 1951), 83, and Louis Berkhof, *Systematic Theology* (Grand Rapids: Eerdmans, 1953), 114.

The Calvinistic-Arminian Standoff

Overemphasizing election to salvation while neglecting election to mission has occasioned debate on topics like God's sovereignty versus humankind's free choice and the logical order of God's decrees to create and redeem. In the Calvinistic-Arminian debates of the post-Reformation period, Arminian Remonstrants at the Synod of Dort (1618-19) rejected some accepted doctrines.[8] The Calvinist majority responded to the Arminians with the five Canons of Dort: total depravity, unconditional election, limited atonement, irresistible grace, and perseverance of the saints.

Debate over divine sovereignty and human freedom will never end. Achieving balance is difficult because we tend to emphasize one pole of the tension while neglecting the other. Yet each emphasis is important to a biblical perspective.

Calvinists have debated the logical order of God's decrees to create and redeem. Stricter Calvinists generally take the supralapsarian (*supra*—before, *lapse*—fall) position, arguing that God chose to redeem persons before He chose to create humankind and to permit the fall. While this position appears biblical in stressing the priority of redemption, it seems to imply that God planned the fall in order to institute redemption. Rather than suggest that God elected the fall, moderate Calvinists take the sublapsarian (*sub*—after, *lapse*—fall) or infralapsarian (*infra*—after, *lapse*—fall) position, implying that God's decree to redeem logically follows His decree to create and to permit the fall.[9]

Baptists and Calvinism

Both General and Particular Baptists appeared in seventeenth-century England. General Baptists reacted against strict Calvinism by holding to a general view of the atonement and stressing freedom of choice. Particular Baptists believed in limited atonement and emphasized God's sovereignty. They minimized the necessity for involvement of believers in evangelism and missions.[10] When Andrew Fuller and William Carey

---

8. Philip Schaff, *Creeds of Christendom*, vol. 1, *History of Creeds* (New York: Harper, 1931), 508-23.

9. R. V. Schmucker, "Infralapsarianism," and F. H. Klooster, "Supralapsarianism," in *Evangelical Dictionary of Theology*, ed. Walter A. Elwell (Grand Rapids: Baker, 1984), 560-61, 1059-60.

In the same dictionary, Elwell recognizes the complexity of the debates over election with reference to the question of the extent of the atonement. Walter A. Elwell, "Atonement, Extent of the," Ibid., 98-100.

10. H. Leon McBeth, *The Baptist Heritage* (Nashville: Broadman, 1987), 32-44, 153-99.

W. L. Lumpkin, "General Baptists," and Eugene Stockstill, "Particular Baptists," in *Encyclopedia of Southern Baptists*, ed. Norman W. Cox, vols. 1-2 (Nashville: Broadman, 1958), 528, 1072-73.

broke with strict Calvinism in 1792, founding the modern mission movement, the Baptist cause began to come alive.[11]

Baptists in the United States divided over missions. The anti-missionary movement spread rapidly across the South and West after the formation in 1814 of the Triennial Baptist Convention, the first nationwide missionary organization of Baptists. Strict Calvinism became the banner of anti-missionary forces. Yet by 1845, Baptists in the South had emerged from the anti-missions crisis to form the Southern Baptist Convention, dedicated to "eliciting, combining, and directing the energies of the denomination for the propagation of the gospel."[12]

Southern Baptist theology, however, retained a distinct, though usually moderate, Calvinistic flavor. Article V of *The Baptist Faith and Message,* "God's Purpose of Grace," for instance, affirms election as "the gracious purpose of God, according to which He regenerates, sanctifies, and glorifies sinners."[13] Though stressing the graciousness of individual salvation, the article is silent with reference to the biblical stress on election as a missionary doctrine.

---

11. Herbert C. Jackson and Lynn E. May, Jr., "Carey, William," Ibid., 231-32.

Shurden recalls the rebuke Carey received from an older preacher during a Baptist associational meeting in England after Carey had pled for Baptists to send missionaries to India. The critic said, "Sit down, young man. If God wants to save the heathen, he is God enough to do it without man's help." Walter B. Shurden, *Not a Silent People* (Nashville: Broadman, 1972), 35.

12. Preface, Constitution of the Southern Baptist Convention. See any yearly Southern Baptist Convention *Annual* (Nashville: Executive Committee, S.B.C.).

For the anti-missions controversy among Southern Baptists see Shurden, *Not a Silent People,* 35-47, and McBeth, *The Baptist Heritage,* 371-77.

13. See the theologies of John L. Dagg, J. P. Boyce, E. Y. Mullins, and W. T. Conner. Conner's theology of election vascillates between a stricter and a more moderate Calvinism. He says:

> To deny election is to affirm that, when God saves a man, he does so without having planned to do so.... In his actual dealings with men in time, does God pass over some without saving them? To ask the question is to answer it.... The next question, then, is this: Did God in eternity plan to pass over those whom he actually does pass over in time? Here again we must say that he did unless we are going to maintain an inconsistency between God's purpose and God's activity. If God's activity is grounded in his purpose, then all that God does he planned to do.

Yet he also says:

> When God passes over men and leaves them in their sins, does he have good ground for doing so? The New Testament makes this point clear. Men are cast off because of their unbelief and their perversity in sin. They are not cast off as an arbitrary matter, nor are they rejected because God does not want to save them.

Also, with reference to human achievement of moral good, Conner recognizes that "finite wills may have to work with [God] to produce some forms of good." Conner, *Gospel of Redemption* (Nashville: Broadman, 1945), 64-67.

A new chapter is being written today on the continuing influence of Calvinism on both Southern Baptists and British Baptists. The new Calvinism takes different forms. In part, it is atavistic, seeking a return to Calvinistic Baptist confessional statements of the seventeenth and eighteenth centuries. Among Southern Baptists this new Calvinism reflects discontent with alleged over-organization in denominational life and with what it regards as shallow evangelism. It emphasizes congregational autonomy but defends congregational government through a plurality of elders. While encouraging churches to associate with one another in Bible conferences, such conferences, in theory at least, are only for fellowship, not to promote organizations or programs.[14]

Restatement

Vigorous debate over election continues because it is an important but difficult doctrine. The following affirmations are aimed at restating a biblical view of election as a missionary doctrine.

Election Stresses God's Sovereignty, Purpose, and Grace

A sovereign God is in full control of the universe and of history. If God is sovereign, history has direction and purpose. Unlike cyclical and atheistic denials of purpose in history, biblical monotheism affirms that history moves toward the achievement of God-intended goals. Biblical election looks to the future confident that God is active in history and that what happens in history matters. Assured that God cannot fail, election affirms that the final victory is His.

Election also says that salvation is by grace (Eph. 2:8-9). We cannot earn it or merit God's free gift (Rom. 6:23). No one is saved just by deciding to become a Christian, as though God's power to save is wholly dependent on the person's will. Rather, believers love God because He first loved them (1 John 4:19)! Persons do not seek God without God's first seeking them, patiently and persistently. In this sense, election is a doctrine for the elect, for the elect recognize, more and more, that they repented and believed, first of all, because of God (1 Cor. 15:10).

---

14. See Albert W. Wardin, *Baptist Atlas* (Nashville: Broadman, 1980), 38-39; James Leo Garrett, "Conner and Resurgent Southern Baptist Calvinism," *Southwestern Journal of Theology* 25 [Spring 1983]: 58-60; *Christianity Today,* April 4, 1980, 50-52, and April 24, 1981, 46-47; McBeth, *The Baptist Heritage,* 699-700, 770-76.

For a statement reflecting something of the posture of resurgent Southern Baptist Calvinism regarding evangelism, see Thomas J. Nettles, "L. R. Scarborough: Public Figure," *Southwestern Journal of Theology* 25 [Spring 1983]: 38. Nettles criticizes Scarborough's personal evangelism on the ground that it "allowed the sovereignty of choice in man to eat up the sovereignty of God."

Election Is Consistent with Human Freedom of Choice

Persons remain responsible and accountable to God for their actions. As sovereign God is not arbitrary. He is a moral God, and His dealings with His creatures are moral transactions. Conner says: "If there is nothing arbitrary in the way God saves a man, then there is nothing arbitrary in his purpose to save him that way"![15]

Several truths are at stake in this stress on the accountability of persons before God.

- God created responsible persons in His own image. Responsibility is God's own gift.

- God wants our willing response (Ex. 35:29; John 4:14; Acts 4:20; 2 Cor. 8:12).

- God relates to persons as persons. He does not treat His people as machines or things. As subjects of His affection, He refuses to compel them, for compelling stunts rather than nourishes the growth of persons, and God wants believers to grow and mature (Eph. 4:13). Instead of displacing the personalities of believers, God works through them. Believers grow in grace through careful, even arduous, Bible study. They are elected through faith, not apart from faith!

- Election is in Christ (Eph. 1:4). The proof that a person is one of the elect is that he repents and trusts in Christ as his Savior and Lord.

- God calls all persons everywhere as long as time lasts (Matt. 28:19-20; 2 Pet. 3:9).

- Persons are lost because of their unbelief, not because God predetermined to pass them by (John 3:18,36; Rom. 6:23).

Election Is to Discipleship as well as to Privilege

God's selection of His people is not only to privilege but also to cross-centered discipleship in furthering His kingdom purposes. Life in God's kingdom is both gift and task. Hyper-Calvinistic paralysis and Arminian activism are false alternatives to kingdom service. Paul should have settled the Calvinistic-Arminian debate before it ever started when he instructed the Philippians, "Work out your salvation with fear and trembling, for it is God who is at work in you, both to will and to work for His good pleasure" (Phil. 2:12-13). God's work enables our work. God takes the initiative but we are still responsible.

God's people easily forget their call to worldwide mission. Even Article V of *The Baptist Faith and Message,* though fittingly headed "God's

---

15. Conner, *The Gospel of Redemption,* 65.

Purpose of Grace," discusses election in relation to individual salvation but says nothing of election as God's missionary calling (Matt. 28:19-20; Acts 1:8).

Lesslie Newbigin, a Christian missionary to India, contrasts the biblical doctrine of election with the Hindu worldview. Hinduism views persons as spiritual monads who can achieve their destiny without others or without a created world. The Bible, in contrast, teaches that persons achieve wholeness only in relation to others and as part of creation, filling the earth and subduing it (Gen. 1:26-30). The doctrine of election, Newbigin argues, arises from this insight concerning human nature. If it were to be pictured according to the biblical view of the truly human, Newbigin says, the gift of salvation would not come to each, direct from above, like a shaft of light through the roof. It would come from the neighbor in the action by which we open the door to invite the neighbor in; but the neighbor would have to be sent (Rom. 10:4). There would have to be one called and chosen to be the bearer of the blessing. The blessing is intended for all. Yet the blessing itself would be negated if it were not given and received in a way that binds each to the other.[16]

Election Is both Individual and Corporate

God works through groups as well as individuals. Just as God called Abraham and Paul, He also called the church at Antioch to launch the Gentile world mission (Acts 13:1-3). Here again, Newbigin reminds us of the importance of the biblical view of the truly human as a life of shared relationships, a life of mutual personal responsibility in the context of shared responsibility for the created world.

Election Is Basic to Christian Motivation for Service

No Christian will serve Christ very long without a sense of divine call. The obstacles and disappointments are too foreboding. A clear awareness of God's call assures us of the importance of ministry in Jesus' name. Having a sense of purpose in life gives the believer courage and boldness in Christian warfare. Convinced that kingdom tasks are God's tasks and assured that God cannot fail, believers know that God will open a way before them, come what may (Rom. 8:38-39; 1 Cor. 10:13).

---

16. Lesslie Newbigin, *The Open Secret* (Grand Rapids: Eerdmans, 1978), 76-78.

PART III

The Christian Life:

THE INDIVIDUAL DIMENSION OF GOD'S PURPOSE

Believers are always becoming, by God's grace, what they already are in Christ.

Issues
Christians Face

The kingdom present is rooted in the transforming power released by the Christ and Pentecost events. The Christian life is first God's doing, then the believer's response.

The Traditional Protestant Approach

Opting for an Alternative Approach

Comparing the Two Approaches

Remembering the Kingdom Context

An Evangelical Concern

The doctrine of the Christian life touches the center of practical Christianity. The fact is simple: no Christians, no Christian movement! The good news is not just something that happened two thousand years ago. The gospel must be proclaimed, believed, and practiced today (Rom. 1:16). The gospel doctrines of Christ's person and work, the Holy Spirit, and the kingdom present come to sharpest application in transformed lives of penitent, trusting sinners. Jesus' call never changes. He still beckons, "Come, follow me" (Matt. 19:21).

When Christians fail to live their faith, they fail everywhere. Yet believers fail. Institutional Christianity has many ways to substitute impersonal routines for personal experience. Our most serious problem is still cheap grace and nominal church membership. Many profess Christian faith and have their names on church rolls; too few do much about it.

The Traditional Protestant Approach

Protestant theology has traditionally constructed its doctrine of the Christian life by focusing on the two chronological stages of Christian experience:

Redeemed! Eschatological Redemption and the Kingdom of God

—136—

justification, defined as beginning the Christian life,

sanctification, defined as continuing the Christian life.[1]

This approach weakens the rich biblical content of justification and sanctification. Guthrie uses the traditional approach but recognizes its inadequacy. He writes, "This way of relating justification and sanctification in a temporal sequence is unbiblical . . . . We *never* leave behind us our need to receive God's forgiveness."[2] The Bible never separates justification and sanctification into differing and successive stages of Christian experience. Sanctification is never viewed as only an experience of growth to be added subsequently to a justification that occurs once for all at the beginning of the Christian life.

In the biblical view nobody can be justified without also being sanctified or sanctified without also being justified. The terms are not synonyms, but the realities they describe are closely related. What the Bible joins, interpreters of the Bible should not separate!

True, the Christian life begins in an experience of initial conversion and continues in a lifetime of struggle and growth. Even so, *justification* and *sanctification* are not the biblical words for designating these successive aspects of the believer's experience.

---

1. Guthrie and Erickson both follow the traditional approach, associating justification with the beginning of the Christian life and sanctification with its continuation. Shirley C. Guthrie, Jr., *Christian Doctrine* (Atlanta: Knox, 1977), and Millard J. Erickson, *Christian Theology* (Grand Rapids: Baker, 1985).

In general, this is the approach of Conner. He treats the Christian life in two chapters, "Becoming a Christian" and "The Christian Life." He departs from traditional practice, however, by insisting that sanctification in the New Testament relates more to becoming a Christian than to Christian growth. Since forgiveness, justification, reconciliation, adoption, regeneration, sanctification, and union with Christ are treated in the chapter on becoming a Christian, the chapter on the Christian life is anticlimactic. W. T. Conner, *The Gospel of Redemption* (Nashville: Broadman, 1945).

Hull adapts the approach to a broadened format. After an opening chapter on the Christian life as a process, his remaining thirteen chapters, each treating a familiar biblical term, are organized into four groups: the choice (repentance, faith, etc.); the change (regeneration, etc.); the consequences (justification, etc.); and the challenge (life, sanctification, and consummation). William E. Hull, *The Christian Experience of Salvation*, vol. 9, Layman's Library of Christian Doctrine (Nashville: Broadman, 1987).

Closely related to the familiar Protestant approach is the evangelical stress on three tenses of salvation, which adds to the beginning and the continuation of the Christian life the third step of final glorification. The note on Rom. 1:16 in the Scofield Bible, for instance, recognizing that salvation is in three tenses, explains tenses as follows: the believer *has been* saved (Luke 7:50; 1 Cor. 1:18; 2 Cor. 2:15; Eph. 2:5,8; 2 Tim. 1:9); the believer *is being* saved (Rom. 6:14; Phil. 1:19; 2:12,13; 2 Thess. 2:13; Rom. 8:2; Gal. 2:19-20; 2 Cor. 3:18); and the believer *will be* saved (Rom. 13:11; Heb. 10:36; 1 Pet. 1:5; 1 John 3:2).

The Baptist Faith and Message (Art. IV, on Salvation) combines familiar Protestant and evangelical approaches, indicating that salvation includes regeneration or justification, sanctification, and glorification.

2. Guthrie, *Christian Doctrine*, 336.

Opting for an Alternative Approach

Instead of the traditional Protestant approach to the Christian life, the approach presented here focuses on the biblical distinction between (1) the Christian life first as God's doing and (2) then as the believer's beginning and continuing response.

This distinction is implicit in biblical language about the Christian life. The great theological realities of the Christian life are God's doing: *God* regenerates, justifies, sanctifies, adopts, and reconciles. God performs these actions. The Bible also uses verbs for which the believer is the appropriate subject: the *believer* repents, believes, worships, follows, obeys, and endures. These verbs describe the believer's responses to God's saving action. Here is a promising approach to the doctrine of the Christian life. *While the Christian life is primarily God's doing, it also involves the believer's beginning and continuing response.*

Other writers have formulated the doctrine of the Christian life along similar lines. Some have distinguished between salvation and conversion, while others have used the terms regeneration and the Christian life to differentiate between God's initiative and the believer's response. One helpful discussion distinguishes between (1) what God does as an accomplished fact and (2) the believer's response as a progressive attainment.[3]

The essential idea is the same in these discussions. Whether beginning or continuing, *believers are becoming by God's grace what they already are in Christ.*[4] Only by keeping this primary emphasis in focus can the amazing grace, the free and joyful spontaneity, and the limitless challenge of Christian living be accorded significant expression.

---

3. Stott uses the terms regeneration and conversion. John R. W. Stott, *Christian Mission in the Modern World* (Downers Grove, IL: InterVarsity, 1975), 114-17.

Bloesch uses the expressions salvation and the Christian life. Donald G. Bloesch, *The Christian Life and Salvation* (Grand Rapids: Eerdmans, 1967). Interestingly, though the title places the Christian life before salvation, Bloesch's discussion begins with salvation and then moves to the Christian life, as one might expect.

Dilday distinguishes between the Christian life as an accomplished fact and as a progressive attainment. R. H. Dilday, Jr., "The Christian Life," leaflet widely distributed by the Baptist General Convention of Texas.

4. Another way of expressing the "am/am becoming" polarity is to speak of the "indicative/imperative" tension in Scripture. Davis, for instance, says that the indicatives of Scripture show that believers "have been tansferred from this present evil age into the kingdom of God's dear Son" (Rom. 6:1-10). The imperatives "show how we are still threatened by this evil age" (Rom. 6:11-13; Eph. 5:8; Col. 3:1-5). The imperatives follow the indicatives "because we can only carry out the commands for holy living through the power of the Holy Spirit." Earl C. Davis, *Life in the Spirit,* vol. 11, Layman's Library of Christian Doctrine (Nashville: Broadman, 1986), 51-52.

Redeemed! Eschatological Redemption and the Kingdom of God

—138—

Comparing the Two Approaches

In order to clarify the difference between the approach followed in this discussion and traditional studies of the Christian life, consider Article 4 of *The Baptist Faith and Message* under the heading, "Salvation":

> Salvation involves the redemption of the whole man, and is offered freely to all who accept Jesus Christ as Lord and Saviour, who by His own blood obtained eternal redemption for the believer. In its broadest sense salvation includes regeneration, sanctification, and glorification.
>
> A. Regeneration, or the new birth, is a work of God's grace whereby believers become new creatures in Christ Jesus. It is a change of heart wrought by the Holy Spirit through conviction of sin, to which the sinner responds in repentance toward God and faith in the Lord Jesus Christ.
>
> Repentance and faith are inseparable experiences of grace. Repentance is a genuine turning from sin toward God. Faith is the acceptance of Jesus Christ and commitment of the entire personality to Him as Lord and Saviour. Justification is God's gracious and full acquittal upon principles of His righteousness of all sinners who repent and believe in Christ. Justification brings the believer into a relationship of peace and favor with God.
>
> B. Sanctification is the experience, beginning in regeneration, by which the believer is set apart to God's purposes, and is enabled to progress toward moral and spiritual perfection through the presence and power of the Holy Spirit dwelling in him. Growth in grace should continue throughout the regenerate person's life.
>
> C. Glorification is the culmination of salvation and is the final blessed and abiding state of the redeemed.

This is a moving summary that follows the traditional approach. When evaluated in the light of the present study, the following comments emerge:

> 1. "The Christian Life" would be a more specific and clear heading than "Salvation." Salvation is a broad term. As used in evangelical writing salvation embraces not only the Christian life but other doctrines as well—Christ, the Holy Spirit, the kingdom present, the church, and

the kingdom consummated.[5] The same is true of other general terms such as redemption and reconciliation.

2. The statement restricts the meaning of regeneration and justification to becoming a Christian and restricts the meaning of sanctification to spiritual growth and struggle.[6] The Bible uses these terms more broadly to describe varying facets of God's saving action throughout the believer's life. Instead of affirming that only God can regenerate and sanctify, the statement merely declares that the believer's response has the double aspect of beginning and continuing, never discussing the gracious divine initiative in Christian experience.

3. The Christian life is treated as merely an individual matter. The inseparable relationship between the individual believer and God's great kingdom purposes is not mentioned in this article, though it is discussed elsewhere in *The Baptist Faith and Message*. Yet salvation is not only a calling to privilege but also a calling that relates to all of life's dimensions.

4. The statement's affirmation that the believer "is enabled to progress toward moral and spiritual perfection," though qualified by the comment that "growth in grace should continue throughout the regenerate person's life," fails to mention that fierce struggle and spiritual warfare are also a part of Christian life.

---

5. Cowen's study of salvation in the New Testament, for instance, includes six chapters: the need for salvation, the purpose of salvation (Christ's death was a propitiation for the sins of the whole world), the basis of salvation (atonement), the application of salvation (initial conversion), the results of salvation (the continuation of the Christian life), and the assurance of salvation. Gerald Cowen, *Salvation: Word Studies from the Greek New Testament* (Nashville: Broadman, 1990).

Dominy's probing analysis of the rich biblical idea of salvation includes three central chapters on the person and work of Christ. His seven chapters are: the human problem, the promise of salvation (the Old Testament), the divine provision (three chapters: incarnation, cross, resurrection), perspectives (terms, pictures), and the consummation. Bert Dominy, *God's Work of Salvation*, vol. 8, Layman's Library of Christian Doctrine (Nashville: Broadman, 1986).

These studies clearly illustrate that salvation is a broader concept in biblical usage than the idea of the Christian life.

6. Sanctification in its traditional sense of progressive sanctification is widely discussed today.

For a discussion of Reformed, Lutheran, Wesleyan, Pentecostal, and contemplative views of progressive sanctification, see Donald L. Alexander, ed., *Christian Spirituality: Five Views of Sanctification* (Downers Grove, IL: InterVarsity, 1988).

For a treatment of Wesleyan, Reformed, Pentecostal, Keswick, and Augustinian Dispensational views of progressive sanctification, see Melvin E. Dieter, and others, *Five Views on Sanctification* (Grand Rapids: Zondervan, 1987).

5. The statement links repentance and faith to initial conversion only, neglecting their never-ceasing importance for the ongoing Christian life.

6. Glorification is a dimension of the final consummation. Strictly speaking, it is not part of what is usually included in discussions of the Christian life. This may explain why glorification is only mentioned in passing.

Remembering the Kingdom Context

The doctrine of the Christian life must be clearly related to God's great kingdom purposes, but this important focus is widely neglected in theological discussion.[7]

Life in the kingdom of God is life in its fullest and most comprehensive dimensions. Consider the sequence of the following topics: the person and work of Jesus Christ, the person and work of the Holy Spirit, the kingdom present, the Christian life, the church, and the kingdom consummated. To catch a vision of the majestic sweep of these mighty redemptive actions is to see the Christian life in a broader and more dynamic biblical perspective.[8]

Consider three comments regarding the topics in this sequence.

- The reality of the kingdom present as a history-changing force is rooted in the transforming power released through the Christ and Pentecost events.

- The Christian life and the church refer to life in the kingdom of God as a present power in history.

- The Christian life and the church anticipate the final and complete triumph of the Redeemer as King of kings and Lord of lords.

An Evangelical Concern

The evangelical approach to the Christian life avoids both naive optimism and enervating pessimism.[9]

7. Howard A. Snyder, *The Community of the King* (Downers Grove, IL: InterVarsity, 1977), especially 21-31.

8. Although Lovelace makes little use of direct reference to the kingdom of God, his volume is a provocative study of evangelical spirituality. Richard F. Lovelace, *Dynamics of Spiritual Life: An Evangelical Theology of Renewal* (Downers Grove, IL: InterVarsity, 1979).

9. Approaches to the Christian life other than an evangelical view are summarized in the following studies: David F. Wells, *The Search for Salvation* (Downers Grove, IL: InterVarsity, 1978); and Erickson, *Christian Theology*, especially, 891-905.

Wells has chapters on conservative thought, neoorthodoxy, existentialism, secularism, liberation theology, and Roman Catholic theology. Erickson refers to liberation theologies, existential theology, secular theology, contemporary Roman Catholic theology, and evangelical theology.

Contrary to the superficial optimism rampant on the current religious scene (with slogans like "God loves you unconditionally," "God wants you healthy and wealthy," "You are great," and the like), evangelical theology stresses the seriousness of the moral and spiritual warfare from which no person ever fully escapes in this life.[10]

Persons apart from Christ are guilty sinners and eternally lost. Struggle and suffering still mark human life, given the superhuman power of evil and our propensity for self-love, self-deception, or other subtle forms of rebellion against God. Only the new birth and the power of Christ and the Holy Spirit can cope with our need.

At the other extreme, unlike the gloom and doom also commonly expressed in contemporary society, God's kingdom can triumph in our lives and in history because of the victory won through the Christ and Pentecost events. Although psychological determinism and secularism deny that human nature can be changed, the gospel proclaims that the old can be made new by the power of God. Although it is possible to promise too much when proclaiming the gospel, it is just as potentially destructive to promise too little!

10. See John F. MacArthur, Jr., *Charismatic Chaos* (Grand Rapids: Zondervan, 1992); Florence Bulle, "God *Wants You Rich" and Other Enticing Doctrines* (Minneapolis: Bethany, 1983); Bruce Barron, *The Health and Wealth Gospel* (Downers Grove, IL: InterVarsity, 1987); and Robert H. Schuller, *Self-Esteem: The New Reformation* (Waco, TX: Word, 1982).

10 *The Christian Life as God's Doing*

The Christian life is God's abundant provision, leaving nothing to be desired. It is a gift of grace— perfect and complete in Christ, embracing the believer's whole experience.

The Christian life is a beginning and a continuing from the standpoint of the believer's response. From the standpoint of God's doing, however, the Christian life is a gift of grace— perfect and complete in Christ, embracing the believer's whole experience. In Christ, believers lack nothing. They are saved, not half-saved (Eph. 2:8). They are saints (1 Cor. 1:2), heirs of God with full family status, not bondservants (Gal. 4:7). Their citizenship is in heaven (Eph. 2:6,19) and their names are written in the Lamb's book of life (Rev. 21:27).

As God's doing, the Christian life is God's initiative.[1] God acts first (John 3:16). He loves us before we love Him (1 John 4:19; cf. Eph. 1:4). All is of grace (Acts 15:11). Credit for the Christian life goes to the God who seeks us before we seek Him (Gen. 3:8-10).

Is this stress on the Christian life as first of all a matter of God's abundant provision, leaving nothing to be desired, not unanimously accepted among evangelicals? Strangely enough, this emphasis is criticized in some circles as legalistic, transactional, fictional, and contrary to the facts.[2]

Because sin breaks relationship with God, becoming a Christian is possible only when that relationship is reestablished. Sin must be confessed. The guilty sinner must be pardoned. The broken filial relationship must be healed.[3]

Biblical Resources: Key Terms

The biblical vocabulary for the Christian life includes key theological terms in evangelical proclamation, such as justification, regeneration, sanctification, and adoption.[4] God, not humanity, is the proper subject of the action when these words are used with their biblical meaning. *God* redeems, saves, reconciles, forgives, justifies, regenerates, sanctifies, adopts, and the like.

Biblical writers poured exhaustless meaning into these terms, and theologians now write whole books on single expressions.[5] Luther's rediscovery of Paul's doctrine of justification by faith sparked the Protestant Reformation. Another of the terms, sanctification, provides a key for understanding the eighteenth-century Evangelical Revival and the theology of John Wesley. Their meaning is immeasurable, but it is necessary to attempt brief definitions.

---

1. H. R. Mackintosh's *The Divine Initiative* (London: Student Christian Movement, 1921) began as a series of lectures to furloughing missionaries. Mackintosh commented, "The title is intended to mark the fact that stress is everywhere laid on one cardinal point, which may be put thus: all that Christians are they owe to the spontaneous love of God [in Christ]" (Ibid., 5).

2. Larson, for one, tends to contrast the theological and relational emphases. Bruce Larson, *No Longer Strangers* (Waco, TX: Word, 1971), 17-21. See also Morris Ashcraft, *The Forgiveness of Sins* (Nashville: Broadman, 1972), 48.

3. See Boyd Hunt, "Atonement," *Encyclopedia of Southern Baptists;* and Paul F. M. Zahl, *Who Will Deliver Us? The Present Power of the Death of Christ* (New York: Seabury, 1983).

4. For a glossary of these and other terms used in the present volume, see Fisher Humphreys and Philip Wise, *A Dictionary of Doctrinal Terms* (Nashville: Broadman, 1983).

5. James S. Stewart, for example, has an epochal volume on Paul's idea of union with Christ in *A Man in Christ* (New York: Harper, 1935).

Justification by grace through faith in Jesus Christ is God's free pardon and full acceptance for Christ's sake of all who turn from sin and trust Christ as Savior and Lord (Rom. 3:21-26; Phil. 3:9). The dual meaning is important: justification is (1) pardon and (2) acceptance into the family of God. Those who are justified have a new status and a new relationship! They had been aliens from the household of God but are now brought near through the blood of Christ (Eph. 2:13).[6]

Regeneration is the imparting of a new heart, a new attitude, a new nature, and a new sense of personal direction and meaning (John 3:1-8).

Sanctification has two meanings: positional and progressive. Positional sanctification says that from the moment of initial conversion believers are set apart for God (1 Cor. 6:11). In God's sight they are at once saints, holy ones. They may still have a long way to go in life ethically and spiritually, but in Christ, for the first time, they are now headed in the right direction.

In this positional sense, sanctification applies to things as well as to persons. Biblical writers regarded material objects such as Old Testament temple vessels or the city of Jerusalem as set apart to God and, therefore, holy. In the absolute sense, of course, only God is holy. When holiness is ascribed to persons or to things it is a derived holiness, a holiness by virtue of association with God. This positional meaning is the most frequent meaning of sanctification in the Bible. It is obviously similar to declarative justification.

The New Testament also speaks of sanctification in a progressive sense. Progressive sanctification is growth in grace (1 Thess. 5:23; 2 Pet. 3:18). Although it is not the customary biblical use of the term, Protestant tradition uses it in this sense. The Protestant neglect of the basic equivalence of declarative justification and positional sanctification is a weakness that merits correction.

Forgiveness, like justification, carries the dual meaning of free pardon and full acceptance. New Testament teaching about justification goes beyond the Old Testament by insisting that Christ's merit is the basis for the believer's new relation to God. Though clarified by the fuller light of New Testament revelation, Old Testament teaching about forgiveness is amazingly profound.

---

6. Unfortunately, Conner, whose theology has so much to commend it and to whom this writer is forever deeply indebted, contrasts the declarative and vital aspects of justification, ruling out the former and opting for the latter, instead of recognizing that the New Testament keeps the two aspects in vital, polar tension. Along with James Denney, Conner tends to equate justification with regeneration. W. T. Conner, *The Gospel of Redemption* (Nashville: Broadman, 1945), 171-77.

The position taken here is that the "legal" aspect of New Testament language is a strength, not a weakness. Declarative justification is a *vital* doctrine!

The Old Testament describes God's forgiveness, especially in the Book of Hosea and in Psalms 32, 51, and 103; Jeremiah 31:31-34 looks forward to a new covenant and a more ample forgiveness. For those who have known the torture of a guilt-ridden conscience—the sleepless nights, the self-hate, the sense of meaninglessness, and more—no word so well describes God's redeeming grace as "forgiveness"!

This is not to suggest that something is gained by sinning. Forgiveness is not making persons as though they had never sinned, for the scars of sin remain. Instead, forgiveness means that sinners are given another chance.

Adoption is the doctrine of a blessed assurance of acceptance with God, an acceptance in the fullest sense of belonging in the family of God (Rom. 8:15-17; Gal. 3:26; 4:7). There are no second-class Christians!

Reconciliation is the cessation of the sinner's active rebellion against God, removal of enmity between God and the person, and the bliss of peace with God (Rom. 5:1,10; 2 Cor. 5:16-21). Those who deny God's wrath and enmity between God and sinners restrict reconciliation to the psychological and social dimension.

According to the Bible, however, God does not love the righteous and the sinful in the same way. To emphasize that wrath is an expression of love is not to deny God's wrath against impenitent sinners. However, as the wrath of God against sin is real, so also is the reconciliation of God to the sinner who trusts in Christ.

In Christian literature reconciliation, like redemption and salvation, is an umbrella term for all that God does in Christ to heal the alienation of sin and to fulfill God's purposes for His creation.

Redemption is the ransoming of the sinner from the slavery of sin to a new life of freedom in Christ (Gal. 4:5). Only the one who trusts in Christ knows what it really means to be "free at last"!

Redemption is also used in a broader sense in theological literature, as when it is said that the Bible is a book of redemption. Used in this manner, redemption refers to all doctrines that deal with God's saving revelation, not just the doctrine of the Christian life.

Salvation is the Greek word for wholeness or health. In Christian theology, as with redemption, salvation has a narrower and a broader meaning.[7] In the more limited sense salvation is God's gift to believers of forgiveness of sins and new life in Christ. In the broader sense, salvation refers to everything God does to fulfill His redemptive purposes in Christ. The phrase *in Christ* expresses the limitless resources for redemption that God provides through Christ. No blessings are conceivable that

7. For the broader significance of the idea of salvation in biblical usage see note 5 above.

God in Christ has not secured for those who trust Him with all their hearts (Eph. 2:4-10). Rather than emphasizing a singular perspective on the Christian life, as do justification or adoption, union with Christ stresses that the essence of Christian experience is a vital relation to and a walk with Christ. Stewart says:

> Everything that religion meant for Paul is focused for us in such great words as these: "I live, yet not I, but Christ liveth in me" (Gal. 2:20); "There is, therefore, now no condemnation to them which are in Christ Jesus" (Rom. 8:1); and "He that is joined unto the Lord is one spirit" (1 Cor. 6:17).[8]

Eternal life sums up the full, abundant, and endless life that God gives through Christ (John 10:10).

These are the most familiar biblical words for the Christian life as God's doing. A question remains: *What is the significance of these words for understanding the Christian life?* Although each term refers to the Christian life as God's doing, they are not mere synonyms. Each has its own distinctive etymology and meaning. Taken together, their variety helps capture the many-colored splendor of God's redeeming action (Eph. 3:10).

In the biblical context, each term describes what God is always doing for the believer from the beginning of the Christian life to the end. This emphasis runs counter to two common views in Protestant theology. Except for sanctification, theologians tend to limit the meaning of these terms to what God does in the person's initial conversion experience. For instance, Conner says, "All these terms are different ways of describing what God does for us at the beginning of the Christian life."[9] Writers have often tried to list the terms in some sort of logical or chronological order.[10] In the biblical view, however, whole Christian life is characterized by the reality these terms describe.

Instead of relating justification, for example, to the experience of initial conversion only, the Bible insists that the believer is justified by grace through faith at every point of the Christian walk (Rom. 5:1). A right relation with God is a relational matter. All blessings of the Christian life are blessings of those in vital faith union with Christ.

Justification in the New Testament often refers to our justification before God at the last judgment. Then, as now, our only plea will be that,

---

8. Stewart, *A Man in Christ,* 147.

9. Conner includes sanctification, focusing on its positional meaning to the exclusion of its progressive sense. He prefers to speak of Christian growth as Christian development rather than as progressive sanctification. Conner, *The Gospel of Redemption,* 194.

10. See *Evangelical Dictionary of Theology,* s.v. "Order of Salvation" (Lat. *ordo salutis*), by G. N. M. Collins.

though we have no righteousness of our own, the living Lord is our righteousness and all of our sins are covered by the blood of Christ (Rom. 5:9).

The following words, almost erased by time, are inscribed on a gravestone on the state capitol grounds in Columbia, South Carolina:

> Yea, Thou wilt answer for me, righteous Lord;
> Thine all the merits, mine the great reward;
> Thine the sharp thorns, and mine the golden crown;
> Mine the life won, and Thine the life laid down.
> Yea, Thou wilt answer for me, righteous Lord!

Historical Perspective

The Christian life as God's doing has been pushed into the background in a variety of ways in the history of Christian theology. Roman Catholic thought has stressed the institutional church, the sacraments, and the monastic life. The Lutheran and Calvinistic emphasis on God's saving action and the believer's response has been undercut by the accompanying stress on infant baptism, union of church and state, and definition of the church more in terms of the clergy (the pure preaching of the Word and the right administration of the sacraments) than in terms of the people of God.

The Christian life as God's doing is best understood in the context of the believers' church tradition that views congregations as spiritual fellowships of baptized, disciplined *believers*. In this setting, the doctrine of the Christian life precedes the doctrine of the church because church membership presupposes personal Christian experience with Christ.

Restatement: Characteristics of the Christian Life as God's Doing

If the point of departure for a biblical understanding of the Christian life is the distinction between the Christian life as God's doing and the Christian life as the believer's response, the clarity of that distinction becomes a primary concern. The following discussion focuses on characteristics of the Christian life as God's doing.

As God's Doing the Christian Life Is a Matter of God's Initiative from Beginning to End

The Christian life is God's gift before it is the believer's response. This truth is important to evangelicals. The Christian life is something God does. It cannot be explained in merely psychological or sociological terms. It is supernatural or miraculous.

Secular theologies have stressed that being Christian does not mean being religious but being human.[11] Evangelicals believe the religious and the human ought never be juxtaposed in this way. Being fully human is to be deeply religious. Being religious means realizing the God-intended potentiality of persons whom God created in His own image and for fellowship with Him, with other humans, and with the self.[12] Leonard Griffith says the purpose of Jesus' ministry was not simply to make people more human but to make them more Godlike.[13]

Since the Christian life is first God's doing, there is no place for human self-righteousness. Salvation is by grace. It cannot be earned by our righteous works. Thus spontaneity and freedom are hallmarks of Christian experience. Believers serve God because they want to! Christians live from the overflow of abundant life in Christ (John 4:14) rather than by the frustrated striving that characterizes systems of salvation by works. Freely receiving, believers freely give. Christian commitment is willing, cheerful commitment, constrained from within rather than compelled from without (Acts 4:18-20; 2 Cor. 9:7).

As God's Doing the Christian Life Is a
Living Relationship between God and the Believer

Like any other living relationship, it must be developed. Graduation from college can be viewed as a status: the graduate frames the diploma, hangs it on the wall, and says, "I have it!" The Christian life is not a "thing" to possess in this manner. It is a status in that the believer is saved and is a child of God, but the Christian life is primarily a living relationship with God in Christ. The status derives from the relationship; everything in the Christian life grows out of the personal relationship.[14]

Personal relationships must be tended. They deteriorate when taken for granted (John 15:5-6). The believer does not trust in Christ as Savior

11. For a summary of the approach to salvation in secular theologies, see David F. Wells, *The Search for Salvation* (Downers Grove, IL: InterVarsity, 1978), 95-117.

Among other insights, Wells observes that for the later Bonhoeffer, the world has "come of age," and "true worldliness" is "unconscious Christianity." Ibid., 102.

12. Notice the uniquely human gift of self-awareness that is lacking in the animal creation.

13. Leonard Griffith, *We Have This Ministry* (Waco, TX: Word, 1973), 21. While ancient Greek ideas of morality stressed self-control or temperance, the biblical ideal is that of passionate devotion to God and His righteous rule (Matt. 6:33).

14. Bruce Larson, *The Relational Revolution* (Waco, TX: Word, 1976. On the positive side, Larson stresses the importance of viewing humans as persons rather than as things. On the negative side, his understanding of the relational emphasis is marred by his inability to see the basic significance of the positional aspect of God's saving act. Instead, he tends to contrast the positional as legalistic and transactional with the relational as vital and personal. See the following section of the present discussion and the stress on the Christian life as believers becoming what they already are in Christ.

for a moment and then forget it. Trust in Christ is a personal relationship—neverending, ever-growing, continuously tested, limitlessly fulfilling!

As God's Doing the Christian Life Stresses That Believers Are to Become in Experience What They Already Are in Christ[15]

While the Christian life as God's work is complete *in Christ* the moment the Christian first believes, at the same time it is also an inexhaustible goal that never ceases to beckon the believer upward and onward. The important words here are *in Christ*.

On the one hand, the believer is immediately and unreservedly accepted. In God's sight and for Christ's sake, the new Christian, though only a babe in Christ, is reckoned an heir, a saint, a full member of God's family! "Therefore having been justified by faith, we have peace with God through our Lord Jesus Christ" (Rom. 5:1). The moment converts believe in Christ they are fully saved, not just half saved.

On the other hand, from the standpoint of Christian character and conduct, the believer has a long way to go following the his initial conversion. The new Christian begins, fails, and fails again. Christian maturity is never an accomplished fact, for each new day brings new beginnings. The ultimate goal in Christ remains limitless. Yet through it all, believers are becoming what they already are in Christ. The believer's love for Christ wells up from within. This radical spontaneity and freedom distinguishes the Christian experience from all oppressive systems of salvation by human achievement.

Zahl points out that ecumenical Christianity in recent years has neglected atonement, justification by faith, substitution, and imputation.[16] Yet, for evangelicals, these emphases are the heart of the gospel. Good works follow justification. The believer strives to please God, not to earn God's favor, but because he *wants* to please God! He has been bought with a price, and "love so amazing, so divine" demands his all. Zahl says: "We are all sinners because we know we are still in a sense the same. We do not have to be surprised at the stubbornness and perseverance of [our sin]. But we are different, because in being regarded as righteous, we start to become as we are regarded."[17]

If believers are to understand themselves, each pole of the tension between "I am a child of God" and "I am becoming a child of God" is indispensable. Believers are both justified and yet also sinners who are

---

15. For a further expression of the importance of this emphasis see the conclusion to this discussion of the Christian life.

16. Zahl, *Who Will Deliver Us?*, 7. See the reference to Hunt's article on "The Atonement" in note 3 earlier.

17. Ibid., 52.

being redeemed. The expression of this dynamic polarity in the familiar hymn, "Like a River Glorious," is striking. Speaking of the peace of God experienced by the justified believer because of Christ (Rom. 5:1), the hymn says:

> Perfect, yet it floweth
> Fuller every day;
> Perfect, yet it groweth
> Deeper all the way![18]

As God's Doing the Christian Life Is One Saving Action of God, not Two

In traditional Protestant theology, justification is identified with the beginning of the Christian life and sanctification with its continuation. However, God's work of salvation is best viewed as one work, not two or more divine actions in succession.

The classical Pentecostal view of two faiths—faith in Christ for justification and a subsequent faith in the Holy Spirit for the baptism in the Spirit and the gift of tongues—is an even more exaggerated version of twofold salvation than the traditional Protestant view. Critiquing the Pentecostal version, Bruner says, "Two is the fatal number in Christian theology." He argues vigorously against "two-stage" views of the Christian life, insisting that adding anything to "simple faith in Christ" for salvation opens the door to legalism. This is true whether in modern Pentecostalism or in the Galatian and Corinthian misunderstandings of the gospel.[19]

Emphasizing the unity of God's saving action is not to belittle the richness of biblical language describing God's saving action. Compromising the unity of God's action denies one of its decisive dimensions. The New Testament gives believers no choice between taking God as justifier and taking Him as sanctifier!

---

18. Frances R. Havergal (1836-79). Cf. Rom. 5:1.

19. Frederick Dale Bruner, *A Theology of the Holy Spirit: The Pentecostal Experience and the New Testament Witness* (Grand Rapids: Eerdmans, 1970), 115,251.

More recently Packer discusses "three main evangelical views of holiness," each of which is a different form of a two-stage version of Christian experience: Augustinian holiness, Wesleyan perfectionism, and Keswick teaching. "The Charismatic Life" is treated in a separate chapter. J. I. Packer, *Keep in Step with the Spirit* (Old Tappan, NJ: Revell, 1984).

We will return to this matter of the inadequacy of two-stage versions of the Christian life in the discussion of the problem of nominal Christianity.

As God's Doing the Christian Life Embraces the Whole of the Believer's Beginning and Continuing Response

Biblical writers use various terms to describe God's acts but all these terms refer to what God is *always* doing for every believer, not to different things He does in separate stages of the believer's experience. God justifies, regenerates, sanctifies, reconciles, not successively but simultaneously throughout the believer's pilgrimage.

The unity of the believer's beginning and continuing response can be compromised, either by overemphasizing initial conversion while neglecting Christian growth, or by a nonbiblical insistence on the believer's need for a second experience in addition to initial saving faith, inevitably minimizing the full significance of the conversion experience. Both a decisive experience of initial conversion and a life of constant growth and struggle are necessary. God saves the believer's whole life, not just a moment of it!

The idea that if one has faith for just a moment he is saved for all eternity is not a biblical view of faith. According to the Bible, faith is inseparable from an abiding, ever deepening personal trust in Christ and walk with Him. Saving faith is persevering faith! Falling away shows that the initial conversion experience was not what it should have been (1 John 2:19). Contrary to popular misunderstanding, there is no way to take Christ as Savior without also taking Him as Lord. The person who is unwilling to acknowledge Christ as Lord is not ready to own Him as Savior.[20]

As God's Doing the Christian Life Is Always an Eternal "Now"

The New Testament constantly proclaims that "now" is always the acceptable time to turn to God (2 Cor. 6:2; Heb. 3:7-8,15; 4:7).

The New Testament distinguishes between two kinds of time: *kairos* time is God's opportune time, *chronos* time is clock or calendar time. *Kairos* time is *chronos* time filled with eternal significance! It is God's

---

20. The difficulty of formulating an adequate theological statement of the principle that to take Christ as Savior is also to take Him as Lord is reflected by the intensity of the ongoing lordship/free grace discussion in evangelical theology.

In a recent phase of the debate among dispensational premillennial writers MacArthur takes issue with Hodges and Ryrie and both of them respond. See John F. MacArthur, Jr., *The Gospel According to Jesus: What does Jesus Mean when He says, 'Follow Me'"?* (Grand Rapids: Zondervan, 1988); Zane C. Hodges, *Absolutely Free! A Biblical Reply to Lordship Salvation* (Grand Rapids: Zondervan, 1989); and Charles C. Ryrie, *So Great Salvation* (Wheaton, IL: Victor, 1989).

For a recent restatement of the importance of keeping Christ's saviorhood and lordship together, see Robert L. Hamblin and William H. Stephens, *The Doctrine of Lordship* (Nashville: Convention Press, 1990), 59-70.

"now." The Christian life as God's doing is always a "now," always an up-to-date experience of God and a relationship with God.

Unlike the human tendency to dwell on past experiences or future intentions while neglecting present opportunities, the Bible stresses our present relationship to God in Christ. "All who *are* being led by the Spirit of God, these are the sons of God" (Rom. 8:14, emphasis added), not just those who were led by the Spirit at some past time or who will be led by the Spirit at some time in the future. The New Testament never substitutes past or future for the opportune present!

As God's Doing the Christian Life Is an Eschatological Existence

The Christian lives in the interim between D-Day (Christ's first coming) and V-Day (Christ's second coming),[21] the time of God's missionary patience (2 Pet. 3:9) as He seeks the furthering of His comprehensive kingdom mission (Matt. 28:19-20; Col. 2:15). Life during this interim is life lived with the assurance of an inheritance in the coming age, the time of the final consummation.

Traditional theology has neglected the New Testament emphasis on eschatological dimension of Christian life, with the result that many believers have an impoverished understanding of the nature of Christian living. Believers have often lost the sense of living in the last days ushered in by the decisive victories of the Christ and Pentecost events.

This loss means a diminished awareness of a number of spiritual realities, such as: the richness of the spiritual resources available through Christ and the Holy Spirit; the intensity and seriousness of the ongoing warfare with evil powers; the certainty that no sacrifice for Christ is ever in vain; and unshakable confidence in the final triumph of the kingdom of God.

The Christian life is the dangerous life of a pilgrim in an alien world. Jesus cautioned His disciples: "In the world you will have tribulation" (John 16:33). Kingdom victories are assured, but they will be costly, for the sign of the cross hangs over every kingdom victory. Yet God is not mocked! The ultimate triumph is Christ's.

---

21. The eschatological dimension of the Christian life includes the facts that the Christian already reigns with Christ during the present interim between Christ's two comings and is destined for life in the consummated kingdom that follows Christ's return. Since the Christian life and the church are the cutting edge of the presence of the kingdom in history, they are already marked by kingdom characteristics such as power and comprehensive mission, a fact often overlooked in traditional discussions of eschatology.

As God's Doing the Christian Life Has both Corporate and Individual Dimensions

The Bible teaches that all of human life is inescapably social.[22] Family relationships are essential to human survival. Socially as well as biologically, Adam and Eve *together* were created in the image of God (Gen. 1:26-28)! Persons are one another's keepers (Gen. 4:9).

This is doubly true of Christian existence. "We are all members of one body" (Eph. 4:25). The love that binds believers to Christ also binds them to one another. After Pentecost those who daily were being saved were added to the assembly of believers *by the Lord* (Acts 2:47)! Individual salvation and church participation go together. Furthermore, the love that binds believers to Christ also sends them into the world with compassion for fellow human beings who are lost without Christ and with a yearning for the healing of society's tragic ills.

In summary as God's doing the Christian life:

- is a matter of God's initiative;
- is a living relationship between God and the believer;
- stresses that believers are to become in experience what they already are in Christ;
- is one saving action of God, not two;
- embraces the whole of the believer's beginning and continuing response;
- is always an Eternal "Now";
- is an eschatological existence;
- has both corporate and individual dimensions.

Since believers have all that is represented by these affirmations working for them, it is no wonder the Bible says, "If any man is in Christ, he is a new creature; the old things passed away; behold, new things have come" (2 Cor. 5:17).

---

22. See the emphasis on the corporate aspect of biblical redemption in the discussion of the church immediately following this section on the Christian life.

11 *The Christian Life as the Believer's Response*

From the beginning of the Christian life until the believer's death, the believer's response to God's saving act in Christ involves never-ending growth and struggle.

Both spiritual and physical growth require effort and discipline. A young Christian can no more achieve spiritual maturity overnight than an infant can walk out of the mother's womb. Yet physical and spiritual growth are different. Spiritual growth, as every Christian soon learns, is not so inevitable as the development of teeth. Growing children become less dependent on parents, but growing believers recognize their deepening dependence on God in Christ for all they are and hope to be.

Biblical Resources: Key Terms

The Bible uses a variety of verbs to speak of the believer's response to God:

Terms for Commitment	*Terms for Growth*	*Terms for Service*
repent	walk	love
turn	run	evangelize
believe	wrestle	witness
trust	study	disciple
enter	eat	serve
open	learn	help
hear	endure	minister
obey		care
follow		
promise		
covenant		
forgive		
hope		
worship		
pray		
praise		

The Bible also uses phrases such as taking up one's cross, making restitution, and eating and drinking the bread and water of life. How long would a complete list be?

Yet the most familiar biblical expressions for the believer's response are *repentance* and *faith*. Faith is the basic term, but faith always implies repentance. These observations have to do with the relation between the two.

1. Repentance and faith are clearly distinguishable. Repentance is turning from self-centeredness to God. Faith is personal trust in and commitment to Jesus Christ as Savior and Lord.

2. Repentance and faith occur simultaneously in Christian experience. Neither the idea of a penitent unbeliever nor that of an impenitent believer is conceivable. Repentance and faith are inseparable.

3. Repentance and faith are responses to God's gracious initiative, not good works to earn salvation. Sinners are saved *if* they repent and believe, not because they repent and believe. Repentance and faith are conditions to salvation, not its grounds. They are God's gifts (Acts 5:31; Eph. 2:8). All the credit for believers' repenting and believing belongs to God. Salvation is His idea before it is the idea of believers.

4. Repentance and faith are inward qualities; hence only God can judge whether or not they are genuine. Persons are easily deceived when attempting to evaluate with finality the response of others.

5. Repentance and faith continue throughout the Christian life. Believers are never done repenting and trusting! The essence of a maturing Christian walk is deepening penitence and trust. "God, be merciful to me, a sinner" (Luke 18:13) is not just the prayer of the new convert. It is also the prayer of the maturing saint.

Historical Perspective

Christian theology through the centuries has neglected the Christian life as the believer's beginning and continuing response for the same reasons it has neglected the Christian life as God's doing. Institutionalism and sacramentalism leave little room for an adequate stress on the personal responses of believers.

Furthermore, neither naive optimism about human perfectibility (as in various holiness theologies) nor inordinate self-depreciation (as in the Calvinism that over-emphasizes human depravity and personal inability while neglecting Calvin's teaching about human responsibility and common grace) provide a balanced context for the study of the believer's response.

Restatement

The following restatement of a biblical doctrine of the Christian life as the believer's response addresses three significant topics:

- characteristics of the Christian life as the believer's response;

- the importance of both initial conversion and a life of growth and struggle;

- the problem of nominal Christians.

Characteristics of the Christian Life as the Believer's Response

As the believer's response the Christian life is possible only because of God's saving action.—All of the credit for the believer's response belongs to God. God draws the response from the believer through His gracious initiatives in Christ (John 6:44). Belief is receiving what God gives, not achieving His rewards. Peck observes that nobody simply decides to become a believer and exclaims, "Well, I did rather well after all." Rather, the believer draws from the Holy Spirit's gracious initiative.[1]

---

1. John Peck, *What the Bible Teaches about the Holy Spirit* (Wheaton, IL: Tyndale, 1979), 94.

The line between faith as a gift and faith as a work, however, is not easily discerned. Frederick Dale Bruner warns against over-emphasizing faith as appropriation. He argues that, in classical Pentecostalism,

> The weight of the gift's transmission is shifted from the Giver's making it men's to men's making it theirs. Hence the gift ceases to be simply received, it is "made one's own" and so at least *in part* even becomes our work. . . . It is our impression that "appropriation" has been the mother of more conditions, if not more misery, than any other word we have encountered in Pentecostalism except, perhaps, the word "full." The notion of appropriation tends to make the believer's faith even more central than God's gift, or to put it another way, to make faith a work.[2]

By responding to God's grace, the believer is becoming what he or she already is in God's sight! The believer works out what God has already worked in (Phil. 2:12-13). God regards the believer as righteous, and the believer's supreme passion is pleasing and glorifying God. The believer, therefore, begins seeking righteousness above all else (Matt. 6:33). Freely forgiven, the believer learns more and more to forgive others.

As the believer's response the Christian life roots in a living relation between the believer and God in Christ.—The Christian life is a voluntary, personal relationship between God and the believer. It is the most intimate and constant of relationships, marked by love and trust, involving the whole person in every moment and dimension. As the parent seeks the child's wellbeing, God seeks the best for believers, yearning for His children to attain "to the whole measure of the fullness of Christ" (Eph. 4:13, NIV). Yet unlike the parent-child relationship, the relationship of the believer to God is voluntary from beginning to end; it cannot be inherited, bought, or arranged by a third party. It is based on a covenant or mutual agreement that requires a lifetime to fulfill, yet remains fragile and requires constant and careful tending.

As the believer's response the Christian life includes both a beginning and a continuing.—This fact is implicit in the personal nature of the response. An adequate theology of the Christian life must recognize the importance of both initial conversion and a life of growth and discipleship. This characteristic will require fuller discussion later.

As the believer's response the Christian life implies a radical change in life attitude and direction.—The biblical view of the Christian life takes seriously the sinner's need for a new heart and outlook: "Therefore if any

---

2. Frederick Dale Bruner, *A Theology of the Holy Spirit* (Grand Rapids: Eerdmans, 1970), 251.

In addition to "appropriation" and "full," Bruner underscores the misery occasioned by the word "more"! Hunger for more than ordinary Christian experiences often drives Pentecostals to seek the super-second experience of Spirit baptism.

man is in Christ, he is a new creature; the old things passed away; behold, new things have come"(2 Cor. 5:17).[3]

Again and again, the plea of the prophet and the apostle is, "Repent! Turn from your idols and renounce all your detestable practices!" (Ezek. 14:6; see also Acts 2:38-40). Jesus began His ministry by echoing the same call (Matt. 3:2).

Essentially the change called for by Scripture represents a turning from self-centeredness to a submission of the self to Christ as Savior and Lord, but the Bible has a variety of ways to describe such change: it is a love for God rather than mammon (Matt. 6:24); a seeking first of the kingdom of God (Matt. 6:33); a loving of God with all the heart (Matt. 22:37). Yet, however it is described, repentance is a reversal of values (John 18:36). The beatitudes (Matt. 5:3-11) and Jesus' teaching about greatness in the kingdom (Matt. 20:25-28) drive home this truth. There is simply no legitimate way to dilute the biblical call to radical transformation.

As the believer's response the Christian life involves discipline and sacrifice.—Although God's gift of salvation is free, following Christ as Savior and Lord costs the believer everything. Some are even called to lay down their lives. No one is called to think first of comfort. In a world where warfare rages between God and the principalities, Christ summons His followers to deny themselves, take up the cross, and follow Him. Living as Christians in a fallen world involves inescapable conflict and struggle.

Although following Jesus is costly, following self is infinitely more costly. In the presence of the King of kings on the day of judgment, none will complain that service to the Master has been too costly. Rather, each will wish to have served the Lord more devotedly. Christ asks much but He gives even more.

As the believer's response the Christian life is public and corporate as well as private and individual.—Jesus described His followers as the salt of the earth and the light of the world (Matt. 5:13-16). Those who acknowledge Christ in this world will be acknowledged by Christ before the Father in heaven (Matt. 10:32). Believing means confessing openly with the lips what one believes in the heart (Rom. 10:9). The good news is for proclaiming and living, not for hiding!

In New Testament days, wherever there were believers there were churches. The inward, heart-response of believers found outward expression in a public profession of faith in Christ, including believer's baptism and church participation.

---

3. Moore's restatement of the doctrine of the Christian life highlights the biblical stress on newness. He has chapters on new creation, new life in Christ, new warfare, new resources, new fellowship, new citizen, new vocation, and new security. H. Guy Moore, *The Christian Life* (Nashville: Convention Press, 1961).

As the believer's response the Christian life is as varied as individuals are different.—Over against what is perennial in Christian practice to stereotype what it means to be a follower of Christ, the New Testament recognizes the endless diversity in persons and the way they respond to Christ.[4] Some individuals are introverts and others extroverts; some are activists, other meditative; some are thinkers, others are doers; some are emotional, others non-demonstrative; some cry, others smile. Personal responses to God's saving act are never exactly alike. Instead of repudiating this diversity in persons, the Holy Spirit cultivates it. His gifts are richly varied (1 Cor. 12:1-24). Without such diversity, the dynamic, exciting unity of the body of Christ becomes a drab, stifling uniformity.

As the believer's response the Christian life is never fully complete or final in this life.—C. I. Scofield is said to have prayed, "Lord, renew my commission. Do not let me serve under an expired commission." As manna in the wilderness had to be gathered fresh daily (Ex. 16:20), so the believer's commitment to Christ requires continual updating. Paul calls for a living sacrifice (Rom. 12:1), but a student once observed, "The trouble with a living sacrifice is that it keeps crawling off the altar!" Hence the importance of the next section.

The Importance of both Initial Conversion and a Life of Growth and Struggle

Approaches to a theology of the Christian life that compartmentalize justification and sanctification also fail to recognize the interrelatedness of initial conversion and a life of continual Christian growth. Believers recognize that life is in constant flux and that yesterday's answers, however hard-won, are often inadequate for today's new problems. So also, consider the beginning and continuing of the believer's response as well as their interrelation.

The beginning: initial conversion.—In the New Testament the believer's response begins with a definite experience of initial conversion.[5] This is the experience in which the individual, in response to God's redeeming initiative in Jesus Christ, deliberately turns from the former way of life to trust in Christ and to follow Him as Lord and Savior.[6]

---

4. Johnson and Malony discuss conversion and personality types. Cedrick B. Johnson and H. Newton Malony, *Christian Conversion: Biblical and Psychological Perspectives* (Grand Rapids: Zondervan, 1982), especially 61-67.

5. See the remarkable study of David F. Wells, *Turning to God: Biblical Conversion in the Modern World* (Grand Rapids: Baker, 1989), and also Billy Graham, *How to Be Born Again* (Waco, TX: Word, 1977).

6. Acts 16:11–18:11 records the conversions of Lydia, the jailer, the Thessalonians, the Bereans, the Athenians, and the Corinthians. Frederick Dale Bruner styles this a little handbook of initial conversion theology (*A Theology of the Holy Spirit* [Grand Rapids: Eerdmans, 1970] 204-6).

In biblical perspective initial conversion combines inward and outward elements. The convert inwardly repents and believes. Acting on God's gracious offer of forgiveness, those who repent acknowledge their sinfulness, commit themselves to Jesus Christ, and trust the promise that they can become children of God through what Christ has done (John 1:12).

Outwardly converts confess Christ before others. They cannot keep their new-found faith to themselves but seek to share their discovery, not only with other Christians but also with non-Christians. They publicly profess faith in baptism, active church membership, and a life of discipleship and service. Inwardly they feed on God's Word; outwardly their new life-style reflects kingdom priorities.

How important is initial conversion? What is lost if its importance is neglected? A meaningful initial conversion experience is vital in two important respects:

1. Conversion speaks to the need for a *decisive break with the old way of life*. Even a child reared in a Christian home should recognize that life outside of Christ gives the priority to self rather than to Christ; self-centeredness enslaves the individual. In initial conversion the believer repudiates inordinate self-interest, with its implied rebellion against God, even when this rebellion is not expressed dramatically.[7]

2. Conversion speaks to the believer's need for a firm *foundation for continuing struggle and growth*. If the experience of initial conversion is confused and vague, the ongoing life falters. Here, no less than elsewhere, well begun is half done. Nothing worthwhile succeeds on the basis of halfhearted commitment, and Christian growth is no exception. Serious commitment is never a static achievement. It stands in need of continual renewal. Jesus repeatedly warned against neglecting kingdom commitments (Luke 9:62; Matt. 25:30).

Experiences of initial conversion fall into two main types, the dramatic or sudden type and the quiet type. Adult conversions are often dramatic. Childhood conversions are more often quiet. Some believers, especially those converted in childhood, are unable to date exactly when they first trusted Christ as Savior. Yet often they know that God's Spirit has mysteriously worked to lead them to trust in Christ as Savior. They also remember distinctly when they gave public expression to this trust through baptism and church participation. "One thing I do know," said the man

---

7. Carr speaks of the value of early conversion experiences for those reared in Christian homes. He points out the need to interrupt the processes of religious education; if these are not checked by a conversion experience, they tend to produce an incurable self-righteousness. Warren Carr, *Baptism: Conscience and Clue for the Church* (New York: Holt, Rinehart & Winston, 1964), 182.

born blind as antagonistic authorities sought to confound him, "I was blind, now I see" (John 9:25).

The experience of initial conversion should never be thought of as a static, merely past event—as something over and done with once for all. New converts have only a limited insight into the significance of initial conversion.[8] Even the most knowledgeable need a growing understanding of their experience. Only as believers grow in grace do they begin to see what sinners they are and how graciously God pursued them and still pursues them (Rev. 3:20).

Furthermore, believers are never done beginning and beginning again. These new beginnings often involve reliving the initial conversion experience. Christians return to where it all started, much as Jacob returned to Bethel (Gen. 28:16-22; 35:1-2), and these journeys are often among life's most cherished experiences.

The continuing: a life of growth and struggle.—The Bible uses various metaphors for Christian growth: eating, drinking, running, going to school, waiting, putting on armor, fighting a good fight, walking, taking a journey, breathing, seeing, planting, watering, cultivating, harvesting, banking, sweeping, cleaning, washing, building, patiently enduring no matter what. Believers are "no longer to be children, tossed here and there by waves, and carried about by every wind of doctrine" but "we are to grow up in all aspects into Him, who is the head, even Christ" (Eph. 4:14-15). As with other Christian doctrines, the problem of living out the doctrine of the Christian life is not a lack of biblical resources.[9]

The need for growth. Initial conversion, important as it is, is only the beginning of the Christian life. New converts, whether children or adults, are babes in Christ.[10] They must journey far on the road to Christian

---

8. Even in the biological realm, despite the phenomenal gains of modern medicine, few babies are born under the full supervision of an attending physician. Yet the situation with reference to initial conversions is far worse. Initial converts receive competent assistance as they enter the Christian life.

9. Maston discusses eight central New Testament passages dealing with Christian growth: 2 Cor. 5:17-21; Rom. 12:2; Eph. 2:11-22; 4:1-3; 4:11-15; Matt. 16:21-25; Col. 3:1-14; and John 14:26; 16:33. T. B. Maston *Real Life in Christ: Biblical Guidance for Walking the Christian Way* (Nashville: Broadman, 1974).

10. Some approaches to the Christian life and church renewal, such as that of the Church of the Savior, Washington, D.C., make mature discipleship a prerequisite for church membership. These forget that mature discipleship is an endless goal and not a static attainment, so that believers never dare think they have arrived. They also forget that the fellowship of believers is where growth in discipleship occurs most effectively. Discipleship is better caught than taught, better caught voluntarily than required legalistically.

For the Church of the Savior story, see Elizabeth O'Connor, *Call to Commitment: The Story of the Church of the Savior, Washington, D.C.* (New York: Harper & Row, 1963), and *Journey Inward, Journey Outward* (New York: Harper & Row, 1968). The first book covers the first eight years of the chronicle, and the second continues it through 1968.

maturity. To remain in infancy is a spiritual calamity. Yet such stress is sometimes placed on initial conversion that the new Christian fails to realize that becoming a Christian is, like a wedding in relation to a marriage, just the beginning. The Christian life is a lifetime filled with change and growth, not just birth.

Resources for growth. The Holy Spirit does not abandon the spiritual infant. Rather, He takes the initiative richly, though never automatically, providing for the growing believer's needs. The Spirit works primarily through Bible study and church fellowship.[11] The adequacy of such provision means that responsibility for failure in Christian growth rests with believers themselves, not with God.

Foes of growth. The *world* (Luke 16:13), the *flesh* (Gal. 5:19), and the *devil* (1 Pet. 5:8) are powerful and persistent, though God's resources for growth leave nothing needful.[12] The need to overcome opposition explains why the Christian life is a life of conflict and struggle, as Bunyan skillfully describes in *Pilgrim's Progress.* Our enemies are fierce but not so strong as the love of God in Christ.

Stages of growth. Lavonn D. Brown likens spiritual growth to physical, mental, and emotional growth.[13] Spiritual life begins in spiritual infancy and moves through stages similar to childhood, adolescence, young adulthood, and mature adulthood. Along the way there can be crises of faith, reflecting the uncertainties and trials of life. Brown correctly observes that the rate of growth varies from person to person. Believers must discover their proper growth rate. Growth may be either too slow or too fast. There are no shortcuts to Christian maturity, and spiritual growth is never a guaranteed ascent toward perfection. Complete maturity is never achieved in this life. Today's maturity at one point or stage is no guarantee of tomorrow's maturity in a different situation.

---

11. The literature here is vast. For popular studies of spiritual growth of new Christians, see Ernest Gordon and Peter Funk, *Guidebook for the New Christian* (New York: Harper & Row, 1972); Russell T. Hitt, *How Christians Grow* (New York: Oxford, 1979); and John and Karen Howe, *Which Way?* (New York: Morehouse-Barlow, 1973).

12. Failure to overcome such foes produces carnal Christians. Davis uses a diagram to distinguish in a general way between natural humans, carnal Christians, and spiritual Christians. A circle has a door at the top leading to God and a door at the bottom opening to Satan. For the unsaved person, the top door is closed and the bottom door is open. For the spiritual person, the situation is reversed: the top door is open and the bottom door is closed. The carnal Christian is shown as having both doors open.

Earl C. Davis, *Life in the Spirit,* vol. 11, Layman's Library of Christian Doctrine (Nashville: Broadman, 1986), 53-55.

13. Lavonn D. Brown, *The Life of the Church*, vol. 13, Layman's Library of Christian Doctrine (Nashville: Broadman, 1987), 56-60. Also helpful is Bruce P. Powers, *Growing Faith* (Nashville: Broadman, 1982), 11-25. Two studies by W. L. Hendricks reflect the relevance of faith for life's different stages: *A Theology for Children* (Nashville: Broadman, 1980) and *A Theology for Aging* (Nashville: Broadman, 1986).

Christian assurance. Assurance is confidence in God's sovereignty in Christ (Rom. 8:38-39) and the certainty of personal and full acceptance with God through Christ (Rom. 8:15-17).[14] These two aspects can be distinguished but are inseparable in Christian experience. Assurance of acceptance with God in Christ is rooted in the certainty of God's sovereignty and Christ's decisive victory over darkness and evil. Believers have confidence in Christ, not in themselves. Because God's promises find their "yes" in Christ alone (2 Cor. 1:20), believers can say assuredly, "I know" (2 Tim. 1:12; cf. Rom. 8:38-39). Christ makes the difference!

This firm confidence in God and His redemption is neither automatic nor easily applied in daily life. Christian pilgrims often waver from anxious doubt (Matt. 6:25-32) or other reasons. Believers question their salvation when they sin, when they fail to grow, when others disappoint them, when they struggle with pain, or when tragedy strikes.

Still Christian assurance is real, though peace and confidence are won at a great price. Assurance comes as quiet, sturdy trust that enables the child of God to walk by faith and not by sight (2 Cor. 5:7; 12:10).

Perseverance. Saving faith is not merely the faith of a moment! Nor is it something static—a possession believers own once they have exercised it. Faith is a relationship of trust with Christ. Faith is a living and personal reality that continues, as all covenanted relationships continue.

The slogan "once saved, always saved" misses the point.[15] The stress should be on perseverance, not just on security. Security is important! The gospel insists that the Holy Spirit completes what He starts (Phil. 1:16) and that the believer is kept by the power of God (1 Pet. 1:5; cf. John 10:28), but perseverance is also important! It is the nature of faith to persevere. Christian commitment takes a lifetime to fulfill. The trials are many; the race is exhausting. Ponder again, for instance, Paul's catalog of perils (2 Cor. 11:21-23). Saving faith, faith that Christ creates and the Holy Spirit sustains, never quits but voluntarily, gladly, and freely endures.[16]

The goal of the Christian life. Central to the believer's growth is a focus on the goal of the Christian life.[17] Three aspects of the believer's goal in Christ are of particular concern.

---

14. Arthur S. Yates, *The Doctrine of Assurance* (London: Epworth, 1952).

15. Boyd Hunt, "The Perseverance of the Saints," in *Basic Christian Doctrines,* Carl F. H. Henry, ed. (New York: Holt, Rinehart, and Winston, 1962), 234-40.

16. Notice the four "all things" in 1 Cor. 13:7-8.

17. The majestic and comprehensive kingdom dimension of the goal of Christian living is treated in the chapters on the kingdom present and the church.

1. The goal of the Christian life is discipleship, and the content of discipleship is Christlikeness.[18] As the Christian's model, Christ defines for
believers what God intends life to be for those whom He created in
His own image and redeemed from sin through the transforming work
of the Holy Spirit. The first Adam failed, as every human fails—with
one great exception! Jesus Christ, the second Adam (1 Cor. 15:22),
lived out a life of perfect obedience to God's will (Heb. 5:8), imaging
finally and perfectly what it means to be a Christian.

2. The goal of the Christian life is relational and involves every dimension of the believer's existence. Christian living expresses itself, first, in
a right relation to God, second, in a right relation to others, third, in a
right relation to self, and, fourth, in a right relation to material things.
No aspect of life is excluded.

    The believer's relation to *God* involves a life of communion with
    God through worship and prayer and through daily conduct that
    pleases Him. Biblical examples include Enoch, who walked with God
    (Gen. 5:24); David, who was a man after God's own heart (Acts 13:22;
    1 Sam. 13:14); and Paul, who could say, "For to me, to live is Christ"
    (Phil. 1:21). The believer's relation to *others* leads to a life of service
    (Matt. 20:26-28). The relation to *self* goes beyond self-denial to self-
    forgetfulness (Luke 9:23; Ex. 34:29). The relation to *material things*,
    viewed as God's good creation, calls the disciple to a life of responsible
    stewardship (Luke 16:10-13).

---

18. For discussions of discipleship, see James M. Boice, *Christ's Call to Discipleship* (Chicago: Moody, 1986); Walter A. Henrichsen, *Disciples Are Made, Not Born: Making Disciples
out of Christians* (Wheaton, IL: Victor, 1974); T. B. Maston, *Why Live the Christian Life?*
(Nashville: Nelson, 1974); and David Watson, *Called and Committed: World-Changing Discipleship* (Wheaton, IL: Shaw, 1982).

For a carefully planned program of discipleship training through groups, see Avery T.
Willis, Jr., *Master Life: Discipleship Training*, vols. 1 and 2 (Nashville: Baptist Sunday School
Board, 1980). The program focuses on taking up the cross, abiding in Christ, living in the
Word, praying in faith, fellowshipping with believers, witnessing to the world, and ministering
to others. It usually involves a six-month training period in a group meeting two hours weekly.

For a one-on-one program of discipleship training, see Billie Hanks and William Shell,
eds., *Discipleship* (Grand Rapids: Zondervan, 1981).

Spiritual formation became a lively topic in American theological circles during the 1970s.
See Richard J. Foster, *Celebration of Discipline: The Path to Spiritual Growth* (New York:
Harper & Row, 1978); Cheslyn Jones and others, eds., *The Study of Spirituality* (New York:
Oxford, 1989); Bill J. Leonard, ed., *Becoming Christian: Dimensions of Spiritual Formation*
(Louisville: Westminster/John Knox, 1990); Lawrence O. Richards, *A Practical Theology
of Spirituality* (Grand Rapids: Zondervan, 1987).

For a stimulating study relating to both discipleship and spiritual formation, see Richard
F. Lovelace, *Dynamics of Spiritual Life: An Evangelical Theology of Renewal* (Downers
Grove, IL: InterVarsity, 1979).

3. The goal of the Christian life is inexhaustible.[19] Christian faith is practiced but never fully achieved, which means that Christian maturity is never static but remains a dynamic tension between being and becoming.[20] Believers are already children of God by faith in Christ, yet—through persevering faith in Christ—they are ever becoming the children they are meant to be by God's grace.

Growth in Christian character and conduct is never automatic. Yesterday's advances can be forfeited today. Past achievements, however stunning, never mechanically guarantee victories today. Believers are, day by day, different persons with different opportunities, distractions, and needs. They must never lay down their armor, as though the battle with evil were over. Paul's "I press on" should be the cry of every saint (Phil 3:14).

Dealing with the Problem of Nominal Christianity

The formation of fruitful disciples has always been a major challenge to believing communities. Even Paul said, "And I, brethren, could not speak to you as to spiritual men, but as to men of flesh, as to babes in Christ" (1 Cor. 3:1).[21] Persons baptized one year often drop out of church life the next. Others attend worship but fail to grow. Many yearn for something "more" than they have yet found in the Christian life.[22]

Christians searching for a deeper faith are often told they should seek a second experience beyond initial conversion in order to discover the highest and best in the Christian life. Two-stage interpretations of the Christian life teach that there is such a second experience, and that it is associated with a further commitment to Christ after initial conversion. Examples of two-stage views include the following:

---

19. For a classic study of Christian perfection, see R. Newton Flew, *The Idea of Perfection in Christian Theology: An Historical Study of the Christian Ideal for the Present Life* (London: Oxford, 1934). See also R. A. Knox, *Enthusiasm* (London: Oxford, 1950) and W. E. Sangster, *The Path to Perfection* (New York: Abingdon-Cokesbury, 1943).

20. While a list of Christian virtues can be called the marks of Christian maturity, the fact is that growth in the exercise of these virtues, due, for one thing, to their inward, attitudinal nature, is impossible to measure. Anyone who attempts to measure such growth, even the individual, is easily deceived by appearances which mask as well as reveal the inner self.

21. Typical of the extensive post-World War II literature about the need for church renewal is Findley B. Edge, *A Quest for Vitality in Religion* (Nashville: Broadman, 1963).

22. In discussing approaches to personal renewal, Edge mentions the usefulness of retreats and conferences. Noting that not every church member would find such meetings helpful, he advises pastors to exercise care to invite those who are "hurting," that is, those who are "feeling the pains of disillusionment" regarding their experience as church members. Findley B. Edge, *The Greening of the Church* (Waco, TX: Word, 1971), 112.

- *Wesleyan perfectionism*

- *Classical Pentecostal and recent charismatic* teaching of a baptism in the Spirit validated by tongues and healing.

- *R. A. Torrey's baptism in the Spirit,* guaranteed by the taking of seven steps, to qualify believers for effective personal evangelism. According to Torrey, however, tongues, healings, signs, and wonders ceased once the New Testament was available and they no longer authenticate the worldwide Christian mission.

- *The Keswick Conference* emphasis on the deeper life, stressing a crisis experience of consecration as the doorway to a Spirit-filled life.

- *The Campus Crusade,* which publishes two booklets, one about initial conversion, the other about tarrying for a crisis enduement with the Spirit before undertaking Christian service.[23]

Each of these perspectives, despite their differences, emphasize the necessity, in the experience of most believers, of two distinct experiences in chronological succession in order to achieve a victorious life.

Why are two-stage approaches to Christian experience so popular? One reason is that the pilgrimage of many believers fits a two-stage pattern. Few committed believers become active, growing Christians early in their Christian experience. Instead, for a longer or shorter period after initial conversion they remain casual about Christ's claim on their daily lives.

Remember, however, that the New Testament never requires a second experience in order to live victoriously, even though Christian experience often unfolds in two or more stages. There is no sound biblical basis for distinguishing the faith involved in initial conversion from the faith exercised by growing believers.

Notice three observations about two-stage Christianity:

1. *Trust in Jesus Christ as Lord and Savior is the sole condition to Christian experience from first to last.* Just as there is no way to be saved without faith in Christ, there is no way to continue in Christian life without faith in Christ. Faith in Christ is the one, all-embracing condition to Christian experience. Two-stage theologies tend to add some supposedly more demanding condition for power in Christian living. Such theologies correctly recognize that faith should be vital and growing and that yesterday's shape of faith is never adequate for

---

23. For discussions of these views see: Donald L. Alexander, ed., *Christian Spirituality: Five Views of Sanctification* (Downers Grove, IL: InterVarsity, 1988); Melvin E. Dieter, and others, *Five Views on Sanctification* (Grand Rapids: Zondervan, 1987); and J. I. Packer, *Keeping in Step with the Spirit* (Old Tappan, NJ: Revell, 1984).

today's new demands. These theologies, however, shift the emphasis from the need for growing and personal faith to some requirement in addition to faith. Paul is adamant at this point: it is to preach another gospel (Gal. 1:6-9; 3:15). Believers never achieve more of the Holy Spirit in power by adding something to faith in Christ.

2. *There is no one, guaranteed key to a once-for-all victorious Christian life.* All such keys invariably promise non-existent shortcuts to abundant living. Jesus was tempted to the end. How can we expect freedom from temptation? Paul clarified this in his Second Epistle to the Corinthians, a veritable manual of spirituality (see especially 2 Cor. 12:7-10).[24] Although many Christians have crisis experiences after initial conversion, the believer's well-being roots especially in his continuing walk with Christ and the daily renewal of his faith.[25]

3. *The Bible knows no elitist class of Christians.* God has one standard, not a low standard for most Christians and a higher one for a select few. We can readily distinguish between new Christians and more mature Christians, but the New Testament never encourages believers to set themselves up as *the* model for others. "Whoever exalts himself shall be humbled, and whoever humbles himself shall be exalted" (Matt. 23:12).

Again and again in the New Testament, the servant who merits the Lord's highest praise is the humble, ordinary, yet faithful believer. When the disciples asked who was the greatest in God's kingdom, Jesus set a child in their midst and said, "Truly I say to you, unless you are converted and become like children, you shall not enter the kingdom of heaven" (Matt. 18:1-3). According to Donald G. Bloesch, "We must strive to think as mature Christians, but we are called to trust and believe as little children."[26]

---

24. Bruner says: "The understanding of 2 Cor. 10-13 provides, we believe, a final key to the inner sanctum of [the New Testament's most serious confrontation with] spirituality." Frederick Dale Bruner, *A Theology of the Holy Spirit,* 303-19.

25. The key New Testament term is "in Christ" and the essential idea is abiding in Christ. Christ is the vine, we are the branches (John 15:5). The believer's hope is in Christ, not in his own maturity. The saint is still a sinner, but he is a sinner whose trust is that Christ will see him through.
Langford says:

> Holiness, as we have defined it, is not a realized state of being or a condition of affairs; it is, rather, a continuously realized and a continuous challenge to realization of the gracious presence of the Holy Spirit; sanctification becomes a process of maturation in which life undergoes constant reshaping through the primacy of the commanding relationship with God.

Thomas A. Langford, "The Holy Spirit and Sanctification: Refinding the Lost Image of Creation," in *The Holy Spirit,* ed. Dow Kirkpatrick (Nashville: Tidings, 1974), 204.

26. Donald G. Bloesch, *The Christian Life and Salvation* (Grand Rapids: Eerdmans, 1967), 140.

In conclusion, the stress in this chapter has been on living the Christian life, not as a new legalism, but as the free, spontaneous, welling up from within, as a spring of water, of God's all-gracious initiative in Christ (John 4:14). As the Spirit energizes the believers life through the Word, the miracle is that he becomes in experience what he already is in Christ.[27] The entire process is morally and spiritually conditioned throughout.

The God revealed in Christ and the Holy Spirit stands at the door and knocks. His posture is a sign of strength, for only the Almighty can deal so gently! Only cross-centered patience can beget in the life of believers the priceless fruit of the Spirit (Gal. 5:22-23) so essential to furthering God's kingdom in history.

---

27. Trees produce fruit because forces work silently and secretly from within. As the waving of the branches in the wind has no direct bearing on productivity, so the fruit of the Spirit in the believer's life results first from the Spirit's energizing, not from the believer's religious activity.

PART IV

The Church:

THE CORPORATE DIMENSION
OF GOD'S PURPOSE

*The Christian life has both an individual
and a corporate dimension. As the corporate dimension of God's purpose, the
church witnesses to Christ, furthering
the great purposes of the kingdom of
God until Christ returns in the ultimate
triumph of God in history.*

12 The Sign and Agent of the Kingdom Present

As God's people on earth, the church lives in dynamic tension. This includes tension between the human aspects of the church and its divinely charged role as sign and agent of the kingdom. The church also experiences the tension between its general aspect as the people of God and its particular reality in gathered churches of believers.

Discussions of the church have been very much alive in the twentieth century, due first to the influence of the ecumenical movement, and, then, following World War II, as a result of the multi-faceted church renewal movement. Despite the voluminous literature on the subject, there is still no consensus. While change, innovation, and experimentation are more the rule than the exception, diligent effort to rethink biblical teaching about people of God is important.

The Church as the Corporate Dimension of Christian Experience

Christian experience is a combination of *individual* and *corporate* aspects. While the doctrine of the Christian life deals with individual aspects, the doctrine of the church treats the corporate aspects.[1] Just as human life itself is inescapably corporate as well as individual, so it is with Christian experience, but in an even profounder sense.[2]

Scripture is emphatic in teaching that God pursues His redemptive purposes by working through groups as well as through individuals.[3] Easter and Pentecost abundantly testify that the risen Christ appeared to *gathered* disciples, to whom He gave the Great Commission, and on whom He poured His Spirit in a new fullness. Passages such as Paul's commendation of the generosity of the churches of Macedonia (2 Cor. 8:1-3) and Jesus' pronouncement of God's rejection of rebellious Israel (Matt. 21:43) indicate that God rewards faithfulness and condemns fail-

---

1. In evangelical theology the individual facet of redemption takes a certain logical priority over the corporate aspect, since the individual's personal relation to God in Christ is the foundation of Christian experience and is logically prior to church membership. Hence, in evangelical studies of Christian doctrine, the chapter on the Christian life typically precedes the chapter on the church. On the other hand, in traditions which practice infant baptism the church is usually discussed first. The one approach regards the church as the fellowship of believers, the other as the realm of redemption. See, for example, Ernest A. Payne, *The Fellowship of Believers* (London: Carey Kingsgate, 1952), and J. Robert Nelson, *The Realm of Redemption* (London: Epworth, 1951).

2. First, regarding the corporate nature of human existence in general, see the earlier discussion of human nature. The Genesis account of creation makes it clear that humanity was created for relationship, not only with God, but also with fellow human beings: "Male and female He created them. And God blessed them; and God said to them, 'Be fruitful and multiply'" (Gen. 1:27-28). Later, Gen. 4 stresses that Cain cannot escape responsibility as his brother's keeper. In the biblical perspective, then, society and its institutions are originally God's creations, intended for humanity's well-being, but now corrupted by the fall and the entrance of sin.

Second, regarding the corporate aspect of the Christian life, see the chapter on the Christian life and the references to Christian experience as both individual and corporate. In a manner which is yet to be understood more adequately, becoming a Christian and vital local church membership go together.

3. In recognition of the corporate aspect of God's redemptive activity, Dominy says:

When we become Christians, we become part of a fellowship composed of other Christians. . . . We enter into the community of faith–the church.

Unfortunately, the communal aspect of salvation is not always appreciated. The church is not always thought to be essential to God's saving activity. Some people have been enthusiastic in praising Christianity and vehement in denouncing the church. It is not uncommon to hear such statements as "I love Jesus but I don't care for the church" or "I can be a better Christian without the church." Some have espoused a "churchless" Christianity.

Bert Dominy, *God's Work of Salvation*, vol. 8, Layman's Library of Christian Doctrine (Nashville: Broadman, 1986), 142-43.

Carmen Conner says:

We need a new word in our vocabulary–*peoplehood*. We have long used brotherhood, childhood, statehood, and other *hood* words. We are just learning to use *personhood*, but it is not enough. We also need *peoplehood* to show that God is glorified both in the individual person and in the community, the people of God.

Carmen Conner, "Christian World View," *The Baptist Program,* April 1989, 15.

To appreciate more adequately how basic the corporate aspect of God's saving activity is, remember that even when God works through individuals, He is working through them as social entities, persons who have been nurtured in and are a part of some community.

ure, not only of individuals but also of groups. To belittle corporate experience is to operate with a less than biblical concept of the nature of God's work in human life.

The corporate dimension of Christian experience demands careful consideration, for a sure way to make shipwreck of the Christian life is to neglect the assembling of believers. United with Christ, believers are united with others who are in Christ. Loving Christ, they spontaneously seek fellowship with others of kindred spirit. Following Christ in discipleship, they discover their wider citizenship in God's far-reaching redemptive kingdom. Thus, the New Testament leaves no room in practice for solitary Christians. The New Testament only uses the word *saint* in the plural. Believers come to realize what Christ has for them only through fellowship with other Christians.

The New Testament speaks of corporate Christian experience in various ways. The Greek word commonly translated "church," means literally an "assembly" or a "gathering." Central New Testament concepts such as "messiah" and "kingdom" inevitably imply the existence of a community of Christ's followers. A messiah without a people is no more a messiah than a kingdom without subjects is a kingdom. Believers without a church are as much a contradiction as citizens without a state.

The most vivid biblical image for the corporateness of God's people is the *body of Christ.* Churches, as well as the church, are a unity of many members in one body with Christ as the head. To deny the body is to deny the head! The "new man in Christ" is never a merely solitary believer. Instead, through Christ, God is creating a new kingdom, a new humanity, a new society, a new race, and, ultimately, a new Jerusalem, new heavens and a new earth.

These expressions show that corporateness in its biblical context is an exceedingly rich concept. This means that the doctrine of the church is a many-dimensioned teaching.

The Main Idea and the Many Facets
of the Biblical Church Idea

The Main Idea

Most New Testament references to the church are to a local church or local churches, and theologians often define the church in local terms. *The Baptist Faith and Message*, for instance, begins as follows: "A New Testament church of the Lord Jesus Christ is a local body of baptized believers . . ." (Art. VI, The Church). Fortunately, the 1963 revision of the statement adds the following sentence at the close of Art. VI: "The New Testament speaks also of the church as the body of Christ which includes all of the redeemed of all ages." The word *church*, then, is used in varied ways in the New Testament.

The main idea of the church is this: *the people of God, redeemed or called out for a special purpose.* The focus is on a living reality, not on a building, an organization, or a place. Through the proclamation of the gospel of Jesus Christ, God is calling out a new covenant people to further His redemptive purposes throughout the world (1 Pet. 2:9-10). Minear identified Ninety-Six New Testament images for the people of God. Two of the more important images are *body of Christ* and *fellowship of the Spirit.*[4]

Many Facets Embracing Dynamic Polarities

Although the main idea of the church is the new people of God called out for a special purpose, this concept has many facets.[5] Some of these facets form pairs or *dynamic polarities.* These polarities look like opposites but stand in creative tension with one another: the church is both divine and human; the church is both general and particular. Each pole is essential to the idea. Their interrelation is not a matter of either-or but of both-and.

Both divine and human.—The church is both divine and human, a spiritual fellowship created by God's Spirit, yet an organization made up of redeemed but imperfect humans. The church has mysterious powers of renewal, for its apparently dead bones keep coming back to life! Still, the church is sadly predictable–marred by factions and lacking commitment to its Lord.

Since the divine aspect of the church defies sociological analysis and explanation, non-Christians often see the church as only another flawed organization. Yet the outward form is not the whole truth about the church. The natural eyes see only the outward form, a form that often disguises more than it reveals of the church's essence as God's creation. In the interim between the first and the second comings of Christ, the source of the church's remarkable vitality remains partially hidden with Christ in God (Col. 3:4).

A biblical view of the church, then, focalizes the divine aspect. The church is more a spiritual fellowship than an institution, more a divinely created community transcending racial and cultural barriers than an association of like-minded people who remain culture bound.

This distinction between the divine and human aspects of the church helps us to fathom something of the mystery of the church. The distinction

---

4. See the section on terminology in the discussion of the biblical resources for the nature and purpose of the church.

5. The comments which follow anticipate the listing of multiple *key emphases* in the restatement of the doctrine of the church's nature and purpose. The number of items in the list indicates that the church is many things!

helps explain why some observers remain hopeful for the church's future while others despair. Those who view the church primarily as a human phenomenon speak of the church's waning influence in today's society.[6]

Before one despairs too quickly, however, it is informative to compare the pessimism of the 1960s about the future of the church with more recent optimism.[7] While theologians in the 1960s were giving up on the congregation, regarding it as an outmoded form of religious experience, more recent studies often picture local congregations as the most pervasive and powerful church organizations in the world.[8] While the church's situation in history often seems precarious, the church is still *God's*

---

6. Zikmund says:

> Christians must stop fooling themselves and admit that the church is marginal. In the late twentieth century ... the Christian church is not at the center of the world [as it is often said to have been, for instance, in medieval society], it is on the edges.

See Barbara Brown Zikmund, *Discovering the Church* (Philadelphia: Westminster, 1983), 101. Zikmund, however, is not ready to abandon the church. Her analysis of the church's role in society today has many keen insights.

Schwarz says:

Many pastors and priests are becoming increasingly uncertain of their role in relation to the members of the congregations they serve. Apart from Sunday morning they have no regular working hours like most people in other professions and they also do not seem to have clearly defined occupational tasks as do medical doctors or fire fighters. So more and more pastors and priests are resigning to do something "worthwhile."

Hans Schwarz, *The Christian Church* (Minneapolis: Augsburg, 1982), 15. Schwarz contends that in such a situation it is more urgent than ever to *rediscover* the origin and purpose of the church.

Evidence for the claim that the church's role in society is diminishing is often found in the numerical decline in the membership statistics of mainline denominations in America in recent years. For discussions of such decline, see: Richard J. Coleman, *Issues of Theological Conflict* (Grand Rapids: Eerdmans, 1980); Richard G. Hutcheson, Jr., *Mainline Churches and the Evangelicals (Atlanta: Knox, 1981); and Dean M. Kelley, Why Conservative Churches Are Growing* (San Francisco: Harper, 1972).

It is interesting to relate the dismal outlook for the church's future on the part of some ecumenical writers today with the pessimistic view of the spiritual vitality of established denominations on the part of older dispensationalists. Ryrie says: "If one were to search for a single term to describe the future of the organized church, the best term would be 'apostasy.'" See Charles C. Ryrie, *The Final Countdown* (Wheaton, IL: Victor, 1983), 69. A less bleak outlook on the church is common in more recent dispensational writing.

7. Guthrie's chapter on the church takes as its point of departure the widespread criticism of the church which marked the outlook of the 1960s. Shirley C. Guthrie, Jr., *Christian Doctrine* (Atlanta: Knox, 1977), 350-75.

Note also the dismal title of Hinson's book. E. Glenn Hinson, *The Church: Design for Survival* (Nashville: Broadman, 1967).

For an indication of an increased evangelical optimism in the 1980s, see John Jefferson Davis, *Christ's Victorious Kingdom: Postmillennialism Reconsidered* (Grand Rapids: Baker, 1986), especially 11. Davis believes that the church will enjoy a "millennium" of vitality and expansion before Christ returns.

8. For instance, the 1980 study conducted by the Rollins Center for Church Ministries, Candler School of Theology, Emory University, Atlanta, asserts the durability of the local congregation and its remarkable ability to survive social and cultural upheavals.

church, gifted through the Holy Spirit with unusual power for renewal and destined for eternal glory.

The distinction between the human and divine aspects of the church shows that the church as a human organization is a mixed body, embracing unbelievers as well as believers. The New Testament makes it clear that it is possible for unbelievers to have their names on a church roll (Matt. 7:21-23; 2 Cor. 13:5; 1 John 2:19). At stake here is the vital truth that it is faith in Christ that saves, not church membership by itself.

The distinction between the human and divine aspects of the church emphasizes that no outward organization can ever be identified immediately with the one church of God. Only God knows the limits of the church as a spiritual reality. Ecumenical programs of church union are not to be confused with the unity of the church as God's people and God's creation. Denominational mergers will not necessarily produce a purer church, nor will dismissing denominational differences as unimportant necessarily unify all believers.

In conclusion, while it is important to recognize that the church is both divine and human, the problem of finding a balance between the two aspects remains. One pole of the tension is often emphasized to the neglect of the other. Activists rush about as though there were no Holy Spirit and everything depended on them. Others, however, so concentrate on the church as a spiritual organism that no significant room is left for the important role of good organization.

Statements such as the following by Bloesch, for instance, do more to confuse than to clarify the indispensability of both the divine and the human aspects of the church:

> Jesus Christ does not need our aid in the completion of his mission. He does not really need the church. . . . We can be instruments of his grace, but he may choose to use other instruments, or he may bestow grace directly.[9]

Over against such imbalance, an emphasis on each of the divine and human aspects is essential. In truth, the Holy Spirit creates the spiritual fellowship which is the church. Yet, in doing so, He chooses to work through the responses of imperfect believers.

---

9. Donald G. Bloesch, *Crumbling Foundations* (Grand Rapids: Eerdmans, 1984), 126. If God bestowed His grace directly, apart from any human instrumentality, as Bloesch seems to allege, there should be records of pagans openly confessing Christ as Savior wholly apart from any influence from other persons, which would also mean wholly apart from the Bible. If such documentation exists, it has been kept remarkably secret.

Conner has a discerning discussion of the two extremes, one of stressing humankind's sufficiency without God, and the other of expecting God to do everything apart from any effort on the part of persons. W. T. Conner, *The Work of the Holy Spirit* (Nashville: Broadman, 1978), 163-76.

Both general and particular.—Not only is the church both divine and human, it is both *general* and *particular.*[10] Sometimes the New Testament emphasizes the people of God in a general sense–all of the people of God of all ages (Matt. 16:18; 1 Cor. 15:9; Eph. 5:25) or the unassembled people of God of a particular time and place (Acts 8:1; 9:31). Ordinarily the New Testament speaks of a specific congregation or specific congregations, assembled or unassembled (Rom. 16:16; 1 Cor. 1:2; 11:16; 2 Thess. 1:4).

Here again, the church is always both general and particular. Although the distinction is clear, it in no way implies separation or antithesis. Instead, the general and particular aspects of the church are inseparable.

The local church is always the full representative in a particular place of the general church, yet the general church is a vague and meaningless abstraction apart from its expression in actual congregations. Milne says:

> The relation between a local company of Christians and the whole of God's people is subtle and has no human parallel, for the local group is not simply one relatively incomplete part of the greater whole. The New Testament teaches rather that the local church, while indissolubly united to the whole people of God, is nonetheless a complete church. All the promises of God obtain for it, and Christ, the head and lord of the church, is as fully present there as in any extended entity (Matt. 18:20).[11]

In the language of the last book of the New Testament, even the least congregation is fashioned by God's Spirit to serve as a golden lampstand in a sindarkened world (Rev. 1:20; cf. Matt. 5:14). Packer says: "Each particular gathering, however small, is the local manifestation of the church universal, embodying and displaying the spiritual realities of the church's supernatural life."[12]

Milne and others, then, miss the biblical idea of the general church when they say that the general use occurs only occasionally in the New Testament.[13] Such an emphasis fails to recognize that both the local and

---

10. In the past some Baptists have feared that acceptance of the general idea of the church opened the door for an undermining of their insistence on a local church polity over against papal, episcopal, and connectional church polities. Yet the general idea of the church as here defended loses its biblical meaning when it is made the basis of some conception of church *polity* which compromises in any way a local church polity.

11. Bruce Milne, *Know the Truth* (Downers Grove, IL: InterVarsity, 1982), 211.

12. J. I. Packer, "The Nature of the Church," in *Basic Christian Doctrines,* ed. Carl F. H. Henry (New York: Holt, Rinehart and Winston, 1962), 246.

For the necessary qualification of "manifestation," see P. T. O'Brien, "The Church as a Heavenly and Eschatological Entity," *The Church in the Bible and the World,* ed. D. A. Carson (Grand Rapids: Baker, 1987), 116.

13. Milne, *Know the Truth,* 211.

For another example of the failure to see the close relation between the general and particular meanings of the church, see the discussion of the "uses of *ecclesia* approach" to a study of the New Testament materials regarding the nature and purpose of the church.

general meanings are implied in every New Testament reference to the church, even when one or the other of the ideas is uppermost.

The Prominence of the Church Theme in Contemporary Theological Discussion

The staggering volume of post-World War II literature related to the doctrine of the church reflects the prominence of the doctrine in recent theological discussion.[14] The immense literature covers such a wide range of issues that it is not only impressive but also bewildering. The relevance and scope of these topics speaks eloquently of the vital importance of the doctrine of the church.

Ecclesiological Studies Since World War II

• Biblical images of the church	• Ministerial burnout
• The nature of the church	• Termination of ministers
• The church as divine	• Leadership
• The church as human	• Lay leaders
• The church and eschatology	• Women in ministry
• The church and the kingdom of God	• Christian education
• The mission of the church	• Spiritual formation
• The functions of the church	• Discipleship
• Worship	• Discipline
• The ordinances	• Small groups
• Church membership	• The church and the world
• Spiritual gifts	• Evangelism

---

14. Macquarrie says: "Probably more gets written on the Church nowadays than [on] any other single theological theme." John Macquarrie, *Principles of Christian Theology*, 2d ed. (New York: Scribners, 1977), 386. Much of the current interest stems from ecumenical and church renewal concerns.

Ecclesiological Studies Since World War II (Continued)

• Church renewal	• World missions
• Liturgical renewal	• Church growth
• The church calendar	• Culture Christianity
• The ministry	• Social action
• Ordination	• The church and ethics
• The pastor's office and role	• Church and state
• Religious liberty	• Third-World Christianity
• The church and revolution	• The form of the church
• Denominations	• The ecumenical movement
• The local church	• Stewardship
• The large church	• The small church
• The church in the inner city	• The church and the city
• Long-range planning	• The church and television
• Church architecture	• Historical studies

The next chapters consider (1) the nature and purpose of the church and (2) the form of the church. The nature and purpose of the church are fundamental since they shape the church's structure. Church forms, therefore, are to be tested by their effectiveness in fulfilling the church's nature and purpose. Apart from good organization, the church can never expect to fulfill its high calling in Christ Jesus.

13 The Nature and Purpose of the Church

The church, as the body of Christ united in the fellowship of the Spirit, is God's people on earth. The church already recognizes the lordship of Christ through worship, nurture, evangelism, and service; but universal recognition of His lordship awaits the triumph of God's kingdom at the return of Christ.

In the discussion which follows attention will first be given to the biblical resources for a study of the church's nature and purpose, then to an historical perspective, and especially to a restating of the doctrine of the church's nature and purpose.

179

Biblical Resources

Two aspects of the biblical teaching about the church require mention: the gradual unfolding of the church idea in the Bible and biblical language for the church.

The Gradual Unfolding of the Church Idea

Since most New Testament uses of the term church occur in Acts and the Epistles, that is, in the part of the record dealing with the event of Pentecost and following events, questions immediately arise concerning the relation of the church idea to the Old Testament and to the teaching of Jesus in the Gospels.

The New Testament idea of the church is rooted in the Old Testament. The Old Testament teaches that Israel is God's people, chosen not only to privilege but also to mission. Yet this important Old Testament teaching is incomplete. The New Testament concept of the people of God transcends the ethnic, political, and cultural limitations of the Old Testament idea of the people of God.

A new and revolutionary concept of the people of God broke into history with the coming of Jesus. Yet, since Jesus seldom used the specific term *church (ecclesia)*, some have questioned whether the church was even in His intention.[1] Although *ecclesia* is used only three times in the Synoptic Gospels (Matt. 16:18; 18:17 [twice]) and not at all in John, the *idea* of the church is everywhere in Jesus' teaching. Consider these factors:

- association of Christ's coming with the coming of the kingdom, implying a kingdom people, a people of the new covenant, the people of God of the last days;

- His calling and training of disciples;

- His sending out the disciples on kingdom mission;

- His establishing baptism and the Lord's Supper;

- His promising the Holy Spirit to guide His followers in their worship and mission;

---

1. For a discussion of the issue and the case for insisting that the church was in Jesus' intention, see R. Newton Flew, *Jesus and His Church,* 2d ed. (London: Epworth, 1943).
   More recently Clowney says:
   > It was once the habit of critics to question the authenticity of Matthew's report [of Jesus' use of *ecclesia* in Matt. 16:18]. Jesus spoke of the kingdom, and knew nothing of the church, they said. Since the discovery of the Dead Sea Scrolls there has been a belated acceptance of the genuineness of the saying.

   Edmund P. Clowney, "The Biblical Doctrine of the Church," in *The Church in the Bible and the World*, ed. D. A. Carson (Grand Rapids: Baker, 1987), 16.

• His charging His community with the Great Commission after His resurrection.

Although Jesus undoubtedly founded the church, it is impossible to say exactly *when* He did so. Everything indicates that His disciples began to understand Jesus' intention for the church only after the resurrection and Pentecost.

Yet, even then, early Christians persisted for a time in their Jewishness. As late as the Jerusalem council (Acts 15), or roughly A.D. 49, Christians were still debating the necessity of circumcision for Gentile converts. Not until the ministry of Paul did the separation between Judaism and Christianity, together with a recognition of the identity of the church as the new covenant people of the last days, begin to take more definite shape.

Terminology

Ekklesia and its translation.—The Authorized Version translates this Greek term "church." It is the most common New Testament term in reference to the corporate aspects of the experiences of believers. Our ecclesiology (the doctrine of the church) is derived from *ekklesia*. Nevertheless, this word raises questions. Is *church* an adequate translation of *ekklesia*? Is a study of this word an adequate way to discover the meaning of the church in the New Testament?

An answer to the question of the adequacy of "church" as a translation of *ekklesia* requires a review of the etymology of the two terms. *Ekklesia*, to begin with, comes from two Greek words, one meaning "to call" and the other meaning "out." It thus refers to *an assembly* of called out or summoned people.

In both secular Greek literature and the Septuagint (the early Greek translation of the Hebrew Old Testament), *ekklesia* has this meaning of an *assembly* of summoned persons. Ancient Greeks used the term in a nonreligious sense to designate an assembly of the citizens of a Greek city-state. A herald or town clerk summoned the citizens to carry on the business of the state. This non-religious use is found even in the New Testament. When Luke describes a pagan riot in Ephesus occasioned by the adverse economic effects of Paul's preaching on the idol-making trade, he used *ekklesia* to describe the unauthorized assembly of the rioters (Acts 19:32, 39, 41).

The Septuagint used *ekklesia* to refer to *an assembly of God's people*– either corporate Israel unassembled or an assembly of Israelites. Numbers 10:1-7 exemplifies both of these uses. Of course, the theological connotation (that is, Israel as God's people) is derived from the context in which the term is used, not from the term itself. Even though *ekklesia* clearly means assembly, the King James Version translates it church—a highly ambiguous term.

The etymology of the English word *church* can be traced to a derivative of the secular Greek word *kyrios*. A *kyrios* in Ancient Greece was a ruler, but the New Testament applied the word to Jesus Christ as Lord.

A derivative of *kyrios* is *kyriakon*, a term used to refer to something as "belonging to a lord." In the Christian era, after church buildings had come into use, *kuriakon* was employed to refer to the buildings in which Christians assembled for their meetings.

By using the term "church" to translate *ekklesia*, then, the King James' translators tended to shift the emphasis from the people of God either to the building in which the people gathered or to the organization they formed. The translators may have avoided translating *ekklesia* as *assembly*, fearing that they would open the door to legitimizing the Separatist and Baptist assemblies of that day as regular New Testament *ekklesiae* (plural). The Anglican translators were unwilling to take this step, for they believed that a bishop in apostolic succession was necessary to an *ekklesia*.

The uses of ekklesia approach to New Testament ecclesiology.— Another question is whether a word study of *ekklesia*—popular among the free churches—is an adequate approach to New Testament ecclesiology? This approach assumes that studying New Testament uses of *ekklesia* is the best way to determine what the New Testament means by "church."[2] This seems reasonable, for *ekklesia* is the most common term in New Testament references to Christians as a group and the term is translated "church" in the Authorized Version.

After surveying some 114 instances of the use of *ekklesia* in the New Testament, the uses of *ekklesia* approach conclude that ninety-three refer to the local idea of the church, while only twelve refer to the church in a general sense.[3]

At this point, however, the approach begins to go awry. Instead of recognizing that the local and general ideas are strictly complementary, it pits one against another, as though an emphasis on the local use required

---

2. For the uses of *ecclesia* approach, see B. H. Carroll, *Ecclesia—The Church* (Louisville, KY: Baptist Book Concern, 1909); W. T. Conner, *The Gospel of Redemption* (Nashville: Broadman, 1945), 268-70; and H. E. Dana, *A Manual of Ecclesiology*, 2d ed. (Kansas City, KS: Central Seminary Press, 1944), 33-69.

The present discussion refers primarily to H. E. Dana.

3. Dana's twelve references for the general idea of the church are: 1 Cor. 12:28; Col. 1:18,24; Eph. 1:22; 3:10,21; 5:23,24,25,27,29,32. *A Manual of Ecclesiology*, 67.

In addition to the local and general meanings of *ecclesia* in the New Testament, Dana also speaks of two other uses: six times it is used in its classical Greek meaning of "assembly" (Acts 7:38; 19:32,39,41; Heb. 2:12; 12:23), and three times in a generic sense (Matt. 16:18; 18:17 [bis]). Ibid.

downgrading, if not a completely denying, of the general use. This approach relegates general references to the church in the New Testament to a future, heavenly reality, or views them as late, vague, and relatively insignificant "spiritual" uses of the term.

Dana, for instance, whose version of the uses of the *ekklesia* approach is especially in view here, refers to the relation of the local and general church ideas as follows:

> The conception presented in Colossians and Ephesians of the church as a universal, spiritual body is practically coextensive and identical with the kingdom, but the prevailing New Testament sense, that of the local church, presents an idea quite distinct from, but definitely related to, the conception of the kingdom.[4]

As a Baptist, Dana wanted to reject any attempt to use the general church idea as the basis for a connectional theory of church *polity*, that is, to subordinate local churches to denominational control.

Unfortunately, New Testament references to the church in a general sense have often been interpreted in order to legitimize connectional or centralized church polities. When Paul referred to the church in a general sense, however, he said nothing about connectional church polity; rather he emphasized Christ's headship over His people. The *nature* of the church as Christ's body is one thing; connectional church *polity* is something else. In its biblical context the general idea of the church has everything to do with the subjection of the whole people of God to the lordship of Christ; it has nothing to do with centralized church polity that subjugates local churches to denominational authorities.

Ekklesia is indeed an important term for the study of the New Testament teaching about the church. As Hort says:

> *Ekklesia* is the only perfectly colourless word within our reach, carrying us back to the beginnings of Christian history, and enabling us in some degree to get behind words and names to the simple facts which they originally denoted.[5]

Furthermore, the *ekklesia* approach accurately concludes that the local congregation is the decisive grouping of God's people for their pursuit of

---

4. Ibid., 66-69.
Dana is influenced by the suggestion that "church" and "kingdom" are "to the ordinary mind notions directly and irreconcilably antithetic," that is, that they are as opposite as monarchy and democracy. In New Testament thinking, however, "church" and "kingdom of God" are not understood according "to the ordinary mind." Rather they are primarily theological, not political, realities, and derive their meaning from the way in which they are used by the biblical writers.

5. F. J. A. Hort, *The Christian Ecclesia* (London: Macmillan, 1897), 2.

their God-given mission in the world in the era between Christ's two advents.

Yet, important as *ekklesia* is, the term by itself is theologically neutral. As Hort says, it is a "perfectly colourless" word. Even the New Testament can use the term to refer to the rioting mob of pagan citizens in Ephesus (Acts 19:32,39,41).

The New Testament *context* gives *ekklesia* a *theological* significance. For this reason, the phrases and modifiers used with *ekklesia* are all-important to understand its Christian and theological associations. When the New Testament modifies *ekklesia* with the phrase "of God" (*tou theou*), the resulting expression takes on new and significant Christian content. The church, let it be said again and again, is *God's* assembly!

Other key New Testament terms.—An even graver weakness of the *ekklesia* approach is that preoccupation with the term *ekklesia* undervalues other New Testament church-related terms that are also essential to understanding the people of God. Three other New Testament images for the church are significant:

- The people of God (1 Pet. 2:9-10);

- The body of Christ (whether referring to the local church, as in 1 Cor. 12:27, or to the church in general, as in Eph. 1:22-23; 5:25);

- The fellowship (*koinonia*) of the Holy Spirit (2 Cor. 13:14).[6]

The church as the *people of God* is God's creation. God called the church to be His people of the new covenant, even as He called Abraham and Israel.

The church as the *body of Christ* is an organism, not merely an organization. The body has many members with diverse spiritual gifts, yet in Christ it is one. Under Christ, the head of the body, each member and each gift are eternally important.

The church as a *fellowship of the Holy Spirit* is a reminder that the church's life and power are not in herself but in the Spirit of God. Fur-

---

6. See Paul S. Minear, *Images of the Church in the New Testament* (Philadelphia: Westminster, 1960), for his discussion of Ninety-six biblical images for the church.

See also *The Interpreter's Dictionary of the Bible* (1962), s.v. "Church, Idea of," by Paul S. Minear, for a later overview of Minear's approach.

A brief, insightful reference to the three images is provided in Bert Dominy, *God's Work of Salvation,* vol. 8, Layman's Library of Christian Doctrine (Nashville: Broadman, 1986), 144-47.

thermore, since the Spirit is never "possessed," the image emphasizes that the church stands ever in need of constant renewal.[7]

Historical Perspective

From post-New Testament times until the rise of the Anabaptist-Baptist wing of the Reformation, sometimes called the Radical Reformation, the church moved toward a clergy-centered, sacramental, connectional, and institutional understanding of itself. Ideas of infant baptism and of bishops, not as local church pastors but as officers who stood in succession from the apostles, began to take shape almost at once after the New Testament period. The notion of the union of church and state soon followed.

Although pre-Reformation church history witnessed important forerunners of the Anabaptist and Baptist movements, their theological emphases took a more permanent form only in Reformation times. The more radical wing of the Protestant Reformation viewed the church as taking shape in congregations regarded as spiritual fellowships of baptized and disciplined believers, gathering for worship and nurture and scattering for witness and service.

The New Testament understanding of the church has had new challengers in modern times. Theological liberalism during the late nineteenth and early twentieth centuries neglected the doctrine of the church. Hordern observes:

Liberals in general had little concept of the Church. To many liberals the churches were simply social organizations of men gathered together because of a common religious and ethical concern. The necessity of the Church was purely practical: men are able to do more when organized than as individuals alone.[8]

---

7. In his well-known study of the nature of the church, LesslieNewbigin links the church as the people of God with the Protestant view of the church, the church as the body of Christ with the Catholic view, and the church as the community of the Holy Spirit with the Pentecostal view. Newbigin argues that when any one of the three images is over-emphasized, its essential biblical meaning is distorted. Each of the images is indispensable to the church's full reality. Lesslie Newbigin, *The Household of God* (New York: Friendship Press, 1954).

Unfortunately, Newbigin's reference to the community of the Spirit image as the Pentecostal view of the church has been taken by Bruner and others as a reference to the twentieth-century Pentecostal movement, while Newbigin appears to have been thinking primarily of "Pentecostal" in a broader sense. Frederick Dale Bruner, *A Theology of the Holy Spirit* (Grand Rapids: Eerdmans, 1970), 31-32.

8. William E. Hordern, *A Layman's Guide to Protestant Theology,* rev. ed. (New York: Macmillan, 1968), 109.

Renewed interest in the doctrine of the church, especially since World War II, is, in part, an intentional corrective to liberal neglect.[9]

Restatement

The Classical and Protestant Approach: The Marks of the Church

Discussions of the nature of the church often revolve around the four classical marks of the church according to the Nicene Creed: the church is holy, one, catholic, and apostolic.[10]

As holy, the church is God's creation, not humanity's. As one, the church represents the one people of God through the ages, the redeemed of the new covenant, in continuity with the redeemed of the old covenant. As catholic, or world-wide, the church knows no racial, national, or cultural boundaries. It embraces converts from every culture—red, yellow, black, brown, white. As apostolic, the church is built on the foundation of New Testament, apostolic authority and is sent into all the world on redemptive mission from God.

Until the Reformation these four marks were interpreted in terms of a clerical, sacramental, church-state, catholic institutionalism. Luther and Calvin re-interpreted the marks and added two distinctively Protestant marks: pure preaching of the Word of God and correct administration of baptism and the Lord's Supper. Guthrie, a Presbyterian, faults this Protestant revision. He bases his complaint on the ground that it does not take seriously the church as mission. He says:

> This classical description of the true church says nothing about the church's having a *task* or *mission* to fulfill.... A too exclusive emphasis on these marks of the church has resulted in the idea that the main function of the church is to care for itself and tend to the needs of its own members.[11]

The four classical and the two Protestant marks of the church fail to define the church as the people of God of the new covenant, that is, in terms of the congregation. Instead, as understood in their historical context, they are associated with the traditional, institutional view of the church.

---

9. The broader story of the recent recovery of the doctrine of the church is inseparable from the history of the ecumenical movement. For an excellent introduction to the shifting theological emphases of the movement, see Lesslie Newbigin, *Sign of the Kingdom* (Grand Rapids: Eerdmans, 1980), especially 1-19.

10. Guthrie's discussion is typical. Shirley C. Guthrie, *Christian Doctrine*, (Atlanta: Knox, 1977), 350-73.

11. Guthrie, *Christian Doctrine*, 364-65.

A Common Baptist Approach: Baptist Distinctives

Especially significant for restating the doctrine of the church from a Baptist perspective is a listing of Baptist distinctives or principles. E. Y. Mullins's *Axioms of Religion* is perhaps the best-known discussion of Baptist principles.[12] He treats six axioms:

- *The theological axiom*—the holy and righteous God has the right to be sovereign;

- *The religious axiom*—all persons have an equal right to direct access to God;

- *The ecclesiastical axiom*—all believers have a right to equal privileges in the church;

- *The moral axiom*—to be responsible the soul must be free;

- *The religio-civic axiom*—a free church in a free state;

- *The social axiom*—love your neighbor as yourself.

In a recent restatement of Baptist distinctives, Anderson speaks of seven principles:

- *The Christological principle*—the lordship of Jesus Christ;

- *The biblical principle*—the authority of the New Testament;

- *The ecclesiastical principle*—a regenerate church membership;

- *The sociological principle*—a democratic order;

- *The psychological principle*—religious liberty;

- *The political principle*—separation of church and state;

- *The evangelical principle*—personal evangelism and world missions.[13]

---

12. E. Y. Mullins, *The Axioms of Religion* (Philadelphia: American Baptist Publication Society, 1908). For a revision of Mullins, see Herschel H. Hobbs and E. Y. Mullins, *The Axioms of Religion* (Nashville: Broadman, 1978).

Mullins calls the principles *axioms* in order to stress that "they are to those who accept Christianity at all self-evident" (Ibid., 74). He adds: "These truths are so obvious when once understood, so inspiring, so self-evident, that the hungering spirit of man seizes upon them as upon the pearl of great price" (Ibid., 78).

Concerning the universal significance of the axioms, he says in his Preface, "God has given to the Baptists of the world a great and sublime task in the promulgation of principles on the preservation of which the spiritual and political hopes of the world depend" (Ibid., 8). Henry Cook, the prominent British Baptist writer, cites this sentence from Mullins at both the beginning and the ending of his widely circulated volume, *What Baptists Stand For,* 3d ed. (London: Carey Kingsgate, 1958), 9,216.

13. Justice C. Anderson, "Old Baptist Principles Reset," *Southwestern Journal of Theology* 31 [Spring 1989]: 5-12. The article reflects an updating of language and includes valuable documentation.

While there was a time in America when Baptists were persecuted for their defense of these principles, today the principles generally find wide acceptance among Christians and others in this country.[14] Yet, important as the principles are for a discussion of historic Baptist distinctives, they do not provide a readily adaptable structure for the broader task of restating the doctrine of the nature and purpose of the church. Consequently, the framework for the following discussion stresses instead what are regarded as key emphases in biblical ecclesiology.

The Present Approach: Characteristics of the Church

The following emphases seek to probe the heart of biblical teaching about the nature and purpose of the church as the new covenant people of God. While these emphases build on a reinterpretation of the classical and Protestant marks of the church and a summary of Baptist distinctives, they are also intended to reflect issues in contemporary discussions of the church's nature and purpose. They assume what was said in the previous chapter about the church as the corporate dimension of Christian experience and the church's polar nature as divine and human and as general and particular.

The church is a redemptive reality.—As the sign and agent of the kingdom of God, the church is the cutting edge of God's pursuit of His redemptive purpose in history. The key biblical word here is *redemption*. In words now familiar among evangelicals, "the Bible is a book of redemption; it is that or nothing at all."[15]

What, then, is the meaning of "redemption"? The term is used here to recognize the biblical distinction between creation and redemption. In the biblical world view, since the Creator and Redeemer are one and same God, creation and redemption are essentially compatible. Since creation was followed by the fall and the intrusion of sin, it is now necessary to speak also of a contingent incompatibility, as well as of an essential compatibility, wherever sin stubbornly persists.

Given this understanding of the redemption of a fallen creation, to say that the church is a "redemptive" reality is to emphasize the *discontinuity* between the church and the world of rebellious humanity as well as the *continuity* between the church and the world as God's redeemable creation.

---

14. See the later reference to Martin E. Marty, "Baptistification Takes Over," *Christianity Today,* September 2, 1983, 33-36.

15. See the opening sentences of the introduction to *The Criswell Study Bible* (1979), xiii. The first paragraph of the introduction continues as follows: "It is not a book of history, science, anthropology, or cosmogony. It is a book of salvation and deliverance for lost mankind."

The discontinuity recognizes such distinctions as the difference between the church and the world, between saved sinners and lost sinners, between a church agenda that includes *both* evangelism and social action, and a church agenda which emphasizes that all persons are already saved so that social action is all that is necessary.

The continuity stresses that fallen creation can find ultimate *fulfillment* only through the redemption from sin made possible by the atoning work of Christ. While sin negates and destroys, redemption frees creation for life abundant by judging sin redemptively.

As a redemptive reality, the church exists in response to the gospel of Jesus Christ.

> The church's one foundation
> Is Jesus Christ Her Lord!
> She is His new creation,
> By Spirit and the Word:
> From heav'n He came and sought her
> To be His holy bride,
> With His own blood He bought her,
> And for her life He died.
>
> —Samuel S. Wesley, 1810-1876

Without Christ there is no church. In Him alone the church discovers its nature and purpose.

Often the church is described as a redemptive fellowship. The truth in the phrase is that the church is a fellowship that grows out of the redeeming work of Christ. It is Christ who redeems. It is Christ who overcomes the destructive barriers that divide and alienate person from person. It is Christ who creates the new humanity, puts a song in the heart, and gives new meaning, challenge, and purpose to life.

Since it is a redemptive reality, the church's agenda in a fallen creation inevitably stresses the logical (as distinguished from chronological) priority of evangelism, or the meeting of humankind's eternal and spiritual needs, over social action, or ministry to the bodily and temporal needs of persons. This observation readily illustrates how the church's nature and purpose determine its structures and programs.

The church is God's creation.—Since only God can redeem, the church as a redemptive reality is always God's creation, not humankind's! Although the church is both a divine and a human reality, in formulating the doctrine of the church, precedence must be given to the former. A variety of significant truths are implicit in this claim.

1. As God's creation the church's primary relation is her vertical relation to God. The church is first a spiritual or redemptive fellowship and, only secondarily, a human organization. O'Brien says:

It is of particular significance that at the beginning of the two Corinthian letters (1 Cor. 1:1; 2 Cor. 1:1; cf. 1 Cor. 10:32; 11:22; Rom.
16:16) the church is described as belonging to the one who brought
it into existence, that is, God, or the one through whom this has
taken place, namely, Christ. Such an *ecclesia* was not simply a
human association or a religious club, but a divinely created entity.[16]

This truth is uppermost in each of the three key biblical images: the
people of God, the body of Christ, and the fellowship of the Holy
Spirit. God is sovereign over His people (1 Cor. 12:28); Christ is the
head of the church, His body (Eph. 1:22); and the Spirit distributes His
gifts to whom He wishes (1 Cor. 12:11). The church is God's church.

2. As God's creation in Christ the church is holy. She is God's possession,
set apart for His use and glory. In Christ she is "without stain or wrinkle or any other blemish, but holy and blameless" (Eph. 5:27, NIV).

3. As God's creation the church is indestructible. Church buildings can
be destroyed, but the church itself, the community of God's people,
cannot be destroyed (Matt. 16:18). Based on this confidence, again and
again in Christian history God's people have demonstrated courage
and boldness in the face of the worst that the enemy could do again
and again in Christian History.

4. As God's creation the church is something new. It is unique, the people
of a new and better covenant (Heb. 7:22; 9:15), the beginning of a new
humanity (Eph. 2:15).

5. As God's creation the church is divinely called out and guided. Beginning with Abraham, the Bible records God's actions in raising up His
people. Jesus plainly identified Himself plainly as the builder of the
church (Matt. 16:18). Always, of course, the Father and the Son work
through the Spirit and the Word. The Reformation insisted, the church
is where God's Word is truly proclaimed.

6. As God's creation the church is gifted through the Spirit for endless
spiritual renewal. This has been discussed in chapter 3.

The church is the people of God.—As a divine-human reality, the
church is both a sinful people and a redemptive creation. The Greek
word for people is *laos*, from which we derive "laity." The church is not

---

16. P. T. O'Brien, "The Church as a Heavenly and Eschatological Entity," in *The Church
in the Bible and the World,* D. A. Carson, ed. (Grand Rapids: Baker, 1987), 92.

When *The Baptist Faith and Message* says that "a New Testament church of the Lord
Jesus Christ is a local body of baptized believers who are associated by covenant in the faith
and the fellowship of the gospel," it fails to say clearly that before believers associate by
covenant they are first drawn together by the Holy Spirit through the gospel (Art. VI, The
Church). The church, it cannot be said too often, is a divine creation before it is a human
association.

first of all an institution or a building but it is people—the people called out for by God for His purposes.[17] Nor are the people of God to be regarded as the laity exclusive of the clergy. The laity include all of the people of God, clergy and laypersons alike.

The church—the redeemed people of God in the interim before the second coming of Christ and the consummation of redemption—is a people who are simultaneously saints yet sinners. They are redeemed but not yet perfected. They are a pilgrim people who walk by faith and not by sight, a people destined for heaven but not yet there.

New Testament writers make no effort to conceal the imperfections of God's people. New Testament communities of faith are at times scarred by division, failure, and lukewarmness. Morrison says that the church "is the only organization that keeps on saying week after week, year after year, age after age: 'We have left undone those things we ought to have done, and we have done those things we ought not to have done.'"[18] Nevertheless, the New Testament also makes it clear that the church is called to something better. Sin is real in the daily walk of God's people, but the power of sin has been decisively broken through the atoning work of Christ and the gift of the Holy Spirit. God's people are called to be overcomers (John 16:33; Rom. 8:37).

Because the church is composed of flesh and blood people whom God has called out and charged with a mission, some kind of church structure is necessary. Whenever God's people gather, some element of organization is inescapable, as is evident in the activities described in Acts 2:41-47. Churches without structure would necessitate people void of finite bodies, individuality, needs, and purpose.

The Reformers' stress on the distinction between the visible and invisible church encourages the escapism that flees the weaknesses of the vis-

---

17. The importance of understanding the church as the people of God has been a major concern in ecclesiological literature since World War II.

Typical of the spate of books by ecumenical writers are: Georgia Harkness, *The Church and Its Laity* (New York: Abingdon, 1962); Alden D. Kelley, *The People of God* (Greenwich, CT: Seabury, 1963); and Hendrik Kraemer, *A Theology of the Laity* (Philadelphia: Westminster, 1958).

From a Roman Catholic perspective especially, see: Walter M. Abbott, ed., *The Documents of Vatican II* (New York: Guild, 1966), 486-525; Hans Kung, *The Church,* trans. Ray and Rosaleen Ockenden (New York: Sheed and Ward, 1967); and Karl Rahner, "The Apostolate of Laymen," in *A Theology Reader,* ed. Robert W. Gleason (New York: Macmillan, 1966), 305-15.

Southern Baptist authors include: Findley B. Edge, *The Greening of the Church* (Waco, TX: Word, 1971) and *The Doctrine of the Laity* (Nashville: Convention Press, 1985); and Kenneth Chafin, *Help! I'm a Layman* (Waco, TX: Word, 1966).

18. Quoted by Robert McAfee Brown, *The Spirit of Protestantism* (New York: Oxford, 1961), 99. Charles Clayton Morrison was the former editor of *The Christian Century.*

ible church and seeks refuge in the perfect but invisible church.[19] Such escapism forgets that the God of the incarnation stoops to pursue His redemptive purposes. It also forgets Paul's stress on the need for order as well as his ardor when, in the midst of his discussion of spiritual gifts, he said, "let all things [in the churches] be done properly in an orderly manner" (1 Cor. 14:40).

The church is indispensable to God's purpose.—To speak of the church as indispensable to God's purpose for His people in the world is to reinforce the earlier emphasis on the church as the corporate dimension of Christian experience. The biblical God works through groups, both small and large, as well as through individuals. In a manner still not adequately grasped by God's people, living the Christian life and vital local church membership go together. Any idea of a churchless Christianity is foreign to biblical teaching about God's purpose for His people.

A problem quickly arises, however, when the question is asked regarding the relation of the indispensability of the church to the matter of a believer's salvation. Is local church membership optional or indispensable so far as a believer's salvation is concerned? The difficulty in formulating an effective answer to this question is reflected in the ongoing lordship/free grace debate among contemporary evangelicals.[20]

Joining a church is optional so far as a person's salvation is concerned, but local church participation is indispensable to a New Testament view of the salvation experience. The important point is that persons are not saved simply by joining a local church. According to the New Testament, professions of faith can be shallow and meaningless (Matt. 7:23; 1 John 2:19), whereas salvation is by a vital, faith relationship with God through Christ.

This is why, in the believers' church tradition, a profession of personal faith in Christ and an initial conversion experience precedes believers' baptism and local church membership. The unconverted do not become

---

19. Dulles faults Brunner at this point as follows:

[Brunner] argued that the Church in the biblical sense is not an institution but a brotherhood; it is "a pure communion of persons." On this ground Brunner rejected all law, sacrament, and priestly office as incompatible with the true being of the Church.

Avery Dulles, *Models of the Church* (Garden City, NY: Doubleday, 1974), 44.

Emil Brunner, *The Misunderstanding of the Church,* trans. Harold Knight (Philadelphia: Westminster, 1953), 35-46.

Trueblood says:

Much of the devotion to the ideal church of our dreams is fundamentally an escape mechanism, which eases our consciences for our failure to work actively for the betterment of the local church to which we belong or ought to belong. . . . Here is the familiar human situation in which perfectionism is really a hindrance to progress. *The abstract best actually becomes the enemy of the concrete good.*

D. Elton Trueblood, *Foundations for Reconstruction* (New York: Harper & Brothers, 1946), 52.

20. For developments in the recent MacArthur/Ryrie phase of the lordship/free grace debate, See footnote 20 on page 138.

Christians merely by being baptized and joining a church. No amount of good works by themselves can ever merit salvation.

In free societies where church and state are separated, as in the United States, this optional or voluntary aspect of church membership assumes a special importance. It becomes a mark of religious liberty.

Although local church participation is in some ways optional and voluntary, in other significant respects it is indispensable to fulfilling God's purposes. *First, local church involvement is inseparable from disciplined Christian living.* As all human existence is inescapably corporate and no one is an island, Christian existence is inescapably corporate. Believers desperately need one another in order to function as Christians and to grow spiritually. Likewise, each believer owes a debt to Christians of the past—missionaries, translators, evangelists, educators, pastors, as well as hymn writers, artists, and a host of others.

Although church membership is not strictly necessary to be a Christian, one cannot live a Christ-honoring life without active church participation. One sure way to make shipwreck of the Christian life is to neglect meaningful local church participation. According to Luke, Jesus attended the synagogue in Nazareth "as was His custom" (Luke 4:16). Similarly the writer of Hebrews admonishes, "Let us not give up meeting together" (Heb. 10:25). Of the early Christian community following Pentecost, it is said that "every day they continued to meet together" (Acts 2:46, NIV). Under the heading, "Is Worship an Obligation or Option?", Lavonn D. Brown says that, for committed believers, congregational "worship is an obligation, not an option. It is not always easy. It requires disciplined effort." As for the meeting between God and His people, "it becomes essential. Where there is no worship, there is no church."[21]

Second, the church is indispensable, not only in the sense that local church involvement is essential to disciplined Christian living, but also because *the task with which God charges believers is too vast for solitary individuals.* God's people must work together in pursuing "the great objects of the kingdom of God" (*The Baptist Faith and Message*, Art. XIV). That is why Jesus gave the Great Commission to the disciples as a group. If, as is often said, the world has yet to see what God can do through a believer wholly yielded to His will, even more, the world has yet to see what God can do through a group of believers earnestly pursuing His comprehensive purpose in Christ. The difficulty remains, however: how can church involvement be both optional and inescapable? One proposal, though it is not offered as a final solution to the dilemma, is that church membership is "a *forced* option," such as breathing. One does not have to breathe, but the consequences of refusing to do so are, to say the least, extreme!

---

21. Lavonn D. Brown, *The Life of the Church*, vol. 13, Layman's Library of Christian Doctrine (Nashville: Broadman, 1987), 72-73.

Another suggestion is that church relationships are like good works: salvation is by faith, but faith in Christ that fails to produce good works is something less than saving faith, as judged by New Testament standards. Although good works are not the root of salvation, they are its fruit. "The only thing that counts," says Paul, "is faith expressing itself through love" (Gal. 5:6); and James flatly states that "faith without deeds is dead" (Jas. 2:26).

In conclusion, then, salvation and church involvement belong together. When Luke says that "the Lord was adding to their number day by day those who were being saved" (Acts 2:47), he specifies that it was the Lord who added new believers: the Lord Himself closely links being saved with church participation, for there is no other way to be a New Testament people of God.

As long as the primary human obstacle to the progress of Christianity in the world is the indifference and lack of commitment of those who bear the name of Christ, just so long will the question of the relation between salvation and meaningful church membership be a crucial Christian concern.

The church is an eschatological community.— *"Eschatology"* comes from two Greek words, *eschata*, last things, and *logos*, doctrine. Eschatology, then, is the doctrine of the last things.

Hoekema observes that there are, broadly speaking, three approaches to eschatology, each with a different view of the coming of God's kingdom: the kingdom is either (1) present, (2) future, or (3) both present and future.[22] The latter is the approach followed here.

---

22. Anthony A. Hoekema, *The Bible and the Future* (Grand Rapids: Eerdmans, 1979), ix. Hoekema presents a lucid, biblically informed interpretation of the latter approach.

For an example of the kingdom as essentially a present reality, see C. H. Dodd, *The Parables of the Kingdom,* rev. ed. (London: Collins-Fontana, 1961), 41, and also *The Coming of Christ* (Cambridge: University Press, 1951), 17, 27. Dodd all but denies Christ's second coming. In a sense his approach is a modified version of the social gospel. His stress is on the Jesus of history and the presence already of a social kingdom hidden within history.

For examples of the futurist approach see especially the dispensational writings of authors such as John Walvoord and C. C. Ryrie. Also, ironical as it is due to the fact that mainline theologians tend to be sharply critical of dispensationalism, traditional Catholic and Protestant orthodoxy has also usually thought of the kingdom primarily in future terms.

See, for instance, Bill J. Leonard, *The Nature of the Church,* vol. 12, Layman's Library of Christian Doctrine (Nashville: Broadman, 1986), 140-51. Although Leonard recognizes that the church is a participant in the life of the kingdom here and now, his stress is on the future. He says: "Eschatology is the study of those ideas and events which relate to the "end of the age," death and judgment, the kingdom of God, and the return of Jesus Christ. It is the quest for the ultimate meaning of the "end times" (145-46)." See also, Ray Summers, *The Life Beyond* (Nashville: Broadman, 1959). Summers is discussing biblical eschatology, yet there is no chapter on the kingdom as a present reality. His study begins with a chapter on the subject of death. For examples of an emphasis on the kingdom as both present and future, see the Hoekema volume cited above, and G. E. Ladd, *The Presence of the Future* (Grand Rapids: Eerdmans, 1974). This approach is often called inaugurated eschatology, but there are so many versions of inaugurated eschatology that the term has little meaning. The approach has come into its own since World War II and is often associated with Oscar Cullmann's famous D-Day/V-Day analogy. See the next footnote.

Basic to the view of the kingdom as both present and future is the *already/not yet,* or D-Day/V-Day, emphasis.[23] Through the decisive events of Christ's first coming, including the outpouring of the Holy Spirit at Pentecost, the kingdom has broken into history in power. The decisive victory has already been won. Already "the last days" are here (Luke 4:14-21; Acts 2:17, cf. Joel 2-3; Heb. 1:2).[24] The beginning of the fulfillment of Old Testament predictions concerning the coming of the great day of the Lord has taken place. Already the powers of Satan and evil have been set at naught (John 12:31; 16:11,33). Already Christ reigns as Lord of history (Matt. 28:18; Acts 2:32-36; Phil. 2:9-11). Nonetheless, the perfection of the kingdom remains in the future and is not yet. The warfare between God and the forces of Satan continues, and in some instances even intensifies.

This "already but not yet" understanding of the kingdom is important for the doctrine of the church. Already, as Lord of history and Lord of the church, Christ charges His people with the limitlessly challenging Great Commission, the marching orders of the kingdom's redemptive mission to the ends of the earth (Matt. 28:19-20). Already God's people find themselves richly gifted for life and mission through the outpouring of the Holy Spirit (Acts 1–2), so that God's provision lacks nothing to justify the church's excuses for failure. Through the church, God is already creating a new humanity (Col. 3:10-11). The church is already an outpost of heaven (Phil. 3:20).

Still the end is not yet. Spiritual warfare between God and Satan continues. Though God has called His people to be the bride of Christ, the Lord has not yet presented to Himself "the church, in all her glory, having no spot or wrinkle or any such thing, but that she should be holy and blameless" (Eph. 5:26-27). The church is still a pilgrim people who press on despite shortcomings and imperfections, "looking for the city which has foundations, whose architect and builder is God" (Heb. 11:8-10).

Yet this already-not yet interim has crucial redemptive significance. The present is the time of God's missionary patience (2 Pet. 3:9), the time of the universal mission of the church. It is the church's opportunity to seek first the kingdom of God and His righteousness (Matt. 6:33).

---

23. The Decisive-Day/Victory-Day analogy is Oscar Cullmann's famous illustration of the already/not yet approach to the coming of the kingdom of God. The analogy is based on the Normandy Invasion which turned the tide of World War II in favor of the Allies. The decisive victory was won but the war went on temporarily.

24. What the Old Testament writers did not anticipate, however, was that the last days would come in two stages separated by a long interim. Reflecting the phenomenon of "prophetic foreshortening," Old Testament prophets did not clearly distinguish between Christ's first and second comings, thus failing to anticipate specifically either the messianic cross/resurrection/Pentecost nature of the first coming or the present, extended, missionary interim prior to the final consummation. See, for instance, Anthony A. Hoekema, *The Bible and the Future,* 9,114, etc.

By way of summary, though the kingdom of God and the church are not the same, they are inseparable. The church is not the kingdom, yet the kingdom is present in the church, and the church participates in the life of the kingdom. As an eschatological community "between the times," the church is the *sign* and *agent* of the kingdom. The priorities and goals of the kingdom determine the priorities and goals of the church. Although made up of imperfect believers, the church points beyond itself to Christ. Its perfection is in Him. As a kingdom people, the church represents the ideal. It is the promise of the fullness of the kingdom that is yet to be and the assurance of final victory.

The church is called to wholistic mission.—The church *is mission!*[25] Some consider this an overstatement because they have a narrow view of mission. The term is sometimes taken to refer only to what the church is sent out into the world to do. Wagner, for example, argues:

> Many things God does through His own people are not properly mission. Worship, prayer, giving, Christian education, fellowship, the sacraments, and numbers of other things that Christians do in obedience to God are not contemplated in holistic mission.[26]

Yet the term need not be limited in this way. Surely it is better to understand the church's mission in terms of *all that Christians do in obedience to God*. Mission, thus, is defined in terms of purpose. The mission of the church is the response of God's people to His purpose for them; and His purpose for them is to become and do all He calls them to become and do.

This means that the church's mission is *wholistic* or comprehensive in scope. God's redemptive purpose in Christ is to sum up *all things* in the Son (Col. 1:20; Rev. 21:5), a purpose broad enough to include the cultural mandate of Genesis 1:26-30: "Fill the earth and subdue it"[27] as well as the sweeping redemptive mandates of Matthew 22:37-40 and Matthew 28:18-

---

25. The basis for this claim is that the kingdom which creates the church is the kingdom of the God who is on redemptive mission in this fallen world. If Jesus can say that "the Son of Man has come to seek and to save that which was lost" (Luke 19:10), then the urgency and centrality of God's redemptive mission is the heart of the gospel.

It should be noticed, however, that to say that the church *is* mission is not to reduce the church to a mere functional reality. The church's mission roots in and includes the church's worship. The church is called not only to do but to be; it exists as well as acts.

26. C. Peter Wagner, *Church Growth and the Whole Gospel* (San Francisco: Harper, 1981), 93. For a similar viewpoint, see also John R. W. Stott, *Christian Mission in the Modern World* (Downers Grove, IL: InterVarsity, 1975), 30.

Incidentally, "wholistic," with its obvious association with the word "whole," is decidedly preferable to the "holistic" spelling.

27. This cultural mandate, part of the biblical account of creation, is never repealed later in the Bible. Instead it is renewed and expanded in Gen. 9:1-7, repeated in Ps. 8:6-8 and Heb. 2:6-8, and continually developed and applied in the extensive and remarkable individual-social-culturalcosmic teachings of Scripture.

20. The concerns of the kingdom, while emphasizing the ultimacy of redemptive issues, are as wide as creation itself!

Since, according to biblical monotheism, the Redeemer and the Creator are one and the same God, a biblically responsible theology must avoid any false dichotomy between the realms of redemption and creation. The world was created good, and as such it is redeemable in Christ. God's certain judgment on sin and evil is no blank condemnation of creation but a recognition that sin corrupts and destroys the well-being that is in creation's best interests. Only in redemption do creation's wounds find healing and its purposes realize lasting fulfillment. Sin frustrates the Redeemer/Creator's intentions, but in redemption creation learns to sing again!

The Bible affirms the ultimate compatibility between kingdom interests and the common life of humanity as designed by the Creator. Contrary to nonbiblical views of a dichotomy between Redeemer and Creator—or between kingdom and creation, church and world, evangelism and social action, and the like—God created persons and charged them with responsibility for the course of civilization. Long-range kingdom concerns cannot but include all of life's God-created dimensions: religious, individual, social, economic, political, cultural, and cosmic. God's people are never off duty; they are always on mission. "Whether, then, you eat or drink or whatever you do," says Paul, "do all to the glory of God" (1 Cor. 10:31).

Believers receive purpose and renewed zeal when they realize that their work is God's work and that the daily walk is the arena of obedience to God. Few visions challenge the church of Jesus Christ like the majestic scope of what *The Baptist Faith and Message* calls "the great objects of the Kingdom of God" (Art. XIV).[28]

Four unchanging functions are involved in fulfilling the church's wholistic mission: *worship, nurture, evangelism,* and *social service.*[29] Ade-

---

28. In the *Baptist Faith and Message, "the* great objects of the kingdom of God" include Articles XI-XVII: evangelism and missions, education, stewardship, cooperation, the Christian and the social order, peace and war, and religious liberty.

29. Although "fellowship" and "proclamation" are sometimes listed as functions in addition to the four just mentioned, they hardly qualify. Since the church itself is the corporate dimension of Christian experience, everything it does with reference to any of the four basic functions involves and furthers fellowship. And since at every point of their existence God creates and sustains His people through the Spirit *and the Word,* each of the four functions inescapably involves an element of proclamation. Neither fellowship nor proclamation, then, as important and essential as they are, can justifiably be considered a discrete function in addition to the four primary functions. Acts 2:41-47 reflects the early Christian community pursuing these four functions and spontaneously discovering its structure as it did so. Members of the community sought *nurture*—"they were continually devoting themselves to the apostles' teaching" (v. 42); they were a caring, sharing, *serving* people—"they were continually devoting themselves to . . . the fellowship" (v. 42); they *worshiped*—"they devoted themselves to . . . the breaking of bread [the Lord's Supper] and to prayer," they preached, and they baptized (vv. 41-42); and they *evangelized*—"the Lord was adding to their number day by day those who were being saved" (v. 47). Other Scriptures also bear out this summary.

quately interpreted, these functions embrace all that God through the Bible encourages His people to do as they assemble and as they scatter in the world. When they gather they worship and nurture; when they scatter they evangelize and serve. Just as all of life is a rhythm of exits and entrances ("your going out and your coming in," Ps. 121:8), so also the life of God's people is a rhythm of gathering and scattering. The church's four functions, then, speak to the total life of God's people, in keeping with the nature of the church's wholistic mission.

How do the functions relate to one another with reference to their relative importance? Worship takes priority over the other functions, since in the teaching of Scripture generally, and in Jesus' teaching specifically, the first and greatest commandment is to love God supremely (Matt. 22:37). Nothing can be right with God's people if the proper God-relation is not in first place.

In a similar manner, evangelism exercises a kind of logical priority over social service, since a person's relation to God, or one's spiritual and eternal well-being, takes theological precedence over material and temporal prosperity. Jesus asked, "For what will a man be profited, if he gains the whole world, and forfeits His soul?" (Matt. 16:26). Even so, a logical priority is not necessarily a chronological priority. Feeding a starving person, for example, takes chronological priority over an immediate effort of personal evangelism.

There are priorities among the functions, but none of the four is expendable. Each is essential if the church is to be the church.

Especially significant, as well as fortuitous, is the fact that the functions do not change! They were the basic functions of churches in the New Testament, and they will be the functions of churches when Christ returns. As historical circumstances change, churches will continually discover and develop new structures to help fulfill these functions; this reflects their vitality and flexibility as living organisms.[30]

The church is gifted for ministry.—No term touches the heart of the nature and purpose of the church more deeply than this word "ministry." Regardless of whichever of the church's varied functions might be in view at any given moment, the singular mission of the church of Jesus Christ is always to minister. Just as it can be said that the church is mission, so it can also be said that the church is ministry. It must not be said lightly, however, since ministry holds a crucial and fundamental place in the Christian revelation. "The Son of Man," Jesus insisted in one of His most

---

30. The urgent need for developing new church structures for today's churches is the theme of the well-known book: Howard A. Snyder, *The Problem of Wine Skins: Church Structure in a Technological Age* (Downers Grove, IL: InterVarsity, 1975).

important sayings, "did not come to be served, but to serve, and to give His life as a ransom for many" (Matt. 20:28).

The distinction between two common uses of the term "ministry" is especially important. On the one hand, using the term in its *verbal* sense, to minister is to serve God and others selflessly for Christ's sake. This is the primary calling of every believer. On the other hand, focusing on the *nominal* use of the term, in ecclesiastical contexts today ministry commonly refers to "the ministry," or to the office and work of the clergy.[31] In the present discussion, the concern is especially with the former, verbal emphasis. Ministry in the latter, substantival sense will be treated in the later discussion of the form or structure of the church.

Humphreys and Wise, discussing ministry in the verbal sense, define it as "the collective name for all the acts of service which the community of faith performs in response to God's call." They go on to add such insights as the following: the very reason for the church's being is that it might serve; the followers of Christ serve both God and others; ministry is self-giving, not selfserving; paradoxically, the greatest Christians are those who serve (Mark 10:43-44); especially important, Christ Himself is the model for ministry; devotion to Christ is the only adequate motivation for ministry; and the resources for ministry "are the gifts which God's Spirit distributes to the church."[32]

Along these lines, underscoring the central truth that Christ Himself is the model for ministry, Erickson perceives that ministry relates first of all to the church's character, not just to what it does. He says:

> We must not limit our study of the role of the church to an investigation of what the church does. . . . The attitude or disposition with which the church performs its functions is also a matter of extreme importance. Since the church is, in its continuing existence, Christ's body and bears his name, it should be characterized by the attributes Christ manifested during his physical incarnation on earth. Two of these attributes are crucial as the church operates in our rapidly changing world: willingness to serve and adaptability.

Concerning the latter, or the willingness to serve, Erickson continues:

> Jesus stated that his purpose in coming was not to be served, but to serve (Matt. 20:28). In becoming incarnate he took upon himself the form of a servant (Phil. 2:7). "He humbled himself and became obe-

---

31. Observe, for instance, the titles of two familiar volumes: H. Richard Niebuhr and Daniel D. Williams, eds., *The Ministry in Historical Perspective* (New York: Harper, 1956), and H. Richard Niebuhr, *The Purpose of the Church and Its Ministry* (New York: Harper, 1956).

Although these titles readily illustrate today's common use of "ministry" in the sense of the clergy, the authors, of course, are well aware that the term has other meanings.

32. Fisher Humphreys and Philip Wise, *A Dictionary of Doctrinal Terms* (Nashville: Broadman, 1983), 71-72.

dient unto death, even death on a cross" (v. 8). The church must display a similar willingness to serve. It has been placed in the world to serve its Lord and the world, not to be exalted and have its own needs and desires satisfied. Although the church may attain great size, wealth, and prestige, it is not here for that purpose. . . . Jesus was not interested in exploiting people. Similarly, the church today will not determine its activity on the basis of what will enable it to prosper and grow. Rather, it will seek to follow its Lord's example of service. It will be willing to go to . . . those who cannot give anything in return.[33]

Ministry, then, in this sense of selfless service to God and to others in Christ's name, is to characterize the life-style of all believers. This is what is intended in the claim that the church *is* ministry. Kraemer, for instance, says that the church "not so much *has* a ministry or ministries, but primarily *is* ministry."[34] The truth in the claim is that God calls the church not only to privilege but also to responsibility. The church exists to serve. It has no authentic existence apart from service. Ministry is its mission!

If ministry, as already emphasized, is to characterize the life-style of every believer, then it follows that *every believer is a minister*! This is the foundational ministry of the church.

It is also the heart of the doctrine of *the priesthood of every believer,* one of the most important and yet least understood doctrines in the New Testament teaching about the church.[35] The doctrine is explicit in pas-

---

33. Millard J. Erickson, *Christian Theology* (Grand Rapids: Baker, 1985), 1067.

34. Hendrik Kraemer, *A Theology of the Laity* (Philadelphia: Westminster, 1958), 136-37. Kraemer, with his Barthian affinities, carries his functional view of the church too far. God loves His people for who they are, not only for what they do.

35. Erickson, for instance, although he has an extended discussion of the doctrine of the church, and although his approach to church polity is baptistic or congregational, nevertheless, he mentions the doctrine of the believer's priesthood only in passing.

Furthermore, he tends to contrast the doctrine with the church's need for a "permanent, resident ministry." He says that, ideally, the universal priesthood should have obviated the need for a settled ministry. See Millard J. Erickson, *Christian Theology* (Grand Rapids: Baker, 1985), 1084-86.

Such contrasting of the ministries of the clergy and the laity raises important questions. Is it really God's intention for the earthly church either that all believers should be chiefs or that there should be no chiefs at all? It would seem that if such were His intention that it would lead to a "nongovernment" view of church polity characteristic of Quakers and Plymouth Brethren, a view which Erickson himself rejects. Ibid., 1082-83.

Regarding the present-day status of the doctrine of the believer's priesthood, Brown says: "The full depths of meaning in the 'priesthood of believers' have not been plumbed by Protestants. It is one of those areas of Protestant thought and life where 'the Reformation must continue.'" Robert McAfee Brown, *The Spirit of Protestantism* (New York: Oxford, 1961), 105.

For two recent restatements of the doctrine of the priesthood believers, see: Timothy George, "The Priesthood of All Believers," in *The People of God: Essays on the Believers' Church,* ed. Paul Basden and David S. Dockery (Nashville: Broadman, 1991), 85-95; and Walter B. Shurden, *The Doctrine of the Priesthood of Believers* (Nashville: Convention Press, 1987).

sages such as Romans 12:1; 2 Corinthians 5:18,20; Hebrews 13:15-16; 1 Peter 2:9-10; and Revelation 1:5-6; 5:9-10; 20:6. It is implicit in many New Testament passages that speak of the status and ministry of every believer.

The priesthood of believers stresses both the believer's privilege and responsibility. The problem is in balancing the two. God's people easily focus on their rights and privileges, insisting that there are no second-class believers ("Do not be called Rabbi, for One is your Teacher, and you are all brothers," Matt. 23:8), that every member of Christ's body is important, that each believer is richly gifted by the Spirit, and that every believer is free to interpret the Bible for himself[36].

These insights are scriptural and important, but believers overemphasize the status and privilege these teachings represent and neglect their calling to minister in Christ's name. Gifts and privileges are not for selfish enjoyment; they are enablements for assigned tasks and reminders that disciples have no excuse for their failure. Christ did God's will supremely while nailed to a cross; none of His followers has any excuse for failure.

Rightly interpreted the doctrine of the believers' priesthood relates to ecclesiology as well as to soteriology and is essential to the crucial churchly issue of the ministry of the laity. This is the aspect of the doctrine that Luther and Calvin missed. Snyder says: "While the reformers affirmed 'the priesthood of all believers,' they applied this emphasis primarily to soteriology (all believers may approach God directly) rather than ecclesiology (all believers are ministers in the church)."

The church is a voluntary people.—This is not to say that the church is merely a voluntary association of like-minded people who decided to get together to start a church.[37] Since the church is first of all God's creation, the full truth is that God takes the initiative in persons coming together to form a church. Before people volunteer God calls. The church is His idea long before it takes shape in human minds.

What the church as a voluntary society is emphasizing is that the church is a spiritual fellowship which functions spontaneously, as "a well of water springing up" (John 4:14), through the presence and energizing of the Holy Spirit. Having created persons in His own image, with freedom and responsibility, God refuses to coerce. He seeks from His people

---

36. The scholarly study of Scripture is essential, but no believer is bound in any *final* sort of way by the work of interpretive specialists. The point is that the Bible can be sorely abused and misused, not only by unlettered people and by enemies of Scripture, but also by scholars who claim to interpret it.

37. Guthrie repeats a familiar misunderstanding of the Baptist position. In discussing the church as God's creation, he says: "According to the Reformed church [in distinction from the churches of the Radical Reformation, such as Baptists], the church is not 'a voluntary association' of believers who get together and decide to form a church." See Guthrie, *Christian Doctrine*, 355.

a free and willing response (Josh. 24:15; John 7:17; 2 Cor. 8:3; Rev. 22:17).[38]

Voluntary Christianity is a special emphasis of the free church tradition. Yet in the United States, with its history of religious liberty, all churches today tend to be free churches, in the sense that there is no state-enforced religion. In fact, the idea of free churches in a free state stands out as the chief American contribution to the history of Christianity. Furthermore, this voluntary nature of American Christianity helps explain the remarkable amount of lay participation in Anerican church life, in contrast to the empty cathedrals of Europe.

Marty speaks of the American stress on voluntary and personal Christianity as "the most dramatic shift in power style on the Christian scene in our time, perhaps in our epoch." Over against catholicization, Marty coins the term "baptistification" to refer to the accent "on decision at *initiation* and decisive *identity*: I should know *what I am doing* in being baptized and I should know *who I am* after my Christian profession and in my Christian experience." Although he stresses the complementarity of the catholic and baptistic styles, he concludes that "for the moment, baptistification is the more aggressive and effective force" in American Christianity.[39]

Whether or not baptistification prevails over catholicization now or in the future, the principle for which it stands is important. Religious liberty, from the baptistic viewpoint, remains a significantly superior social value, simply because other values cannot be *freely* appropriated without religious liberty.

The church is in the world, but not of the world.— The church is both *in* the world yet *not of* the world (John 17:13-15; 16:33b). The relationship between the church and the world is a dynamic polarity involving both the church's *identification with* and its *separation from* the world.

Guidelines for interpreting this polarity are a part of the doctrine of the ongoing warfare between the kingdom present and the evil principalities and powers. These guidelines recognize that even though the evil powers were decisively defeated through the Christ-Pentecost events, they continue to struggle fiercely against the forces of righteousness which represent God's kingdom.

Robert E. Webber has written at length on the relation of the church to the world. He distinguishes but criticizes three traditional models of churchworld relations: the *separational, identificational,* and *transforma-*

---

38. For different meanings of voluntarism, as well as the distinction between voluntarism and voluntaryism, see James Leo Garrett, Jr., E. Glenn Hinson, and James E. Tull, *Are Southern Baptists "Evangelicals"?* (Macon, GA: Mercer, 1983), especially, 227-29.

39. Marty, "Baptistification Takes Over," 33-36.

tional models. The separational model excuses withdrawal from the world; the identificational model justifies compromise with evil; and the transformational model ignores the seriousness of sin.

Webber argues that no one traditional models is, by itself, flexible enough to respond to the changing situations of God's people in history. For instance, no model is adequate to cope with the difference between free churches existing where religious liberty prevails and struggling churches amid persecution and repression, or the difference between wealthy churches in affluent societies and penniless churches trapped in abject poverty due to grossly unjust economic circumstances.

Thus, while the pre-Constantinian period of Christian history called for implementing aspects of the separational model, the radically different postConstantinian era required the church to identify with culture whenever possible, something unthinkable during repressive regimes.

Webber goes on to claim that an *incarnational* model preserves the essential truths of the three traditional models but avoids their narrowness and rigidity. He argues that in the incarnation Christ "identified with the world; was separate from the ideologies that ruled it; and by his death, resurrection, and second coming assured its transformation."[40]

In distancing itself from the world without withdrawing from it, the church is called to purify itself and exercise a significant prophetic function in society. Snyder helpfully suggests four ways in which the church can fulfill its prophetic function: (1) create a reconciling community; (2) recognize the true enemy; (3) renounce the world's idea of truth, goodness, and beauty; and (4) promote justice for all in society.[41]

In effect, then, the church is called to serve, under God, as the world's conscience. Always, however, its summons is to exercise this role as the servant church. If it is to remain true to itself it can never exercise its role in a legalistic, coercive, or triumphalist fashion.

Furthermore, if the church is to serve as the world's conscience, it must be a disciplined church. Yet, in church life today, high standards of discipleship remain more the ideal to which believers are called in Christ

---

40. Robert E. Webber, *The Secular Saint: The Role of the Christian in the Secular World* (Grand Rapids: Zondervan, 1979), 188. See also his later discussion in *The Church in the World* (Grand Rapids: Zondervan, 1986). Webber's approach can be compared with Richard Niebuhr's classic, widely used, yet more complex, analysis of the options in church/world relations. Niebuhr's five categories are: Christ against culture; the Christ of culture; Christ above culture; Christ and culture in paradox; and Christ the transformer of culture. H. Richard Niebuhr, *Christ and Culture* (New York: Harper, 1951). Niebuhr, it is important to recognize, regards the first two as either/or options, and the other three as closely related *median* models. When this fact is understood, the relation between Webber's and Niebuhr's models is more readily apparent.

41. Howard A. Snyder, *The Community of the King* (Downers Grove, IL: InterVarsity, 1977), 106-16.

rather than a description of the life-style of most church members. Unfortunately, this problem has no textbook solution. No greater challenge faces the church than the call to deepen the commitment of Christ's followers.[42]

The church stands in need of continual renewal.—Although some observers in the 1950s and 1960s despaired for the future of the institutional church, many now believe not only in the possibility of church renewal, but also in the church as God's chosen agent for furthering His kingdom. As the fellowship of pilgrims living between D-Day and V-Day and the cutting edge of the kingdom of God in history, the church needs the Holy Spirit's constant refreshing.

The church is called to become what it already is: God's creation, the body and bride of Christ, the community of the Holy Spirit. Requirements for renewal are demanding because they are personal and relational. Renewal is never automatic, as though God's presence and empowering could be assembly-lined or taken for granted.

Where Christians are numerous and churches enjoy political favor, church membership merits public approval. In such situations the church is tempted to affirm uncritically the values and attitudes of society. So it is that the world invades the churches. Instead of exercising their prophetic function, the churches accommodate themselves to culture, lowering themselves to the status of social clubs, business enterprises, political power structures, and conservers of dominant cultural life-styles.

The only hope for the church in its pilgrim walk is constant renewal. Sometimes the church lapses so grievously that its prophets despair that it can ever live again; then the Spirit of God moves over the valley of dry bones, and God's people rise to live anew (Ezek. 37:1-14).

---

42. MacGorman suggests six reasons for the widespread abandonment of church discipline today:

1) The well-documented abuses of the past, in which harsh and vindictive punishment was often meted out to those who deviated from established norms, has left a negative legacy. 2) The level of Christian commitment in our churches is so low that the capacity to administer discipline has been lost. 3) Large church memberships have made impossible the pastoral care that is prerequisite to consistent and salutary discipline. 4) The multiplicity of churches and denominations in our communities has made the withdrawal of fellowship improbable, for excluded members would be accepted readily into other congregations. 5) There is the desire to protect the innocent members of an offender's family. 6) In a society that has become increasingly litigious, there may be the fear of a lawsuit with a heavy indemnity.

J. W. MacGorman, "The Discipline of the Church," in *The People of God: Essays on the Believers' Church*, Paul Basden and David S. Dockery, eds. (Nashville: Broadman, 1991), 82.

MacGorman, whose article is a study of 1 Cor. 5:1-13, is primarily addressing the problem of the toleration by churches of "flagrant wrong in their members" (Ibid., 83). However, his second reason for the lack of church discipline today, which points up the low level of Christian commitment in the churches, focuses on the heart of the larger church discipline problem.

In conclusion, much about the church remains a mystery. It could not be otherwise, for the church is the Spirit's creation and His work is always characterized by an element of mystery: "The wind blows where it wishes and you hear the sound of it, but do not know where it comes from or where it is going. So it is with everyone born of the Spirit" (John 3:8).

This mystery helps explain why key aspects of the church's nature and purpose can only be expressed in polar terms. The church is both: divine and human, an organism and an organization, indispensable and optional, corporate and individual, free and responsible, voluntary and yet submissive to God's sovereignty, in the world but not of the world, already God's people yet becoming God's people.

To affirm an element of mystery, then, is simply to recognize that the final truth about the church can never be fully expressed. It is not to despair. Instead it is to celebrate that the church is a living and not a dead reality.[43]

---

43. Drawn from Brown who says: "A book about the church can never be finished." Robert McAfee Brown, *The Significance of the Church* (Philadelphia: Westminster, 1956), 96.

14

The Form
of the Church

*Church form should facilitate Christ's rule over His
body and free believers to further "the great objects
of the kingdom of God."*

Biblical Resources: Biblical Principles Controlling
Church Form
The Importance of Principles versus Details
Three New Testament Principles
Christological: Jesus Christ is Lord of the Church
Organic: the church's form grows out of its nature
Voluntary: order and freedom are complements
Historical Perspective: Traditional Types of Church Polity
Episcopal
Papal
Connectional
Nongovernmental
Congregational
Restatement: Features of Congregational Polity
Defining a Local Church
*The Local Church as the Decisive Grouping of
God's People*
Regenerate Church Membership
The Church as a Democracy
Ministry I: Structuring a Church's Basic Functions
Ministry II: Equipping the Laity
Ministry III: Ordination and Leadership
The pattern of New Testament leadership
The flexibility in New Testament leadership
The Ordinances
The Autonomy and Interdependence of Local Churches
Evaluating Denominational Divisions
Religious Liberty

Given the preceding discussion of the nature and the purpose of the church, the question concerning the form of the church is quick to follow.[1] People on mission require structures.

This chapter is an overview of congregational polity from a Southern Baptist perspective. The presentation begins by indicating the biblical resources, continues with a reference to a historical perspective, and concludes with a restatement of the main features of a congregational polity.

Biblical Resources:
Biblical Principles Controlling Church Form

Few details regarding church form are recorded in the New Testament. One explanation of this fact is that many of the polity question which vex Christians today did not exist in New Testament times. Churches were young and principles and problems of polity unfolded slowly.

We assume, for instance, that one reason why Paul did not refer to deacons until Philippians 1:1, and then with only a passing reference, was that the role of deacon at that time was in the process of developing.[2]

Similarly, the Book of Acts makes no reference to pastors, bishops, or (church) elders until Acts 11:30, and again with only a passing reference. A possible explanation of this lack of earlier references is that the Jewish assemblies from which the first Christian converts came had rulers and elders, and this fact prepared the way for a ready Christian acceptance of pastoral leaders. Apparently the role itself created no problems. Had it been controversial, it would likely have been mentioned earlier.

Since few specifics regarding church structure are detailed by the New Testament, some writers today simply assume that Scripture reflects no single type of church polity. Robert McAfee Brown concludes that New Testament Christianity included elements of each of the three main tra-

---

1. This statement assumes Christian presuppositions. As Trueblood observes:

> That the idea of a churchless Christianity is not intrinsically absurd is evident when we realize that, in most of the world's religions, there has never been anything identical with what we mean by the Church. It is wholly possible to have shrines and priestly orders and scriptures and ceremonies without the existence of gathered communities of ordinary men and women whose faith is nurtured by a living fellowship. Even orders of monks and nuns can exist without the concurrent existence of gathered churches. . . . It is a bit shocking to note that the ancient Greeks and Romans who were, in some ways, highly religious, possessed nothing even similar to what we mean by a church. . . . The more carefully we study the origins of Christianity, the more we realize that, in the beginning, the Church, far from being something added, was absolutely intrinsic. The New Testament, in fact, is so saturated with the reality of group life that individual religion is the exception rather than the rule.

D. Elton Trueblood, *The Future of the Christian* (New York: Harper, 1971), 20-21.

2. Phil. 1:1 is the first use of the noun "deacon." The noun is not used in Acts 6, even though a deacon-type of role is under discussion.

ditional types of polity: congregational, presbyterian, and episcopal.[3] Even Erickson, a Baptist, says that "there is so much variation in the descriptions of the New Testament churches that we cannot discover an authoritative pattern." Later, however, Erickson maintains that "the congregational form of church government most nearly fulfills the principles" that the New Testament lays down.[4]

The Importance of Principles versus Details

Although the New Testament gives few details about church form, it does yield guiding and controlling principles that strongly indicate a congregational polity. These principles are more lasting and significant than detailed descriptions could ever be.

Far from abandoning believers in their search for appropriate church structures, the New Testament gives much more help than God's people have learned to use. The New Testament provides no detailed instructions concerning polity because church structures were never meant to be rigid and inflexible. That the New Testament reveals principles rather than lists of descriptive details indicates that God's people are *expected* to adapt the details of church structure creatively to constantly changing historical circumstances.

The emphasis on principles signifies that the New Testament offers guidance in the only manner consistent with the personal and spiritual nature of Christian experience. Rather than dictating detailed answers to polity questions, God richly gifts His people with the Word and the Spirit, equipping them to discover appropriate forms to realize the church's purpose. *How else would it be possible to grow responsible church-persons?*

Yet the principles approach also indicates that the freedom of believers to innovate and improvise in developing church structures has very definite limits. Structures are intended to reflect the principles, not negate them.[5] Howard A. Snyder undervalues these principles when he

---

3. Robert McAfee Brown, *The Spirit of Protestantism* (New York: Oxford, 1961), 101. Surely, though, Brown would not argue that sacerdotalism, papal institutionalism, apostolic succession of bishops, union of church and state, and the like are taught or seriously implied in the New Testament as clearly as is congregationalism.

4. Millard J. Erickson, *Christian Theology* (Grand Rapids: Baker, 1985), 1085-86.

5. Writing on the theme of the irresponsible shifting of patterns of church order among twentieth-century American Baptists, Hudson says:

> The one thing that is apparent, whether one looks to Clarke, Mathews, Hovey, or McNutt, is the fact that none of them had clear words of guidance for the task of ecclesiastical construction. As they saw it, the churches of the twentieth century were on their own, free to experiment and to improvise to their heart's content on a purely pragmatic basis, quite divorced from any theological or biblical considerations.

Hudson notes that by the twentieth century "the door was already open to ecclesiastical innovations and improvisation, for the notion of a structured church life had been badly undermined during the course of the nineteenth century." Winthrop Still Hudson, ed., *Baptist Concepts of the Church* (Philadelphia: Judson, 1959). Hudson's personal references are to William Newton Clarke, Shailer Mathews, Alvah Hovey, and W. R. McNutt.

belittles turning to the Bible for direction about church organization. He maintains that "all institutional . . . structures are man-made and culturally determined."[6] This position drives too large a wedge between Scripture and matters of church form.

Biblical principles set boundaries on appeals to *tradition* and *expediency*. Tradition, in the sense of biblically grounded insights of other Christians, can be a priceless teacher. Expediency, in the sense of effective structural changes to meet changing and often temporary historical conditions, can be important. The church needs good organization. Tradition and expediency, however, must give way to the final authority of Scripture (the teaching of the apostles, Acts 2:42). Congregations today often find it easier to follow tradition or expediency than to heed Scripture. This helps explain the disarray and blind experimentation that often frustrate the church's pursuit of its God-given goals.

Three New Testament Principles

New Testament churches must be organized on New Testament principles. The following discussion identifies three New Testament principles of church polity which reflect the central Christological and redemptive theme of Scripture.

The Christological principle: Jesus Christ is Lord of the church.— Everything that the church is and does roots in Christ, in His redemptive reality and work, and in His purposes for His people. The church is His: Christ is the church's foundation (1 Cor. 3:11), builder (Matt. 16:18), and head (Eph. 5:23). The church has no higher calling than to glorify Christ (Phil. 2:9-11).

Unless Christ has priority, nothing in the church can be what it ought to be. Seeking first the righteousness of the kingdom (Matt. 6:33) means putting Christ ahead of all else. It means giving the vertical, God-human relation precedence over the horizontal, person-to-person relation. Christians are to please Christ in all things.

Strangely, however, the significance of Christ's lordship over church government is often overlooked. Yet the strongest argument for congregational polity is the implementation of Christ's lordship of the congrega-

---

6. Howard A. Snyder, *The Community of the King* (Downers Grove, IL: InterVarsity, 1977), 159. Snyder's Free Methodist background helps to explain his position. Admittedly, a careful balance between scriptural principles and polity practices today is not easily maintained, and Snyder's discussion, despite the above demurrer, has much to commend it.

Bill J. Leonard, a Baptist, tends to take a position similar to Snyder's. He writes, "There seems to be no end to the forms of the church. No one structure contains all the diverse elements of ecclesiastical energy and integrity. . . . In a sense, all Christian groups may correctly claim to be 'Bible-believing Christians.'" Bill J. Leonard, *The Nature of the Church*, vol. 12, Layman's Library of Christian Doctrine (Nashville: Broadman, 1986), 119-20.

tion. Consider the following implications of Christ's lordship for church government:

1. *Because Christ is Head of the church, congregations must be free to go directly to Him* without the formal interposition of any mediating authority such as bishops or synods! Christ is the only Mediator. This is the theological basis for the doctrine of congregational autonomy.

2. *Because Christ is Head of the church, churches are not only autonomous but also interdependent.* Christ is the common bond uniting churches with one another in nature and calling.

3. *Since Christ is Lord of individual believers as well as of the congregation, individual believers, too, must be free to go directly to Christ.* This is the heart of the venerable doctrine of the priesthood of all believers, over against all notions of the necessity for any formal, clerical, or priestly mediation between believers and Christ, as though the clergy had an entrance to God denied to the laity.

4. *As the Lord of His people, Christ is the model for their discipleship and ministry.* Since Christ Himself took the form of a servant (Mark 10:45; John 13:4-5; Phil. 2:7), churches, too, are to stress the servant spirit in all that pertains to Christian life and action (1 Cor. 13, especially 4-7). Christ shapes the form of the church from within, as He transforms the inner spirit and attitude of God's people.

5. *Since Christ is the head of the church, He is its sole authority.* Some play off Christ against the Bible, as though it were necessary to choose between them. Properly understood Christ and Scripture are not two authorities but two complementary aspects of the church's one, primary authority.

The preface of *The Baptist Faith and Message* states both that "the sole authority for faith and practice among Baptists is Jesus Christ" and also that "the sole authority for faith and practice among Baptists is the Scriptures of the Old and New Testaments." Both statements are true. The apparent contradiction is merely two ways of saying the same thing.

For believers who live on this side of the closed biblical canon, there is no way to take seriously the authority of Christ without also taking seriously the authority of Scripture, and vice versa. In order for God's people today to determine the will of their Lord, the primary authority is the living Christ as He speaks through Spirit-illumined Scripture. Tradition, reason (or human wisdom in general apart from Scripture), and individual opinion are authorities subordinate to Scripture.

The organic principle: the church's form grows out of its nature.— "Let the church be the church!" Nature precedes form. Form is subordinate to function, and church form should let the church be the church. The church is first an organism and secondarily an organization. Christ is the Head of the church, and good organization should help Christ guide His people. When congregations adopt forms inconsistent with their nature, they betray themselves and hamper their kingdom purpose.

Church structures should help congregations fulfill their essential functions—worship, nurture, evangelism, and service. Structures are servants: they are to serve the church's nature and purpose. Organization is not the end but the means. While church work can easily become perfunctory and tedious, it assumes a fresh importance when the God-given eternal and redemptive purpose it is meant to serve is remembered.

The voluntary principle: order and freedom are to complement each other in the church.—First, to begin with *order* or organization, many throughout Christian history have feared that church organization stifles the Spirit.[7] Groups as diverse as Quakers, anti-missionary Calvinists, and Plymouth Brethren have refused to assign a significant role to organization in God's achievement of kingdom purposes in the world. Yet good organization is necessary if congregations are to be effective.

Order is scriptural. Jesus called disciples, taught them patiently, and sent out the seventy two-by-two on a special witnessing mission. He carefully organized the feeding of the five thousand, giving attention even to saving the leftover fragments (Mark 6:39).

At Pentecost, 120 disciples gathered. Later three thousand believers were counted, baptized, and incorporated into church life. Paul likened the church to the intricately organized human body (1 Cor. 12:12). "Let all things," he said, "be done properly and in an orderly manner" (1 Cor. 14:40).

Orderliness is implicit in God's call for excellence. Jesus says, "Be perfect, as your heavenly Father is perfect" (Matt. 5:48). Paul admonishes the Ephesians "to work in a manner worthy of the calling with which you have been called" (Eph. 4:1). His concern is that the body of Christ might be built up "until we all . . . become mature, attaining to the whole measure of the fullness of Christ" (Eph. 4:12-13, NIV). In all such calls, no room is left for cheapness or shoddiness as believers respond to the Master's summons.

Orderliness is also implicit in the corporate dimension of Christian experience. Any group experience, secular or religious, involves organization. Even the most primitive expressions of family life reflect an element of organization. The same is even more true when numbers of families combine to form tribes, when tribes join to form states, and so on.

---

7. Lavonn D. Brown, *The Life of the Church*, vol. 13, Layman's Library of Christian Doctrine (Nashville: Broadman, 1987), 144-47.

Order is to be effective. Effectiveness is more than efficiency. It means doing the right things, not just doing things right. Effective structures major on the qualitative rather than on the quantitative. They undergird and further the church's pursuit of kingdom values. The modern drive for efficiency is often more interested in maintaining institutions than helping persons (Matt. 6:26). Such preoccupation with efficiency while neglecting effectiveness is a reminder of how easily organization, like any other tool, is abused. In selfseeking hands efficiency manipulates rather than edifies. In fact, evil forces are often more efficient than forces of righteousness. The achievement of kingdom goals requires time, skill, and patience, but evil's disruptive and destructive ends can be accomplished at times with the touch of a button.

Organization in itself is incapable of furthering redemptive purposes. A sure way to disappointment in kingdom enterprises is promoting the program while neglecting what only God by His Spirit can accomplish. However, while kingdom goals can never be easily or automatically achieved by organization alone, in the hands of a Spirit-led people of God, good organization is indispensable to effective kingdom service.[8]

Second, a congregation must balance order with *freedom* in order to be the people that God intends. Of course, the freedom that God's people need is not just any freedom; it is the freedom which only the Holy Spirit gives. "Where the Spirit of the Lord is," Paul says, "there is liberty" (2 Cor. 3:17).

The Spirit liberates because the Spirit is sovereign and free: "The wind blows where it wishes" (John 3:8). Paul says that the Spirit apportions His gifts to each believer individually "as he wills" (1 Cor. 12:11). The Spirit also liberates because He gives life, and redemptive freedom is inescapably rooted in vitality. Life in Christ liberates, just as sin enslaves. "It is the Spirit who gives life," says Jesus (John 6:63), and Paul refers to the Spirit as "the Spirit of life" (Rom. 8:2).

God asked Ezekiel, "Can these bones live?" The Lord then answered His own question: "Come from the four winds, O breath, and breathe into these slain, that come to life." So Ezekiel prophesied to the breath, and, as the breath responded, the corpses came to life (Ez. 37:1-10)! Without the Spirit our church structures are dry bones, but they come alive when God's Spirit breathes upon them.

The point to be remembered is that when order is balanced with *freedom*, the Holy Spirit enables the responses of God's people in kingdom life and service to be both *voluntary* and *flexible*. Neither coerced

---

8. Sullivan, who discusses the need for sound organizational principles, also treats the difference between disorganization and good organization. James L. Sullivan, *Baptist Polity as I See It* (Nashville: Broadman, 1983), 57-60,67.

responses nor responses incapable of adapting readily to change are adequate to implement effectively the furthering of enduring kingdom goals.

First, regarding the *voluntary* aspect of the Christian's free response, Jesus says, "Freely you received, freely give" (Matt. 10:28). Paul echoes this emphasis when he appealed for generous giving: "Let each one do just as he has purposed in his heart; not grudgingly or under compulsion; for God loves a cheerful giver" (2 Cor. 9:7). Paul, a Hebrew of the Hebrews (Phil. 3:5), remembered that Israel's offerings for the building of the tabernacle were willing offerings ("All the Israelite men and women who were willing brought to the Lord freewill offerings for the work of the Lord," Ex. 35:29, NIV).[9]

A moment's reflection underscores why the voluntary response of God's people is important. Their experiences must be voluntary to be redemptive. If experiences are to contribute to their spiritual development, they must be freely encountered. Actions that are less than voluntary are less than fully human and personal. David Little says, "Clearly, 'ought language' or 'should language' is invariably reserved for beings regarded as free to choose deliberately."[10]

The implication of this emphasis for church government is plain. Believers must have free, direct, and personal access to Christ, unfettered by the imposition of sacerdotal rituals or hierarchical authorities, if commitment is to be voluntary. In the New Testament, congregations are fellowships of believers, not sacramental institutions under clerical control.

Especially noteworthy is the fact that as free the responses of God's people have a redeeming quality of *spontaneity*. The woman who anointed Jesus before His crucifixion took no thought of the monetary value of the ointment. When the disciples were indignant at what they perceived as indefensible waste, Jesus rebuked them with the words, "Why do you bother the woman? For she has done a good deed to me. . . . I say to you, wherever this gospel is preached in the whole world, what this woman has done shall also be spoken of in memory of her" (Matt. 26:6-13).

Such memorable spontaneity is the free overflow of a grateful heart! Out of gratitude for God's amazing grace in Christ, God's people will do willingly what they could never be forced or paid to do (Acts 5:41)! Kingdom actions exhibit a royal bearing, a dignity, a charm, a disarming lack

9. In a similar vein, Edge speaks of the "ought-overflow" tension as he discusses motivating God's people for mission. Significant involvement in church renewal, he says, is marked by "a minimum of the sense of 'oughtness' and a maximum of that nebulous thing called 'overflow.'" The ideal, then, is to minister for the sheer joy of ministering! Findley B. Edge, *The Greening of the Church* (Waco, TX: Word, 1971), 141-44.

10. *The Westminster Dictionary of Christian Theology,* 1983 edn., s.v. "Freedom," by David Little.

of self-awareness, a grace that can only be explained as the mark of Christ on the lives of His own.

Another fruit of the Spirit's gift of freedom, along with voluntariness, is *flexibility*. Openness to God's speaking through the Word and the Spirit, willingness to let God revise our most cherished plans day by day, and readiness to adapt to new and changing situations are important characteristics of a New Testament people of God. As a organism living in a changing historical framework, the church must adapt to new situations. Forms that proved effective in one generation and culture are not necessarily effective in a different context.

The Book of Acts records the exciting story of the earliest churches crossing one cultural barrier after another. Some New Testament churches, to be sure, adapted more readily than others. The church at Jerusalem failed to send Paul on his Gentile world mission, and this privilege passed to the fledgling congregation at Antioch (Acts 13:1-3).

This need for adaptability requires the church to keep its organizational life as simple as possible. God's people are to travel lightly. With an irrevocable commission to take the gospel to the ends of the earth, impediments to their mobility must be avoided.

In conclusion, considerations like these underscore how important it is that the New Testament provides guiding and controlling principles for church polity rather than prescribing organizational details.

Historical Perspective: Traditional Types of Church Polity

In the course of church history five broad types of church polity have developed: episcopal, papal, connectional, nongovernmental, and congregational.[11]

---

11. Two brief introductions to polity types are: G. Hugh Wamble, *The Shape of Faith* (Nashville: Broadman, 1962) and Richard W. Harmon, *Baptists and Other Denominations* (Nashville: Convention Press, 1984).

Wamble has seven chapters: Episcopal, Congregational, Lutheran, Christian (Disciples), Methodist, Presbyterian, and Baptist. Harmon has six chapters: Lutheran, Episcopal, Methodist, Presbyterian, Churches of Christ, and Pentecostal. He also includes a bibliography.

For a broader, more systematic approach to the diverse polity types, see Erickson, *Christian Theology*, 1071-83. Erickson discusses Episcopal, Presbyterian, Congregational, and Nongovernment types of church government.

Sullivan employs categories of his own to name the varying types of church polity. His six labels are: informal or unstructured; independent and isolationist; hierarchical; delegated; related; and directed and balanced. The latter is his name for Southern Baptist polity. In discussing Southern Baptists his emphasis is on the workings of the Southern Baptist Convention. His discussion of the local church as such is limited to ten pages. Sullivan, *Baptist Polity as I See It,* 70-93.

Episcopal Polity

Episcopal polity is church government by bishops (Greek, *episcopoi*, overseers). According to Cyprian (d. 258), the church is in the bishop, and without a bishop there is no church in a real sense.

Episcopal polity stresses church tradition (especially the ecclesiastical developments of the first five Christian centuries), the sacraments (especially baptism and the eucharist), and bishops as successors to the apostles. The more familiar episcopal communions, often called catholic (small "c") churches, are the Greek Orthodox, the Anglican, and the Swedish Lutheran churches.

Papal Polity

A later development of the episcopal type, *papal* polity is peculiar to Roman Catholicism. The Roman bishop is regarded as the chief bishop or pope, and the church is understood as a hierarchical and priestly institution, elaborately structured with seven sacraments,[12] and undergird with the doctrine of papal infallibility and the claim that the Roman Catholic church is the one true church.

Connectional Polity

A third, broad type of polity characterizes the classical Reformation tradition, represented in varied ways by Lutheran, Reformed (Continental European background), Presbyterian (Scottish background), Congregational (as distinguished from Baptists), Methodist, Christian (or Disciples), and some Baptist groups.

It is a *connectional* type of church government in the sense that denominations of this type regard themselves as churches made up of member congregations lacking full structural autonomy. The denomination holds title to the congregation's property, ordains ministers, assigns ministers to congregations, and determines the congregation's practice of the ordinances.

Methodists, despite their affinity for their Anglican forebears, are viewed as connectional rather than episcopal for two reasons: (1) British Methodists have no bishops, as American Methodists do; and (2) the bishops in American Methodism, unlike Anglican bishops, are not regarded as successors to the apostles.

Congregationalists, despite their name, follow a connectional rather than a congregational polity in three important ways: (1) their denomina-

---

12. The seven sacraments, accepted also by the Eastern churches, are: baptism, confirmation, the eucharist, penance, extreme unction, holy orders, and matrimony.

tional structure limits congregational autonomy;[13] (2) they accept the practice of infant baptism; and (3) in Colonial America they practiced the union of church and state, with the state often persecuting non-Congregationalists.

The American Baptist Churches U.S.A., formerly the American Baptist Convention and, before that, the Northern Baptist Convention, is an example of a Baptist group which is increasingly connectional in its polity.

Nongovernmental Polity

As the name implies, this type of polity minimizes church organization. Erickson, from whom the term "nongovernmental" is derived, attributes this type to the Quakers and Plymouth Brethren.[14]

Congregational Polity

Congregational polity is typically represented by Baptist groups. It is described more fully in the restatement of the doctrine of church form which follows.

Restatement: Features of Congregational Polity

Given the convictions represented here that congregational polity is clearly reflected in the New Testament and that it is widely recognized today for its viability throughout the world, the next question concerns its main features. Since there are varieties of congregationalism,[15] this

---

13. Wilshire says: "'Ministerial standing' is held by associations (sometimes by conferences) which cooperate in the ordination or installation." L. E. Wilshire, "Congregationalism," in *Dictionary of Christianity in America*, ed. Daniel G. Reid (Downers Grove, IL: InterVarsity, 1990), 311.

14. Erickson, *Christian Theology*, 1082-83.
The widespread influence of the Plymouth Brethren movement, especially in England and America, is reflected by the popularity of the Scofield Reference Bible (1909, 1967). According to Scofield, the church (understood as the company of the redeemed only and sharply distinguished from Christendom or the churches of mainline denominations, which, it is believed, are increasingly apostate and include many members who are not genuine Christians) is viewed as a parenthetical reality between Christ's first coming and the pretribulational rapture (removal) of the church from the world. As pretribulational, the rapture takes place prior to the final, seven-year period of tribulation immediately preceding the second coming. With the church, or true believers, removed from the world at the beginning of the tribulation, God's purpose during the tribulation and the millennium reverts to the fulfillment of Old Testament promises to *earthly*, national Israel, according to the unique dispensational interpretation of these promises. The church, as a *heavenly* people, is with the Lord in glory.

15. For an indication of the varieties of congregationalism, see Donald F. Durnbaugh, *The Believers' Church: The History and Character of Radical Protestantism* (New York: Macmillan, 1968). Durnbaugh ranges beyond congregationalism as such. He deals with: medieval sectarians, radical reformers, separatist Puritans, free church Pietists, New Testament restorationists, and contemporary expressions.

discussion focuses on Southern Baptist practice.[16] A number of topics call for consideration:

- defining a local church;

- the local church as the decisive grouping of God's people;

- regenerate church membership;

- the democratic functioning of church structures;

- ministry I: structuring the church's basic functions;

- ministry II: equipping the laity;

- ministry III: ordination and leadership;

- the ordinances;

- local church autonomy and interdependence;

- evaluating denominational divisions;

- religious liberty.

For a further study of the believers' church, see James Leo Garrett, Jr., ed., *The Concept of the Believers' Church* (Scottdale, PA: Herald, 1969). This volume contains the thirteen addresses prepared for the Conference on the Concept of the Believers' Church held in Louisville, Kentucky, in 1967. Some twenty-five different church bodies were represented by the participants.

16. For something of the diversity in views of the church and its polity among English and American Baptists, see Hudson, *Baptist Concepts of the Church.* The following views are discussed in the volume: The Philadelphia Tradition, John Gill's view, Andrew Fuller's view, the Backus-Leland tradition, the individualism of F. Wayland, and Landmarkism. Hudson contributes a concluding essay on "Shifting Patterns of Church Order in the Twentieth Century."

For varied Southern Baptist views of the church and its polity, see Donald E. Lewis, "Some Basic Southern Baptist Concepts of the Church" (Th.D. diss., Southwestern Baptist Theological Seminary, 1968). Lewis treats: the Charleston tradition, the Separate Baptist concept, the concept of the Regular Baptists of Virginia, the concept of J. L. Dagg, Landmarkism, and the tradition of the Southwest.

For varied Southern Baptist theological and regional traditions, see Bill J. Leonard, *God's Last and Only Hope: The Fragmentation of the Southern Baptist Convention* (Grand Rapids: Eerdmans, 1990), 31-39. Following Shurden, Leonard discusses: the Charleston tradition, the Sandy Creek tradition, the Georgia tradition, and the Landmark tradition. He then adds two other traditions: the evangelical denominational tradition and the Texas Baptist tradition. He concludes with a section on the question, "A Southern Baptist Synthesis?," in which he postulates a Grand Compromise which until the 1970s "kept the SBC theologically conservative and historically Baptist while allowing for surprising diversity in the churches."

Defining a Local Church

At the heart of congregational polity is the local church. First, then, a definition of a local church calls for attention.

Article VI of *The Baptist Faith and Message* discusses "The Church," first as a local body, then in a general sense:

> A New Testament church of the Lord Jesus Christ is a local body of baptized believers who are associated by covenant in the faith and fellowship of the gospel, observing the two ordinances of Christ, committed to His teachings, exercising the gifts, rights, and privileges invested in them by His Word, and seeking to extend the gospel to the ends of the earth.

> This church is an autonomous body, operating through democratic processes under the Lordship of Jesus Christ. In such a congregation members are equally responsible. Its Scriptural officers are pastors and deacons.

> The New Testament speaks also of the church as the body of Christ which includes all of the redeemed of all ages.[17]

The matter of congregations of like faith and order cooperating with one another in common endeavors is dealt with forthrightly in Article XIV, "Cooperation":

> Christ's people should, as occasion requires, organize such associations and conventions as may best secure cooperation for the great objects of the Kingdom of God. Such organizations have no authority over one another or over the churches. They are voluntary and advisory bodies designed to elicit, combine, and direct the energies of our people in the most effective manner. Members of New Testament churches should cooperate with one another in carrying forward the missionary, educational, and benevolent ministries for the extension of Christ's Kingdom. Christian unity in the New Testament sense is spiritual harmony and voluntary cooperation for common ends by various groups of Christ's people. Cooperation is

---

17. Two examples of briefer definitions highlight the key ideas in typical Southern Baptist ideas of the local church.

Sullivan says that the definition which many Baptists have learned is that "a church is a body of baptized believers, bound together voluntarily by the common bond of love for Jesus Christ [and] working together under God's Holy Spirit to do his work on earth." Sullivan, *Baptist Polity as I See It,* 19.

Brown says:

Years ago I memorized a definition of church for my ordination service. I still find satisfaction in it. Simply, yet comprehensively, the church is "a body of baptized believers bound together voluntarily to carry out Christ's divine commission to disciple, baptize, and teach (Matt. 28:19-20)."

Brown, *The Life of the Church,* 14.

desirable between various Christian denominations, when the end to be attained is itself justified, and when such cooperation involves no violation of conscience or compromise of loyalty to Christ and His Word as revealed in the New Testament.[18]

In addition to these statements, two comments regarding a definition of a local church can help to keep the matter in perspective. First, recall the earlier emphasis on the church as a voluntary people. A local church is a great deal more than a group of like-minded people deciding to get together to start a church. The church is first God's idea and creation. He first calls out the people and plants the idea! The grand initiative is His.

Furthermore, the local and general church ideas are closely related. The local church is representative in a particular place of all of God's people. Paul reminded the churches in Achaia to inspire the churches in Macedonia by giving financially as they had promised (2 Cor. 9:1-5). He sought to correct worship and behavioral abuses at Corinth by appealing to "certain traditions which must be maintained by all of the churches of God" (see 1 Cor. 1:2; 11:2,16; 14:34,36; 16:1).[19]

The Local Church as the Decisive Grouping of God's People

As fare local churches, so fares the work of the kingdom of God! This is the crucial importance of the local church.

God's people group in various ways, and every gathering of God's people in Jesus' name has something of a "churchly" nature. Each group represents God's people everywhere and is gifted with Christ's presence by the Holy Spirit (Matt. 28:20), whether two or three gather (Matt. 18:20) or thousands meet in an international assembly (Acts 2:5-12).

Of all these groupings, however, the local congregation is the decisive grouping of God's people for furthering God's great redemptive purposes. This is true for various reasons: (1) the local church is accessible, meeting where the members live; (2) it meets frequently, at least every

---

18. The act in 1845 by the senate and house of representatives of the state of Georgia to incorporate the Southern Baptist Convention includes the following: "said corporation being created for the purpose of eliciting, combining, and directing the energies of the Baptist denomination of Christians, for the propagation of the gospel."

Article II of the Constitution of the Southern Baptist Convention concerns the purpose of the Convention. The article says: "It is the purpose of the Convention to provide a general organization for Baptists in the United States and its territories for the promotion of Christian missions at home and abroad and any other objects such as Christian education, benevolent enterprises, and social services which it may deem proper and advisable for the furtherance of the Kingdom of God."

The charter and constitution of the Convention can be found in any Southern Baptist Convention *Annual*.

19. Kenneth S. Hemphill, *Spiritual Gifts: Empowering the New Testament Church* (Nashville: Broadman, 1988), 121.

Lord's day when this is at all practicable, providing opportunity for participation and spiritual nurture; (3) it offers the possibility for a diversity which is not afforded by small groups, since it often bridges the gaps between generations, races, economies, and cultures; and (4) it is more personal and flexible than general bodies, such as associational, state, national, and international gatherings, which tend to be less personal because they are characteristically large and assemble less frequently.

For these and other reasons, no other grouping of God's people is so effective as the local church in enlisting, nurturing, and equipping believers for kingdom service. Edge contends that what happens on the crucial battleground of the world "depends on what first happens in the local church." After noting the neglect of the local church by the lay academy movement that flourished in Europe after World War II, he asks: "How did they hope to make any significant and continuing impact on the world? There needs to be a base from which the people of God invade the world, a place of continuing fellowship, a place where those who are 'coming alive' are taught and equipped."[20]

Regenerate Church Membership

By definition a local church is a congregation of the people of God. Implicit here is the idea that a local church is a congregation of those who have personally trusted in Jesus Christ as their Lord and Savior.

Broadly speaking, there are two views of church membership: (1) mainline, ecumenical denominations, viewing the church as the realm of redemption, baptize infants into the sphere where redemption is taking place; (2) believers' churches understand congregations as fellowships of those who have already made professions of faith.[21]

One issue here is the essentially voluntary nature of Christian experience and church membership, over against views that persons become members of the church in some preliminary way through the efficacy of the sacrament of infant baptism. In the Baptist view, only acts involving personal choice have Christian redemptive and moral value. Individuals must be free to deal personally with God—willingly, with understanding, and without constraints.

The distinction between the church as the realm of redemption and the church as the fellowship of believers has played an important role in the history of denominations. Justice C. Anderson writes:

20. Edge, *The Greening of the Church*, 16-19.
21. For a discussion of this basic distinction, see J. Robert Nelson, *The Realm of Redemption* (London: Epworth, 1951).

The Baptist interpretation of the New Testament doctrine of the church has been one of the most important contributions of the denomination to Christian history. Along with the Anabaptist movement of the sixteenth century, it spawned the "Free Church" sector of Christian ecclesiology. The cardinal principle of Baptist ecclesiology, and logically, the point of departure for church polity, is the insistence on a regenerate membership in the local congregation. Their rejection of infant baptism, their practice of believer's baptism, and their various limitations on participation in the Lord's Supper are logical conclusions of their belief that the New Testament requires a pure church, composed of true believers.[22]

Even so, regenerate church membership in an important sense remains the ideal. The New Testament makes it clear that not all professions of faith are genuine (for example, the parable of the soils, Matt. 13:1-23) and that not all believers grow in grace as they should (1 Cor. 3:1-3). There is a difference between empty and genuine professions of faith, but only God can distinguish between them with certainty.

Furthermore, not all evangelicals, despite their common emphasis on the necessity of a born-again experience, agree about what constitutes regenerate experience. Witness, for instance, the Ryrie-MacArthur exchange over salvation by grace versus lordship salvation and the varied views of sanctification championed by diverse evangelicals.[23]

Southern Baptists agree in principle that a profession of personal faith in Christ is prerequisite to church membership, but they are of different minds about the relative importance of initial decisions for Christ as compared with discipleship emphases.[24] Suffice it to say that the ideal of regenerate church membership includes both an initial profession of faith in Jesus Christ as Lord and Savior as prerequisite to church membership and a continuing, growing commitment to Christ. This continuing com-

---

22. Justice C. Anderson, "Old Baptist Principles Reset," *Southwestern Journal of Theology* 31 [Spring 1989]: 8.

Regarding studies of the concept of believers' churches, see the references to James Leo Garrett and Donald F. Durnbaugh in footnote 15.

Anderson's emphasis on regenerate church membership as the cardinal principle of Baptist ecclesiology presupposes the principle of Christ's lordship which is stressed in the present discussion.

23. For recent developments in the free grace/lordship salvation discussion, see 138 n.

For discussions of some of the varied evangelical approaches to sanctification, see: Melvin E. Dieter, *Five Views on Sanctification* (Grand Rapids: Zondervan, 1987); and Donald L. Alexander, ed., *Christian Spirituality: Five Views of Sanctification* (Downers Grove, IL: InterVarsity, 1988).

24. Since evangelism and discipleship are terms with varying meanings, their use is always to a certain extent confusing. Readers easily read content into a writer's use of the terms which he did not intend. The terms are used loosely here simply to indicate that in the past evangelism and discipleship have not always been recognized as inseparable, twin emphases in the church's fulfillment of the Great Commission.

mitment is manifested in a life of discipleship nurtured by participation in the community of believers. The New Testament presents salvation as both a gift and as a continuing responsibility.

The ideal of a regenerate and committed membership challenges every believers' church. To the extent that, by God's grace, the ideal is realized, to that extent the church becomes the people of God it is intended to be.

The Church as a Democracy

Democracy means different things to different people—self-government, social equality, the right to pursue selfish interests. *E pluribus unum* ("of many one") is the ideal of secular democracies, but their citizens often remain self-centered, more preoccupied with their individual rights and privileges than with the well-being of fellow citizens.

Congregational polity gives democracy a theological application, for the lordship of Christ confronts the believer's self-interest. For this reason, since the church is a democracy under God, Sullivan calls it a "theo-democracy." The purpose of the church, he says, is to use "democratic processes to find the will of God instead of the will of men."[25]

The democratic nature of church structure and practice is to be firmly grounded in the doctrines of the lordship of Christ and its corollary, the priesthood of all believers. These doctrines emphasize the believers' direct access to Christ as Lord and Savior and their equal responsibility under Christ. Conner maintains that the "Christian cannot recognize any

---

For the Mullins-Scarborough tradition of personal evangelism, see: E. Y. Mullins, *Talks on Soul Winning* (Nashville: Sunday School Board, Southern Baptist Convention, 1920); and L. R. Scarborough, *With Christ after the Lost* (Nashville: Sunday School Board, Southern Baptist Convention, 1919). Even though the Mullins-Scarborough tradition has frequently been faulted for a neglect of an adequate emphasis on discipleship, the plain fact is that more often than not those who followed in its train were loyal and dedicated people whose evangelism grew strong churches firmly committed to the furthering of "the great objects of the kingdom of God" (Baptist Faith and Message, art. XIV).

For an emphasis on discipleship, see: Charles W. Deweese, *A Community of Believers* (Valley Forge, PA: Judson, 1978); E. Glenn Hinson, *The Integrity of the Church* (Nashville: Broadman, 1978); and G. Temp Sparkman, *The Salvation and Nurture of the Child of God* (Valley Forge, PA: Judson, 1983).

For the current recognition of the importance of both emphases, and for an evangelism that results in churches as well as a discipleship which evangelizes, see: Findley B. Edge, *The Greening of the Church*; Delos Miles, *Church Growth—A Mighty River* (Nashville: Broadman, 1981); and Ebbie C. Smith, *Balanced Church Growth* (Nashville: Broadman, 1984).

25. James L. Sullivan, *Rope of Sand with Strength of Steel* (Nashville: Convention Press, 1974), 40.

master in the spiritual realm, in the realm of conscience, without to that extent denying the Lordship of Jesus. This necessarily makes the church a democratic organization."[26]

New Testament congregations exercized their democratic privileges. Sullivan summarizes four such New Testament references:

> 1) Most of Paul's letters were addressed to churches, not just to church leadership, as seen in Rom. 1:7. 2) Acts 6:2-3 clearly indicates that "the twelve apostles called the whole group of disciples together and said, . . . choose seven men among you." 3) Acts 10:47 mentions Peter's referral of the matter of accepting certain brethren as prospects for baptism with the words, "Can any man forbid water, that these should not be baptized?" 4) As Dr. A. T. Robertson pointed out, in Tit. 1:5 in which Paul was urging Titus to "appoint church elders in every town," the word "appoint" had its original meaning "to vote by show of hands," indicating audience participation in the process.[27]

The democratic process is the most effective means available to congregations for determining God's guidance. Included in the process are careful Bible study, deliberation, and prayer with reference to the business at hand, followed by vote of the congregation to determine the will of the majority. This is not to deny that the majority can be wrong! However, even though the democratic process is not infallible, it is still the best way for a congregation to seek God's leadership in matters not specifically dealt with in Scripture. If a church later decides that the majority vote had been wrong, it can repeat the Bible study, deliberate again, pray more, and vote again!

A distinct advantage of the democratic process is that prayerful decision by a majority vote takes seriously the responsible participation of church members in the congregation's affairs. How else can lay persons be more effectively encouraged and practiced?

Even so, not all Christians—not even all evangelicals—are agreed about the strength of the case in favor of the democratic process. Those who approach questions of church government from papal, episcopal, or connectional viewpoints often reject the claim that the church is essen-

26. W. T. Conner, *Christian Doctrine* (Nashville: Broadman, 1937), 267.

27. Sullivan, *Baptist Polity as I See It*, 24-25. This volume is indispensable as a practical approach to an understanding of Southern Baptist church polity.

See also Brown, *The Life of the Church*, 133-34. Brown uses the terms "congregational" and "democratic" interchangeably.

Both Sullivan and Brown emphasize that democratic procedures sometimes take more time than authoritarian decisions. But, since responsible group thinking is usually more reliable than independent, individual thinking, Sullivan comments that the fact that it is slower need not be considered a weakness!

tially a democracy. Writing from a typically Anglican perspective, evangelical Watson says:

> The church is not a democracy with equal votes for every member on all decisions. The clear principle of headship is true both for the human family and for the family of God, the church. . . . In no sense was [the selection of the "pastoral elders" or pastoral assistants in Watson's congregation] an election. The church is not a democracy, and the elders have always been ultimately by appointment.[28]

In a similar vein, Carson rejects the idea that churches in the New Testament established decisions "by mere majority approval."[29]

Conner, however, argues that the Holy Spirit indwells every believer, not simply the church's official class, in order to make known the will of Christ. Each believer's understanding of God's will "is limited by his spiritual perception, not by his official position."[30]

According to congregational polity, congregations practice democratic procedures in their general bodies, such as associations and conventions, as well as in their individual affairs. Only on this basis can churches hope to achieve a balance between their autonomy and their interdependence.

Ministry I: Structuring the Church's Basic Functions

In the earlier discussion of the church as "gifted for ministry" it was said that "no term touches the heart of the nature and purpose of the church more deeply" than the word "ministry." Furthermore, concerning the close relation between the church's ministry and its functions, it was also said that "regardless of whichever of the church's varied functions might be in view at any given moment, the singular mission of the church is to minister."

Regardless of how the church's varying functions are distinguished, the church must never forget its call to minister! The primary business of the church is not institutional self-preservation. The church's calling is first to worship and serve God, and next to think of others before itself (Matt. 22:37-40). No church can please God when its interests are turned primarily inward upon itself or when it is caught up in an activism that has more to do with meetings and programs than with ministry.

Next to the significance of Christ's lordship for church polity is the importance of churches allowing their four basic functions to determine

---

28. David Watson, *I Believe in the Church* (Grand Rapids: Eerdmans, 1978), 87,269,292.
29. D. A. Carson, "Church, Authority in," in *Evangelical Dictionary of Theology,* Walter A. Elwell, ed. (Grand Rapids: Baker, 1984), 230b.
30. Conner, *Christian Doctrine,* 268.

their organizational priorities and structures. These essential functions are worship, nurture, evangelism, and service.[31] Since these functions are indispensable to the church's nature and purpose, congregations are under a biblical mandate to effect their actualization in the life and work of God's people.

Because the church's primary function is to worship,[32] worship structures assume a certain priority over other structures; and because evangelism merits a logical (though not always a chronological) priority in eternal kingdom concerns over service (Matt. 16:26), service ministries should not overshadow evangelistic efforts.

To illustrate something of what is involved in the ever new task of effectively structuring the congregation's basic functions, consider Young's approach to church planning. He identifies twenty-two principles for planning, programming, and evaluating the structures that shape church life. These fall into four categories: basics, people, programming, and structure/function. "Church life," he says, "should not be a series of kneejerk, emotional responses to situations. It should be guided by broad, general principles."[33]

Young's first of the basic principles is obedience to Christ. Following the leading of the Holy Spirit, however, can at times appear foolish or risky, since any proposals to change church structures easily provoke opposition and divisiveness.

Next he turns to the principles that relate to people. Churches that take this principle seriously "put people into, not take them out of, important things." Recognizing that "all of people's needs are not 'religious'" and appreciating that people are different, these churches seek to discover, develop, and utilize each person's unique spiritual gifts.

With regard to programming, his point of departure is that "the church's primary task is not its own organizational growth." Concerned with the church's too frequent tendency to proliferate church programs, Young says that "if a program cannot sustain itself without 'propping up' by the staff, we should let it die."

---

31. See 181-82. Footnote 30 explains why fellowship and proclamation are not included in the list.

32. As indicated earlier "the first and greatest commandment is to love God supremely (Matt. 22:37). Nothing can be right with God's people if the proper God-relation is not in first place" (52). Is it a right God-relation, for instance, that it fuels the fires of evangelism and missions? Without worship evangelism is reduced to human efforts to proselytize.

33. Doyle L. Young, *New Life for Your Church: A Renewal Handbook for Pastors* (Grand Rapids: Baker, 1989), 57-102.

Concerning structures and functions, he emphasizes the importance of pastoral supervision, qualified by the use of a pastoral team.[34] Insisting that every Christian is a minister, he says:

> [The pastoral team] is not just trying to "get people involved." It is not getting big crowds to come hear the professionals hold forth on theological subjects. It is creating the structures and environment where people's gifts are elicited and nurtured, and where places of ministry (not necessarily empty slots in the organization) are found.[35]

Young's title, *New Life for Your Church: A Renewal Handbook for Pastors,* indicates that congregational vitality and renewal are at stake in identifying and structuring the basic functions of the church. Wherever one looks today there are dying congregations that once prospered. Congregations lose their direction and drift as readily as individual believers. Churches must rediscover worship, nurture, evangelism, and service.

There are no panaceas for renewal, but efforts to rekindle commitment to first things is worth whatever price is involved. After all, if the church's organizational life is a matter of God's people implementing the lordship of Christ, the church's business is the King's business, and the rewards are eternal.

When members are convinced that the church's business is God's business, their spirit and attitude improves. This is easily forgotten, and meaningful reminders are indispensable. When a congregation neglects its basic functions to focus on worldly standards of success, such as budgets, buildings, and bodies, inevitably its people, as well as unchurched people, become disenchanted and too easily conclude that the church is nonessential.

Ministry II: Equipping the Laity

Of the themes prominent in church renewal literature since World War II, none has received more attention than the matter of the ministry of the laity, including closely related topics such as the priesthood of all believers and spiritual gifts.

---

34. The pastoral team, as Young employs the expression, represents "the spiritual leaders of the congregation." The team to which he personally refers included the pastor (himself), the Sunday School director, the assistant Sunday School director, and an additional layman. The team met monthly, and Young says: "We were the pastoral team. I knew it, and they knew it. These men, with no formal training, had tremendous spiritual gifts for ministry. It was the closest thing that I have experienced to the New Testament's idea of a shared, team ministry. And it worked well, both for the church and for me as pastor" (Ibid., 98).

35. Ibid., 99.

Strictly speaking, the laity includes all of God's people. It is used here in the qualified sense of lay persons rather than clergy. The problem here is that speaking of lay persons as "ministers,"[36] runs counter to the common use of "minister." The use of "pastor" and "minister" interchangeably is so deeply rooted in daily speech that the likelihood of changing it seems unrealistic. Trueblood writes, "If Dr. Jones is *the* minister of the First Presbyterian Church of Centerville, it follows that the ordinary members of the church are *not* ministers."[37] The advocacy of the ministry of the laity must proceed despite this difficulty.

When church renewal leaders[38] suddenly awakened after World War II to the fact that secularism had deeply penetrated modern culture, they began to realize how isolated and insulated from society the churches were.[39] They recognized that if the church was to penetrate the world as the earliest Christians did, laypersons must abandon their spectator roles and become aggressively involved in witness in the market place.

For this to happen, pastors must be more than professional clergy; they must be enablers of the laity in ministry. Instead of themselves being *the* minister, or the one paid by the congregation to do the work of the church,[40] first-century pastors were congregational leaders who facilitated the equipping of the laity for ministry. According to Paul, church leaders were gifted "for the equipping of the saints for the work of service, to the building up of the body of Christ" (Eph. 4:12).

---

36. Trueblood, however, carries this truth too far when he says that it "erases the distinction between laymen and ministers." D. Elton Trueblood, *Your Other Vocation* (New York: Harper, 1952), 30.

While the New Testament stops short of answering all of today's questions regarding ordination, it leaves no doubt concerning the distinction between the congregation and congregational leaders.

One of the contributions of Hemphill's study of spiritual gifts is his recognition of the gift of leadership. Referring to 1 Thess. 5:12-22, he says: "Even though all members must minister, God has called out some individuals for leadership functions and they must be esteemed for their hard labor." Hemphill, 38.

37. James R. Newby, ed., *The Best of Elton Trueblood* (Nashville: Impact Books, 1979), 134.

38. Although it is now somewhat dated, the following volume is an indispensable introduction to and resource for the study of the post-World War II church renewal movement: Bob E. Patterson, ed., *The Stirring Giant: Renewal Forces at Work in the Modern Church* (Waco, TX: Word, 1971). Patterson provides a compilation of passages from one hundred books and nineteen periodicals, representing the best in church renewal literature from 1952 to 1970.

39. There were other dimensions to the problems facing the churches, such as civil rights, the resurgence of world religions, and a new awareness of the evil aspects of colonialism which further complicated mission strategies for crossing cultural barriers with integrity.

40. In Roman Catholic ecclesiology, the clergy continue to a significant extent to remain the rulers and the laity the subjects. Congar says: "Lay people will always be a subordinate order in the church." See Yves Congar, *Lay People in the Church* (Madison, WI: Bloomsberry, 1985), xxiii. Later Congar acknowledges that in the last few decades some Roman Catholics have made the "veritable discovery that lay people are not outside the church" (Ibid., 49).

Brown is convincing as he speaks of the pressing need to recover the ministry of the laity. He says:

> No wonder the task of the church remains too great for her. The professional clergy [alone] will never be able to do what the church is called to do. The laity, the new people of God, is the greatest unused resource available to the church.... The primary ministry of the laity must be performed in the world.... Therefore, on Monday the church is where you are as a Christian layperson: on the job, at home with your family, in your leisure hours, in the shop, in the office, on the farm, in the health club, or at the social gathering. The minister as clergy can be at only one place. Laypeople must become the minister of the church in the world during the week. This is where most of their time is spent.... What is the primary aim of the church then? Is it to enlist and train laypeople for its organizations and services? Or is it to put theologically capable laypeople out in the world for service? . . . The greatest need of today's church is a new emergence of strong, capable laypeople.[41]

In a similar manner, Edge argues that "the primary responsibility for God's ministry in the world rests upon the shoulders of the layperson and not upon the shoulders of the clergy."[42] He says:

> What is needed is . . . a radical change in the congregation! If lost people are not being won, if unreached people are not being reached, if needy people are not being helped, if the sick are not being visited—if the work of God is not being done . . . —it is the fault of and the responsibility of the [laity] whom God has called to be His ministers! [The idea that the congregation can pay the pastor and other staff members to fulfill the church's ministry] is the most heinous and the most irresponsible heresy that the mind of man ever perpetrated on the Word of God.[43]

Such statements indicate that the greatest single hindrance to the furtherance of God's kingdom is the failure of churches to implement the practice of the priesthood of all believers. The failure is doubly tragic in

---

The neglect of the ministry of the laity is not merely a Catholic problem, however. Protestantism falls short, too. Even the definition of the church in the theology of Luther and Calvin, with its stress on the church as the place where the Word of God is purely preached and where baptism and the Lord's Supper are rightly administered, is a definition of the church in terms of the role of the clergy. The congregation remains secondary.

41. Brown, *The Life of the Church*, 48-50.

42. Findley B. Edge, *The Doctrine of the Laity* (Nashville: Convention Press, 1985), 45. Also by Edge, see *The Greening of the Church*.

43. Ibid., 46.

that it not only represents a limitation in the church's outreach, but also reflects a waste of the rich gifts for ministry with which the Holy Spirit has endowed His people.

Yet, as urgent as the concept of the ministry of the laity is, the difficulty of implementing it in practice must not be ignored.[44] Edge says:

> We are in danger of losing the battle for the ministry of the laity by default. For more than twenty-five years this doctrine has been proclaimed from pulpits, in books, and in journals. But the fact that a biblical truth is discussed does not at all guarantee that it is incorporated into the life and work of the churches. We are in danger of talking the ministry of the laity to death.[45]

Yet, pastors who seek to honor the vision without adequately understanding the crucial role of appointed or set-apart church leaders can suffer a loss of their sense of identity. Consequently, Hemphill says:

> In recent years we have seen a healthy and biblical emphasis on the shared ministry of staff and church members. I rejoice in this discovery. The biblical teaching on spiritual gifts will offer even greater encouragement to the layperson in ministry. We must not allow this discovery to unnecessarily depreciate the work of those men and women called out by God for leadership roles in the church.[46]

The importance of balancing the ministries of laity and leadership in the congregation is a priority item in church renewal.

Despite problems, however, many congregations have experienced new life as members have discovered their gifts and put them to use in ministry. Tillapaugh tells the story of the Bear Valley Baptist Church in

---

44. Edge gives a great deal of attention to "practical proposals" for implementing the ministry of the laity. His main emphasis is on the congregations' formation of small groups, especially what he terms "searching groups." See Findley B. Edge, *The Greening of the Church,* 107-89.

A volume stressing the importance of small groups in the discipling process is Lawrence O. Richards and Gib Martin, *A Theology of Personal Ministry: Spiritual Giftedness in the Local Church* (Grand Rapids: Zondervan, 1981), 228.

Hinson speaks of three vehicles for the renewal of the church: the small group (so effectively used by Wesley), the retreat, and education. Through such vehicles a "dynamic nucleus" begins to take shape in the congregation, a nucleus concerned to transmit the life of Christ to others through contagion more than a formal process. E. Glenn Hinson, *The Church: Design for Survival* (Nashville: Broadman, 1967), 77-81.

Of special importance in any discussion of ways to implement the ministry of the laity is the role of the Sunday School. Though critics of the Sunday School are many, Brown says: "In larger churches, Sunday School classes come nearest to being able to offer caring, personal ministry. . . . Nothing has ever taken the place of the fellowship and individualized ministry of the Sunday School class in the larger church." Brown, *The Life of the Church,* 26,147. Edge disagrees. Edge, *The Greening of the Church,* 126.

45. Ibid., 10.

46. Hemphill, *Spiritual Gifts,* 29.

Denver.[47] Less dramatic, but not less impressive, is the story of multitudes of lay people whose Christian experience has reached new levels of vitality and meaning by using dormant gifts and discovering others they never knew they had. Lay ministry opens many opportunities for Christian witness, but equipping the laity is still under-developed.[48]

Ministry III: Ordination and Leadership

New Testament leaders were just that! They were leaders, not officers in any official sense. In church affairs, establishing leadership roles involves the recognition of proven qualities of moral and spiritual leadership in an individual, not the conferring of authority based on status.

A study of leadership roles in the New Testament indicates both an unfolding *pattern* and a notable *flexibility*. There is significant form and order but no hierarchical rigidity. Radical New Testament critics once conjectured that from an earlier charismatic type of ministry there developed in the New Testament era the rigid episcopal structure which they found in the Pastoral Epistles and attributed to second-century Christianity. Today, however, without denying that there was an element of development, scholars often recognize the importance of set apart leadership roles in the earliest New Testament congregations.[49] Without gifted leadership there can be no effective building "on the foundation of the apostles and prophets, Christ Jesus himself being the corner stone" (Eph. 2:20) or a responsible passing on of the church's rich and living heritage (Acts 2:42; 2 Tim. 2:2).

The pattern of New Testament leadership.—Leadership in the New Testament is both general and local. General leadership roles include apostles, prophets, evangelists, and teachers. Local church leadership

---

47. Frank R. Tillapaugh, *Unleashing the Church: Getting People out of the Fortress and into Ministry* (Ventura, CA: Regal, 1982). The book begins with the story of how rapidly the Bear Valley Baptist Church has grown. This needs to be remembered when in his foreword to the volume Vernon Grounds writes: "Unleash the church! Forget about bringing people in. Focus on getting people out where there are sin and pain and need" (Ibid., 5).

48. In addition to resources already mentioned, two books by Pinson highlight the challenging ministry possibilities open to the people of God. William M. Pinson, Jr., *The Local Church in Ministry* (Nashville: Broadman, 1973), and *Applying the Gospel* (Nashville: Broadman, 1975).

49. Hemphill, for instance, heads his chapter on the significance of 1 Thess. 5:12-22 for a study of New Testament teaching regarding spiritual gifts, "An Early Look at Ministry Structure."

He says: "The consideration of this passage is important for our study for several reasons. It is acknowledged to be one of Paul's earliest letters and it contains a significant passage which addresses the concerns of the ongoing ministry of a local community." He insists that Paul's first concern was that the members of the community give proper respect to their leaders. Hemphill, *Spiritual Gifts*, 18,25.

roles include pastoral and deacon roles, involving ordination, or setting apart by the congregation.

The distinction between pastors and deacons was functional rather than official. Their authority was inherent in their proven qualities of spiritual leadership, not in their offices.[50] They were recognized as leaders because they had proven resourceful in nurturing and guiding God's people. In no sense were they formally interposed, as though by some divine necessity, as mediators between God and His people.

In congregational polity the ordination of pastoral and deacon types of leaders is not a denominational prerogative but the responsibility primarily of the local church. It involves the gathering of the congregation, including at times unofficial representatives from fellow congregations, to set apart publicly the leaders whom the congregation recognizes as called by God to serve.

Without question, unresolved tensions in ordination doctrine and practice remain. For Southern Baptists these tensions include questions as to: 1) which staff members in multiple-staff congregations and which leaders in the denomination generally, whether local, associational, state, national, or international, are to be ordained; 2) and the relation of women in ministry to ordination. Behind these matters is the ongoing concern to probe afresh the essentials of a biblical theology of ordination, especially as it relates to current issues.[51]

The New Testament refers to the pastoral type of role with varied terms, such as pastor, bishop, and elder. Indications are that some congregations may have had a plurality of pastors (Acts 14:23). Functions associated with pastoral leadership include teaching, oversight, and caring. At the heart of all that pastors did was the equipping of the laity for ministry. Pastoral leadership was regarded as entitled to respect and financial support.

Pastor roles did not conflict with the equality before God of all His people. Set-apart ministers were not regarded as constitutive of the church, as though there were *the* channel through which Christ's life flowed to the congregation, or as though they alone were the authoritative teachers of God's word.

---

50. This fact helps to explain why some Baptists, such as C. H. Spurgeon, who was never ordained, minimize the practice of ordination. Baptists generally, however, have practiced ordination, sensing that it is justified by the biblical emphasis on the importance and dedication of God-called leaders.

51. For examples of such probing, see the following essays: Fisher Humphreys, "Ordination and the Church," and Sharon Hodgin Gritz, "The Role of Women in the Church," in *The People of God: Essays on the Believers' Church,* ed. Paul Basden and David S. Dockery (Nashville: Broadman, 1991).

J. B. Lightfoot, though himself an Anglican, says with reference to 1 Corinthians 12:28 and Ephesians 4:11 that "there is an entire silence about priestly functions: for the most exalted office in the Church, the highest gift of the Spirit, conveyed no sacerdotal right which was not enjoyed by the humblest member of the Christian community."[52]

The deacon type of role stressed "serving" (*diakoneo*), a general term that says more about character and commitment than it does about specific function. Deacons were lay leaders who served the congregation in a variety of ways. Women were included in the serving role.[53]

Since the New Testament records few details about church form,[54] apparently the existence and validity of leadership roles was not a divisive issue among early Christians. Most early believers were already familiar with the role of congregational leaders in the synagogues.

The flexibility of New Testament leadership.—The use in the present discussion of the terms "pastor type" and "deacon type" are a recognition that congregations today have leadership roles that are of modern origin and are not directly mentioned in Scripture.[55] Additional roles of the pastoral type in the local church include a wide variety of ministries, such as minister of education, minister of music, minister of youth, counseling minister, church administrator, and church visitor. Additional roles of the pastoral type beyond the local church include associational, state, conventionwide, and mission field ministries, such as director of missions, department head, agency head, institutional head, teacher, chaplain, and missionary. Additional roles of the deacon type include ministries such as Sunday School director, church training director, choir director, church clerk, church treasurer, and presidents of men's and women's organizations.

52. Quoted by P. E. Hughes, "Priesthood," in *Evangelical Dictionary of Theology*.

53. For a summary discussion of these leadership roles, including New Testament references, see H. E. Dana, *A Manual of Ecclesiology*, 2d ed. (Kansas City, KS: Central Seminary Press, 1944), 245-78.

54. Phil. 1:1 is the earliest specific reference to the role of deacon and Acts 11:30 is the first direct reference to pastoral leaders.

55. Stressing that the lack of *specific* biblical precedent for some of today's ministerial roles need not eliminate entirely the sense of a measure of biblical precedent, Humphreys says:

Christians naturally look to the Bible for precedents for their own forms of service. It is no good for an historically alert scholar to point out that it is an anachronism to speak of "professors" or "youth ministers" in the Bible. At an intellectual level this comment is correct, but at the level of lived experience, the need for biblical precedents means that people gain a sense of assurance by identifying themselves with people in the Bible; . . . the cash value of this identification is simply this: "God has called me to do my work as a teacher or president or whatever, just as long ago He called those whose stories I read in the Bible." It is psychologically insensitive to deny the appropriateness of such language.

See Humphreys, "Ordination and the Church," in *The People of God: Essays on the Believers' Church*, 293.

Nor is this the end! As new needs arise, new roles are discovered and developed, guided always by the controlling principles of the New Testament.[56] Remarkable though it is, in the midst of constant change, the New Testament pattern of two basic kinds of set-apart leaders continues to prove an effective solution to the leadership needs of God's people.

The Ordinances

Southern Baptists understand baptism and the Lord's Supper as symbolic ordinances rather than as sacraments conveying special grace. Since Christ Himself ordained them, these ordinances of His are not *mere* symbols: they are divinely given pictures dramatizing 1) His death and resurrection, 2) the believer's death to sin and resurrection to new life through trust in Christ, and 3) the believer's daily sustenance and renewal through vital faith union with Jesus Christ.

The effectiveness of observances of the ordinances is never automatic, but is mediated by the Holy Spirit through Scripture and through the disciplined response of believers. While the ordinances are not saving sacraments, neither are they empty rituals.

In keeping with the symbolism of death and burial to sin and resurrection to new life through faith in Jesus Christ, *baptism* is immersion in the name of the Father, Son, and Holy Spirit. It is the believer's public confession of Christ and open identification with a community of God's people. As symbolizing initial conversion and the beginning of the believer's walk with Christ, it precedes church membership and participation in the Lord's Supper.

Observance of *the Lord's Supper* is an act of obedience to Jesus Christ, who said: "Do this in remembrance of me" (1 Cor. 11:24; Luke 22:19). It memorializes His shed blood, broken body, and resurrection. It also celebrates the certainty of Christ's return and final triumph. Jesus said that He would "never again eat it [the Supper] until it is fulfilled in the kingdom of God" (Luke 22:16), and Paul, also looking forward to the second coming, says, "As often as you eat this bread and drink the cup, you proclaim the Lord's death until He comes" (1 Cor. 11:26). As believers eat the bread and drink the cup, these symbolic actions picture their trust in Christ to supply every daily need and their commitment to follow Him wherever He leads.[57]

Rather than serving as a convenient agenda items for gatherings of general bodies, such as associations or conventions, or for informal, small

---

56. See 190-96.

57. Spivey says of B. H. Carroll that "at the Lord's Supper he emphasized commemoration more than fellowship." James Spivey, "Benajah Harvey Carroll," in *Baptist Theologians,* eds. Timothy George and David S. Dockery (Nashville: Broadman, 1990), 318.

groups, such as retreats, the observance of the ordinances, as also with ordination, is more appropriately a local church matter. This restriction is fitting because the corporate dimension of Christian faith is usually experienced most responsibly and profoundly at the congregational level.

The Autonomy and Interdependence of Local Churches

Since all of Baptist life is to reflect the democratic or voluntary principle, congregations are to seek a balance between their local autonomy and their interdependence with other congregations and general bodies of like faith and order.

Autonomy.—As autonomous, each congregation is free from any authoritarian interference from the outside in governing its own affairs. Consequently, each church holds title to its property, ordains ministers and deacons, calls its own pastor, observes the ordinances, determines its doctrines and its constitution and bylaws, and elects its officeholders.

Also as autonomous, the congregation's relation to general bodies, such as associations, state conventions, and the national convention, is voluntary. Local churches retain their primacy and sovereignty as creators of general bodies. They are free to cooperate or not to cooperate. No formal surrender of independence or delegation of essential authority is involved. Voluntary cooperation is one thing; structured, hierarchical centralization is quite another. Here again the importance of the voluntary principle is obvious.

Interdependence.—Local churches, however, are not only autonomous, they are also interdependent, as their inwardly compelling drive to create general bodies indicates. For a variety of purposes the Holy Spirit, working through Scripture and its witness to Christ, draws congregations together. Such interdependence gives expression to "the tie that binds our hearts in Christian love."[58] Just as Christians need one another in congregational fellowship, churches need one another in order to take the gospel to the ends of the earth, to give mutual aid in distress and adversity, and to deliberate together about common beliefs and the great issues of kingdom advance.

While observance of the Supper, as an act of the community of God's people at worship, has a profoundly corporate dimension, Jesus did not say, "Do this as an expression of your unity and your fellowship with one another," but rather, "Do this in remembrance of Me." Congregational unity and fellowship are involved in the observance of the Supper, as they are in all that the church does, but they are by-products. Yet the emphasis on the Supper as Christ-centered commemoration is just that, a matter of emphasis. Without such an emphasis, however, something is lacking in the quality of the fellowship experienced when the Supper is observed.

58. Hymn, "Blest Be the Tie," John Fawcett, 1782.

The interdependence of congregations *of like faith and order* introduces the modern concept of the denomination and calls for an explanatory word about the existence of Southern Baptists as *a denomination*. It also necessitates a distinction between a denomination and a convention.

The second article of the Constitution of the Southern Baptist Convention reads as follows:

> It is the purpose of the Convention to provide a general organization for Baptists in the United States and its territories for the promotion of Christian missions at home and abroad and any other objects such as Christian education, benevolent enterprises, and social services which it may deem proper and advisable for the furtherance of the Kingdom of God.[59]

Strictly speaking, the Southern Baptist Convention is an annual meeting, not of churches as such, but of messengers from congregations in cooperation with the convention. The convention assembles for the purposes of inspiration and business. "Denomination," then, is a broader concept than "convention." The Southern Baptist denomination is composed of Southern Baptist churches and their enterprises.

In addition to the annual nationwide convention, churches also cooperate through associations and state conventions. Here again, these general meetings are not composed of churches but of messengers from cooperating churches.

These general bodies are creations of the churches and exist to serve the churches. Each general body has its own identity. In keeping with the voluntary principle, each is autonomous, just as congregations are. There is no constituted, hierarchical centralization. No general body is inferior or superior to another. General bodies recommend to the churches and to one another, but they do not prescribe.

With reference to functions, associations are geographically closer to the churches than other general bodies. They help congregations in starting new churches and in disciplining congregations that break fellowship with sister churches. State conventions, since they cover larger geographical areas than associations, represent more congregations. Consequently, they assist the churches in more ambitious projects, such as establishing colleges and publishing state papers. The national convention helps the congregations in even more demanding endeavors, such as home and world missions, publishing, theological seminaries, study commissions, and denominational planning and promotion. On a worldwide level, Southern Baptists fellowship with other Baptist groups through the Baptist World Alliance.

---

59. See any *Annual* of the Southern Baptist Convention.

Such voluntary interdependence and cooperation is a high calling, yet difficulties arise. Each entity develops its own character and tends to go its own way, so that working together requires constant dialogue and readjustments. No organization or agency stays on its given course automatically, any more than persons do. Older institutions often serve their day and lose their reason for existence. New ministry challenges require novel structures. Vigor, vision, and willingness to change are costly.

Even so, the challenge of voluntary cooperation is worth the struggle it involves. When *The Baptist Faith and Message* speaks of "Cooperation" in art. XIV, it says: "Christ's people should, as occasion requires, organize such associations and conventions as may best secure cooperation *for the great objects of the Kingdom of God.*" Were Southern Baptists compelled by this vision (Matt. 6:33), who could estimate what God would do through them?

Evaluating Denominational Divisions

The necessity for evaluating the legitimacy of the modern multiplicity of denominations is inescapable after a century of mainline Christianity's preoccupation with the ecumenical movement.

On the one hand, the assumption that denominational divisions are inherently sinful is commonplace. Even a writer as insightful as S. C. Guthrie asks what can be done about the glaring contradiction between our affirming the unity of the church and the brokenness of the church, which he says we practice. His answer is: "We can give up all attempts to excuse or explain away the scandalous contradiction between our faith and our practice. We can acknowledge the sinfulness of our divisions."[60]

On the other hand, other writers, including some who are ecumenical, focus on the spiritual unity of believers and stress that oneness in Christ is compatible with a constructive and responsible approach to the existence of different denominations.

Four reasons for adopting this latter stance can be cited.

1. *Denominational diversity can provide a system of valuable checks and balances among God's people that is impossible in one-church situations.*—No single denomination can legitimately pretend to have a permanent corner on all of the truth, any more than one believer can justifiably claim to have every gift of the Holy Spirit! When this system of checks and balances works, denominationalism furthers the quest for the wholeness of the Christian faith. Where would Christendom be today without the historical contribution of such groups as the Quakers?

---

60. Shirley C. Guthrie, Jr., *Christian Doctrine* (Atlanta: Knox, 1977), 363-64.

Responsible denominational pluralism can help to serve as a corrective to the overemphases and neglects of particular denominations.

Much is sometimes made of the fact that Christian unity is from God, yet diversity is also God's gift for humanity's well-being. Both unity and diversity, adequately understood, are important.[61] The true church can never be fully encompassed by any of its earthly expressions, not even by a fully ecumenical church, were all denominations somehow to unite in one organization. Could anyone seriously think that the state of the church and its effectiveness in society would be improved by the development of such a single denomination?

2. *Denominational differences are often substantive.*—For instance, affirmations of the voluntary principle, of believer's baptism, and of the church as a fellowship of believers rather than a sacramental institution into which infants are incorporated before any personal commitment of faith are important to those in the Baptist tradition. Denominational traditions can compromise their own integrity by trying to merge with differing traditions in a way that discards hard-won treasures worth preserving.

3. *Christianity appears to have thrived more where there is a diversity of denominations than where one-church ideas have prevailed.*[62]—Christianity has experienced its greatest expansion in the last four hundred years, despite having been exposed to its greatest denominational fragmentation. To recognize this is not to place a premium on division at the expense of unity. Both unity and diversity are important.

4. *The oneness of believers in Christ is more basic than what can be accomplished when significantly differing denominational identities are merely merged.*—Interdenominationalism, whether liberal or conservative, is no better path to spiritual vitality and maturity than denomina-

---

61. To further pursue this claim, see: William R. Estep, *Baptists and Christian Unity* (Nashville: Broadman, 1966), 168-69; John Macquarrie, *Christian Unity and Christian Diversity* (Philadelphia: Westminster, 1975), 16-17; Russell E. Richey, ed., *Denominationalism* (Nashville: Abingdon, 1977); W. R. White, *Baptist Distinctives* (Nashville: Sunday School Board, Southern Baptist Convention, 1946); Barbara Brown Zikmund, *Discovering the Church*, vol. 9, Library of Living Faith (Philadelphia: Westminster, 1983), 82-85.

A volume by Kelley reflects the recent increased awareness of ecumenical deficiencies on the part of observers of American mainline churches. Dean M. Kelley, *Why Conservative Churches Are Growing* (New York: Harper, 1972).

62. Macquarrie says: "It is interesting to notice that Christianity seems to have thrived much more vigorously in countries where there has been denominational diversity than in countries where the great majority of the people are embraced within a single church." He then goes on to cite the examples of Spain and Sweden. John Macquarrie, *Christian Unity and Diversity*, 16-17.

tionalism. No finite form can monopolize the discovery and effective use of the gifts of God's Spirit.

For reasons such as these, despite the seeming erosion of denominational commitment in the twentieth century, it is hardly responsible to speak of the death of denominationalism. McBeth says, "I regard the Baptist denomination as a still viable expression of the Christian faith. While I value the modern ecumenical movement and rejoice in the spirit of brotherhood which increasingly prevails among believers of different labels, I do not yet see the denomination fading away."[63]

The real evil is not necessarily denominational diversity, but lovelessness, contentiousness, divisiveness on the one hand, and arrogant claims to the keys to the kingdom on the other hand. Granted that a lack of brotherly love, a spirit of bitter competitiveness, and the senseless multiplication of church divisions are indefensible, this still does not mean that the only alternative is a repudiation of all denominational differences. Quite to the contrary, it just may be that for God's people the most promising way to a wider expression of their unity in Christ is the gaining of a new appreciation for the responsible diversity in God's family. Trueblood says:

> You cannot be a member of *the church* unless you are sharing actively in the life of *a church*. . . . There is no vital religion in the world today that is not sectarian and there cannot be. . . . Separation into denominations is often as beneficent as it is inevitable. . . . Conscious membership [in a worthy tradition] is the most powerful single stimulus in all behavior.[64]

Religious Liberty

Vital to congregational polity, as was indicated above in the emphasis on the church as a voluntary people, is the doctrine of a free church in a free state.[65] As with other aspects of contemporary society, global as well as American, the problems involved in church-state relations have grown more complex. It just could be that in the days ahead society will be more hostile and that Christians in this country and elsewhere will pay a heavier price for their loyalty to Christ.

In times of social upheaval such as the present, churches face a multiplicity of challenges which they have not faced before.

---

63. H. Leon McBeth, *The Baptist Heritage* (Nashville: Broadman, 1987), 5.

64. D. Elton Trueblood, *Foundations for Reconstruction* (New York: Harper, 1946), 53-55,57. This book, by the way, is an invaluable discussion of the significance of the ten commandments for life today.

65. See William R. Estep, Jr., "Church and State," in *The People of God: Essays on the Believer's Church*, 267-76.

One of God's calls to His people in times of turmoil is to remember that some things do not change! Especially, God's nature and faithfulness do not change; but also His primary purpose for His people remains as unchanging as the canon of Scripture itself!

Yet, it is easy for churches to forget their purpose and to drift in whatever direction the push of the current is strongest for the moment. In this situation Dale has some significant words regarding the way ahead if church renewal is to become a reality for a congregation. He says:

> There are four ways to revitalize a church, organizationally speaking. The easiest change is policy change. You simply adjust the way you do things.

A second strategy is to change personnel. Firing the minister or electing new lay leaders is a common approach. Another change tactic is to create new program structures. Reorganization plans are familiar in institutions of all kinds.

Change policy. Change people. Change programs. Each of these approaches has its advocates. But the approach I suggest is the most basic of all—clarify purpose.

The fourth way to revitalize a church is to define and act on its fundamental purpose. A new dream awakes a congregation. A poster motto challenges: "Aim for the sun. You may not reach it, but you will fly higher than if you never aimed at all."[66]

---

66. Robert D. Dale, *To Dream Again* (Nashville: Broadman, 1981), 5. Also by the same author, see *Keeping the Dream Alive: Understanding and Building Congregational Morale* (Nashville: Broadman, 1988).

PART V

The Kingdom Consummated:

GOD'S ULTIMATE PURPOSE

The consummation of God's redemptive activity has individual and cosmic aspects. The individual part deals with death and the intermediate state before the second coming of Christ. The cosmic dimension concerns the second coming of Christ, the final resurrection, the last judgment, and heaven and hell or the eternal future of God's creatures and His creation.

The Life Beyond

Several initial matters require discussion before considering the doctrines associated with the second coming of Christ. These topics include the nature of biblical prediction, the importance for life today of the doctrine of a future existence, and the two teachings associated with the individual aspect of the consummation, namely, physical death and the intermediate state.

As the Bible opens with a vision, it also concludes with a vision.[1] It begins with a majestic vision of the creation of the heavens and the earth and ends with an awesome vision of the consummation of history, including the return of Christ, the resurrection of the dead, the final judgment,

---

1. Meyer says: "As the Bible ends in an Apocalypse, an unveiling of the future, so it begins with an Apocalypse, an unveiling of the past." *F. B. Meyer*, Great Pulpit Masters, vol. 6 (New York: Revell, 1950), 11. Robert G. Lee provides the introduction for the volume.

and the creation of the new heavens and the new earth. In the measured words of the solemn and venerable Gloria Patria:

> Glory be to the Father, and to the Son, and to the Holy Ghost; As it was in the beginning, is now, and ever shall be world without end! Amen.

Introductory Matters

The Kingdom Consummated and Eschatology

Unfortunately discussions of eschatology are usually restricted to topics related to kingdom consummated. Even writers who emphasize that the kingdom is a present as well as a future reality still tend to limit the use of the term to matters related to the future consummation.

According to the approach taken in the present discussion, all of God's redemptive activity, from its inception to its consummation, is eschatological. The Old Testament presents an eschatology of anticipation; eschatology between the Christ-Pentecost events and the second coming of Christ is the eschatology of the kingdom present; and the eschatology of the life beyond is the eschatology of the kingdom consummated.

In turning to the latter topic, it is necessary to distinguish between individual and cosmic aspects of the kingdom consummated. The *individual* dimension of the life beyond deals with the intermediate state (the question of what happens to Christians who die before the second coming of Christ). The *cosmic* dimension of the world beyond involves four major biblical themes of the final consummation: the second coming, the resurrection, the judgment, and the eternal futures of God's creation and His creatures.[2]

The question of a millennial order, whether regarded as occurring before or after the second coming, is also discussed in the following pages, though it is not a separate topic in any of the great creeds and confessions of Christendom.

The Nature of Biblical Prediction

Serious study of the doctrine of the kingdom consummated raises a question: What is the nature of biblical prediction of future events?

---

2. One of the more balanced and judicious summaries of the doctrine of the kingdom consummated is Mennonite David Ewert's, *And Then Comes the End* (Scottdale, PA: Herald, 1980).

See also Carl E. Armerding and Ward Gasque, eds., *Dreams, Visions, and Oracles* (Grand Rapids: Baker, 1977); Millard J. Erickson, *Christian Theology* (Grand Rapids: Baker, 1985); Anthony A Hoekema, *The Bible and the Future* (Grand Rapids: Eerdmans, 1979); and Stephen Travis, *The Jesus Hope* (Downers Grove, IL: InterVarsity, 1974).

Three topics call for treatment: the distinction between prophecy and prediction; the fact of biblical prediction; and, especially, the conservative debate about the nature and extent of prediction.

The distinction between prophecy and prediction.—Those who write most about biblical prediction seldom distinguish between prediction and prophecy. In fact, books on prediction are often entitled as discussions of prophecy.[3] Yet *prediction* or foretelling is not the dominant aspect of biblical prophecy. *Prophecy*, the broader of the two concepts, is proclaiming God's message to instruct and guide His people (Mic. 3:8; 6:8).

The fact of biblical prediction.—Over against the tendency in radical biblical criticism to deny the fact of biblical prediction, the Bible does make predictions. Old Testament prophets repeatedly predicted a great day of the Lord (Gen. 49:10; 2 Sam. 7:12-16; Ps. 83:3-4; Isa. 7:14; 9:6-7; Jer. 31:31; Joel 2:28; Mic. 5:2). Jesus predicted His death and resurrection, the approaching outpouring of the Holy Spirit, a future era of Christian missions, His second coming, and the like (Matt. 16:21; 17:22-33; 20:18; 24:2,30). The New Testament echoes and enlarges on Jesus' predictions (Acts 1:11; Phil. 3:20; Heb. 9:28).

The conservative debate regarding the nature and extent of biblical prediction.—Conservatives continue to disagree about the nature and extent of biblical prediction. Broadly speaking, the debate is between *dispensationalists* and *non-dispensationalists* (historical premillennialists, amillennialists, and postmillennialists).[4] Dispensationalists often assume that biblical prediction provides a detailed timetable for future events. Non-dispensationalists believe the Bible provides profound, general certainties about God's sure promise to fulfill, finally and gloriously, His redemptive purpose in Christ, but they understand the Bible to minimize the listing of specific names, places, and dates regarding the course of future events.

There is great variety, of course, within each of the two groups. Among recent writing dispensational premillennialists, Walvoord, Ryrie, and others associated with Dallas Theological Seminary give attention to detailed prediction. Grace Theological Seminary dispensationalists, such

---

3. Notice the confusion of the two terms in the following title: J. Barton Payne, *Encyclopedia of Biblical Prophecy: The Complete Guide to Scriptural Predictions and Their Fulfillment* (Grand Rapids: Baker, 1980).

4. More will be said later concerning the millennial options. It should be indicated at once, however, that in the present study dispensationalism is not regarded as a heresy. In its distinctive tenets, as reflected in the Scofield Reference Bible, it does represent a departure from patristic, reformation, and evangelical theology, particularly with reference to the place of the church in the outworking of God's redemptive purpose. Furthermore, its attitude toward nondispensational evangelicals has sometimes been negative and even harsh. Yet its basic position with reference to the themes of individual redemption is soundly evangelical.

In recent years, historical premillennialists such as Ladd, amillennialists such as Hoekema, and postmillennialists such as Davis are united in their firm rejection of a Walvoord-Ryrie type of predicting the future.

as Hoyt, together with other mild dispensationalists of varying sorts, speculate less about such topics as the temporal nearness of the second coming, the exact roles of specific modern nations in preparing for the final battle of Armageddon, and the personal identity of the antichrist.

Dispensational Armageddon calendars. Ryrie's timetable for history's climaxing events includes the following: the failure of the present church dispensation in furthering God's redemptive purposes, since mainline denominations are becoming increasingly apostate; the return of the Jews to Palestine and the establishing of the state of Israel (May 14, 1948), in express fulfillment of Old Testament predictions; the "rapture" (snatching up to heaven) of the true church before the seven-year tribulation immediately preceding the second coming of Christ; with the church removed from the world, during the tribulation and the millennium God shifts His primary dealings from the church to Israel as an earthly, warring, national, political power; the formation by the Gentiles during the tribulation of a ten-nation confederacy, the beginnings of which may already be taking place in the creation of the European Common Market; the establishing by this confederacy of a league with Israel, which is soon broken as the confederacy wages war against Israel; the appearance of the antichrist; armies from the West are joined by armies from the East in battle against God at Armageddon; Christ returns to the earth to establish national Israel's thousand-year earthly, political reign by force over the nations of the world; Israel rebuilds the temple; and more.

Armageddon calendars are constructed with the help of daily newspaper headlines, and they must be revised as the headlines change.[5]

---

5. Charles C. Ryrie, *The Final Countdown: God's Blueprint for Future Events,* rev. ed. (Wheaton, IL: Victor, 1982).

Wilson documents the constant revisions of Armageddon calendars to fit changing newspaper headlines. Dwight Wilson, *Armageddon Now! The Premillenarian Response to Russia and Israel since 1917* (Grand Rapids: Baker, 1977). Wilson's reference to premillenarians, however, is misleading. Since his focus is on the older stance of Moody Bible Institute and Biola College, "dispensationalist" or "dispensational premillennialist" would be more accurate in his title than "premillenarian." Wilson's own background is Assembly of God dispensationalism. His study, which is well done, grows out of his Ph.D. dissertation at the University of California, Santa Cruz. He ends his research, for the most part, with the Six-Day War of 1967 and the publication of Hal Lindsey's *The Late Great Planet Earth* (1970). He omits a discussion of Ladd's appearance on the scene and the lack of interest on the part of post World War II historical premillennialists in the construction of Armageddon calendars.

Whereas Ryrie and other timetable dispensationalists appear overly concerned with an earthly, military-type annihilation of Israel's political enemies, and an earthly, military-political reign of national Israel over other nations during the millennial period, the Bible's central concern is with the gospel, that is, with humankind's spiritual and redemptive needs.

For Ladd's initial attack on Scofield Bible dispensational premillennialism, see George Eldon Ladd, *Crucial Questions about the Kingdom of God* (Grand Rapids: Eerdmans, 1952). A second printing of Ladd's work was soon necessary.

For further critiques of timetable dispensationalism, see Hoekema,'*The Bible and the Future,"* 194-222; Travis, *The Jesus Hope,* 80-91; John P. Newport, *The Lion and the Lamb* (Nashville: Broadman, 1986), especially 101-2; and Robert G. Clouse, "The Danger of Mistaken Hopes," in *Dreams, Visions, and Oracles,* eds. Carl E. Armerding and W. Ward Gasque (Grand Rapids: Baker, 1977), 27-40. As will be noted later, some recent writers in the timetable tradition are modifying its claims.

The non-dispensational evangelical view of biblical prediction.—Two convictions of many evangelicals regarding biblical prediction merit mention. *First,* many evangelicals are convinced that biblical prediction does not emphasize detailed history written beforehand. The Bible is not silent about future events, but it does not spell out a detailed timetable. For instance, Paul indicates in Romans 9-11 that God is not finished with believing Israel, His chosen people. Yet Paul makes no specific reference to any future for Israel as an earthly, political nation.

Humanly speaking, biblical prediction is not specific history written beforehand because present language and experience are inadequate to describe future events. Old Testament predictions of the Messianic Age, for instance, refer to the Messiah as the son of David and to His people as Abraham's descendants. There was simply no humanly understandable way to predict fully the incarnation and Pentecost events before they took place. To recognize Christ as Savior and Lord and to confess that the Holy Spirit is God requires new dimensions of divine self-revelation.

The future which the Old Testament anticipated was beyond anything humanly conceivable at the time the predictions were made. Old Testament predictions of the coming Messiah were indeed remarkable, but they lacked the specificity that would have enabled Old Testament saints to recognize Jesus Christ as the promised One when He came.

There are exceptions to the rule. In early New Testament times, by the aid of the Holy Spirit, select saints in Israel such as Simeon, Anna, John the Baptist, and even Peter had profound momentary glimpses into Christ's identity before the cross, resurrection, and Pentecost events. For the most part, however, even those devout Jews most familiar with Old Testament predictions failed to recognize Jesus as their promised Messiah.[6]

One way in which the biblical writers used the language available to them to speak of the future was to employ symbolic and apocalyptic terms, as in the Book of Revelation. How else could the awesome grandeur of last things have been portrayed? The moon turns to blood, the four horsemen ride, the new Jerusalem descends from heaven—such is the veiled, figurative language common in biblical apocalyptic writing.

---

6. Ryrie misses the point when he speaks of Jesus coming the first time just as He was promised. He speaks of Old Testament predictions being fulfilled to the last detail, of biography written in advance, of Old Testament forecasts of Jesus' death, and the like, and emphasizes the odds against all of these predictions being fulfilled in exact detail.

The point is, however, that we have no indication of any Jew understanding these details *before* the coming of Christ. See the later discussion of the biblical resources for the doctrine of the second coming and the reference to the phenomenon of foreshortening which characterizes Old Testament prediction.

Ryrie, *The Final Countdown*, chap. 3, "He Came as He Promised."

Most non-dispensational evangelicals would probably agree in essence with Mueller that biblical prediction "is the dawn that heralds the coming day, but does not reveal it."[7]

Second, from a positive perspective, non-dispensational evangelicals tend to concur that biblical prediction yields enough knowledge about the future to ground firmly the believer's confidence in the ultimate triumph of God's kingdom. One important reason for such vital certainty is the fact that *the expectation of what God will do grows out of the knowledge of what He has already done.* God is true and faithful as well as almighty. He has already won the decisive victory through the Christ and Pentecost events, guaranteeing the full and final triumph of His redemptive purpose in Christ.

The Importance of the Doctrine of the Kingdom Consummated for Life Today

The secular theology, which has been influential among ecumenical Catholics and Protestants since World War II, stresses the importance of this world but says little of the world to come.[8] Its emphasis falls on the righting of present injustices in society. Any attempt to underscore the importance of the life beyond is dismissed as an effort to flee the social and ethical responsibilities of this life.

In what ways, then, is it true that the biblical emphasis on the certainty of the ultimate victory of God's kingdom is crucially important for living the Christian life today?

1. Belief in the consummation is a reminder that *this world is temporary and is passing away.*—Jesus asked, "What will a man be profited, if he gains the whole world, and forfeits His soul?" (Matt. 16:26). Since life in the present is momentary, He calls His followers to store up treasure, not on earth, but in heaven where things endure (Matt. 6:20; cf. 2 Cor. 4:16-18). It is easy to conceive of regrets at the final judgment, when disciples are faced with reminders of their often half-hearted commitment to Christ in this life. It is impossible to think seriously of any follower of Christ feeling that His kingdom service had been too costly!

2. Belief in consummation says that *today's decisions shape a person's eternal destiny.*—Some believers build with gold, silver, and pre-

---

7. *International Standard Bible Encyclopedia*, 1929 ed., s.v. "Parousia," by John Theodore Mueller, 2249a.

8. For an introduction to the secular emphasis, see the following: John A. T. Robinson, *Honest to God* (Philadelphia: Westminster, 1963); Colin W. Williams, *Where in the World?* (New York: National Council of Churches, 1963), and *What in the World?* (New York: National Council of Churches, 1964); and Harvey Cox, *The Secular City* (New York: Macmillan, 1965).

cious stones, and their work endures. Others, however, build with wood, hay, and stubble, and their work is lost (1 Cor. 3:12-15).

3. Belief in the consummation says that *to live for heaven is to resist evil and to fight against injustice more aggressively now.*—Over against the idea that Christ's soon coming renders it useless to work sacrificially to make this a better world in which to live, belief in heaven seeks to realize as much of heaven on earth as possible. To pray as Jesus teaches His followers to pray is to ask that God's "will be done *on earth* as it is in heaven" (Matt. 6:10).

4. Belief in the consummation underscores Jesus' counsel that *believers need not fear "those who kill the body, but are unable to kill the soul"* (Matt. 10:28).—Faith in the life to come delivers those who trust in the risen Lord from an inordinate fear of death or of anything created and temporal. The real loss, the peril most to be feared, is not physical death but spiritual death.

5. Belief in the consummation stresses that, even in the worst of times, *believers should dream of and courageously live for the great objects of the kingdom of God.*—They need never despair! Evil's present victories are temporary. A great day is coming when righteousness will prevail once and for all, a day when "the earth will be filled with the knowledge of the glory of the Lord as the waters cover the sea" (Hab. 2:14).

Physical Death

Death and the intermediate state are the *individual* aspects of the kingdom consummated. Those who die before the second coming of Christ are brought one by one to face in some measure the realities of the eternal order.

Physical death and dying have fascinated Americans in recent years. Since the 1960s, a whole new science has begun to unfold, the science of thanatology or the study of the social and psychological dimensions of death, dying, and bereavement.

Along with the rapid proliferation of books on the subject, schools at varying levels have initiated courses on death and dying. Elementary school children take tours of funeral homes and cemeteries. Films that portray persons in what was once the privacy and sanctity of their dying moments are casually viewed, even by church groups, with little more than passing curiosity. This new preoccupation with death distinguishes the present generation from its predecessor, with its euphemisms for death and its struggle to avoid facing the subject.[9]

---

9. In 1968 Guthrie wrote: "It is considered bad taste to talk about dying in our time. Death has replaced sex as the subject too obscene for polite society. (Now we say "passed on" instead of "died," and "memorial park" instead of "graveyard"—just as we once said "limbs" instead of "legs.")" Shirley C. Guthrie, Jr., *Christian Doctrine*, (Atlanta: Knox, 1977), 377.

Biblical Resources

A summary of the biblical resources for the study of physical death calls for three observations. First, *the Bible clearly distinguishes between physical death and spiritual death*. While physical death is the cessation of vital bodily functions without the human possibility of resuscitation, spiritual death is sin, or alienation from God's forgiveness and mercy, both now and eternally. Paul referred to spiritual death in writing to the Ephesians, "You were dead in your trespasses and sins" (Eph. 2:1); and to the Romans, "The wages of sin is death, but the free gift of God is eternal life in Christ Jesus our Lord" (Rom. 6:23). In the Romans passage the contrast between the eternal death of the lost and the eternal life of the saved, between hell and heaven, is emphatic.

Second, *the Bible is primarily concerned with redemption, or God's remedy for spiritual death, not with physical death*. In contrast to the preoccupation of traditional theology with physical death as *the* result of sin, the biblical focus is on salvation from sin and spiritual death. Our *first* problem is sin, not mortality. Christ died on the cross to save us from sin. Believers still die physically, but, when they understand the Bible and when their hearts are right with God, physical death is robbed of its sting (1 Cor. 15:55).

Third, although *the Bible* is concerned primarily with redemption from sin, it *never minimizes the seriousness of physical death*.[10] Some reasons for this include the following:

1. Human beings do not just die, as animals do; rather, they have to die. J. S. Whale says:

> Human death may not be explained and dismissed as a purely natural phenomenon, a biological fact which touches man as closely as it touches the bird or the beaver. Death cannot be a purely natural fact for one who is not a purely natural being, but a person made in God's image. . . . There is a world of difference between "dying" (a purely zoological fact, admittedly), and "having to die" (which is

---

10. Contrast the seriousness with which the Bible regards physical death with this statement from the cover of a popular Christian magazine: "The best motivation for providing loving care is knowing that Christians don't die; they merely pass from human care to God's care." *Christianity Today,* April 24, 1981. The magazine, quite obviously, did not intend the statement to be taken as it stands, but as it stands, without any attempt at explanation, it sounds like Mary Baker Eddy, not the Bible.

Guthrie faults both the false pessimism which assumes that death has the last word, and the false optimism which fails to take death seriously enough. His example of the latter is the pagan Platonic doctrine of the soul's *innate* indestructibility and immortality, a doctrine which views physical death, not as the Bible does, but as the *escape* of the soul from the evil prison house of a mortal body, a view which miserably fails to recognize that in Gen. 1, and elsewhere in Scripture, God created the body and saw that as such it was good. Guthrie, *Christian Doctrine,* 379-83.

uniquely and poignantly human). . . . It is the supreme illustration of the incomprehensibility of our world.[11]

Contemporary American funerals often romanticize death, viewing it as springtime when seeds are planted (fall into the ground and die) and flowers bloom, or in terms of the metamorphosis by which worms turn into butterflies. Yet the Bible never plays with death in this manner.

2. Death is the great leveler. It is no respecter of persons. No one, not even pharaohs, escape it. With all solemnity the Book of Hebrews says, "It is appointed for men to die once and after this comes judgment" (Heb. 9:27).

3. In the sense that physical death seals one's destiny forever, it is coldly final. Nowhere does the Bible offer persons a second chance in the life to come.[12]

4. Death often comes, not as a friend, but as a foe. The discussion in the next section recognizes that death can come as a friend, as when it brings a faithful believer release from years of agonizing infirmity and pain. Even so, death, since it wears different faces, can also come as a foe. First, it separates loved ones. Persons are loathe to leave behind those dear ones with whom they have shared the joys and the ills of life through many years. "Love," says Whale, "makes death an immemorial agony."[13] Second, death separates us from God-given tasks we often perform with a full heart but which remain unfinished. Whale says that death is tremendous because life is. Third, death comes as a foe because it comes as a stranger. It is a path one has not trod before. As unknown, its way is foreboding. Fourth, it comes at times lingeringly and with great pain. Fifth, at other times it wrenches loved ones away ruthlessly, as in war, famine, disease, earthquake, fire, flood, and cruel accident. The old English word for grief in death is "bereft." It is a strong word. Death often plunders, robs, rends.

For reasons such as these, the final stage of dying for the Christian can hardly be mere acceptance.[14] There must be an element of acceptance

11. J. S. Whale, *Christian Doctrine* (Cambridge: University, 1941), 174.

12. A strange anomaly in the premillennial view is that it offers some people a chance for salvation *after* the second coming of Christ, thus compromising the teaching regarding the finality of this life in determining eternal destiny.

13. Ibid., 173.

14. According to Kubler-Ross's ground-breaking study, the five stages of death are denial and isolation, anger, bargaining, depression, and acceptance. The author recognizes, though, that these stages do not exist in strict chronological sequence or in complete exclusion from one another. Elisabeth Kubler-Ross, *On Death and Dying* (New York: Macmillan, 1969), chaps. 3-7.

for the child of God, in the light of death's inevitability and the believer's deep trust in the Father's providence. Yet in other ways the Christian may well remain a rebel against physical death, the thief and the foe, until the very end.

Historical Perspective

While the Bible focuses primarily on God's redemptive activity in resolving the problem of sin or spiritual death, Christian thought has traditionally focused on explaining physical death as the result of sin. As a consequence, traditional theologians have had much to say concerning physical death as a divine punishment but little to say to help humans cope redemptively with the agonies of dying.

Restatement

A restatement of a Christian view of physical death revolves around the response to two issues especially: first, since traditional theology has focused on death as the result of sin, the question concerning the relation between physical death and sin is inescapable; second, the familiar claim that physical death is man's greatest enemy also bears close examination.

Physical death and sin.—The basic question here is whether Adam and Eve were created with mortal bodies.[15] From a simple reading of Genesis 1–2, the conclusion appears inescapable that they were created with finite and mortal human bodies. Different kinds of living things were created to reproduce each after its kind. This suggests the beginning and ending of the life cycle, with its stages of growth concomitant with the processes of decay and death. Ostensibly the plants created were plants such as the ones we know. Since they were good for food (1:29), apparently eating them was essential to human survival. Adam and Eve were commanded to "be fruitful and multiply" and to "fill the earth, and subdue it" (1:28), injunctions which appear to apply to earthly life as we know it. Especially important is the fact that "God formed man of dust

---

15. Erickson appears to be of two minds with reference to the relation between sin and bodily mortality. On the one hand, he says that Adam before the fall "was mortal in the sense of being able to die; and when he sinned, that potential or possibility became a reality." On the other hand, Erickson says ambiguously that "physical death came from man's sin; it was not part of God's original intention for humankind."

He also says that "physical death is one of the evils countered and overcome by Christ's resurrection. He was himself delivered from physical death." Jesus was raised from the dead, but He was not delivered from dying. In evangelical theology generally, and contrary to Pentecostal teaching regarding healing, just as Christ does not deliver us from dying, neither does He always deliver us from sickness and suffering. Bodily healing and exemption from calamity were no more included in the atonement than was deathlessness. Erickson, *Christian Theology,* 1170-71.

from the ground" (2:7; cf. 3:19; Ps. 104:29; 1 Cor. 15:47), which is clearly indicative of mortality.

There is not the slightest suggestion in Genesis 1–2 that the world God created was anything other than this temporary earth which began and which is passing away. Apparently it was created to provide a testing ground for human creatures, whom God placed here on probation, since the devotion He desires is a free and willing response from those He created in His own image.

The assumption that the earth before the fall was an eternal New Jerusalem without death, crying, hunger, or pain (Rev. 21:4) lacks biblical justification. The fall was a fall into rebellion against God, with resulting exclusion from the garden of innocence, not a fall from heaven to earth, nor from an immaterial, immortal existence to a material, this-worldly existence.

Notice, however, that the issue here is not what God could have done. God is almighty. He could have created Adam and Eve with deathless, resurrection bodies. That He could have done so is not in question. The question is not what God could have done but what the Bible says He did do.

Remember also that there is a vast difference between saying that Adam and Eve were created mortal and suggesting that human death is a merely natural phenomenon. As already indicated, the Bible takes human physical death too seriously to allow any conclusion that it is no more than a mere, passing, biological concern.

Several *additional biblical considerations* reinforce the idea that Adam and Eve were mortal before the fall. First, it is this perishing, physical body, made from the dust of the ground, that is regarded as God's good creation. Hence Paul can say that the believer's mortal body is "a temple of the Holy Spirit," and admonish believers to "glorify God in your body" (1 Cor. 6:19-20; Rom. 12:1).

Second, the Bible often views physical death as the normal end of a long and fruitful life (Gen. 35:29). For the elderly, death can sometimes bring sweet release from years of pain and infirmity.

Third, physical death, as in the case of Stephen's martyrdom (Acts 7:58, to cite but one biblical example), can be offered to God as an act of discipleship. That which is the direct result of sin cannot as such be so offered.

Fourth, Jesus was without sin and yet He had a mortal body. He died. He was fully human and mortal (He was also fully God and immortal!) and yet He had no sin, simply because sin is an intruder and an alien in human nature. Sin is in no way essential to human nature. Persons fell into sin; they were not created sinners.

Fifth, and especially important, the New Testament firmly rejects as pagan the Gnostic dualism that regards the material order as cursed and inherently evil (Col. 2:23). One of the main problems with the traditional teaching that physical death is wholly and only the result of sin is that it reflects the pagan view of the sinner's mortal body is a curse rather than is God's good creation spoiled.

The traditional view is in line with a medieval, dualistic, Roman Catholic type of thinking that regards sexual relations between husband and wife for any purpose other than procreation as sensual and displeasing to God. This traditional view, however, conflicts with the biblical view that this temporary earth, despite its natural disasters and suffering, is God's good creation (Gen. 1:31).

Refusal to attribute human's creaturely mortality solely and directly to the fall into sin is by no means to hint that we have a complete solution to the persistent problem of the existence of death and natural evil in God's good creation. In the end, human dying can be no more rationally explained than any other aspect of pain or suffering, which is not, so far as we can tell, directly the result of a person's sin.

The Bible stops short of attributing all suffering, sickness, and death in the natural order directly to human sin (Luke 13:1-5; John 9:1-7). It recognizes that God can use pain and death redemptively (as in Jesus' death on the cross, Stephen's martyrdom, and the like) but that for God to use sin redemptively would be to do evil that good might come, thereby contradicting and compromising His righteous nature.

Paul asks, "What shall we say then? Shall we continue in sinning, that grace may abound?" His answer is an adamant, "God forbid!" (Rom. 6:1-2, KJV). Nothing good ever comes to the sinner directly because of sin. The fall was a fall, not an achievement. Any person would be better for all eternity if he or she never sinned. What else could the sinlessness of Jesus mean!

Yet sin and death are closely related. That they can be related is indicated first by exceptional *instances in the Bible where physical death is explicitly said to be a divine punishment for wrong doing.* The extermination of the Canaanites in Israel's conquest of the promised land is viewed, at least in part, as a judgment of God on the blatant wickedness of the Canaanites (Deut. 9:4). Among other examples, the deaths of Ananias and Sapphira are reported in the New Testament as immediate consequences of their having lied to God (Acts 5:1-10). Who could fail to be grateful that their case is highly exceptional!

Second, also reflecting a relation between sin and death are *such matters as hastening one's death through intemperance* or bodily abuse, *fatal accidents due to carelessness* or neglect, and the like.

Third, sin also *tends to aggravate a person's anxiety about the future and death*. This appears to be the meaning of Genesis 3:14-19. The idea is clearly expressed in Isaiah 57:20-21: "The wicked are like the tossing sea . . . . 'There is no peace,' says my God, 'for the wicked.'" Of course, the reverse is also true. As with Adam and Eve in the garden, anxiety intensifies the temptation to sin. In their frailty, instead of seeking the God whose goodness they scorn, persons are tempted to overreach their creaturely limitations and to seek to become as God (Gen. 3:1-5).

Is physical death our greatest enemy?—Ladd says:

> If Jesus is not raised, redemptive history ends in the *cul-de-sac* of a Palestinian grave. Then . . . death is stronger than God; death is stronger than God's word. God's acts are proven futile in the face of man's greatest enemy—[physical] death.[16]

Quite to the contrary, however, the Bible is emphatic that human's greatest problem is not mortality but sin. Death, to be sure, can at times present itself even to believers as a dreaded foe. Paul's message is that those who trust in Christ need not be anxious about death! He even regards death as one of the believer's possessions in Christ (1 Cor. 3:21-22). That is, what is a liability for the unbeliever is, in a sense, an asset for the believer. Death delivers unbelievers into eternal lostness, but it ushers believers into the radiance of God's presence through Christ.

Consequently, Paul faced martyrdom calmly and quietly. Believers who are anxious about dying could well read repeatedly such passages as Romans 8:28-39; 14:8-9; 2 Timothy 4:6-8; and Psalm 23. Such assurance can never come from philosophical reasoning alone. As Conner says, "This confident assurance concerning death and life beyond death is not to be found except where men have found communion with the living God through faith in Christ."[17]

---

16. George Eldon Ladd, *I Believe in the Resurrection of Jesus* (Grand Rapids: Eerdmans, 1975), 144. Surely Ladd misconstrues Paul's stress on the resurrection of Christ.

When Paul says that "if Christ had not been raised, your faith is worthless" (1 Cor. 15:17), and the like, he is not at all suggesting that the essence of biblical redemption is merely the conferring of immortality.

Christ died and rose again to save sinners from the horror of an eternal hell, not merely to save mortals from the grave!

Continued existence beyond death roots originally in persons being created in God's image, that is, in God's work as creator. Unbelievers, as well as believers, continue to live beyond the grave. God's work in redemption deals first with the sin problem.

What Paul is saying is that Christ's resurrection is God's vindication of His Son. If Jesus was not the Son of God, if God was not in Christ reconciling the world to Himself, then we are yet in our sins (2 Cor. 5:19)!

17. W. T. Conner, *The Gospel of Redemption* (Nashville: Broadman, 1945), 306.

By way of conclusion, one observation should be clear—Christians have yet to develop an informed, well-rounded, fully biblical doctrine of physical death.

Intermediate State

If an adequate doctrine of physical death is not easily achieved, the same is even more true of the doctrine of an intermediate state.

The presentation here is a stammering attempt to respond to inescapable and often pressing questions about what happens to those who die during the present interim before the second coming of Christ, the final resurrection, and the last judgment. In effect, the doctrine wrestles with the awkward idea of an *intermediate* heaven and hell. If the Bible reveals few detailed answers to many of the questions people ask about heaven and hell, such as the nature of the eternal bodies of the saved and the lost, it reveals even less about the state of persons in an intermediate heaven and hell.

Yet the fact that our knowledge of the subject is limited should not be used as an excuse to avoid facing forthrightly the problems it raises. Some of the most poignant questions encountered in Christian ministry relate to dilemmas people face about what happens to their loved ones at death. The following discussion then, is not intended as idle speculation but as an effort to take seriously the practical and honest queries of troubled believers. While adequate answers are elusive, the questions beg for response. To remain silent would be insensitive.

Biblical Resources

The concern here is especially with the New Testament witness regarding the intermediate state of believers. (The Old Testament yields few details about the life beyond, and what the New Testament has to say concerns believers especially.) Regarding the fate of unbelievers in the intermediate state, Jesus' parable of the rich man and Lazarus hints that, as believers immediately experience bliss at death, unbelievers are at once exposed to torment (Luke 16:19-31; cf. Heb. 9:27; and 1 Pet. 4:6).[18] This is essentially the extent of the references to the state of unbelievers at death before the final consummation.

The primary New Testament clue to the intermediate state of believers is the repeated insistence that they are *with Christ* in a *conscious existence* that is *far better* than anything experienced in this life. Jesus encouraged the thief on the cross with the brightest of hopes: "Truly I say to you, today you shall be with Me in Paradise" (Luke 23:43). He also

---

18. Although the ideas of *sheol* in the Old Testament and *hades* in the New Testament, and similar biblical themes, are closely related to a discussion of the intermediate state, these topics are dealt with later in relation to the doctrines of heaven and hell.

cried out to the Father from the cross, "Father, into Thy hands I commit My spirit" (Luke 23:46). As Stephen was stoned to death he called on the Lord, saying, "Lord Jesus, receive my spirit!" (Acts 7:59). Just before he was driven out of the city to be stoned, Stephen said: "Behold, I see the heavens opened up and the Son of Man standing at the right hand of God" (Acts 7:56). Paul's confidence in the face of death was that he would be "at home with the Lord" (2 Cor. 5:8). Hence his desire, which was tempered by his zealous commitment to his call to be an apostle as long as he was permitted to live, was "to depart and be with Christ, for that is very much better" (Phil. 1:23).

Jesus' story of the rich man and Lazarus also suggests a heightened quality of conscious experience in the intermediate state. The poor man died and "was carried away by the angels to Abraham's bosom," where he was conscious and active (Luke 16:22). The same thing is further indicated by the conversation of Moses and Elijah with the transfigured Christ (Luke 9:30), by the statement that Jesus preached to the dead (1 Pet. 4:6), and by references to the redeemed as they worship gloriously in heaven (Rev. 5:13; 6:9-11; 14:13; 15:2-4; 19:1-8).

One question that is quick to arise, however, concerns the meaning of references to the believing dead as "sleeping" (Matt. 9:24; John 11:11; Acts 7:60; 1 Cor. 15:51; and 1 Thess. 4:14). How is sleeping related to an active, conscious relationship with Christ?

New Testament references to the death of believers as sleep are best understood from the standpoint of those who are still living. Although those who remain in this life cannot communicate at will with the deceased, this does not mean that the righteous dead have ceased to exist. Sleep is a condition of living persons! The references might also suggest that the separation between the living and the dead is temporary, and that ultimately, after the final consummation, all believers will once again be joyously reunited.[19]

---

19. Noting that Jesus spoke of death as a sleep, Conner says: "By this he did not mean a state of unconsciousness; but doubtless he meant a state of rest as compared with the trouble and turmoil of this life." Conner sees this as an indication of a new outlook of quiet confidence and certainty with reference to death which grew out of the deepened sense of communion with God in this life which Jesus made possible.

Ryrie refers to the use of the term "sleep" with regard to the intermediate state of the righteous dead as a metaphor. He says: "The object of this metaphor is to suggest that as a sleeper does not cease to exist while his body sleeps, so a dead believer continues to exist even if those who remain alive cannot communicate with him." Ryrie, *The Final Countdown*, 82.

Wessel refers to Old Testament references to death as sleep. He says: "Sleep is also used metaphorically of death as is evidenced by the oft recurring phrase in the OT historical books, 'he slept with his fathers' (cf. also Job 14:2; Jer. 51:39)." *Baker's Dictionary of Theology*, 1960, s.v. "Sleep," by Walter W. Wessel.

Primarily, of course, the life beyond death is not something for believers to dread. They are at home with the Lord in an existence superior to anything experienced in this life. This is the basic New Testament witness.

Historical Perspective

Instead of referring to an intermediate state, traditional theologians have usually spoken of a disembodied state,[20] reflecting the widespread view that between death and the final resurrection souls exist without bodies. This idea has to do essentially with one's view of the body-soul relation. At stake is the biblical understanding of human personhood as an embodied existence and the Bible's stress on the life beyond as *resurrection* life, not merely the continued existence of innately immortal souls!

Interestingly, adherents of this view generally stress that disembodied souls are nonetheless conscious. Hoekema, for instance, speaks of disembodied souls as having "very close fellowship with the Lord," or a richer communion with Christ than anything experienced here on earth.[21]

The problem with this view, however, is that of conceptualizing how the existence of disembodied souls can be characterized as a superior form of existence, especially in light of the New Testament stress on the importance of *the resurrection of the body* if heaven is to be heaven, but also remembering that the body is the instrument of self-conscious experience for human beings.

These difficulties are so great that some theologians speak of souls sleeping until the final resurrection. Few advocates of death as disembodiment, though, are willing to press logic so far.[22]

Other writers simply reject out of hand any idea of an intermediate state. They think of an individual's death as the occasion for that person's final resurrection, just as though the second coming of Christ had already taken place. The basis for this interpretation is found in a non-temporal view of the life beyond. Travis says:

> At death we pass beyond the earthly measurements of time. So to discuss how many years may pass between death and resurrection is really to miss the point. All who die in faith are firmly grasped by

---

20. Recently, however, discussions sometimes combine the two expressions. Hoekema, for instance, speaks of the intermediate state but still understands it in terms of a period of disembodinent, a state in which the soul is separated from the body. Hoekema, *The Bible and the Future,* 95.

Trentham expresses the essence of the older disembodied view when he defines physical death as "the escape of the soul from the body." *Encyclopedia of Southern Baptists,* s.v., "Death," by Charles Trentham.

21. Hoekema, *The Bible and the Future,* 107.

22. For one view of soul sleeping, see Oscar Cullmann, *Immortality of the Soul or Resurrection of the Dead?* (London: Epworth, 1958), chap. 4, "Those Who Sleep."

Christ's love, and will not be conscious of any passage of time until the moment when Christ returns.[23]

This understanding of the life to come, however, runs counter to the seriousness with which God takes *history* according to the Bible. To say that heaven is not aware of earth's temporal distinctions, or the difference between past, present, and future, is to rob God's mighty redemptive acts in history of their abiding reality. They are reduced from decisive once-for-all achievements that alter and shape the course of history to mere temporal manifestations of eternal dimensions.

Restatement

From the discussion so far it is evident that there is no simple answer to persistent questions about what happens to believers at death.[24] Building on the New Testament emphasis that during the intermediate state believers are at home with the Lord in a fuller sense than at present, the following restatement first assumes the legitimacy of two presuppositions, then suggests the possibility of three different meanings of resurrection, and concludes with a reference to the relation in Christ between living and dead believers.

Two presuppositions.—The first presupposition is that of a unitary view of the body-soul nature of human existence. When God created persons in His own image, He created them as body-soul creatures, as unique, self-aware creatures, existing in relation to Himself and to one another, and different from angels or animals. Souls without bodies or bodies without souls are less than whole persons. From the biblical perspective, for believers to have a fuller existence in the intermediate state involves their being whole persons, not partial persons.[25]

---

23. Travis, *The Jesus Hope*, 69.

Along the same line, Cotterell says: "Words like 'before,' 'after,' and 'until' don't really apply to the eternal world to which we go when we leave this one." Peter Cotterell, *What the Bible Teaches about Death* (Wheaton, IL: Tyndale House, 1980), 97.

Brunner says: "The New Testament bears witness both to departing and being with Christ and to the appearing of the glory of Christ and His world of the Resurrection as one and the same hope." Emil Brunner, *The Christian Doctrine of the Church, Faith, and the Consummation,* vol. 3, *Dogmatics,* trans. David Cairns and T. H. L. Parker (Philadelphia: Westminster, 1962), 393.

24. Obviously there is no simple way around all of the problems involved in describing the intermediate state. One is faced either with the difficult notion of *an intermediate heaven,* or the idea of a resurrection life which at the same time is not yet the final resurrection life, or one speaks of *two different heavens,* one void of resurrection reality and the other realizing it fully!

25. Over against a unitary view of the body-soul relation such as the present discussion presupposes, Erickson, in defending a disembodied view of the intermediate state, argues for a kind of dualism. He says: "The human being is capable of existing in either a materialized (bodily) or immaterialized condition. We may think of these two conditions in terms of a dualism in which the soul or spirit can exist independently of the body.... Just like matter and energy, the materialized and immaterialized conditions of the human are interconvertible." While indicating that the experience of God in the disembodied state is less intense than the relation to God in the final consummation, he nevertheless insists that "they are of the same qualitative nature." Erickson, *Christian Theology,* 1184. Implied in this position is a suggestion that the resurrection of the body has no significant bearing on the quality of one's relation to God, which simply emphasizes again that there are no easy answers to questions about the intermediate state.

At stake in the stress on whole persons is the biblical emphasis on the believer's relation with Christ in the intermediate state as something *better*. A heightened consciousness at death on the part of body-soul creatures is hardly conceivable without some kind of embodiment, some creaturely organ of consciousness and self-awareness. Acceptance of the idea that disembodied human souls are as vividly self-conscious as though they were clothed with resurrection bodies would require at least some hint of biblical support to justify its defense. Yet such support is wanting.[26]

Since the Bible yields few details about existence in the intermediate state, the main argument for the position presented here is that it is the option most consistent with biblical presuppositions. From a New Testament perspective, it is easier to believe that God supplies His people with some kind of intermediate resurrection body at death than to think of them as existing in any fulfilling sense without bodies. On what possible biblical grounds could a bodiless existence be thought of as a better or higher form of relation to God than we now experience?[27]

The second presupposition of the view of the intermediate state outlined here is that temporal distinctions are real for the eternal order. If angels in heaven rejoice over a sinner who repents, then heaven is aware of events transpiring on earth. To deny this empties the incarnation, and all of the biblical mighty acts of God, of any real significance as a historical events. It is to think of them instead as mere pictures of divine realities that take place all the time. If this is true there is no intermediate state and the final resurrection is no longer viewed as a truly future event.

---

26. In fact, the idea seems more consistent with Platonic idealism or Mary Baker Eddy spiritualism than it does with biblical realism.

27. Three further comments merit mention. First, for those who find it difficult to conceptualize the possibility of an intermediate body beyond death, a body which would be in continuity with the present body which lies molding in a grave, it may be of some help to remember that a person's identity is not dependent on the particular particles which make up his or her body at any given moment. Body particles continually change. In this sense, the individual can have a body which bears his or her personal identity but which is made up of different "particles" than those in the grave. All interpreters are agreed that the resurrection body is *a different kind* of body from the body in the grave (1 Cor. 15:44), even though personal bodily identity persists. Second, concerning writers (such as Hoekema, referred to earlier) who cite Rev. 6:9 as an indication of souls existing in the intermediate state without bodies, it should be noted that these "souls" in heaven wear robes, sing, praise, cry out, sit on thrones, and do other such things. Not a great deal is to be made of this fact, though, since reference to heavenly things with earthbound language inevitably involves some use of figurative language. It should be clear, however, that the souls under the altar are not pictured as mere ideas! A third comment is similar to the second. It is helpful to put together indications outside the Book of Revelation that believers in the intermediate state have bodies of some kind. Each of the passages cited above as indicating that believers in the intermediate state have consciousness also suggests that they have some kind of bodily form. The story or parable of the rich man and Lazarus, for instance, says that when the beggar died "the angels carried him to Abraham's side" (Luke 16:22). At the very least, such references indicate how difficult it is for us to think of an existence in heaven which is far better than our present existence but which is bodiless. Lewis spoils us. He imagines that existence in heaven is more solid, not less substantial! C. S. Lewis, *The Great Divorce* (New York: Macmillan, 1946), especially chap. 3.

Different meanings of resurrection.—If the final resurrection is a really future event, on what basis can it be said that the intermediate state is for believers a kind of resurrection fullness? The answer is that resurrection has different meanings in the Bible. There is ample precedent for the claim that the Bible uses many of its key terms in different ways. Salvation can mean either that one has been saved, or that one is being saved, or that one will be saved. Satan's defeat by Christ can mean either that Satan was defeated at the cross, or that he is being defeated whenever kingdom victories are achieved in history, or that he will be defeated finally when Christ returns. Likewise eschatology can mean either the Old Testament promise of the future, or the presence already of the future through Christ's first coming, or the final, culminating realization of the future at the second coming of Christ.

In a similar manner the Bible employs varied meanings of the believer's resurrection. Believers are already risen in the sense that they receive eternal, resurrection life at conversion (John. 3:16,36; 11:25-26; Eph. 2:6). In an intermediate sense believers have a fuller resurrection life one by one at death. According to 2 Corinthians 5:1-5, Paul shrinks from the thought of being unclothed at death and speaks instead of being clothed with a heavenly dwelling.[28] In a yet fuller sense believers are raised at the final resurrection when Christ returns and redemption is consummated (1 Cor. 15:52).[29]

No one interpretation of the intermediate state has so far won anything like unanimous acceptance, so that diversity of opinions continues to prevail. Yet surely there can be a broad consensus that in the biblical view the believing dead are more alive and conscious in Christ after death than they were in their present existence. They are now, in a fuller sense than was ever true on earth, *with Christ the Lord*. Destiny, to be sure, is not final until history itself is final, but whatever else death is, it is for the believer a portal to a sunrise more glorious than any this earth has known.[30]

---

28. F. F. Bruce, "The Idea of Immortality in Paul," in *A Companion to Paul,* ed. Michael J. Taylor (New York: Alba House, 1975), especially 132.

29. Conner says: "We have a foretaste of the blessedness of redemption in this life; we enter upon a fuller possession of that blessedness at death; we come into full possession of it after judgment." Conner, *The Gospel of Redemption,* 344. Regarding the believer's embodiment during the intermediate state, he says: "Whether we get our resurrection bodies at death or at the consummation of the age, the doctrine of the resurrection gives us the assurance that salvation is for the whole man." He also distinguishes between individuals being brought to eternity at death and humanity as a whole being brought to eternity at the second coming (Ibid., 316).

The matter of the possibility of varied meanings of the resurrection of believers will be discussed again in relation to the doctrine of the general resurrection at the time of the second coming of Christ.

30. Contrary to this view, Finger writes: "The dead in Christ are in some passive state. Perhaps it is not wholly unconscious. It may well approximate pleasant dreaming. It is a 'rest from their labors.' Their sufferings are over. Nevertheless they still exist within the tension of the 'already/not yet.' Until Christ's cosmic victory is consummated, they too will not experience the fullness of his presence and the fulfillment of their individual destinies."

Thomas N. Finger, *Christian Theology: An Eschatological Approach,* vol. 1 (Nashville: Nelson, 1985), 141. Finger is perplexed by Phil. 1:23 and simply insists that Phil. 3:20-21, with its focus on the *parousia,* eliminates the possibility of an intermediate, conscious fellowship with Christ which is "better."

The relation between living and dead believers.—What, then, is the relation in Christ between living and dead believers? This is the question raised by the phrase, "the communion of the saints," in the third article of the Apostles' Creed. First it will be helpful to indicate what the phrase does not mean, and then to suggest what it does mean.

Concerning what the topic does not mean, all forms of occultism or spiritualism, such as the attempts of the living to communicate with the dead, are to be firmly rejected.[31] Also lacking in biblical support are prayers for the dead, as in Roman Catholic and Anglican communions, and baptism for the dead, as in the Mormon church.[32]

What the topic does mean involves taking seriously the basic truth of a oneness of believers in Christ that defies the limits of death. It must be said at once, however, that the oneness of believers referred to here is something far more significant than anything necessarily denied by the existence in this life of multiple denominations. The reference is not to the ecumenical notion of the organizational unity of all living believers but rather to a relation in Christ between living and deceased believers. For instance, is the president of an evangelical seminary justified in invoking the unseen presence of deceased former presidents of the institution as he prays at a founder's day program?

As limited as we are in answering such a question, two emphases pointing to a positive response seem biblically reasonable. First, earth is real to heaven. Many biblical passages indicate as much, even though they fail to give specific indication of the extent of the saints' knowledge of earth's events (Luke 15:7,10; Heb. 12:1-2; and Rev. 6:9-11).

Moreover, the unity of living and dead saints which is in view here is a oneness *in Christ*. That is, the believer's sense of the nearness of those who are already with the Lord is one with his sense of the Lord's nearness through the Word and the Spirit. The communion of living believers is with the Lord; it is with deceased believers through the Lord. It is He they worship, not saints in heaven!

In conclusion, the death-defying communion of the saints is a reminder that Christ's kingdom is eternal, that heaven's chief concern for believers is with their commitment to kingdom priorities, and that the labor of believers in kingdom service in this life is never lost. Hence, the communion of the saints in Christ is significant and real. Through it

---

31. In a strange passage, Phillips reports the late C. S. Lewis appearing to him and speaking to him. J. B. Phillips, *Ring of Truth* (New York: Macmillan, 1967), 118-19.

32. Regarding the latter, the sole text is 1 Cor. 15:29: "Otherwise, what will those do who are baptized for the dead? If the dead are not raised at all, why then are they baptized for them." *The Criswell Study Bible* comments concerning this verse: "Biblical doctrine should not be built on any verse as obscure as this one." Commentaries can only make a wide variety of guesses as to what the verse might mean.

believers today are bonded with Abraham, Moses, Mary, Peter, Paul, Augustine, Luther, Bunyan, Carey, Ann Judson, Fanny Crosby, and a host of others. No wonder that the Book of Hebrews says that "since we have so great a cloud of witnesses surrounding us, let us also lay aside every encumbrance, and the sin which so easily entangles us, and let us run with endurance the race that is set before us, fixing our eyes on Jesus, the author and perfecter of faith" (12:1-2).

16 *The Second Coming of Christ*

The New Testament uses rich and varied language to teach that the next great act of God in human history is the second coming of Christ.

With the topic of the second coming, focus now shifts from *individual* and intermediate concerns to the *cosmic* dimensions of the final consummation. A great day is coming! The Bible never allows us to forget that God is guiding history toward an ultimate climax, toward a grand fulfillment of His purpose in Christ Jesus for all creation. This awesome expectation colors everything of which the Bible speaks. What God has begun in Christ He is bringing to full completion.

Efforts of the biblical writers to describe the breathtaking grandeur of their vision of God's final victory beggars human language. Often they employ apocalyptic and symbolic imagery as they attempt to describe the indescribable. Some of the passages which merit careful study if one is to appreciate the majesty of the Bible's cosmic hope include the following: Isaiah 60; Daniel 7; Matthew 24–25; Romans 8:18-25; 1 Corinthians 15; Ephesians 1:15-23; Philippians 2:1-13; 1 Thessalonians 4:13-18; 2 Peter 3:8-13; and Revelation 6:1–22:21.

Four major themes present themselves in the biblical doctrine of the cosmic aspect of the final consummation: the second coming of Christ, the final resurrection, the last judgment, and eternal destinies, or the doctrines of heaven and hell.

The first major theme is the second coming of Christ, the unmistakable center of the biblical hope for God's final victory. In the sobering words of *The Baptist Faith and Message*, Article X:

> God, in His own time and in His own way, will bring the world to its appropriate end. According to His promise, Jesus Christ will return personally and visibly in glory to the earth; the dead will be raised; and Christ will judge all men in righteousness. The unrighteous will be consigned to Hell, the place of everlasting punishment. The righteous in their resurrected and glorified bodies will receive their reward and will dwell forever in Heaven with the Lord.

Any serious questioning of the crucial importance of the doctrine of Christ's second coming to Christian teaching is indefensible. Dominy says:

> It would be difficult to overestimate the significance of this hope. . . . Apart from the hope of final victory the struggle with sin is inconclusive, death remains an undefeated foe, and the problem of suffering is insoluble. What Paul said about Christ's resurrection, we may also say about His coming. "If only for this life we have hope in Christ, we are to be pitied more than all men" (1 Cor. 15:19).[1]

Yet, at no point in theological discussion is it more true than here that the excesses of extremists are used by those who minimize, or even deny, the doctrine of the second coming to justify their disinterest. A comparable situation prevails with reference to the doctrine of the Holy Spirit.

At times, though, excuses for ignoring the doctrine are even less substantial. Those who are disinterested seek to avoid the topic with a flippant, "Who said He was absent?" Yet, rather than implying that Christ is now absent, the biblical stress on Christ's return takes seriously the fact that the Christ who is coming again is the same Jesus who died on the cross, rose again, and now works in history through the Holy Spirit. In the two-advent eschatology of the New Testament, Christ has already come once, is now victoriously present, and is also yet to come a second time.

Others attempt to play down the doctrine of Christ's return by objecting that the term "second coming" is not a biblical expression. Yet even if the New Testament does not use the precise words, the idea is thoroughly biblical. Besides, the clear reference in Hebrews 9:28 to Christ's

---

1. Bert Dominy, *God's Work of Salvation*, Layman's Library of Christian Doctrine, vol. 8 (Nashville: Broadman, 1986), 155-56.

appearing "a second time" is biblical justification enough for referring to Christ's return as His second coming.

Biblical Resources

Old Testament hope centered broadly on a single great day of the Lord yet to come.[2] No clear distinction was made between a first and a second coming of the Messiah. Instead, Israel's future was telescoped into the hope for one great divine deliverance and judgment, one great day of the Lord.[3]

Not until the coming of Christ did it become clear that the last things would come in two stages, that they would be inaugurated with the first advent of Christ and consummated with His second advent. Given this New Testament perspective of two comings of Christ and looking back to the Old Testament, interpreters can *now* see references in the Old Testament which relate to Christ's first coming (e.g., Isa. 53) and references which relate to His second coming (e.g., Dan. 7). What is missing in the Old Testament itself, when it is viewed apart from later New Testament disclosures, is a specific distinction between the two comings with a clear indication that a long interim would intervene between them.[4]

New Testament studies of Christ's return are abundant in conservative theological circles. Familiar topics in the discussions include: 1) characteristic terms for Christ's return, 2) key New Testament passages, 3) typical ways of describing the event, and 4) the debated issue of signs of His coming. In addition, there are related issues such as a coming tribulation, the future role of Israel as a nation, the appearance of an antichrist, and the question of a millennium. For the following summary of New Testament resources, it will suffice for the present to refer briefly to the general concerns. The related issues will be treated later.

First, regarding New Testament terms for the second coming, six expressions are especially significant:

---

2. For a guide to the study of biblical predictions, see J. Barton Payne, *Encyclopedia of Biblical Prophecy* (Grand Rapids: Baker, 1980). For Old Testament prophecies with reference to Christ, see 665-68.

3. Instead of a reference to telescoping, Hoekema speaks of prophetic perspective or prophetic foreshortening. Anthony A. Hoekema, *The Bible and the Future* (Grand Rapids: Eerdmans, 1979), 9-12,114.

Conner refers to a loss of time perspective. W. T. Conner, *The Gospel of Redemption* (Nashville: Broadman, 1945), 325-26.

4. Payne, and others with a special interest in Old Testament prediction, often have problems with this fact of the Old Testament's telescoping of the time of Christ's two advents. Although Payne recognizes prophetic foreshortening in some places in the Old Testament, he adds: "Yet Old Testament prophecy does not invariably telescope Christ's two advents." Sadly, though, he does not document the exceptions. Payne, *Encyclopedia of Biblical Prophecy*, 139.

• *parousia*, presence (1 Thess. 2:19);

• *epiphaneia*, epiphany, appearing, manifestation (1 Tim. 6:14);

• *apokalupsis*, revealing (1 Cor. 1:7);

• *erchomai*, coming (Matt. 24:30; 1 Cor. 11:26; 16:22);

• *hemera*, day (Phil. 1:6; 2:16);

• *elpis*, hope (Titus 2:13).

Such a variety of terminology reflects the dynamic and thought-provoking style of the writers as they gave witness to the profound, many-sided truths of divine revelation. The variety is a reminder that the mysteries of God's ways with humankind cannot be reduced to neat, final verbal formulas!

Second, concerning key New Testament passages relevant to an in-depth study of the second coming, note the following: Matthew 16:27-28; 24:1–25:46; Mark 8:38; John 14:3; 21:22; Acts 1:11; Romans 2:1-16; 1 Corinthians 1:4-9; 4:5; 15:23; Colossians. 1:5; 3:4; Philippians 3:20-21; 1 Thessalonians 1:10; 4:13-18; 5:1-11; 2 Thessalonians 1:5-10; 2:1-8; 3:6-13; 1 Timothy 6:14; 2 Timothy 4:8; Titus 2:13; Hebrews 9:28; James 5:7-8; 1 Peter 1:7-13; 2 Peter 3:10-14; 1 John 2:28; 3:2-3; Jude 14-16; and Revelation 16:15; 22:7,12,20.

Third, familiar New Testament phrases and images to describe the second advent include the following: Christ comes suddenly, with great power, as lightning, on the clouds, with His holy angels, with a loud shout and trumpet blast; He raises the dead; He gathers His saints from the four corners of the earth; He visits final judgment on all unrighteousness and injustice, and casts the devil and His angels into the bottomless pit; He makes all things new, establishing His sovereignty over all creation and reigning as King of kings and Lord of lords forever and ever, as all heaven rejoices: "Worthy is the Lamb, that was slain to receive power and riches and wisdom and might and honor and glory and blessing" (Rev. 5:12)!

Ewert comments on the range of language employed in biblical descriptions of the second coming as follows:

> Some of [the language] is borrowed from the Old Testament, some from Jewish apocalyptic, some from the political world in which the writers lived, or from ordinary life. All of it, however, has been employed by the biblical writers under the inspiration of the Spirit, to portray the triumph of our Lord at the end of the age.[5]

5. David Ewert, *And Then Comes the End* (Scottdale, PA: Herald, 1980), 90. Ewert's influence throughout the present discussion of Christ's return is gratefully acknowledged.

Fourth, New Testament references to the signs of Christ's coming will be dealt with below in connection with the discussion of the time of Christ's return.

Historical Perspective

Reference to the inadequacy of certain historical approaches to the doctrine of the second coming should alert believers to pitfalls to avoid in the study of the second coming. Some of the misplaced emphases include the following.

First, the chiliastic or millennial teachings of the earliest church fathers tended to neglect a recognition of the Christian's present ethical and social responsibility with reference to the full sweep of God's great redemptive, kingdom purpose in Christ, and to picture the millennial future after Christ's return in overly materialistic terms.

Second, although chiliasm dropped into the background with the beginning of the Constantinian era, the New Testament hope of the second coming was not restored to its proper place in Christian theology. The creeds and confessions of the period affirm the hope of a final consummation of history, but the church's teaching about the end of history tended to lose sight of the close *redemptive* relation between Christ's first and second comings.

Instead of recognizing that the Christ who returns is the same Savior and Lord who came the first time, the inclination of the great theologians of the Constantinian period was to contrast the purposes of the two advents. They easily assumed that Christ came the first time to save, and that He will come the second time to judge.

Third, since the latter part of the nineteenth century, discussion of the Christian hope in American evangelical theology has been so preoccupied with the millennial issue that the crucial doctrines of the second coming, the resurrection, the judgment, and eternal destinies have been neglected. Many of the books dealing with the millennial theme hardly mention these major topics of a biblical doctrine of the final consummation.

Fourth, throughout Christian history, there have been repeated efforts to date Christ's return. Despite sharp New Testament warnings to the contrary, again and again extremists have brought the discussion of the second coming into disrepute with highly speculative efforts to forecast the future.

Fifth, if the weakness of conservative extremists is the inclination to speculate unduly about the exact time of Christ's return, the secular error is the opposite. Recent academic theology tends to treat the promise of the second coming as a first-century myth, emptying it of any specific historical significance. Christ's return is viewed, not as His personal coming to earth to consummate history, but as a *symbol* of His presence already within believers or of some vague concept of innate, human immortality. Any idea of a cosmic divine intervention to end history is dismissed out of hand. Rather, the historical present is somehow taken up into God's timeless eternity as individuals die one by one.

Restatement

As developed here, the restatement of the doctrine of Christ's return revolves around three topics: the nature and purpose of the second coming, the time of the second coming, and the millennial issue.

The Nature and Purpose of the Second Coming of Christ

The first, and by far the most important, aspect of the doctrine of Christ's return is the biblical teaching regarding the nature and purpose of His coming. Yet conservative discussions about the future often dwell at length on the millennial issue, or on the time of His coming, unduly ignoring the underlying and significant matter of the nature and purpose of the event.[6] An exception is Vos, who recognizes that the second advent is "the momentous event."[7]

In order to underscore the aptness of Vos' description, the discussion which follows revolves around eight observations regarding the nature and purpose of the second coming.

First, the indispensable clue to the nature and purpose of the second coming is the nature and purpose of the first coming! *The key to what God will do is what He has done.* God is faithful. He can be counted on. He is not capricious nor arbitrary, acting one way one time and a contrary way another time. Hebrews 13:8 refers to Jesus Christ as "the same yesterday and today and forever."

Christ's first coming set the stage for and guarantees the nature and certainty of His second coming. As the first coming was momentous, so also will be the second coming. As redemption from sin was the theme of the first coming, so also will be the theme of the second coming. The pur-

---

6. Hoekema is typical, even though his book on the subject is one of the best in the area. Out of seven chapters devoted to the second coming, he gives less than two pages to the manner or nature of Jesus' coming, indicating only in passing that Christ's return will be personal, visible, and glorious. Hoekema, *The Bible and the Future*, 171-72.

7. Geerhardus Vos, *The Pauline Eschatology* (Grand Rapids: Eerdmans, 1930; reprint 1960), 76.

Grier employs the expression as the title for his discussion of the second coming, a popular work which has gone through several printings. W. J. Grier, *The Momentous Event* (Belfast: Evangelical Book Shop, 1945; Carlisle, PA: Banner of Truth Trust, reprint 1976).

Despite his title, Grier devotes only his first brief chapter of slightly over three pages to the momentous event itself. The remaining discussion wrestles with the time of Christ's coming and the millennial question.

poses Christ consummates are the purposes for which He died and rose again, and for the pursuit of which He poured out the Holy Spirit, the Giver of life, through whom He is present with His people, and through whom He also inspired the Scriptures in order to guide His people.

Discussing the basis on which the best is yet ahead for believers, Travis says:

> The one who will meet us at the end is not some unknown, fearsome figure, but Jesus. . . . So we can face the future with confidence—not because we have a crystal ball in which to see all the details, but because the future is in the hands of one we know.[8]

Before moving to the next point, it should be noted that the continuity between Christ's two comings means, for one thing, that they are not to be divorced. One way to divorce them is to take the Old Testament as the major clue to the nature and purpose of the second coming, just as though there were no Christ-Pentecost events or New Testament.

This cannot be! Whatever else the future is, it is a New Testament future, not merely an Old Testament future. As Christian, the future is spiritual and redemptive, not primarily national and military. The Christ who returns is the Savior, the one who bears in His body the marks of the cross, and whose weapon is the Word of God, the sword of the Spirit.

The two advents are not simply to be contrasted, as when it is said that Christ came the first time in humiliation but that He will return in glory, or that He came the first time as Savior but will return as Judge.[9] There is truth in such statements, to be sure, but it is easily overdone. The New Testament stress is not on contrast but on continuity.

Although the first coming was costly in terms of the humiliation of the incarnation and the cross, it was also glorious and triumphant. Essential to the New Testament gospel is the recognition that Christ's life, death, and resurrection were a victory won once and for all, that He bestowed the Holy Spirit in power, that He already reigns from His throne in heaven, and that the promise of His return in glory is unshakable. In this

---

8. Stephen Travis, *The Jesus Hope* (Downers Grove, IL: InterVarsity, 1976), 32.

9. Conner's first point in discussing the purpose of the second coming is that "Christ is not to return to save the world, but to judge it." Yet, though Conner here strangely reverts to the traditional focus on the second coming as judgment, his second point is that when Christ returns He comes as Redeemer: He returns "not to establish a temporal kingdom on earth, but to consummate the mediatorial kingdom and usher in the eternal kingdom." W. T. Conner, *Christian Doctrine* (Nashville: Broadman, 1937), 308.

Grier says: "The historic Protestant position is not millenarian. It insists that the second coming of Christ is the signal for the final and general judgment." Oddly, though the context refers also to the general resurrection, this concluding statement mentions only the judgment. Grier, *The Momentous Event*, 31.

The New Testament knows of no role change when Christ returns. He came the first time as Savior and Judge, and He returns in the same dual role.

sense, the good news of Christ's first coming and the redemption He achieved is "the only thing that has ever really happened" in history,[10] and as such is the indispensable clue to the meaning of all history from God's perspective.

The second coming is the consummation of all that Jesus inaugurated through His first coming. All that is yet to be is grounded in the decisive, once-for-all Christ and Pentecost events at the center of all history.

Second, at the heart of Christ's return as an event is the Person who comes. The event is momentous because the Person is momentous. Christian hope is the Jesus hope! Travis says: "The end of the world is no mere event, but a meeting with a Person."[11]

Too often today's discussions stress the accoutrements of His return— the lightning, the holy angels, the shout, the trumpet sound. Or they debate such issues as the future of national Israel, the role of the 144,000 during the tribulation, the identity of the antichrist, and the nature and purpose of a millennium.

These are secondary concerns. At the forefront of the event is Christ Himself. To see Him, to be exposed to His presence—this is primarily what the second coming is all about. Longenecker says:

> It is the return of Christ, therefore, that is the focus of the futuristic message of the New Testament. Any attempt to shift this focus, whether in theory or in practice and for whatever reasons, can rightly be called "sectarian" because it alters the thrust of the biblical proclamation.[12]

Third, the purpose of the second coming is the consummation of God's redemptive purpose in Christ. D-Day has taken place, V-Day is coming. Jesus will reign, and every knee will bow and every tongue confess that He is Lord (Phil. 2:6-11). According to the Book of Revelation, at the sounding of the seventh trumpet loud voices in heaven proclaim: "The kingdom of the world has become the kingdom of our Lord and of His Christ, and He will reign forever and ever" (Rev. 11:15).

The second coming gives emphasis and focus to the fact that Christianity is significantly forward looking. It is a religion of hope, a hope

---

10. Dorothy L. Sayers, *The Man Born to Be King* (New York: Harper, 1943), 22.

11. Travis, *The Jesus Hope*, 55.

For the biblical emphasis on the one who comes, recall the discussion of the biblical terms for Christ's return: the *parousia* is Christ's coming, the *epiphaneia* is Christ's appearing, the *hemera* is the day of the Lord, and so forth.

12. Richard N. Longenecker, "The Return of Christ," in *Dreams, Visions, and Oracles*, eds. Carl E. Armerding and W. Ward Gasque (Grand Rapids: Baker, 1977), 149.

Nowhere else in the New Testament is Christ more central to the Christian hope than in the Book of Revelation. Yet it remained for Summers to highlight the fact through the title he selected for his commentary on Revelation. Ray Summers, *Worthy Is the Lamb* (Nashville: Broadman, 1951).

which the New Testament describes as "a living hope (1 Pet. 1:3), a good hope (2 Thess. 2:16-17), and a blessed hope (Titus 2:13)."[13] This hope is also a sure hope, since it springs from the decisive victory which God has already accomplished through the Christ-Pentecost events.

Yet the Christian hope remains a hope. Christians do not live in the past. Their longing is not a nostalgic escapism, a sentimental yearning to return to "good old days." Rather, the biblical God is up front, beckoning His people forward. His young people see visions and His older persons dream dreams (Acts 2:17). Travis says: "The Christian life means looking forward to the coming of Christ, like runners straining for the finishing tape."[14]

Consequently, the crucial question concerns underscoring what it is that the New Testament looks forward to primarily. What is the central content of the Christian hope? The clear and indisputable answer, despite the fact that it is so sadly neglected in conservative writings, is that the New Testament looks forward to the four grand and major aspects of the final consummation: the second coming, the general resurrection, the last judgment, and eternal destinies.

The New Testament views Christ's return as the time when the warfare between the forces of righteousness and the powers of darkness will be decisively terminated, when believers will be gathered together from the four corners of the earth in full and glorious reunion with their blessed Lord and fellow Christians, when wickedness will be judged, and when history will be brought to its climax as the new heavens and the new earth are ushered in. It goes without saying, of course, that these are developments which only the triune God Himself can bring to pass.

Manley's perspective illustrates a more limited way of viewing the content of the Christian hope. He says that the purpose "most immediately connected with the *parousia*" in the New Testament is the gathering together of all believers.[15] He supports his view with data such as the following: Jesus speaks of gathering the wheat at harvest time (Matt. 13:30); the same word is used with reference to His lament over Jerusalem: "How often I wanted to gather your children together" (Matt. 23:37); Paul writes concerning the coming of our Lord Jesus Christ and our being gathered to Him (2 Thess. 2:1); and, in John's Gospel, as Christ has gone to prepare a place for His own, so He will return to gather believers to be with Himself, so that they may be where He is (John 14:3).

Obviously, Manley's view is not without significant biblical support. Yet, though it is a very comforting and beautiful emphasis for individual

---

13. Ewert, *And Then Comes the End*, 174-75.
14. Travis, *The Jesus Hope*, 93.
15. G. T. Manley, The Return of Christ (London: InterVarsity, 1960), 47.

believers, it fails to do justice to the broader individual, corporate, and cosmic dimensions of Christ's return.

The question of the purpose of the second coming is difficult for premillennialists with their emphasis that when Christ returns He will establish an earthly, temporal and temporary, utopian, millennial order. Such a view tends to subordinate crucial, transhistorical, redemptive concerns, such as the final resurrection, the last judgment, and eternal destinies to earthly, utopian concerns.[16]

Fourth, Christ's coming again is the major event in a complex of events. Ewert says: "The return of Christ is not simply one of a dozen other themes in this area of biblical teaching; it is the very heart and center of our hope."[17] Longenecker says:

> It is not, after all, learned discourses on "the signs of the times" that form the apex of eschatological preaching, else Christianity becomes only another form of esoteric Gnosticism. Nor is the Christian's "blessed hope" a deliverance from the Tribulation, the arrival of the Millennium, the redemption of the 144,000, the establishment of the New Jerusalem, or anything of the like. . . . It is, therefore, the return of Christ that should be preeminent in the Christian's expectation and in His proclamation regarding the future.[18]

To emphasize that the second coming is the major event in a complex of events makes sense only when it is understood in the context of the points already underscored: 1) the biblical clue to the meaning of the second coming is the nature of the first coming; 2) the significance of the event derives first of all from the majesty of Him who comes; 3) and the purpose of the Christ's return is *redemptive*, not primarily earthly, national, political, social, or military. Without this focus the discussion of the second coming is sure to be sidetracked by secondary concerns.

To say the same thing in another way, the main issue dividing dispensational from non-dispensational evangelical views of the second coming is not the literal versus the figurative interpretation of the Bible. Conservatives are agreed, not only that the Bible sometimes employs figurative language, but also that the starting point in all theological construction is the literal, historical-grammatical meaning of Scripture which the authors intended. The issue dividing dispensational and non-dispensa-

---

16. Erickson says: "The first major feature of the premillennial system is an earthly reign of Christ that is established by His second coming. . . . This reign means that there will be complete peace, righteousness, and justice among men." Millard J. Erickson, *Contemporary Options in Eschatology: A Study of the Millennium* (Grand Rapids: Baker, 1977), 91.
17. Ewert, *And Then Comes the End,* 80.
18. Longenecker, "The Return of Christ," 149-50.

tional evangelicals regarding the second coming is whether it is primarily a redemptive and Christian event or a national, political, Jewish event.

Fifth, Christ's return is a certain event. Its certainty roots 1) in the clear New Testament teaching that Christ is coming again, 2) in the decisiveness of the victory achieved by God through the Christ-Pentecost events occurring at the first coming, and 3) in the faithfulness and reliability of God. Biblical writers are one in their firm conviction that God is guiding history toward its culmination in Christ.

Such certainty is far more important to the New Testament writers than a knowledge of the precise time of Christ's coming. The thought of believers standing one day in Christ's presence is utterly astounding and takes precedence over secondary questions concerning the day and the hour of His return. Bruce says: "The time of its occurrence does not matter so much as the fact that its occurrence is assured."[19]

Sixth, the second coming of Christ is a real event. It does not have to be demythologized.[20] Even though in some respects it is supernatural and transhistorical, at the same time it really happens. At stake here is the seriousness with which the biblical writers take the historicity of God's redemptive revelation. The mighty acts of God on which biblical proclamation rests actually happened. Just as Christ's first coming was an event in history, so the second coming of "this Jesus" (Acts 1:11) will be a real event.

Sloan says that Christ's coming is "no vaguely distant, final term of secular history."[21] History does not just fade away. God Himself draws the final curtain when and as He will. Over against the demythologizing of Bultmann, Thiselton says:

> The *parousia* in the New Testament remains a genuinely future event. It is not a mere linguistic cipher calling attention to man's condition in the present.[22]

---

19. Everett F. Harrison, ed. *Baker's Dictionary of Theology* (Grand Rapids: Baker, 1960), s.v. "Eschatology" by F. F. Bruce, 193.

20. The modern denial of Christ's personal return to the earth takes a variety of forms. Dodd says that the idea of an end to history "is no more than a fiction designed to express the reality of theology within history." And again: "All that the church hoped for in the second coming of Christ is already given in its present experience of Christ through the Spirit." C. H. Dodd, *The Apostolic Preaching and Its Developments* (London: Hodder & Stoughton, 1936), 82,73.

Bruce refers to a 1957 statement of Beasley-Murray's that the denial of Christ's personal return to earth had become "a new orthodoxy" among academic theologians in Britain. Harrison, *Baker's Dictionary of Theology,* 192.

21. Robert B. Sloan, Jr., *The Favorable Year of the Lord* (Austin, TX: Scholar Press, 1977), 165.

22. Anthony C. Thiselton, "The *Parousia* in Modern Theology," *Tyndale Bulletin* 27(1976):39.

Also at stake in the historical reality of the second coming is its personal nature. The Christ who comes again is the Christ who has already come, who arose bodily from the grave, and who ascended personally and bodily into heaven. Hence, *The Baptist Faith and Message* stresses that Christ will return "personally and visibly in glory to the earth" (Art. X). This is the public nature of the event: "And every eye will see Him" (Rev. 1:7). Again, in graphic detail Paul writes that Christ will come with a loud command, with the voice of the archangel, and with the trumpet call of God (1 Thess. 4:16).

Seventh, the coming of Christ is a cosmic event, both in the scope of the event and also in its apocalyptic nature. With reference to the former, the second coming touches and involves all creation. Thiselton says:

> Christian eschatology is set in cosmic terms, not simply in terms of the individual's moment of death. It is a symptom of our modern individualism that we hear protests to the effect that the threat of imminent individual death is more real to the average Christian than the expectation of the *parousia* of Christ. To make this protest at all is to confess a certain degree of self-centeredness. The great questions which concerned Jesus and Paul were not questions about their own personal identity, so much as questions about the destiny of the Church and the world, and especially the cosmic purposes of *God*. How and when will God vindicate His name? How and when will God be true to His promises?[23]

The role of all creation in the consummation will be dealt with further in the discussion of the new heavens and the new earth.

Also, remembering that apocalyptic language uses a cosmic vocabulary, the return of Christ is a cosmic event in the sense that Scripture freely uses apocalyptic language to describe it. Luke 21:25-27 says:

> There will be signs in the sun and moon and stars, and upon the earth dismay among nations, in perplexity at the roaring of the sea and the waves, men fainting from fear and the expectation of the things which are coming upon the world, for the powers of the heavens will be shaken. And then they will see the Son of Man coming in a cloud with power and great glory.[24]

Two things should be said here regarding the second coming as apocalyptic. First, the use of apocalyptic language heightens the sense of the

---

23. Ibid., 52.
24. For brief summaries of the apocalyptic language used to describe the second coming, see Richard N. Longenecker, "The Return of Christ," 158-60, and Ewert, *And Then Comes the End,* 86-90.

suprahistorical aspects of Christ's return. The consummation is the work of God, not merely of humans; only God's power can bring it to pass. As suprahistorical the consummation is also vastly beyond the descriptive powers of ordinary human language. The use of apocalyptic language emphasizes the *awesomeness* of what is yet to be.

Second, the use of apocalyptic language is a reminder that God employs the catastrophes of history as vehicles in the furthering of His purposes of redemption and judgment. That the final manifestation of Christ in His role as Redeemer and Judge could occur in connection with some unprecedented cataclysmic upheaval seems to be suggested by Jesus Himself (Matt. 24).

Remember, however, that although God uses the catastrophic dimension in the execution of His purposes, His kingdom is spiritual and redemptive, so that its purposes cannot be furthered primarily by the sudden, the overwhelming, or the cataclysmic. Jesus' wilderness temptations clearly demonstrated this fact. God's kingdom comes savingly when persons willingly respond to His love and patient forbearance, not when they are drivenor compelled. Apocalyptic language is not the main language of Scripture.

Eighth, the second advent is a glorious and triumphant event. This emphasis is primarily by way of a summary of the preceding points, as well as an anticipation of the discussion of the remaining major events of the final consummation, namely the final resurrection, the last judgment, and eternal destinies.

Christ's second coming is final Victory Day. While His coming is delayed, the martyrs under the altar in glory call in a loud voice, "How long, O Lord, holy and true, wilt thou retrain from judging and avenging our blood on those who dwell on the earth" (Rev. 6:9-10). Even the rocks cry out for Him to reign (Luke 19:40). And the Book of Revelation ends with a solemn invocation: "Amen. Come, Lord Jesus" (Rev. 22:20).

The Time of the Second Coming

The second topic involved in formulating the doctrine of Christ's return concerns the time of its occurrence. Three issues are to be discussed: 1) reasons for recent speculation; 2) the Bible and signs of Christ's return; and 3) guidelines for dealing with the time question.

Reasons for recent speculation.—Since speculation regarding the time of Christ's return has escalated noticeably among American conservatives in recent years, as is clearly indicated by the phenomenal popularity of Hal Lindsey's *The Late Great Planet Earth* and John F. Walvoord's revised *Armageddon, Oil, and the Middle East Crisis*,[25] the question arises as to why there is such special interest.

Two explanations of the recent fascination with Armageddon calendars come readily to mind. The first grows out of the proliferation in recent years of threats to human survival. Following the use of the atomic bomb in World War II, humankind has been increasingly haunted by the specter of nuclear extinction. Meanwhile, other menaces have kept pyramiding: the population explosion, famine and hunger, disease, pollution, economic injustices, the energy crisis, the diminishing of natural resources, festering alienations in the human community, increasing crime and violence, war, terrorism, natural calamities, and the like. Cults feed on humankind's fears and uncertainties. Astrologies thrive. Satan worship is blatant and open. By any test, along with other similar periods in human history, these are indeed apocalyptic times.

A second explanation of a quite different kind is the fact of the establishing of the state of Israel, May 14, 1948, and the assumption that it signals the nearness of the end according to biblical prediction. Since 1948, each new crisis in the Middle East, especially the Six-Day War of 1967, resulting in Israel's occupation of Jerusalem, and the Persian Gulf War of 1991, has sparked renewed insistence, on the part of timetable dispensationalists especially, that the end of history is near.

In addition to these explanations, the continuing wave of endtime speculation reflects humankind's inordinate fear of the unknown, his insatiable curiosity regarding the future, and his inflated confidence, veiled at times by the claim that forecasts are based on a literal interpretation of Scripture and that predictions can be made with precision concerning future course of world events.[26] Biblical scholars should have learned long ago that "the important thing is not that Christ's return is near, but that it is *intended*— by a God whose faithfulness is well-known."[27]

The Bible and signs of the time of Christ's return.—Next it is necessary first to refer briefly to the New Testament approach to the matter of signs of Jesus' coming. Three questions especially merit attention: 1) what is Jesus' teaching with reference to the signs of His coming?; 2) did the New Testament writers change their minds during their own lifetimes concern-

---

25. Hal Lindsey, *The Late Great Planet Earth: A Penetrating Look at Incredible Prophecies Involving This Generation* (Grand Rapids: Zondervan, 1970), and John F. Walvoord, *Armageddon, Oil, and the Middle East Crisis: What the Bible Says about the Future of the Middle East and the End of Western Civilization* (Grand Rapids: Zondervan, 1974; revised, 1990). Also see Charles H. Dyer, *The Rise of Babylon: Sign of the End Times* (Wheaton, IL: Tyndale House, 1991).

26. Robert G. Clouse, "The Danger of Mistaken Hopes," in *Dreams, Visions, and Oracles,* eds. Carl E. Armerding and W. Ward Gasque (Grand Rapids: Baker, 1977), 27-39, and Ewert, *And Then Comes the End,* chaps. 1-3.

27. Travis, *The Jesus Hope*, 50.

ing the chronological nearness of Christ's return?; and 3) regarding New Testament references to such topics as a future for national Israel, a great tribulation, and an antichrist, are these references specific enough to enable believers today accurately to predict when the second coming is chronologically near?

The amount of space allotted to these questions in the pages which follow reflects the inordinate amount of attention which they receive in current evangelical literature rather than their importance to the writers of the New Testament. It also reflects the conviction that the questions are of sufficient interest to evangelicals to merit the consideration given to them here.

First, concerning Jesus' teaching with reference to the signs of His coming, two observations require comment. One of these relates to the kind of phenomena which Jesus regarded as signs of the end of the age. In Matthew 24, which is typical of His other references, He speaks of such matters as deceivers, wars, famines, earthquakes, persecutions, apostasies, false prophets, an increase in wickedness, the preaching of the gospel to all nations, the abomination that causes desolation, seemingly unequaled distress, false Christs, false signs and miracles, cataclysmic disorders, and wickedness as in the days of Noah. What is important here is an awareness of what these phenomena have in common, namely, that each of them is a aspect of ordinary history.

Another observation involves the tension between the present and the future in Jesus' teaching regarding the signs of His coming. On the one hand, He says that when His followers see the signs they can know that the end of the age is near, even right at the door. He even adds that "this generation" will not pass away until these things have happened. Yet, on the other hand, He also stresses that His coming will be sudden, that no one knows the day and hour of His coming, not even the angels, and that His coming will be unexpected.

Furthermore, with each of these types of sayings, He appears to refer both to the destruction of Jerusalem in the first century as well as to the final consummation at the end of history. Yet He gives no clear indication as to when He is referring to the one and when to the other.

In the light of these considerations, the conclusion seems justified that Jesus' references to the signs of His coming were given, not to indicate a precise date for His return, but: 1) to warn His followers that trouble and distress would continue to be their lot as long as history continued, 2) to caution them against preoccupation with attempts to determine the precise time of His coming, and 3) to assure them of God's faithfulness to the end. On this basis, Ewert speaks of "the signs of the times for all times."[28]

---

28. Ewert, *And Then Comes the End,* 31.

Jesus' prediction that the gospel would be preached "in the whole world as a testimony to all nations" before the end would come (Matt. 24:14) is especially significant. The reference should not be taken to teach that the day of Christ's return can be hastened by intensified evangelistic efforts.[29] Rather, the gospel is to be preached in every generation, with full assurance that God will not allow His purpose for its world-wide proclamation to fail. Instead of a defeatist preoccupation with the darkness and the difficulties of the hour, Jesus called His followers to heroic commitment and endurance whatever the circumstances.

Second, concerning the question as to whether New Testament writers had a change of mind during their lifetime regarding the chronological nearness of Christ's return, there is no denying that some people in New Testament times expected an immediate return of Christ. There were scoffers who asked why Christ delayed His return (2 Pet. 3:3-4), and the Thessalonians were distressed when some of their fellow believers died before the occurrence of the *parousia* and the final resurrection (1 Thess. 4:13). On the basis of such references, even Paul is sometimes said to have changed his mind from an earlier expectation that Christ would return while he was still alive (1 Cor. 15:51) to a belief that he would die before the second coming (2 Cor. 5:1-10).[30] What are we to make this claim? Did Paul and other New Testament writers change their minds on the subject?

---

29. Ladd once wrote:
> Here is the thing that thrills me.... If God's people in the English-speaking world alone took this text [Matt. 24:14] seriously and responded to its challenge, we could finish the task of world-wide evangelization in our own generation and witness the Lord's return.

George Eldon Ladd, *The Gospel of the Kingdom* (Grand Rapids: Eerdmans, 1959), 136.
    Wright says: "It seems, therefore, [on the basis of 2 Pet. 3:12] that the time of the Second Coming lies partly in our hands." J. Stafford Wright, "Times and Seasons," in *Dreams, Visions, and Oracles,* eds. Carl E. Armerding and W. Ward Gasque (Grand Rapids: Baker, 1977), 173.
    Rottenberg, who is less specific than Ladd and Wright, nonetheless says: "Yet, a world in need is always waiting for a Christianity that lives and moves and has it full being from a vision of the future of the Lord, and through its mission seeks to hasten the day of the coming of the kingdom." Isaac C. Rottenberg, *The Promise and the Presence* (Grand Rapids: Eerdmans, 1980), 89-90.
    Yet neither Matt. 14:14 nor 2 Pet. 3:12, the primary passages for the idea that the day of Christ's return can be hastened by increased evangelistic efforts, should be interpreted in a manner which compromises the New Testament insistence that the time of the second coming is wholly in God's hands. Gasque says: "He may, according to the divine purposes that we do not understand, delay his return." W. Ward Gasque, "Of This We Can Be Sure," in *Dreams, Visions, and Oracles,* eds. Carl E. Armerding and W. Ward Gasque (Grand Rapids: Baker, 1977), 145.
    30. Efird speaks of Paul sharing "the belief of the early Christians that Jesus would return within their lifetime" and includes him in a reference to "the ways the later New Testament writers tried to deal with the disappointment and embarrassment that ensued when it became rather clear they had been wrong in their belief at this point." James M. Effird, *End-Times: Rapture, Antichrist, Millennium* (Nashville: Abingdon, 1986), 10,46.

Without questioning a certain "progress of doctrine" on the part of biblical writers,[31] the issue is how "progress" is to be understood. Is it a progress from false to true, so that the later insight negates and supplants the earlier, or is it a progress from bud to flower, so that the later developments are implicit from the beginning?

Rather than suggesting that Paul and other New Testament writers were at first mistaken regarding the time of Christ's return, it is far better to explain their strong belief in the "nearness" of the *parousia* as growing out of a profound awareness that it was *the next main event* in the outworking of God's mighty acts of redemption.[32]

Accordingly, the second coming *loomed large* on the horizon of all their thinking! They saw that what God was doing in Christ was the center and meaning of history. They found themselves living day by day in the light of eternity, living as though each day were their only day (Rom. 13:11-14).

On this basis, if remaining alive until Christ returned was in a sense a possibility for Paul, since God's times are in God's hands, this does not mean that it was a positive expectation. Paul was not a date-setting, apocalyptic fanatic. He knew well that God alone appointed the time of Christ's coming and that it was incalculable by humans.

Third, the remaining question regarding the biblical view of the signs of Christ return asks whether or not New Testament predictions pertaining to a future for the Jews, a final tribulation, and an antichrist are sufficiently specific for us to know precisely the time of His coming. Do the New Testament predictions with reference to these topics justify drawing up an Armageddon calendar?

Regarding the Jews, it is essential to distinguish between the people and the nation. Ewert, a historical premillennialist, has this to say regarding a future for *national* Israel in the New Testament:

---

31. An invaluable resource at this point is: Thomas Dehany Bernard, *The Progress of Doctrine in the New Testament* (Boston: Gould and Lincoln, 1870) an American edition, drawn from the second London edition with improvements [n.d.]. L. R. Scarborough's copy of the book in the Roberts Library at Southwestern Baptist Theological Seminary, Fort Worth, Texas, is inscribed by Scarborough: "A great book."

32. In addition to the second coming, Robinson speaks poetically of five other acts in the biblical drama of redemption:

—the first when God gathered a nation out of Bedouin tribes, the second when He raised up prophetic teachers with their fragments of truth, the third when exile purged and disciplined the religious consciousness of Israel, the fourth when the tragedy of the Cross of Christ brought man's sin face to face with God's grace, the fifth, when the Holy Spirit began the creation of a fellowship not yet achieved, the inauguration of the kingly rule of God.

H. Wheeler Robinson, *The Christian Experience of the Holy Spirit* (London: Nisbet, 1928), 183.

It may come as a surprise to some readers that we have not included the establishment of the state of Israel as a sign of the times. The reason for the omission is a simple one: the New Testament nowhere foresees the reestablishment of the state of Israel.

Ewert insists that the hope which Paul holds out for the people of Israel in Romans 11:25-27 is a hope for salvation in the same way that Gentiles are saved, and not a hope for national, political restoration.[33]

With reference to the additional topics of the great tribulation and the antichrist, let it suffice to suggest that they function in the New Testament to indicate precisely what Jesus taught regarding the signs of the times in general: believers do not escape trouble and suffering, but God is faithful, and in the end the final word with reference to the time of the end is His.

Guidelines for dealing with the time question.—By way of a summary of the implications of what has been said so far regarding the time of the second coming, the following guidelines are suggested to help believers in their wrestling with questions concerning the time of His coming?

First, *no one knows the time* when Christ will return (Matt. 24:36). Believers who take this claim seriously are not easily deceived by date setters. They know, as *The Baptist Faith and Message* says, that God will bring the world to its appropriate end "in His own time and in His own way" (Art. X). Nowhere does the New Testament provide an early warning system to take the surprise out of the time of Christ's return.

---

33. Ewert, *And Then Comes the End*, 36.

Ewert cites Ladd: "Possibly the modern return of Israel to Palestine is a part of God's purpose for Israel, but the New Testament sheds no light on this problem." But this is not all that Ladd says. He also claims:

The salvation of Israel must be through the new covenant made in the blood of Christ already established with the church, not through a rebuilt Jewish temple with a revival of the Mosaic sacrificial system. Hebrews flatly affirms that the whole Mosaic system is obsolete and about to pass away. Therefore the popular Dispensational position that Israel is the "clock of prophecy" is misguided.

George Eldon Ladd, *The Last Things* (Grand Rapids: Eerdmans, 1978), 28.

Interestingly, Averbeck, Whitcomb, and others at Grace Theological Seminary, Winona Lake, Indiana, an influential center of dispensational theology, not only deemphasize the significance of 1948 with reference to signs of Christ's return, but oppose the prediction fever with its "intensifying of imminence" in general. Their reason for minimizing the predictive significance of the reestablishment of the state of Israel is that what is important to the New Testament is not the mere reorganization of the nation but Israel's return to God through repentance and trust in Christ. Richard E. Averbeck, "Is Modern Day Israel the Israel of the Last Days?," *Spire* 9 [Fall 1981], 3-5; John C. Whitcomb, "This Generation Will not Pass Away," *Spire* 9 [Spring 1981]: 5.

Second, since *Christ's coming will be sudden and unexpected*, it seems reasonable to leave its time so utterly in God's hands that it could occur at any moment.[34] Biblical references to a widespread conversion of the Jews, a great tribulation, and an antichrist are simply not specific enough to justify completely ruling out the possibility of an any-moment return of Christ. Quoting Bengel, Grier says: "It accords with the majesty of Christ that during the whole period between His ascension and His [final] advent, He should without intermission be expected."[35]

Third, *believers are to be ready* to meet Christ. To be ready means to wake from sleep (Rom. 13:11), to watch (Matt. 13:32-33), or to purify one's self as He is pure (1 John 3:3). Believers are on business for the King, and the King's business requires haste, especially His royal commission to take the gospel to the ends of the earth (Matt. 28:19-20). "Expectation," says Thiselton, "is not so much a state of mind as an attitude which is expressed in certain conduct."[36] To expect a person is to do the appropriate things by way of preparation for his or her coming!

It must be noted, however, that the Christian's sense of urgency in witness and ministry is grounded in Christ's lordship over the believer's life and not in speculation concerning the chronological nearness of Christ's return. The disciple's first need is a right relation to Christ. Therein is the only adequate motivation for sustained and sacrificial Christian service.

Fourth, *the believer's anticipation of Christ's coming is a blessed hope* (Titus 2:13). It is a joyous, even if solemn, expectancy, not a nervous anxiety. "Amen. Come, Lord Jesus" (Rev. 22:20)!

---

34. The question as to whether Christ's return is an "any moment" coming receives considerable attention from Ladd. In order to refute the dispensational position regarding an "any moment" rapture prior to the tribulation and the second coming, he rightly argues against separating the rapture from the second coming, but, unfortunately, goes on to insist that the second coming cannot be "any moment" since it must be preceded by the tribulation and related events. An entire book is devoted to the discussion. George Eldon Ladd, *The Blessed Hope* (Grand Rapids: Eerdmans, 1956). Contrary to Ladd, the stress on the elements of uncertainty and surprise with reference to the time of Christ's return is too deeply rooted in the New Testament for an any-moment return of Christ to be dismissed easily. By assuming that the tribulation will serve as an early warning system that the second coming is chronologically near, Ladd seems to forget that the Bible does not allow dogmatic statements to the effect that any particular point in history *must* be viewed as the beginning of the end.

By the way, Payne, a premillennialist, argues that we could be in the tribulation now! He says: "It is said that more believers have laid down their lives for Christ during the twentieth century than in any other period of history." J. Barton Payne, *Biblical Prophecy for Today* (Grand Rapids: Baker, 1978), 27. Payne's "it is said" could be referring to Travis, *The Jesus Hope,* 112.

35. Grier, *The Momentous Event,* 11-12.

36. Thiselton, "The *Parousia* in Modern Theology," 52-53. See also Ewert, *And Then Comes the End,* 180.

The Millennial Issue

The third topic involved in restating the doctrine of the second coming is the millennial issue.[37] Four considerations present themselves in the effort to summarize the subject: the term "millennium"; the biblical basis for a millennium; the four major schools of millennial thought; and the current status of millennial discussion.

The term "millennium."—The term "millennium" is derived from the Latin, *mille*, thousand, and *annus*, year. The theological use of the term is rooted in Revelation 20:1-10, where the expression "a thousand years" occurs six times and refers to a reign of Christ with His saints for a thousand years, during which Satan is at first bound but at the end of which he is loosed and leads a final rebellion against Christ and the saints. "Chiliasm," derived from the Greek *chilia*, thousand, and *ete*, year, is a synonym for millennialism.

The biblical basis for a millennium.—The sole explicit biblical basis for the idea of a millennial reign of Christ with His saints is Revelation 20:1-10. Ladd, a historical premillennialist, readily acknowledges that "the only place in the Bible that speaks of an actual millennium is this passage."[38] Premillennialists find indirect support for their views elsewhere in Scripture, but Revelation 20:1-10 remains the only direct reference to a millennial reign.

The four major schools of millennial thought.—Since World War II, four leading millennial views have established themselves among theological conservatives on the American scene: historical premillennialism (posttribulationism), dispensational premillennialism (pretribulationism), postmillennialism, and amillennialism.

---

37. In order to sort out the facts concerning the millennial issue, a good place for students to begin is with introductory studies such as: Robert G. Clouse, ed., *The Meaning of the Millennium: Four Views* (Downers Grove, IL: InterVarsity, 1977); Millard J. Erickson, *Christian Theology*, vol. 3 (Grand Rapids: Baker, 1985), by the same author, *Contemporary Options in Eschatology*; and Hoekema, *The Bible and the Future*. For commentaries on the Book of Revelation especially oriented to the millennial issue, see: G. R. Beasley-Murray, et al, *Revelation: Three Viewpoints* (Nashville: Broadman, 1977), and John P. Newport, *The Lion and the Lamb* (Nashville: Broadman, 1986).

38. George Eldon Ladd, "Historic Premillennialism," in *The Meaning of the Millennium*, ed. Robert G. Clouse (Downers Grove, IL: InterVarsity, 1977), 32. Ladd goes on to explain why he does *not* find references to the millennium in Matt. 25:31-46 and 1 Cor. 15:23-26 (where he does find room for "an interim kingdom if not a millennium"), passages sometimes cited by others in support of a millennial reign of Christ (Ibid., 38-39).

Erickson, also a premillennialist, agrees that Rev. 20:1-10 is the only explicit reference to a millennial reign of Christ with His saints, but he is quick to add that the premillennial view of two resurrections (of believers before the millennium and of unbelievers after the millennium), which he finds explicitly expressed Revelation 20, is *intimated* "in a number of places" elsewhere in Scripture (including Dan. 12:2). His concern is to emphasize that premillennialism is not based on only one passage.

Two lines of investigation are especially important if these millennial options are to be understood: first, from the historical perspective there are matters of labels, origins, and development; second, from the theological viewpoint there are questions concerning tenets, strengths, and weaknesses.

First, the attempt must be made to place the discussion in historical perspective, a pursuit which has been sadly neglected. Little scholarly work has been done on the subject, partly because of the tendency in the theological academy to assume that only the untrained and fanatical are concerned with the subject.[39] This picture is changing, however, and increasingly significant, brief historical insights are surfacing. In the light of this fresh historical interest, two observations are in order.

First, today's student should be aware of the fact that the labels now used for the different millennial options are of recent origin. The repeated references to the chiliasm or premillennialism of the early church fathers, for instance, easily leaves the impression that the fathers had access to the same millennial views which are available today, and that they deliberately opted for the premillennial view over against the other positions. Such an impression is unfounded and confusingly misleading. Yet, only now are discussions beginning to take more serious note of the recent origin of the presently familiar labels and definitions.

Marsden, for example, observes that "clear distinctions in terminology between 'premillennial' and 'postmillennial' do not seem to occur before the nineteenth century" and amillennialism was "not so termed until the twentieth century."[40] This startling observation is a clear reminder that the now commonly recognized millennial positions were not labeled and distinguished from one another formerly as they are today.

Erickson also speaks up, pointing out the difficulty modern writers have in identifying accurately the millennial views of earlier theologians. He says:

> It has not always been possible to distinguish amillennialism from postmillennialism, since they share many common features. Indeed, various [earlier] theologians who [did] not [address] the particular issues which serve to distinguish the two views from one another— among them are Augustine, John Calvin, and B. B. Warfield—have been claimed as ancestors of both camps. . . . It is likely that postmil-

---

39. A notable exception to the lack of scholarly work in the area of millennial views in general is Leroy Froom, *The Prophetic Faith of Our Fathers,* 4 vols. (Washington, DC: Review and Herald, 1946-54). This multiple-volume history of prophetic interpretation by a Seventh-Day Adventist is an encyclopedia of details. Unfortunately it basically antedates the fundamental changes in American millennial thinking occurring since World War II.

40. George M. Marsden, *Fundamentalism and American Culture* (New York: Oxford, 1980), 240, note 4.

lennialism and amillennialism simply were not differentiated for much of the first nineteen centuries of the church.[41]

Similarly, Weber emphasizes that if the renewed interest in premillennialism in the nineteenth century is to be understood, it is quite necessary to distinguish between the *historicist* (not to be confused with historic or historical premillennialism, terms which came into use especially in America after World War II) premillennialism of the first part of the nineteenth century and the quite different *futurist* or dispensational variety of premillennialism which spread so rapidly, especially in America, in the latter nineteenth and early twentieth centuries.

In America in the first half of the nineteenth century, the most famous historicist premillennialist was William Miller, the pioneer of Seventh-Day Adventism. Premillennialists of Miller's historicist type believed that biblical prediction in Daniel and Revelation previewed the course of the entire church age.

Starting with the reference in Daniel 7:25 (cf. Rev. 13:5) "a time, times and half a time" (3-1/2 years, or 42 months, or 1,260 days), by using a sort of "millennial arithmetic," they first interpreted the 1,260 days as 1,260 years, and then, by adding 1,260 years to the year A.D. 538, their date for the rise of the papacy, they arrived at 1798, the year of the Pope's exile from Rome! Whereupon they enthusiastically announced to the world that the predictions of Daniel 7:25 and Revelation 13:5 had now been exactly fulfilled.

Encouraged by their initial success, they next started with Dan. 8:14 and the reference to 2,300 days, and again interpreting the days as years, they calculated that Christ's second coming would occur 2,300 years after the desolation of the sanctuary by Nebuchadnezzar in 457 B.C. (Ussher's chronology), or about 1843.

When Christ failed to return in 1843, Miller revised the date to October 22, 1844, only to be mistaken a second time. The interesting fact is that, despite the "Great Disappointment" of the Millerites, their failure in predicting the time of Christ's return did little if anything to impede the rapid acceptance, especially in America, in the latter part of the century of the new, *futurist* premillennialism of the Darbyite, dispensational variety, which was as interested in relating biblical prediction to current events as was the historicist variety.[42]

---

41. Erickson, *Christian Theology,* 1212-13.
42. Timothy P. Weber, *Living in the Shadow of the Second Coming: American Premillennialism, 1875-1982,* (New York: Oxford, 1979; enlarged ed., Grand Rapids: Zondervan, 1983), 14-16.
The discussion here draws heavily from Weber, who formerly taught church history at the Conservative Baptist Theological Seminary, Denver, Colorado, but now serves as the David T. Porter professor of church history at the Southern Baptist Theological Seminary, Louisville, Kentucky. His book grew out of his doctoral studies at the Divinity School of the University of Chicago, where Martin Marty was his advisor.

Second, a further invaluable historical contribution concerns the fresh insights regarding the origin and development of the today's main millennial options, remembering that today's labels for these options did not exist in earlier times.

In the interests of objectivity and brevity, the following summary builds on the findings reported by both Clouse and Weber.

Clouse perceptively heads his brief sketch of historical concerns, "Different Views at Different Times." Beginning with the second and third centuries of Christian history, although the evidence is variously interpreted by different writers, he contends that a kind of *chiliasm*, or what is now known in a loose sense as historical premillennialism, was the dominant eschatological outlook. As proponents of the early chiliasm he cites in passing the names of Justin Martyr (100-165), Irenaeus (130-200), and Tertullian (160-220).

The fourth century witnessed a dramatic shift in millennial outlook. Since the Constantinian establishment in the Roman Empire (312) had brought an end to the persecution of Christians, and had even conferred on them favorable public status, the eschatological emphasis in Christian thinking understandably shifted from the "hard times" focus of chiliasm to the "Christ reigns despite problems" stress of what is now called amillennialism.

Consequently, Augustine (354-430) interpreted Christ's millennial reign as referring to the present church age. His view, in essence, was retained by Luther and Calvin, which means that, though chiliasm or a premillennialist type of thinking never did completely disappear, amillennialism became the prevailing outlook of the church for nearly fifteen hundred years.

In the eighteenth century the eschatological outlook shifted again, reflecting in part the heightened cultural optimism regarding the future of humankind which was characteristic of the expansionist Enlightenment period in the Western world. This time it was postmillennialism which attracted "the leading [biblical] commentators and preachers of the age."

Weber adds that most of the credit for this shift should go to Jonathan Edwards (1703-58), who believed that the preaching of the gospel and the use of the ordinary means of grace would usher in a glorious millennial era *before* the return of Christ. Weber explains that as strange as this optimism must have sounded when Edwards voiced it in public lectures in 1739, the coming of the Evangelical Revival under the Wesleys in

England, and two massive religious awakenings in America seemed in the eighteenth century suddenly to bring the millennium within reach.[43]

From the latter part of the nineteenth century until World War II, as was anticipated in the above reference to the two kinds of nineteenth-century premillennialism, the most pervasive and popular eschatological outlook among American evangelicals was the dispensational premillennialism (pretribulationism) of Darby and the Scofield Reference Bible.

Following World War II, however, along with the sweeping, revolutionary social and cultural changes associated with the war, as well as the widely publicized revival of religion experienced by American churches, dispensational premillennialism noticeably declined in influence. With the proliferation of new Bible translations and evangelical study Bibles, the dominant influence of the Scofield Bible waned. The militant, separatist fundamentalism of the 1920s was also forced to take the defensive as a "new evangelicalism" began to assert itself with the founding of the Fuller Theological Seminary, the rise of Billy Graham, the establishing of the magazine, *Christianity Today*, and the like.

In the place of dispensational premillennialism, modified versions of "historical" premillennialism and fresh interpretations of amillennialism gained rapidly in popularity. Eventually, in the 1980s, even evangelical postmillennialism experienced a measure of rejuvenation. Hence it is that the four most familiar millennial options on the American scene currently are historical premillennialism, dispensational premillennialism, amillennialism, and postmillennialism.

Second, having reviewed something of the historical background of the varying millennial views, it is now in order to consider them from a theological viewpoint, and to inquire concerning their main tenets, strengths, and weaknesses. The intention, of course, is to focus on the more important emphases, bypassing for the most part the endless variations in detail introduced by individual writers. To facilitate the achievement of this end, the individuals chosen to represent each of the views are, with one exception, those chosen by Clouse. These are: George Eldon *Ladd*, historical premillennialism; Herman A. *Hoyt*, dispensational premillennialism; John Jefferson *Davis* (instead of Loraine Boettner), postmillennialism; and Anthony A. *Hoekema*, amillennialism.[44]

---

43. Robert G. Clouse, "Introduction," in *The Meaning of the Millennium: Four Views*, ed. Robert G. Clouse (Downers Grove, IL: InterVarsity, 1977), 9-13, and Weber, *Living in the Shadow of the Second Coming*, 13-14.

44. Clouse, *The Meaning of the Millennium*. The discussions in Clouse, however, should be updated as follows.

To begin with *premillennialism*, or the view that Christ's return precedes His millennial reign, it is necessary first to distinguish between historical premillennialism and dispensational premillennialism.[45]

Before proceeding further, an explanation is in order regarding the term "historical" premillennialism. Often the term is understood merely to signify that historical premillennialism is more deeply rooted in Christian history than dispensational premillennialism. While dispensational premillennialism is fairly recent, originating with John Nelson Darby (1800-82) in the nineteenth century, historical premillennialism is said to

---

Ladd's outline of historical premillennialism reflects his confrontation with the dispensational fundamentalism of the 1950s more than it does the views of historical premillennialists in the 1980s and since. There is less tendency today, on the part of both historical and dispensational premillennialists, to polarize the two kinds of premillennialism. Ladd's discussion does, however, indicate the inclination on the part of the new historical premillennialism to find common ground with evangelical amillennialism. More will be said regarding these matters as the discussion continues.

Hoyt's version of dispensational premillennialism should be updated with discussions such as: Robert Saucy, "The Crucial Issue between Dispensational and Non-Dispensational Systems," *Criswell Theological Review* 1 [Fall 1986]: 149-65, and Craig A. Blaising, "Developing Dispensationalism, Two Parts," *Bibliotheca Sacra* 145 [April-June 1988]: 133-40, and [July-September 1988]: 254-80. Such articles represent a softening of the tendency in older dispensationalism to contrast national Israel and the church in the outworking of God's purpose.

Hoyt, chancellor and professor of Christian theology emeritus, Grace Theological Seminary, Winona Lake, Indiana, is a leader in one of the foremost American centers of dispensational theology, though he might not be as well known as John Walvoord and Charles Ryrie of Dallas Theological Seminary, whose Armageddon calendars have given them wide publicity (regarding Armageddon calendars see the above discussion on the nature of biblical prediction).

Hoekema's presentation of amillennialism should be supplemented with his later discussion in *The Bible and the Future*. Also, in a subsequent article, Hoekema seems to qualify somewhat his earlier stress on the continuity between this earth and the eternal new earth. Anthony A. Hoekema, "Heaven: Not Just an Eternal Day Off," *Christianity Today*, September 20, 1985, 19.

Boettner's case for postmillennialism in the Clouse volume is seriously dated. Essentially he uses material from his earlier study, *The Millennium* (Philadelphia: Presbyterian and Reformed, 1958). For an informed, more recent defense of postmillennialism, see John Jefferson Davis, *Christ's Victorious Kingdom: Postmillennialism Reconsidered* (Grand Rapids: 1886). For a discussion of recent Christian Reconstructionism, with its theonomic version of postmillennialism, see H. Wayne House and Thomas D. Ice, *Dominion Theology: Blessing or Curse?* (Portland, OR: Multnomah, 1988).

45. Terminology for the different millennial options varies with different writers. Erickson, a historical premillennialist, avoids speaking of two premillennialisms, referring instead simply to premillennialism and dispensationalism. His hesitancy to speak of dispensationalism as a kind of premillennialism may be indicated in his initial discussion of dispensationalism, which is separate from his treatment of premillennialism, and which lists dispensationalism as one of six modern non-evangelical approaches to eschatology, along with liberalism, A. Schweitzer, C. H. Dodd, R. Bultmann, and J. Moltmann.

He also treats millennial and tribulational views separately, as though the topics had no direct relation. Yet historical premillennialism is posttribulational and dispensational premillennialism is pretribulational. Any exception to this association of views can be regarded as incidental. Midtribulationism, for instance, is essentially a variant of pretribulationism. Erickson, *Christian Theology*, 1162-64, 1209-12, 1218-20.

have probably been "the dominant millennial view during the early period of the church [A.D. 100-300]."[46]

Reference to the distinction between the older premillennialism of the early church fathers and that of nineteenth-century dispensationalism has been common in millennial discussions since before World War II, but this is not all that is involved in the use of the term historical premillennialism today.

Instead, since the early 1950s the term has come increasingly to be employed to refer to the recent type of premillennialism popularized in America especially by Ladd, and reflecting his vigorous reaction to what he perceived as a lack of scriptural support for several of the key emphases of the dispensational premillennialism.[47] Although pre-World War II posttribulational premillennialists, such as Henry Alford (1810-71), are sometimes cited as examples of historical premillennialists, the term *as it is now used* is of post-World War II origin and better fits contemporaries such as Millard J. Erickson, Robert H. Gundry, Alan F. Johnson, Dale Moody, Robert H. Mounce, George R. Beasley-Murray, and John P. Newport.[48]

While these writers believe that there is an element of historical continuity between their views and the chiliasm of early church fathers, they

---

46. Erickson, *Christian Theology,* 1209. Erickson, however, as noted above, avoids the use of the terms historical premillennialism and dispensational premillennialism, speaking instead simply of premillennialism and dispensationalism.

Clouse, who uses the term historic premillennialism, says:

> Expressed in a form that has been called historic premillennialism, this hope [hope as taught in the Book of Revelation] seems to have been the prevailing eschatology during the first three centuries of the Christian era, and is found in the works of Papias, Irenaeus, Justin Martyr, Tertullian, Hippolytus, Methodius, Commodianus, and Lactantius.

Walter A. Elwell, ed. *Evangelical Dictionary of Theology* (Grand Rapids: Baker, 1984), s.v. "Millennium, Views of," by Robert G. Clouse.

47. See George Eldon Ladd, *Crucial Questions about the Kingdom of God* (Grand Rapids: Eerdmans, 1952; reprint, 1954), and Ladd, *The Blessed Hope.*

Ladd's specific criticisms of the dispensational premillennial teachings of the Scofield Reference Bible heralded the break of the post-World War II new evangelicals from the fundamentalist movement of the 1920s. See George M. Marsden, *Reforming Fundamentalism: Fuller Seminary and the New Evangelicalism* (Grand Rapids: Eerdmans, 1987). Marsden's volume is a history of Fuller Theological Seminary's first forty years.

48. Clouse, Weber, and George are typical of writers who recognize a post-World War II significance of the term historical premillennialism.

After describing the rise of dispensational premillennialism in the nineteenth century, Clouse speaks of its rapid spread in America "among millions of conservative Protestants" during the first half of the twentieth century. He then adds that "the new view [dispensational premillennialism] replaced the older [early nineteenth century, posttribulational] premillennial outlook to such an extent that when George Ladd restated the historic interpretation in the midtwentieth century it seemed like a novelty to many evangelicals." Elwell, *Evangelical Dictionary of Theology.*

do not make much of the point.[49] Their use of the term historical premillennialism tends rather to distinguish their position from that of dispensational premillennialism. In today's American context, the term implies the importance of drawing the distinction between historical premillennialists as post-World War II neoevangelicals and dispensational premillennialists as heirs of the fundamentalist movement of the 1920s.

Turning now to the basic distinction between the two premillennialisms, *historical premillennialism* is the view that the second coming of Christ precedes an earthly, Christian, utopian reign of Christ for a thousand years or for a complete period of time, during which Satan is at first bound, but at the end of which Satan is loosed and leads a final rebellion against "the camp of the saints and the beloved city" (Rev. 20:9). On the basis of Revelation 20:4-6 historical premillennialists also argue for two resurrections, a resurrection of the righteous at the beginning of the millennium and a resurrection of the wicked at the end of the millennium.

Dispensational premillennialism is more complex than historical premillennialism. While the two premillennialisms agree regarding a return of Christ prior to the millennium, a Satanic rebellion at the end of the millennium and two resurrections, dispensational premillennialism includes additional beliefs which significantly distinguish it from historical premillennialism.

Two of dispensationalism's distinctive beliefs especially merit mention. First, it differentiates the rapture, or the return of Christ at the

---

Weber also comments on the new interest in historical premillennialism. He says:

> Such divisions [among premillennialists] have actually intensified since World War II when posttribulationism experienced a renaissance. Premillennialist biblical scholars such as George E. Ladd, Robert Gundry, and Robert Mounce have challenged some of dispensationalism's most fundamental hermeneutical and exegetical arguments. In their effort to undercut dispensational interpretation, they use some of the methods of modern mainstream biblical scholarship. In short, many people within more moderate evangelical circles are finding in posttribulationism a way of retaining their basic premillennialist orientation while entering, at least to some degree, the world of modern biblical scholarship.

Weber, *Living in the Shadow*, 241. Weber documents his viewpoint.

Referring to the growing interest in eschatology since World War II, George says:

> In evangelical circles this growing interest in the future has been accompanied by a rediscovery and revision of the premillennial view. Some scholars have espoused a view usually called historical premillennialism.

David C. George, "Summary," in *Revelation: Three Viewpoints,* G. R. Beasley-Murray, et al (Nashville: Broadman, 1977), 229.

49. Erickson says:

> Much of the millennialism [of the early period of the church]—often termed "chiliasm," from the Greek word for "thousand"—had a rather sensuous flavor. The millennium would be a time of great abundance and fertility, of a renewing of the earth and building of a glorified Jerusalem.

Erickson, *Christian Theology,* 1209.

beginning of the final tribulation period to snatch believers out of the world, from the second coming of Christ at the end of the tribulation period to lead the Jews in triumph at the battle of Armageddon and establish their reign during the millennium. Second, with believers taken out of the world at the time of the rapture, it holds that the focus of God's purpose during the tribulation and the millennium shifts from believers to the *nation* of Israel. In these ways dispensational premillennialism places greater stress on the fulfillment of Old Testament promises for a national Israel and on a more detailed scheme of end time events, than does historical premillennialism.

Having generally distinguished the two kinds of premillennialism, the differences between them can be further clarified by comparing them at four significant points. The comparison is made on the basis of the way in which the two options are presented in Clouse, with Ladd speaking for historical premillennialism and Hoyt for dispensational premillennialism.[50]

First, the two premillennialisms can be compared at the point of their diverse approaches to biblical hermeneutics. For one thing, they differ with reference to the way the Old and New Testaments are to be related. Ladd's historical premillennialism stresses the New Testament, emphasizing that the New Testament is the key to the Old Testament, that the church fulfills God's Old Testament promises to Israel, and consequently that the millennial age is essentially Christian and has nothing to do as such with the restoration of national Israel in Palestine as the dominant, political and military world power. Hoyt's dispensational premillennialism, however, emphasizes the authority of the Old Testament in millennial matters, insisting that the Old Testament is the key to the meaning of the millennial reign referred to in Revelation 20:1-10, that God's Old Testament promises to Israel of *national* glory in Palestine are yet to be fulfilled, and, consequently, that the millennial age has a distinctly Old Testament and Jewish character.

Furthermore, dispensational premillennialists insist that the basic difference between them and nondispensationalists is that they interpret the Bible "literally" while others do not.[51] Others, they say, explain away the Old Testament promises to national Israel. Yet, the problem of biblical

---

50. Ladd, "Historic Premillennialism," and Herman A. Hoyt, "Dispensational Premillennialism," in *The Meaning of the Millennium*, ed. Robert G. Clouse (Downers Grove, IL: InterVarsity, 1977), 17-40, 63-92. Hoyt responds to Ladd (Ibid., 41-46) and Ladd responds to Hoyt (Ibid., 93-94).

51. In addition to the dialogue between Ladd and Hoyt in the Clouse volume regarding the "literal" interpretation of the Bible, the recent study of dispensationalism by Poythress devotes several informative chapters to the theme of "what is literal interpretation?" See Vern S. Poythress, *Understanding Dispensationalists* (Grand Rapids: Zondervan, 1987), especially chaps. 5-13.

authority is not the real issue. As a theological conservative, Ladd is as insistent on the plain, natural, literal, or historical-grammatical meaning of Scripture as is Hoyt.[52]

The more basic difference between the two kinds of premillennialism grows out of their divergent understandings of the nature of God's redemptive purpose as disclosed in Christ and the New Testament. Historical premillennialists say that the New Testament gospel, which is the same for the Jew as for the Gentile in its offer of salvation, is definitive in dealing with millennial questions.[53]

Dispensational premillennialists, on the other hand, says that the fulfillment of God's Old Testament promises to national Israel—essentially unaltered by anything Christ has taught or done—is central in determining one's millennial view. Hoyt says: "The literal method of approach to the teaching of the premillennial, dispensational doctrine of the kingdom is absolutely basic." He then quotes Walvoord:

> [Dispensational] premillennialism is founded principally on interpretation of the Old Testament. . . . The [dispensational] premillennial interpretation offers the only literal fulfillment for the hundreds of verses of prophetic testimony.[54]

The remaining points of comparison between the two kinds of premillennialism are subordinate to the first. The second point of comparison concerns the differing roles attributed to national Israel and the church during the final tribulation and the millennium. Dispensationalists, identifying the kingdom of which Jesus spoke with the fulfillment of Israel's national expectations, say that when the Jews rejected Jesus' offer of the kingdom, the offer was withdrawn, and the fulfillment of Israel's earthly

---

Poythress, professor of New Testament at amillennial Westminster Theological Seminary, an independent Presbyterian seminary, is interested in exploring opportunities for rapprochement and growth in mutual understanding between dispensationalism and covenant theology (Ibid., 1-2). Work on the book during a 1983 sabbatical involved study at Dallas Theological Seminary and firsthand dialogue with the faculty there.

52. Throughout his presentation of historical premillennialism, Ladd insists that the interpretation of the Bible for which he is contending is "the natural reading." George Eldon Ladd, "Historic Premillennialism," 17,18,32,33,35.

53. Whether or not historical premillennialism is consistent in the application of this principle when it posits an earthly, millennial utopia *after* the second coming of Christ and the final resurrection of believers, a utopia which ends in a violent apostasy and rebellion led by Satan, is a further question which will be raised later.

54. Hoyt, "Dispensational Premillennialism," 67.

political dreams was postponed until the millennium.[55] In other words, dispensational premillennialists tend to contrast the present church age, which is New Testament and Christian, with the future millennial age which is Old Testament and Jewish.

Historical premillennialists, on the other hand, deny that the kingdom was postponed, insisting that it is a spiritual and redemptive kingdom founded on the Christ-Pentecost events, that it is both present and future, that it is the instrument for the fulfillment of the Old Testament promises to Israel, and that the future millenial kingdom is Christian and not Jewish.

A third point of comparison pertains to the extent to which the Bible is believed to predict the detailed course of future events. Dispensational premillennialists often place more stress on the formation of Armageddon calendars and their constant updating in the light of rapidly changing current events than do historical premillennialists. Even Hoyt, who usually reflects the inclination of the faculty at Grace Theological Seminary to cool the predictive fever, says: "The movement of events in our day suggests that the establishment of the kingdom is not far away."[56] Commenting on the dispensational proclivity to predict the future, Weber says:

> Dispensationalism's current problems go beyond that of datesetting. There is also the tendency to be excessively concerned with the *details* of prophetic fulfillment.[57]

A fourth point of comparison is that dispensational premillennialists are pretribulationists, while historical premillennialists are posttribulationists. Dispensational premillennialists characteristically believe in a two-stage return of Christ, which separates the secret rapture of the church out of the world at the beginning of the tribulation from the later return of Christ to

---

55. According to the New Scofield Reference Bible, the note on Matt. 11:28 says:
> The new message of Jesus. The rejected King now turns from the rejecting nation and offers, not the kingdom but rest and service to all who are in conscious need of his help. It is a pivotal point in the ministry of Jesus.
Regarding this teaching, Hoyt says:
> In a peculiar sense the mediatorial kingdom has been placed in a position of abeyance or suspension during the period extending from Pentecost to the return of Christ. This means that it is not [yet] being experienced in the full sense as described in Old Testament prophecy (Ibid., 90).
56. Ibid., 63.
57. Referring to Lindsey, Walvoord, and Ryrie, Weber goes on to say:
> All three authors believe that they can identify the participants in end-time events among today's nations and have detailed scenarios of the future. . . . They believe that the Bible contains a detailed and discernible plan for the end of history. Thus they would be remiss if they did not try to show how it is being worked out. Briefly stated, dispensational premillennialism is inherently guilty of historical and theological "overassurance."
Weber, *Living in the Shadow*, 242-43.

earth with His saints at the end of the tribulation to triumph at the battle of Armageddon and to establish the millennial kingdom.

The idea of a pretribulational rapture of believers out of the world is important to dispensational premillennialists, since the nation of Israel, not the church, plays the central role during the tribulation and the millennium.

Historical premillennialists, on the other hand, do not deny the rapture, but believe that the return of Christ and the rapture of believers to meet the Lord in the air occur simultaneously.

In conclusion, as these comparisons show, the two premillennialisms are notably different. Historical premillennialists, since they are more open to differences in millennial interpretation among theological conservatives, coexist on the same faculties with amillennialists and postmillennialists. Dispensational premillennialists, however, have tended in the past to follow a separatist line, insisting that theirs is the biblical view and that to question it is to compromise a high view of biblical authority.[58]

Ironically, however, fundamentalists who are amillennialists are just as insistent that theirs is *the* biblical view.[59] In the past, neither of these two different kinds of American fundamentalist millennialism has been shy about charging one another with heresy.

Turning next to a consideration of the strengths and weaknesses of the two premillennialisms, their strength is that, in addition to a commitment to take Scripture seriously and to stress the return of Christ personally to the earth, they are realistic in their estimate of what the gospel of Christ

---

58. Ladd opens his response to Hoyt in the Clouse volume as follows:
    Hoyt's essay reflects the major problem in the discussion of the millennium. Several times he contrasts nondispensational views with his own, which he labels "the biblical view" (pp. 69,70,84). If he is correct, then the other views, including my own are "unbiblical" or even "heretical." This is the reason that over the years there has been little creative dialogue between dispensationalists and other schools of prophetic interpretation.

George Eldon Ladd, "An Historic Premillennial Response," in *The Meaning of the Millennium*, ed. Robert G. Clouse (Downers Grove, IL: InterVarsity, 1977), 93.

Fortunately, creative dialogue between millennial views has increased since the 1950s and 1970s. See the earlier note on updating the discussions in Clouse.

59. See, for instance, *The Standard Bearer,* a Reformed semi-monthly magazine, published by the Reformed Free Publishing Association, Inc., Grandville, MI 49418.

Both the amillennial Westminster Theological Seminary, Philadelphia, Pennsylvania, the seminary founded J. Gresham Machen, leader of the fundamentalist movement in the 1920s and 1930s, and the dispensational premillennialist Dallas Theological Seminary, Dallas, Texas, founded by Lewis Sperry Chafer, also a leader in fundamentalist circles, are self-styled "fundamentalist" seminaries. Westminster speaks for a Reformed, covenant theology approach, while Dallas, its particular archrival, speaks for dispensational theology.

For a Dallas Seminary critique of covenant theology, see Charles C. Ryrie, *Dispensationalism Today* (Chicago: Moody, 1965; ninth printing, 1974), chap. 9. For a Westminster critique of dispensational theology, see John H. Gerstner, *Wrongly Dividing the Word of Truth: A Critique of Dispensationalism* (Brentwood, TN: Wolgemuth & Hyatt, 1991).

can be expected to accomplish in history prior to the second coming. In militant opposition to the excessive evolutionary optimism of liberalism regarding humankind's ability to solve problems through education and technology, premillennialists have emphasized humankind's helplessness in sin apart from Christ and have viewed the second coming of Christ as the only final hope for history.

The events of the twentieth century have proved the premillennialists' estimate of history far more accurate than the liberals'. As a result, for many theological conservatives *prior to World War II*, premillennialism and theological conservatism came to be practically synonymous terms.

A weakness of the two premillennialisms is the lack of specific biblical support for an earthly, millennial utopia *after* Christ's second coming and before the inauguration of the eternal order. This weakness has several aspects. First, as already noted, premillennialists themselves acknowledge that the only place in the Bible that refers directly of a millennium is Revelation 20:1-10, a passage especially difficult to interpret, as the ongoing millennial debate readily testifies.

Second, what the New Testament does emphasize is that Christ's return ends history and ushers in the eternal states. Ladd says: "I admit that the greatest difficulty to any premillennialism is the fact that most of the New Testament pictures the consummation as occurring at Jesus' parousia."[60] A preoccupation with premillennial concerns pushes into the background the New Testament focus on the second coming, the resurrection, the judgment, and eternal destinies. Such imbalance compromises the awesome finality which the New Testament associates with Christ's return, and leaves the door open for further salvation experiences during the millennium and *after* the second coming.

A third aspect of the lack of biblical support for a millennial interim after the *parousia* is the want of a biblical rationale for such a millennium. The purpose for the delay in Christ's return during the present era is that today is the time of God's missionary patience (Matt. 28:19-20; Acts 1:8; 2 Pet. 3:9). Yet a rationale for extending history and delaying the final consummation for another thousand years *after* Christ returns is another matter. Since this want of a purpose which a millennial period would serve is a major unresolved topic in the ongoing millennial debate, the subject will be further discussed at the conclusion of the present section on the millennial issue.

Postmillennialism, the third of the major millennial options, is the view of the millennium as a gradual Christianization of society through the

---

60. George Eldon Ladd, "An Historic Premillennial Response [to Amillennialism]," in *The Meaning of the Millennium*, ed. Robert G. Clouse (Downers Grove, IL: InterVarsity, 1977), 189-90.

Redeemed! Eschatological Redemption and the Kingdom of God

—294—

spread of the gospel prior to the second coming of Christ. Evangelical postmillennialists do not speak of eliminating evil entirely from society, but of reducing it to a minimum.

Some writers attribute the postmillennial view to Augustine, but, in its modern sense, it began to come into its own with Daniel Whitby (1638-1726).[61] Some of the names associated with postmillennialism in the past include Matthew Henry, John and Charles Wesley, Jonathan Edwards, David Brown, Charles Hodge, B. H. Carroll, B. B. Warfield, A. H. Strong, and the earlier W. T. Conner.

Ewert, himself a historical premillennialist, speaking of evangelicals, suggests that postmillennialism "was probably the most popular [understanding of the millennium] in America at the turn of the twentieth century."[62] A clear distinction should be made, of course, between evangelical postmillennialism, with its stress on what God accomplishes through evangelism and missions, and the liberal social gospel movement, with its naive and humanistic commitment to inevitable evolutionary progress.

Postmillennialism experienced a near eclipse during the period of the two world wars of the twentieth century. Writing in 1975, Kantzer says: "The postmillennial view for all practical purposes has dropped out of sight."[63] Yet, since World War II it has made something of a comeback, rallying support from such writers as Loraine Boettner, J. Marcellus Kik, Donald G. Bloesch, and John Jefferson Davis. Even Pinnock has spoken up. Reviewing Erickson's three-volume *Christian Theology*, he notes Erickson's silence with reference to the kingdom of God and the wholistic scope of God's redemptive purpose in Christ. Pinnock says:

> Sooner or later we will need an evangelical systematic theology which will legitimate rather than discourage the work of culture reclamation we are already starting to engage in. I do not think liberation theology has much to offer, since it is in the last analysis a thinly disguised religious version of Marxist politics. I think we are going

---

61. Bloesch says:
> The real heyday of postmillennialism was in the seventeenth and eighteenth centuries, which witnessed the flowering of the evangelical movements of Pietism and Puritanism. In the early Evangelical vision the future of history belongs to Jesus Christ, and his kingdom will be manifested in power and glory before his coming again. . . . Both Pietists and Puritans saw this millennial hope as the fulfillment of the great commission and this accounts for their intense preoccupation with world missions and evangelism.

Donald G. Bloesch, *Essentials of Evangelical Theology*, vol. 2 (San Francisco: Harper, 1979), 193.

62. Ewert, *And Then Comes the End*, 112.

63. Kenneth Kantzer, "Unity and Diversity in Evangelical Faith," in *The Evangelicals*, eds. David F. Wells and John D. Woodbridge (Nashville: Abingdon, 1975), 59.

to need the old Calvinistic eschatology called postmillennialism. This is the hope which places victory rather than defeat before our eyes.[64]

Whatever strength there is in the majestic scope of the postmillennial vision of God's kingdom purpose, however, its weakness is its tendency to neglect the realism of the Bible with reference to human sinfulness and the seriousness of the continuing warfare between the powers of light and the forces of darkness.

Amillennialism, the fourth millennial option, is represented by Hoekema in the Clouse volume. This is the view that Christ's millennial reign with His saints is a redemptive reality *prior* to the second coming, both in heaven as the intermediate state, and on earth as the powerful, though veiled, presence of the kingdom of God in history.

Although the amillennialism of today is in historical continuity with similar beliefs in other centuries, in certain important respects it is largely a post-World War I phenomenon. Erickson says:

> When postmillennialism began to fade in popularity in the twentieth century, amillennialism was generally substituted for it, since amillennialism is much closer to postmillennialism than is premillennialism. Consequently, amillennialism has enjoyed its greatest popularity in the period since World War I.[65]

During the 1930s especially, amillennialism gained increased public attention through its emphasis on the church as the instrument of God's pursuit of His redemptive purpose in history and its vigorous critique of the older dispensational theology, with its subordination of the role of the church to the role of national Israel in the outworking of God's purpose for history.

Yet, unlike dispensationalism, which has been a widespread popular movement, amillennialism, until the 1970s, was something of a classroom movement. George, for instance, commenting on the treatment of the Book of Revelation in Southern Baptist circles, says that popular interpretations of the Book have tended to be influenced by dispensational premillennialism, while Southern Baptist scholars have tended to be amillennial.[66]

This situation, however, has changed dramatically since the 1970s, as the once dominant dispensational premillennialism began to face new challenges due to the rise of the neoevangelicals, to the proliferation of

---

64. Clark H. Pinnock, "Erickson's Three-Volume Magnum Opus," *Theological Students Fellowship Bulletin* 9 [January-February 1986]: 30.
65. Erickson, *Christian Theology*, 1213.
66. George, "Summary," 224-27.

other Bible translations than the King James, and to the publication of numerous study Bibles in competition with the Scofield Reference Bible.

The strengths of amillennialism are the simplicity of its definition and its emphasis on the main redemptive themes which the New Testament associates with Christ and His two advents.

A weakness of amillennialism is the frequent failure of its advocates in the past to recognize that the issue dividing millennialists is not a literal versus a symbolic approach to the interpretation of Scripture. No theological conservative, whatever his millennial position, is ever justified in taking figuratively what the Bible intends to be taken literally! [67]

Current status of the millennial debate.—The final topic related to the millennial issue is an assessment of the current status of the constantly changing face of millennial discussions. Five comments are in order.

The first comment is that *each of the four major schools of millennial thought gives evidence of vitality.* The millennial debate is alive and thriving! This is so, as has been noticed, even with postmillennialism, though it continues to play the least significant role.

One sign of vigor is the amount of writing on the subject, not only by theologians, but also by historians and sociologists, whose concern is essentially academic. Another sign is the increasing effort to communicate across the lines dividing the options, which means that positions are constantly restudied, modified, and restated. Another indication of vigor is the interest of the laity.[68]

A second comment in assessing the current status of the millennial discussion concerns evidence that the *heated rhetoric of past discussions has cooled somewhat and that many evangelicals evidence a quickened desire to stress the substantial points where they are agreed.* Following are some examples of this reaching out for common ground.

---

67. Hoekema does his concern to take the Bible seriously a disfavor when, in commenting on Hoyt's failure always to interpret the Bible literally, he says: "Dispensationalists sometimes interpret nonliterally, and nondispensationalists sometimes interpret literally." Anthony A. Hoekema, "An Amillennial Response," in *The Meaning of the Millennium*, ed. Robert G. Clouse (Downers Grove, IL: InterVarsity, 1977), 107.

To make such a statement Hoekema refers to literal interpretation in some other sense than responsible historical-grammatical interpretation.

See also Jones' chapter, "Is Prophetic Language Literal or Figurative?" Russell Bradley Jones, *What, Where, and When Is the Millennium?* (Grand Rapids: Baker Book House, 1975), 53-64.

68. An example of academic interest in the subject is: Michael Barkun, *Crucible of the Millennium: The Burned-Over District of New York in the 1840s* (Syracuse, NY: Syracuse University, 1986).

An example of lay interest is: R. G. Currell and E. P. Hurlbut, *The Ruler of the Kings of the Earth* (Phillipsburg, NJ: Presbyterian and Reformed, 1982). The book is amillennial.

Bloesch appeals for a millennial approach which takes into account the valid insights of postmillennialism and premillennialism within the framework of a modified amillennialism.

Several historical premillennialists are speaking up, including Ladd, Erickson, Kantzer, and Newport. Ladd insists that "the New Testament nowhere expounds a theology of the millennium" as such. Erickson acknowledges that his own historical premillennial perspective provides "relatively little rationale for the millennium" for which he contends. Kantzer speaks for many when he stresses the "common allegiance to Jesus Christ as the Lord of history" on the part of evangelical proponents of each of the millennial views, and appeals for a cessation of "the acrimony, narrowness of spirit, and unfairness with which too many" have defended their views in the past. Newport grants that "in many ways [the ethos of historical premillennialism] is . . . like that of amillennialism. The millennium, in other words, plays a much less crucial role in [the historical premillennial] approach." Further testimony to the growing cordiality in relations between historical premillennialists and amillennialists is clearly apparent in the response to one another of Ladd and Hoekema in the Clouse volume. Each indicates agreement with practically all that the other has to say!

Robert Saucy, a dispensational premillennialist, speaks of noteworthy developments which "have worked to bring closer, if not total agreement, on many points of prior disagreement" between dispensationalists and nondispensationalists.[69]

The third comment in assessing the current status of millennial discussions among conservatives relates to the *difficulty of interpreting Revelation 20:1-10*. Why is this passage hard to interpret, and what principles should govern its interpretation?

Reasons why conservatives remain divided over the meaning of Revelation 20:1-10 include the fact that they bring to the task of biblical interpretation in general widely varying theological and interpretive presuppositions.[70] Furthermore, concerning the interpetation of the Book of Revelation, even though its central meaning and message are clear, namely that despite opposition Christ reigns and His final triumph

---

69. Ladd, "Historic Premillennialism, 39; Erickson, *Christian Theology,* 12-24; Kenneth Kantzer, "Our Future Hope: Eschatology and Its Role in the Church," *Christianity Today,* Christianity Today Institute Supplement, February 6, 1987, 14; Newport, *The Lion and the Lamb,* 106; Ladd, "A Historical Premillennial Response [to Amillennialism]," and Anthony A. Hoekema, "An Amillennial Response [to Historic Premillennialism]," in *The Meaning of the Millennium,* ed. Robert G. Clouse (Downers Grove, IL: InterVarsity, 1977), 189-91, 55-59; and Saucy, "The Crucial Issue," 150.

70. One ready indication of the sociological and theological diversity of American evangelicals is Webber's careful listing of fourteen different kinds. Robert E. Webber, *Common Roots: A Call to Evangelical Maturity* (Grand Rapids: Zondervan, 1978), 32.

is sure, yet, beyond this basic theme, questions regarding interpetation quickly multiply.[71]

With reference particularly to the difficulty of interpreting Revelation 20:1-10, the fact that it is the sole, *explicit* passage regarding a *millennial* reign of Christ, whether before or after the return of Christ, means that there is no *direct* help for understanding the passage from elsewhere in Scripture. In addition, the passage itself is too innovative and brief to be completely self-explanatory.

In ten brief verses, four intriguing topics are mentioned in passing only: (1) the no less than six references to the thousand years; (2) the binding of Satan for a thousand years, so that he should no longer deceive the nations (vv. 1-3); (3) the millennial reign of Christ and the saints, with references to a coming to life of martyrs and saints at the beginning of the thousand years and to a coming to life of "the rest of the dead" at the end of the thousand years (vv. 4-6); and, (4) the release of Satan at the end of the thousand years, his work in deceiving the nations, the fire from heaven aborting his attack on the camp of the saints, and his final destruction (vv. 7-10).[72]

Some of these themes are unique, such as the references to the thousand years and the two resurrections separated by the thousand years. Other themes are found elsewhere in the New Testament, some more than once, but in different contexts and without the reference to the thousand years. These include: the binding of Satan; Christ's reign; the reign of saints with Him; the resurrection of the believing and the unbelieving *as a single event;* Satan on the loose, deceiving the nations, and warring against the saints; and Satan destroyed.

---

71. Newport, for instance, lists seven different methods of for interpreting the Book of Revelation. The book can be viewed variously as: 1) encouragement for first-century Christians—the preterist-historical background or contemporary-historical view; 2) a symbolic portrayal of truths for each age and for the end of history—amillennial; 3) a forecast of the development of history—the historicist or continuous-historical view; 4) a forecast of Christian triumph in history before the second coming of Christ—postmillennialism; 5) a statement of eternal theological principles—symbolic, idealist, spiritualist principles view; 6) a forecast of the very last days of history—extreme future or dispensational premillennial view; and 7) a document intended to encourage, inform, and challenge first-century Christians and Christians of every generation, to teach eternal theological principles, and to portray the last days of history and beyond—the combination approach, the synthesis view, the prophetic-apocalyptic perspective, the moderate futurist view, and historical premillennial or covenant-premillennial approach. Newport, *The Lion and the Lamb*, 14-15, 79-112.

72. Something must be said about the special difficulty of Rev. 20:7-10 for premillennialism, but also for postmillennialism. For anyone interested in the problem, see Arthur H. Lewis, *The Dark Side of the Millennium: The Problem of Evil in Rev. 20:1-10* (Grand Rapids: Baker, 1980).

Referring to the mixture of saints and sinners in the millennial society according to Revelation 20, Lewis says: "So serious is this darker side of the picture that it may prove to be the 'Achilles heel' of the entire [premillennial] system of interpretation" (Ibid., 5)!

In the light of the brevity and complexity of the passage, the lack of agreement among conservatives regarding its interpretation is readily understandable. Conservatives agree on many principles governing biblical interpretation, but this significant concord does not automatically resolve long-standing differences over the meaning of these verses. It does help, however, to emphasize *what is not the problem*. It demonstrates, for instance, that the problem is not a denial that the Bible is the inspired Word of God, nor that the heart of the biblical message is the gospel of Christ, nor that the clue to difficult biblical passages is what the Bible clearly teaches generally,[73] nor that the Bible is to be interpreted literally, naturally, historically, grammatically, and contextually—not spiritualized or explained away.

A fourth comment in assessing the status of millennial discussions calls attention to a *possible breakthrough in interpreting the relation of Revelation 20 to Revelation 21–22*.[74] In recent years, both amillennial and historical premillennial writers have begun to speak of the thousand years of Revelation 20:1-10 as an "end-historical" event, that is, an event with significance for both history and the final consummation. On this basis Revelation 21:9–22:5 is understood to describe the millennium as well as the eternal new earth, so that the millennium is viewed less as a discrete interim between the second coming and the eternal order, and more as a manifestation of the new heavens and the new earth.

The end-historical terminology is not entirely new. Berkouwer, referred to by Johnson as a nonmillennialist, used the expression in the early 1960s.[75] In recent years, however, certain American historical premillennialists have employed the term to emphasize, as Johnson says,

---

73. For a classic and widely used statement of the evangelical viewpoint regarding what the Bible as a whole teaches, see John R. W. Stott, *Basic Christianity* (Grand Rapids: Eerdmans, 1958). The book has been reprinted repeatedly.

Since the millennium is not a major biblical theme, and not an article of belief in any of the major confessions of faith, Stott does not discuss the topic.

74. This reference to a possible breakthrough is more meaningful when placed in the context of a 1975 statement by Kantzer:

> Premillennialism, generally in the past merely tolerated in the church, has managed to disassociate itself from bizarre features of a former chiliasm and is the characteristic stance of the majority of American evangelicals. At the same time, it has ceased its rapid gains of the early middle part of the century *and has probably come to a sort of stalemate with amillennialism*, both being accepted as legitimate within the framework of consistent evangelicalism.

Kenneth Kantzer, "Unity and Diversity in Evangelical Faith," 59 (italics added).

75. G. C. Berkouwer, *The Return of Christ*, trans. James Van Oosterom (Grand Rapids: Eerdmans, 1972; Dutch ed., *De Wederkomst van Christus, I and II*, Kampen, The Netherlands: J. H. Kok, 1961,1963), 299.

that the millennium "is at once the final historical event of this age and the beginning of the eschatological kingdom of Christ in eternity."[76]

Johnson continues his discussion by dealing with "the sequence question." Inquiring whether the succession beginning with Revelation 19:11 and running through 22:6 is chronological, he asks:

> If the Millennium is a true eschatological, historical event like the person and ministry, and resurrection of Jesus, may not 21:1ff. be viewed as the full manifestation of the kingdom of God, a partial manifestation of which will be realized in the thousand-year reign of Christ and the saints, during which Christ will defeat all His enemies, including death (1 Cor. 15:23-28)?[77]

In the light of this end-historical development, it would seem that the gap between the historical premillennial view and the amillennial view may be lessening somewhat. There appears to be less emphasis in historical premillennial circles on the millennium as an interim event and more recognition of the New Testament stress on the second coming as a final event.

Berkouwer attributes the idea (but not the term), to Cullmann, whom he quotes as follows:
> [The Book of] Revelation [in 20:1-10 does not] intend to identify this thousand-year period with the whole period of the Church between Christ's ascension and his return. Revelation thinks rather of a specifically eschatological kingdom to be realized only in the future. It is, so to speak, the very last part of Christ's lordship, which at the same time extends into the new aeon.

Berkouwer's *added* comment is: "So the millennium is an end-historical category" (Ibid.). For the Cullmann reference, see Oscar Cullmann, *The Early Church*, trans. A. J. B. Higgins and S. Godman (London: SCM, 1956), 119.

76. Alan F. Johnson, *Revelation*, Bible Study Commentary (Grand Rapids: Zondervan, 1983), 183.

Johnson attributes what he calls the end-historical type of premillennialism to Cullmann, even though Cullmann does not use the term in the passage cited by both Berkouwer and Johnson (see the documentation in the preceding footnote).

Newport, citing Johnson, also makes use of the end-historical emphasis. First, in a reference to Rev. 11:15, he says that "this kingdom involves the millennial kingdom and its blending into the eternal kingdom (chs. 20—22)." Later he says that "the historical premillennial view is also called the "end-historical" view." Newport, *The Lion and the Lamb*, 228,294.

Beasley-Murray, though he does not employ the end-historical label, nonetheless says that "it is likely that [John's] description of the city of God in Revelation 21:9–22:5 is given as a revelation of the kingdom both in the millennial age and in the new creation." However, by stressing the earthly nature of the millennial kingdom, he retains the notion of the millennium as a discrete interim before the new heavens and the new earth. Beasley-Murray, *Revelation: Three Viewpoints*, 63.

Similarly, Ladd, in the Clouse volume, fails to make use of the end-historical emphasis. He also argues for a millennium which is "an interim kingdom, between this age and the Age to Come." Ladd, "An Historic Premillennial Response [to Amillennialism]," 190.

It may be that Johnson is the first American historical premillennialist to utilize the endhistorical emphasis.

77. Ibid., 184.

A fifth comment in assessing the status of millennial discussions concerns the *need to evaluate carefully the varying rationales for the different millennial views*. Saucy, a dispensational premillennialist, says that the "one basic and rather comprehensive issue" that distinguishes dispenationalists from nondispensationalists is their different views of "God's purpose and plan for biblical history."[78] This is surely correct. What could be more crucial for one's understanding of the Bible than the way in which God's purpose for history is viewed?

Remember, however, the close relation between God's purpose for history and God's purpose for a millennium. The latter reflects the former. At its heart, the millennial discussion among evangelicals is an attempt to determine what the Bible teaches about the nature of God's great redemptive purpose for history.

To begin with dispensational premillennialism, Walvoord and Ryrie maintain that God has a *broader* purpose for His now fallen creation than His purpose to provide redemption through Jesus Christ. Instead of saying that the Bible is a book of redemption,[79] as evangelicals generally contend, these writers regard redemption as a *reductive* idea and stress instead that the Bible is the book of God's glory.[80]   What is inadequate in this view is the implied suggestion that God's glory centers elsewhere or more widely than in Christ as Redeemer. In the Bible, however, to

---

78. Saucy, "The Crucial Issue," 155.

Ladd agrees. Acknowledging that the truth of the Lord's return has often been a subject of controversy, regarding the familiar millennial options, he says: "These several views embody different philosophies of history." George Eldon Ladd, *Jesus Christ and History,* Contemporary Christian Thought Series (Downers Grove, IL: InterVarsity, 1963), 15.

79. The first paragraph of the introduction to *The Criswell Study Bible* is:

The Bible is a book of redemption. It is that or nothing at all. It is not a book of history, science, anthropology, or cosmogony. It is a book salvation and deliverance for lost mankind.

W. A. Criswell, ed., *The Criswell Study Bible* (Nashville: Nelson, 1979), xiii.

80. Ryrie, *Dispensationalism Today*, 46-47, 101-5, and Saucy, "The Crucial Issue," 161-62. Saucy explains:

Although not denying that non-dispensationalists also see the glory of God as the chief end of all things, dispensationalists have insisted that the limitation of the *means* of that glorification to spiritual redemption which is often done by non-dispensationalists is an unwarranted reduction of the many facets of God's historical work.

Saucy then cites Walvoord:

All the events of the created world are designed to manifest the glory of God. The error of covenant theologians is that they combine all the many facets of divine purpose in the one objective of fulfillment of the covenant of grace. . . . The various purposes of God for Israel, for the church which is His body, for the Gentile nations, for the unsaved, for Satan and the wicked angels, for the earth and for the heavens have each their contribution. How impossible it is to compress all of these factors into the mold of the covenant of grace! (Ibid.)

For the Walvoord quote, see John F. Walvoord, *The Millennial Kingdom* (Findlay, OH: Dunham, 1959), 92.

behold Christ the Redeemer is to behold the glory of God in all of its full-ness (Col. 1:15-20).[81]

Why is it that some dispensational premillennialists insist that God's purpose for history is broader than the intent to provide redemption through Christ? They answer that they do so in order to justify establish-ing a millennial order that is more an earthly, Jewish, political, utopian Eden than a redemptive reality in an evangelical New Testament sense.[82]

Turning next to historical premillennialists, we find that the matter of a rationale for the millennium is a thorny problem for them also. They seek to hold to a discrete, earthly, millennial interim between Christ's sec-ond coming and the inauguration of the eternal order, an interim that is neither history as we know history nor the eternal new heaven and new earth. While Ladd characterizes the millennium as a New Testament and Christian order,[83] however he still is not clear about the sense in which the nature and purpose of the millennium are redemptive.

Ladd frankly acknowledges that there is no clear New Testament rationale for the millennium. Yet he proceeds to suggest three purposes which he believes the millennium serves: (1) the millennium is the time of Christ's messianic rule, when He will put all of His enemies under feet (1 Cor. 15:22); (2) the millennium is the disclosure of Christ's messianic kingdom *in history,* over against His present reign as invisible and inward and the eternal new heavens and new earth which are beyond history; and (3) Satan's success in arousing a rebellion against the city of God at the end of the millennium shows that sin is not due to a bad environment

---

81. This is not to charge with heresy any millennialists who speak of God's purpose for history as broader than "just" His purpose to redeem in Christ. It is easy to assume that there is no deliberate intention to subordinate Christ as redeemer. Evangelical millennialists are, after all, conservatives who work with a basically orthodox Christology.

Yet, surely the notion that redemption in Christ is a reductive idea is quite mistaken. Harrison is on firm biblical ground when he says: "No word in the Christian vocabulary deserves to be held more precious than Redeemer." Walter A. Elwell, ed., *Evangelical Dic-tionary of Theology* (Grand Rapids: Baker, 1984), s.v. "Redeemer, Redemption," by E. F. Harrison.

Over against any tendency to view God's purpose to redeem as narrow or limited, the argument above in the chapter on the kingdom present is that only in redemption, not apart from it, can God's intention for creation find its highest fulfillment.

82. Saucy prefers to speak of a theocratic kingdom rather than of God's glory as the focus of God's comprehensive purpose for history, but his view appears to be essentially the same as that of Ryrie and Walvoord. He speaks of the socio-political salvation of the nations, the restoration of the nation of Israel to a central position during the millennium, and the like. Saucy, "The Crucial Issue," 164.

83. Beasley-Murray is emphatic at this point:

The kingdom that is to come . . . is a "Christian" kingdom of Christ. . . . There is no question of a reversal to old covenant religion in the earth. . . . The kingdom of Christ is not a kingdom of the Jewish nation. . . . We are not at liberty, in interpreting the revelation of God given to us in the Bible, to read the Old Testament as though the New Testament did not exist.

Beasley-Murray, *Revelation: Three Viewpoints,* 68-69.

but to the sinful human heart, thus fully vindicating God's justice in His punishment of sinners at the final judgment.[84]

This list of purposes, however, fails to justify the necessity for a millennial interim. What Ladd ascribes to the millennium has either already taken place in Eden or will be accomplished in the new heavens and the new earth, especially when the end-historical nature of Revelation 20—22 is remembered.

With reference to Ladd's first rationale, according to the New Testament generally the time when Christ triumphs climactically over His enemies is at His second coming. Ladd cites 1 Corinthians 15:22 in support the millennium as the time when Christ's enemies are subdued, but he himself questions this interpretation of the passage.

Similarly with the second rationale, the time when Christ fully manifests His reign to this world is when He returns to establish the new heavens and the new earth. This is the importance of the second coming as personal, visible, and to this earth. Ladd's expectation that Christ, after He returns and before the final consummation, will establish a millennial kingdom within history, makes the second coming an interim rather than a final event. No historical premillennialist in recent years, to this writer's knowledge, has attempted to describe in detail what conditions would or could prevail in such an interim. Finally, with reference to Ladd's third rationale for a millennium, Genesis 3 has already demonstrated once and for all that sin is not due simply to a bad environment. Furthermore, the partial success of Satan's revolt at the end of the millennium (Rev. 20:7-10) is hardly necessary to demonstrate the sinfulness of the human heart (a fact indisputably evident every day of human history) or to vindicate the justice of God's punishment in the day of judgment. Instead, Ladd's view of Satan's revolt gives the millennium an even more enigmatic nature. How can the millennium be viewed as an era of utopian peace and righteousness under the reign of Christ when the hearts of multitudes ("the number of them is like the sand of the seashore," Rev. 20:8) smolder in rebellion?

Postmillennialists find it even more difficult to establish a biblical rationale for their millennial view. Their overly optimistic view of the extent of kingdom progress which can be expected in history on New Testament principles is not easily reconciled with the fact that the New Testament qualifies its call to expect great things from God with repeated reminders of the subtle sinfulness of the human heart and the certainty

---

84. Ladd, "Historic Premillennialism," 39-40.
Johnson and Newport give similar lists of purposes for a historical premillennial millennium. See Johnson, *Revelation*, 184-85, and Newport, *The Lion and the Lamb*, 296-97.

of the ongoing, fierce warfare between the kingdom of God and the kingdom of darkness.[85]

A biblical rationale for the amillennial view flounders on the references to the thousand years in Revelation 20:1-10 and on the negative nature of the name "amillennialism." It is simply inadequate to say, as the term "amillennial" does, that there is no millennium (in a premillennial or postmillennial sense). Recent advocates of amillennialism have suggested positive alternative labels such as "realized millennialism" or "historical millennialism,"[86] but the problem is deeper than a simple change of name. So long as the idea of a millennium continues to be thought of as biblical (Rev. 20:1-10 is in the Bible!), amillennialism will have difficulty substantiating its claims to biblical authority.

In conclusion, this discussion of the millennial issue has sought to highlight the strong points and the weaknesses of each of the familiar millennial options as they are currently formulated. Regarding the way ahead, the conclusion appears inescapable that a convincing key to the meaning of Revelation 20:1-10, one widely acceptable to evangelicals, is yet to be discovered.

When such a key is found it will surely conserve the dispensational premillennial concern for biblical authority, the historical premillennial stress on the gospel of Christ (including, of course, the promise of Christ's sure return) as the only final hope for the salvation of fallen humankind, the older postmillennial vision of the global missionary challenge of the gospel, and the amillennial underscoring of the decisiveness of the Christ-Pentecost events at the heart of history and the majestic finality of the second coming at the consummation of history. For the present no one of these views by itself gives promise of an ability to fill the void left by the absence of any of the other views.

---

85. In his recent restatement of the postmillennial view, Davis moderates postmillennial optimism somewhat. While he expects "a time prior to the return of Christ when a revitalized Christianity will become the world's dominant religion and most powerful moral and intellectual influence," he nonetheless does not "expect that all will be converted or that sin will be entirely eliminated prior to the eternal state." He even expects "a brief period of apostasy and sharp conflict between Christian and evil forces" immediately prior to Christ's return.

Davis, *Christ's Victorious Kingdom*, 11,14.

86. Jay E. Adams, *The Time Is at Hand* (Philadelphia: Presbyterian and Reformed, 1970), 7-11, and Arthur H. Lewis, *The Dark Side of the Millennium*, 6.

17 *The Final Resurrection*

Biblical faith is not content to affirm the shadow existence of an immortal soul. Rather, biblical realism stakes its claim on the resurrection of Jesus Christ and affirms the resurrection of the body—a resurrection with cosmic, corporate, and individual dimensions.

Biblical Resources
Historical Perspective
Restatement
    The Universality of the Resurrection
    The Uniqueness of the Christian View
    The Certainty of the Resurrection
    The Time of the Resurrection
        The issue of the intermediate state
        Is the final resurrection one or more than one?
    The Nature of the Resurrection of the Body
    The Resurrection as Corporate and Cosmic

"Behold, I tell you a mystery," wrote Paul in words still fresh and startling: We shall not all sleep, but we shall all be changed in a moment, in the twinkling of an eye, at the last trumpet; for the trumpet will sound, and the dead will be raised imperishable, and we shall be changed. For this perishable must put on the imperishable, and this mortal must put on immortality (1 Cor. 15:51-53).

Whence this astounding hope? Above all, of course, it is hope grounded in Christ's own resurrection from the dead. "If Christ has not been raised, your faith is worthless"; and not only that but "you are still in your sins. . . . But now Christ has been raised from the dead, the first fruits of those who are asleep" (1 Cor. 15:17,20).

Hunter says, "We are living in a world in which, for all its sin and sadness, Christ has left one vacant tomb in the wide graveyard of the earth."[1] We live on this side of God's Decisive-Day! Christ's first coming and the

---

1. A. M. Hunter, *Interpreting Paul's Gospel* (London: SCM, 1954), 126.

305

outpouring of the Holy Spirit have changed everything. Great as this good news is, however, we may never forget the price paid to make it possible. It is no light matter for a disciple of Christ to confess: "I believe. I believe in the resurrection of the body. I believe in the life everlasting. Amen!"

Biblical Resources

Contrary to a common misunderstanding, the Old Testament does not regard death as the end of personal human existence. After all, belief in existence beyond death was strong in ancient, middle-east in religion general. Yet the Old Testament does not say a great deal about the resurrection of the body. The place of the dead, or *sheol*, which corresponds in the Greek to *hades*, is often pictured as a place of gloom (Job 10:21-22; Ps. 6:4-5; Isa. 38:18-19), though in moments of clearer vision even Old Testament saints could trust that God in His goodness and steadfast love would not abandon His people in *sheol*.

In 2 Samuel 12:23, for instance, David voices confidence in the continuity of life beyond the grave; Enoch and Elijah were both translated; Isaiah 26:19 and Daniel 12:2 clearly assert the resurrection of the body. Although passages such as Ezekiel 37:1-14 and Hosea 6:1-2 speak of resurrection, they refer to the hope of exiled Jews for a national restoration of Israel.

Beyond these references, some New Testament passages attribute resurrection teaching to the Old Testament (see Mark 12:18-27; Acts 2:24-36; 13:30-41). According to Hebrews 11:13,16 (NIV), the epitaph of all Old Testament saints is that "all these people were still living by faith when they died. . . . They were longing for a better country—a heavenly one." Yet, not all Jews in Jesus' day believed in the resurrection (Mark 12:18-27; Acts 23:6-8).

In the New Testament Christ's own resurrection is the watershed leading to the changed view of the resurrection of the body which marks its pages. Yet, even before His resurrection, Jesus clearly taught the hope of resurrection.

* Jesus countered the Sadducees' denial of the resurrection by referring to the Pentateuch, the only part of the Old Testament the Sadducees accepted (Mark 12:18-27).

* Jesus spoke of the resurrection of the dead, some to life and some to judgment (John 5:25-29).

* Jesus reassured Martha and Mary at the tomb of Lazarus with His claim, "I am the resurrection and the life" (John 11:25).

- Jesus taught that to trust in Him is to experience already the eternal life of the age to come (John 3:36).

Similarly, Paul taught that the gift of the Spirit is a down payment or first fruit of the life to come (Rom. 8:11; 2 Cor. 5:4-5; Eph. 4:30).

The primary datum, however, is that Jesus not only taught the resurrection of the dead, but that He rose bodily from the grave. Everywhere in the New Testament belief in the resurrection of the body is firmly rooted in the fact of the resurrection of Jesus Himself. Jesus' resurrection was first; we are sure to follow (Acts 26:23; 1 Cor. 15:20; Col. 1:18). Paul is confident: "He who raised the Lord Jesus will raise us with Jesus and will present us with you" (2 Cor. 4:14). Further passages include Acts 24:15; Romans 6:5; 8:11,18-25; Philippians 3:10-11,20-21; 1 Thessalonians 4:16-17; Hebrews 6:2; and Revelation 20:4-6,11-15.

Historical Perspective

Although the great creeds and confessions of Christendom readily affirm the general resurrection, questions such as what happens to the individual at death, the relation of the resurrection of the body to the philosophical idea of the *innate* immortality of the soul, and the continuity in personal identity from this life to the next have received varied treatment.

Modern liberalism, inspired by Platonic arguments for the soul's innate immortality, speaks more often of the survival of personality than it does of the resurrection of the body. More recently, twentieth-century secular and humanistic skepticism tends to dismiss the whole biblical teaching about the final consummation as mere make-believe, leaving the door open for bizarre notions of life-after-life in a nether spirit world, such as those proposed by Kubler-Ross.[2]

Restatement

Thoughts occasioned by a person's affirmation of belief in the resurrection of the body, assuming that the biblical basis for the affirmation is taken seriously, depend in part on how recently one has stood by the open grave of a loved one who was torn away suddenly and tragically. Recall the gloom of the disciples as they laid the body of Jesus in the tomb, or their elation upon finding the tomb empty and the Lord Himself risen and alive. Belief in the resurrection of the body is no mere dry-as-

---

2. Elisabeth Kubler-Ross, ed., *Death: The Final Stage of Growth* (Engelwood, NJ: Prentice Hall, 1975). Also see Frances Adeney, "Hope in Reincarnation: Elisabeth Kubler-Ross and the Life after Death," Spiritual Counterfeits Project *Newsletter* 8 [August-September 1982]: 1-4.

dust philosophical abstraction. It touches life at its crucial center: "If we have hoped in Christ in this life only, we are of all men most to be pitied" (1 Cor. 15:19)!

Of importance for a grasp of the biblical idea of the resurrection of the body is a reminder of the magnitude of the issues involved. These issues include belief in:

•The almightiness and constancy of God as revealed in Christ;

•Life beyond death;

•The worth of individual persons as creatures made in God's image and for eternity;

•The resurrection, not only of believers to life but also of unbelievers to judgment;

•The resurrection as God's concern for the quality of life, not merely its quantitative extension;

•Both the continuity and the discontinuity between present existence and future existence.

The doctrine of the resurrection of the body affirms that God's love breaks through the boundaries of death. His love is not just a love for the moment. The doctrine also says that the values and relationships of Christian experience are for eternity. They are worth the sacrifices involved in the daily commitment to seek first God's kingdom and His righteousness.

In turning now to a restatement of the doctrine of the resurrection, the following topics call for discussion:

•The universality of the resurrection;

•The uniqueness of the Christian view of the resurrection of the body;

•The certainty of the resurrection;

•The time of the resurrection;

•The nature of the resurrection body;

•The resurrection as corporate and cosmic as well as individual.

The Universality of the Resurrection

Although the doctrine of the resurrection of the body centers in the resurrection of believers, it should be understood from the outset that the New Testament speaks explicitly of the universality of the resurrection. In John 5:29 (NIV) Jesus speaks of a time when "those who have done evil will rise to be condemned" (KJV, "unto the resurrection of damnation"). In Acts 24:15 (cf. also Dan. 12:2) Paul refers to a resurrection of both the righteous and the wicked.

In addition to these direct references, the universality of the resurrection is implicit elsewhere in Scripture. The reference to a "first" resurrection of the martyred saints and holy ones in Revelation 20:4-5 implies a second resurrection of unbelievers, whose fate is the second death or the lake of fire (Rev. 20:6,14), even though there is no direct reference to a second resurrection. Matthew has several hints of a universal resurrection (5:29-30; 10:28; 12:41-42; 25:31-46). A possible Pauline reference occurs in 1 Corinthians 15:22-24.[3]

Since these references relate to the universality of judgment, they raise another question: Does not a universal judgment imply and necessitate a universal resurrection? Although the New Testament answers in the affirmative, such an answer involves a conceptual difficulty, due to the fact that resurrection reality in the New Testament is usually associated with believers and their resurrection to glory. The resurrection of unbelievers, on the other hand, is a resurrection to shame and to condemnation. In view of this distinction between resurrection to glory and resurrection to shame, it seems evident that the doctrine of a universal resurrection requires two distinct dimensions: a resurrection to fullness of life, and a resurrection involving little more than reanimation. According to Harris, "There is another, special sense of resurrection [other than glorification], referring . . . to the resuscitation of dead persons and their appearance before God in some undisclosed bodily form that permits continuity of personal identity."[4]

The modern mind has trouble reconciling a resurrection to condemnation with a God who is the Father of all mercies. Yet the idea of a resurrection to condemnation is grounded in Scripture and cannot be lightly jettisoned.

Although the resurrection of unbelievers is clearly affirmed by the New Testament, the primary focus is on the resurrection of believers. Harris explains, "The New Testament stresses the benefits that accrue from believing rather than the deprivation that results from refusal to believe."[5] Since this is so, the New Testament ventures very little information about the resurrection body of unbelievers. Conner says:

> As to the nature of the resurrection body of the wicked, we are left almost entirely in the dark. About all that we learn is the fact that

---

3. For a discussion of these matters see Murray J. Harris, *Raised Immortal* (Grand Rapids: Eerdmans, 1985), 174-76.
4. Ibid., 177,271.
5. Ibid., 184.

the wicked are raised and that they rise to a resurrection of shame and condemnation. Possibly in some ways their bodies will conform to their depraved and deformed spirits, but we are not told; and where nothing is revealed and we have no suggestions in experience as to which way to go, we had better practice a reverent silence.[6]

The Uniqueness of the Christian View

The biblical view of the resurrection of the body is different from the Greek view of an innately immortal soul set free from imprisonment in a corrupt and decaying body. When Paul preached the bodily resurrection of the dead at Athens, the philosophers sneered (Acts 17:32).[7]

According to the Platonic tradition in ancient philosophy, physical death is the escape of the innately immortal, deified soul from the prison house of the mortal body. The human problem is not seen as sin but as creatureliness and mortality. Persons need to escape from bodily limitations in order to become free, immortal, godlike spirits. Death should be welcomed as a way of escape from the futile confines of this life into the larger, wider spirit-world.

The biblical view of the resurrection of the body takes an altogether different view of these matters.

1. The Bible views death realistically, recognizing the tragic and painful aspects that often characterize physical dying. In this sense it avoids the euphemism of the Greek view.

2. The Bible views the body, and the temporal material order in general, as originally God's good creations, firmly rejecting the Platonic and Gnostic contempt for the body and earthly existence.

3. The Bible views the resurrection as including public, corporate, and cosmic aspects. The Greek view is preoccupied exclusively with private and individual aspects of the life beyond.

4. The Bible views the impenitent sinner, who dies without Christ, as eternally lost. Paul repudiates the Greek view that the human dilemma is mortality or creatureliness. The human problem is not death but death without Christ.

5. The Bible centers human hope in the redeeming power and grace of God in Christ. People's hope in themselves is no hope at all.

---

6. W. T. Conner, *The Gospel of Redemption* (Nashville: Broadman, 1945), 319-20.

The comment of *The New Scofield Reference Bible* is simply: 'The resurrection body of the wicked dead is not described" (1 Cor. 15:52, note 2).

7. On the difference between the biblical and Greek views of the nature of body and soul see Harris, *Raised Immortal,* 201-5.

The Certainty of the Resurrection

Belief in the doctrine of the resurrection, as with all Christian belief, is grounded in the integrity and divine authority of Scripture. According to the foundational biblical witness, Christ's own resurrection marks the grand turning point in the Christian understanding of death and the life to come. Christ's resurrection guarantees the resurrection of believers (1 Cor. 15:20). Rather than some vague philosophical notion about the ability of the human spirit to survive death on its own, belief in the resurrection of the body is a clear biblical teaching based on the historical fact of Jesus' resurrection.

The confidence of the biblical writers in the final resurrection is further reinforced by their strong conviction that persons have worth to God, a worth rooted in persons as creatures created in God's own image and as creatures for whom Christ died. Paul was sure that nothing in all creation could separate believers "from the love of God that is in Christ Jesus our Lord" (Rom. 8:38-39).

God never forsakes or abandons His own. His love is steadfast, not momentary; it never ends (1 Cor. 13:8). If the Old Testament saint could exclaim, "And I will dwell in the house of the Lord forever" (Ps. 23:6), how much more can the Christian celebrate with George Matheson the "love that wilt not let me go."[8] Earth's kingdom values are eternally precious to heaven!

The Time of the Resurrection

Although the major confessions of faith generally agree that Christ will raise believers when He comes again (1 Cor. 15:23; Phil. 3:20-21; 1 Thess. 4:16), diversity prevails about details of the time of the final resurrection, as was readily evident in the discussion of the millennial issue. Two questions especially are discussed.

The issue of the intermediate state.—The first question regarding the time of the resurrection concerns the state of believers who die before the final resurrection. In the earlier discussion of the intermediate state, the suggestion was made that the most adequate way to handle the difficulties this question raises is to speak of three levels or stages in the actualization of the believer's resurrection. The three levels are:

- Believers already have eternal life, and in this sense are already risen (John 3:26,36; 11:25-26; Eph. 2:6);

- Believers at death are raised bodily one by one in an interim or intermediate sense (2 Cor. 5:1-10; Phil. 1:23);

---

8. See the hymn, "O Love That Wilt Not Let Me Go," George Matheson, 1842-1906.

- Believers will be raised in the fullest sense at the final resurrection, when God's redemptive purpose in history will be consummated once and for all (1 Cor. 15:22).

Concerning the distinction between the first of these levels and the other two, Harris writes:

> We may therefore speak of two stages by which the Christian's resurrection is realized or of two tenses of Christian resurrection. There is a future somatic or "outward" resurrection, and a past spiritual or "inward" resurrection.

Concerning the distinction between the second and third levels, he says:

> Paul's belief that in His resurrection state Christ possessed a glorious body (Phil. 3:21) would more naturally imply that active, personal communion "with the Lord" (2 Cor. 5:8b) [at death] involved the believer's possession of a spiritual body than that such fellowship should be experienced between a bodiless spirit and its embodied Lord. And it is at least open to doubt whether Paul ever countenanced the notion of a disembodied, sentient soul capable of sustaining personal relation. . . . 2 Cor. 5, written from the perspective of the individual Christian, envisages transformation at death, while 1 Cor. 15, expressing the corporate hope of the Church, places the resurrection at the second advent.[9]

Is the final resurrection one event or more than one?—The second question about the time of the resurrection relates to the premillennial separation between the believers' resurrection and the resurrection of unbelievers, with the former taking place before the millennium and the

---

9. Harris, *Raised Immortal,* 98,100-101.

In 1980, citing earlier materials by Harris, Travis says:

> Harris argues that from the time he wrote 2 Cor. 5:1-10 Paul believed the resurrection body to be received at death. The parousia thus became for Paul not the moment of resurrection but the moment of open manifestation of a previously hidden state of embodiment. Thus there is still an intermediate state, but not an awkwardly disembodied one.

Travis then continues:

> Aldwinckle also believes that the intermediate state will involve an embodied existence: "The idea of being in Christ as only half a person does not make sense." In that case the general resurrection at the parousia would denote not our passing from a disembodied to an embodied state, but our entry into full communion with the whole body of the faithful.

Travis attributes the same view to F. F. Bruce. Stephen H. Travis, *Christian Hope and the Future* (Downers Grove, IL: InterVarsity, 1980), 110-11.

> It should be noted that when discussing the time of the believer's receipt of his immortality as a child of God, Harris says:

> It is clear that the only unambiguous testimony places the receipt [of immortality] at the time of the resurrection, be that at the individual believer's death or on the Last Day.

latter after the millennium.[10] Amillennialists, on the other hand, viewing the millennium of Revelation 20 as a present, spiritual, earthly-heavenly reality, believe that the resurrection of believers and unbelievers will occur simultaneously when Christ returns. Hoekema and Summers argue that Revelation 20:4-6 is a disputed passage, and that established exegesis interprets passages which are more difficult in the light of the passages which are less controversial. They conclude that Revelation 20 is not an adequate scriptural basis for denying the general resurrection as a single event, which is the dominant view of the Bible as well as of the history of Christian theology.[11]

This debate as to whether believers and unbelievers are raised at the same time or at different times is hardly of major concern. Premillennialists, amillennialists, and postmillennialists relate the final resurrection to the return of Christ and the consummation. This is the important matter.

The Nature of the Resurrection of the Body

"But someone will say, 'How are the dead raised? and with what kind of body do they come?'" (1 Cor. 15:35). This ageless question about the resurrection body is really two questions. It concerns not only the nature of the resurrection body of believers, but also, the nature of the resurrection body of unbelievers?

The New Testament clue to the nature of the resurrection body of believers is the resurrection body of Jesus Christ. At Jesus' resurrection the tomb was empty (Luke 24:3), yet Jesus' body was not merely resuscitated

---

10. George Eldon Ladd, "Historic Premillennialism," and Herman A. Hoyt, "A Dispensational Premillennial Response [to Historic Premillennialism]," in *The Meaning of the Millennium*, ed. Robert G. Clouse (Downers Grove, IL: InterVarsity, 1977), 37-38,44-45.

While Ladd readily acknowledges that the idea of the millennium intervening between the two resurrections is found only in Rev. 20:4-6,12-13, Erickson says:

> We should also observe that while the two resurrections are spoken of explicitly only in Rev. 20 there are other passages which hint at either a resurrection of a select group (Luke 14:14; 20:35; 1 Cor. 15:23; Phil. 3:11; 1 Thess. 4:16) or a resurrection in two stages (Dan. 12:2; John 5:29). . . . These texts fit well with the concept of two resurrections.

Millard J. Erickson, *Christian Theology*, (Grand Rapids: Baker, 1985), 1217.

Dispensationalists add further refinements, such as the distinction between the rapture of the church out of the world prior to the tribulation and the return of Christ at the end of the tribulation and the beginning of the millennium. See *The New Scofield Reference Bible*, Rev. 19:19, note.

11. Anthony A. Hoekema, *The Bible and the Future* (Grand Rapids: Eerdmans, 1979), 240-45, and Ray Summers, *The Life Beyond* (Nashville: Broadman, 1959), 83-92.

but rather resurrected and transformed.[12] He was not readily recognized by His disciples (Luke 24:16,37; John 20:14; 21:4). He could pass through closed doors (John 20:19,26). He could vanish from sight (Luke 24:31). Yet He was recognized (Matt. 28:17; Luke 24:31; John 20:16,20,28; 21:12). He ate with the disciples (Luke 24:43). He broke bread and gave it to them (Luke 24:30). He urged them to see His hands and feet and to touch Him (Luke 24:39; John 20:27).

The appearances of the risen Christ had the quality of something more than mere physical manifestations. For one thing, Jesus' reported appearances were to believers, or, as in the case of Saul on the Damascus Road, He appeared to an unbeliever for the purpose of his conversion (Acts 9:5). This fact suggests that faith or spiritual perception, and not mere physical vision, was required in order to see the risen Christ.

Because resurrection involves both transformation and continued personal identity, Paul described the resurrection body of believers through the analogy of the seed and the plant. He says:

That which you sow, you do not sow the body which is to be, but a bare grain, perhaps of wheat or of something else. But God gives it a body just as He wished, and to each of the seeds a body of its own (1 Cor. 15:37-38). Relating this analogy to the resurrection, he continues: "So also is the resurrection of the dead. It is sown a perishable body, it is raised an imperishable body" (1 Cor. 15:42).

Commenting on this remarkable analogy, Cotterell says:

> The illustration used by Paul is a very helpful one. . . . I'm not a particularly good gardener, but in Ethiopia I grew a lot of eucalyptus trees from seed. The seed is a tiny black speck, but now, just outside Addis Ababa, or two hundred miles to the south where I lived a couple of years, you can see today what grew from those tiny black seeds. Now what grew was *not* a series of enormous black spheres,

---

12. For the discussion between Geisler and Harris regarding Jesus' resurrection body see: Norman L. Geisler, *The Battle for the Resurrection* (Nashville: Nelson, 1990), and Murray J. Harris, *From Grave to Glory* (Grand Rapids: Zondervan, 1990).

Erickson distinguishes rather sharply between Jesus' resurrection and His ascension, and hence between His resurrection body and His ascension body. He says:

> In the case of Jesus, however, the two events, resurrection and ascension, were separated rather than collapsed into one [as they will be in the case of the resurrection bodies of believers]. So the body that he had at the point of resurrection was yet to undergo a more complete transformation at the point of the ascension. . . . We might say, then, that the Easter event was something of a resuscitation, such as that of Lazarus, rather than a true resurrection, as will be the case for us. Jesus' postresurrection body may well have been like the body with which Lazarus came out of the tomb—Lazarus could still and presumably did again die. If this was the case with Jesus, he may have needed to eat to remain alive.

Erickson, *Christian Theology,* 777.

but fine, sweeping trees, not black, but brown and green and silver
in the highland winds. Not ugly, but beautiful. Not sullenly immo-
bile, but vibrantly alive, growing.[13]

Resurrection, then, involves radical transformation and glorification.
Paul anticipates that Christ "will transform the body of our humble state
into conformity with the body of His Glory (Phil. 3:21). John says,
"Blessed are the dead who die in the Lord" (Rev. 14:13), as he paints dramatic pictures of the new existence of saints in glory.

Many lesser questions about the nature of the resurrection body
remain unanswered. What kind of a body will those have who died in
infancy? What kind of a body will those have who died in their advanced
years and whose bodies were crippled almost beyond recognition by dev-
astating disease?

Such details are not revealed, but believers are not dismayed. They
share Paul's hope that "our present sufferings are not worth comparing
with the glory that will be revealed in us" (Rom. 8:18). They know they
can trust the God revealed in Christ Jesus who cares infinitely and whose
goodness never fails.

One question with a sure answer regards the continuity of personal
identity in the life to come. Will believers recognize one another in glory?
Yes, clearly yes. The essence of the doctrine of the bodily resurrection is
the continuity of personal identity.

The body is instrumental to the person. The resurrection of the body
is the resurrection of the person! Just as Jesus' followers recognized the
risen Jesus, the saints will recognize one another in heaven. Otherwise,
not only would the resurrection body lack continuity with the present
body, but believers would know less in heaven than they know on
earth![14]

Further biblical support for the assurance of recognition in heaven was
mentioned in the discussion of the intermediate state. Even the fact that
the names of the saints are written in the Lamb's book of life (Rev. 21:27)
attests that they will know as they are known (1 Cor. 13:12).

How far can the assertion of personal identity be pressed? What about
the male-female distinction, for instance? Jesus said that in heaven
believers will be as angels, that they will neither marry nor be given in

---

13. Peter Cotterell, *What the Bible Teaches about Death* (Wheaton, IL: Tyndale House,
1980), 98.
14. Cotterell quotes George McDonald: "Shall we be greater fools in Paradise than we
are here?"!
Cotterell contends for the possibility that our powers of recognition will be even greater,
not lesser, in that we will "recognize" people we have never known before!
Ibid., 91,95.

marriage (Matt. 22:30). Does this imply that we will be androgynous creatures? Traditionally a common answer has been in the affirmative. Referring to Jesus' comment, however, Harris writes:

> This contrast suggests that the resurrection body will be without sexual passions or procreative powers, not that the resurrected righteous will be sexless (since sexual identity is an essential part of personality, and personality is retained in resurrection).[15]

The Resurrection as Corporate and Cosmic

Emphasis on the resurrection body of the believer should not obscure the fact that the resurrection has corporate and cosmic dimensions as well as an individual aspect. Because of God's action in Jesus Christ, believers are a body, a community, a kingdom. On the day of resurrection, in the twinkling of an eye, the whole body of believers will be gathered in Jesus' presence, a grand reunion of the people of God, never again to be separated.

Resurrection is no mere, solitary, individual experience. The New Testament visions of heaven are pictures of throngs from every nation—red and yellow, black, brown, white—glorifying and praising God. If it could be said in Old Testament times with reference to the congregation of Israel, "Blessed are those who have learned to acclaim you" (Ps. 89:15, NIV), what will it be to come to Mount Zion, to the heavenly Jerusalem, the city of the living God . . . to come to thousands upon thousands of angels in joyful assembly, to the church of the firstborn, whose names are written in heaven . . . come to God, the judge of all men, to the spirits of righteous men made perfect, to Jesus the mediator of a new covenant, and to the sprinkled blood that speaks a better word than the blood of Abel (cf. Heb. 12:22-24, NIV)!

Harris notes that whenever a New Testament writer "adds the qualification 'of the dead' to the term resurrection, the word 'dead' is always a plural (*nekroi*), never a singular." He adds that the corporate dimension of resurrection life is further confirmed outside of a resurrection context "by such ideas as 'a new earth in which righteousness dwells' (2 Pet. 3:13), 'the holy city, New Jerusalem' where God will dwell with His people (Rev. 21:23,10-14), and the marriage supper in honor of the Lamb (Rev. 19:9)."[16]

---

15. Harris, *Raised Immortal*, 123.
Harris lists five features of the resurrection body of believers: (1) of divine origin; (2) spiritual (free of sinful propensities, without physical instincts, amenable to the Spirit's guidance); (3) imperishable, glorious, and powerful; (4) angel-like; and (5) heavenly (heaven is its natural habitat). Ibid., 124
16. Ibid., 233-34.

Regarding the cosmic aspect of the resurrection, Scripture indicates that God's purpose in Christ extends to the natural creation. The Christ who changes our lowly bodies to be like His glorious body exercises a "power that He has even to subject all things to Himself" (Phil. 3:21). The entire creation looks forward to resurrection day when "the creation itself also will be set free from its slavery to corruption into the freedom of the glory of the children of God" (Rom. 8:21). To speak further of this cosmic dimension would be to anticipate unduly the later treatment of the doctrine of heaven and the new earth.

These are some features of the biblical doctrine of the resurrection of the body. Their discussion should have emphasized the same truth that became clear in the study of the second coming: Jesus Christ is the primary object of Christian hope, not just an event or a series of events but a Person. Resurrection life is life in and with Christ. Life with Christ in the consummation is nothing less than life in its resurrection fullness and indescribable abundance.

The Last Judgment

At the end of history God will manifest the charac-
ter and destiny of each person and group through
the same Lord Jesus Christ who came to save.

In its biblical perspective, judgment is a reassuring word as well as a solemn word! In a world gone wrong through sin, a world where human cruelty makes life unbearable for unnumbered multitudes and where the human misuse of creation turns even the environment against us, no day of final reckoning or vindication would be a cause for despair. Instead of blindly fearing judgment, any thinking person dreads the thought of a day of no judgment!

In a purposeful universe, where responsible persons are governed by a righteous and merciful God, a day of final reckoning is morally inevitable because personal accountability is God's way of making us into the kind of responsible persons He created us to be. Scripture is clear: "It is appointed for men to die once and after this comes judgment" (Heb. 9:27). Travis says:

> Although the suggestion that we should drop the idea of divine judgment is superficially attractive, it leads in fact not to the liberation of man but to his belittling. To deny that all people are responsible *for* their actions and responsible *to* God is to deny an essential part of human personality and to reduce us to the level of machines.

318

> The prospect of judgment may even be welcomed because it assures
> us that God treats all our actions as significant.

If the idea of judgment is removed, then ultimately *no* actions are significant.[1]

Judgment as administered through Jesus Christ is, first of all, intended to produce repentance and to bring sinners to salvation. Forsyth argues that judgment "always means the dawn of the kingdom more than the doom of the world."[2] In Jesus' parable of the talents, attention first focuses on the indescribable blessing accorded to the faithful servants in terms of the Master's priceless benediction, "Well done, good and faithful servant" (Matt. 25:20-23). After all, "God did not send the Son into the world to judge the world, but that the world should be saved through Him" (John 3:17).

Biblical Resources

A basic Old Testament belief is that God is righteous, that He blesses nations or individuals who practice righteousness (Isa. 3:10) and punishes those who live unrighteously (Mic. 6:8). Most Old Testament references to divine punishment center on temporal calamities—war, flood, famine, earthquake, and pestilence. Increasingly, however, later Old Testament prophets spoke of the coming day of the Lord—a day of judgment on the wicked, whether Gentile or Israelite, as well as a day of deliverance for God's faithful, covenant people (Joel 2:28-3:21; Amos 5:16-20; Zeph. 1:7-9). The prophets were not concerned with charting the detailed course of future events but with calling God's people to repentance and to obedience in their covenant commitment to Him.

In the New Testament the idea of the last judgment takes definite shape. In addition to general references to the certainty of punishment for wrongdoers, such as Jesus' warnings of hell fire (Matt. 5:22; Luke 16:19-31; John 15:6), and to the certainty of future blessing for those who remain faithful (Matt. 6:20), there are also specific references to the last judgment.

Jesus speaks of the sheep and goat judgment at the last day (Matt. 25:31-46), Paul of the judgment seat of God (Rom. 14:10) or of Christ (2 Cor. 5:10), and John of the great white throne judgment (Rev. 20:11-15). This day of future judgment is associated with death (Heb. 9:27), with the second coming of Christ (Matt. 16:28; 1 Cor. 4:5; 2 Thess. 1:5-10; Jas. 5:8-9), or with the final resurrection (John 5:28-29). It is designated as the day of the Lord (1 Thess. 5:1-3), a day of judgment (Matt. 11:24; Acts 17:31;

---

1. Stephen H. Travis, "The Problem of Judgment," *Themelios* 11 [January 1986]: 53.
2. P. T. Forsyth, *The Justification of God* (New York: Scribner's, 1917), 198.

2 Pet. 2:9; 3:7; 1 John 4:17), the day of God's wrath (Rom. 2:5), the day when God will judge (Rom. 2:16), the judgment to come (Acts 24:25), or the coming wrath (1 Thess. 1:10).

Conservative interpreters differ about secondary questions such as the number of judgments, but they agree that the second coming of Christ brings with it final judgment.

Historical Perspective

Traditional Christian orthodoxy customarily affirms a final judgment, yet it has not always been careful to maintain the biblical balance between God's mercy and His wrath, or to recognize that both believers and unbelievers will be judged. Medieval Roman Catholic theology, for instance, tended to dwell more on the condemnation of unbelievers than on the blessedness of the faithful,[3] while older Protestant orthodoxy too often regarded wrath as more characteristic of the divine nature than mercy.

"God must be wrathful, he may be merciful," remained a common Protestant assertion until recently.[4] D. L. Moody's ministry was revolutionized when as a pastor in Chicago he discovered, through the guest ministry of Henry Moorhouse in 1868, the crucial importance of John 3:16 for Christian proclamation.[5]

Modern liberalism, on the other hand, overreacting to orthodoxy's stress on wrath to the neglect of love, has emphasized God's love to the neglect of biblical teaching about the last judgment.[6]

---

3. Guthrie refers to medieval paintings of the last judgment as portrayals of "a day of gloom and doom on which Christ, with clinched fist and a sword, sternly separates those on the right, who are floating upward into rosy clouds, from those on the left, who are being dragged down by hideous demons into all kinds of excruciating torture."

S. G. Guthrie, *Christian Doctrine* (Atlanta: Knox, 1977), 389.

4. A. H. Strong, *Systematic Theology*, 3 vols. (Philadelphia: Judson, 1907), 196.

Regarding this tendency in Protestant theology, Richardson says: "Only a certain kind of degenerate Protestant theology has attempted to contrast the wrath of God with the mercy of Christ." Alan Richardson, *An Introduction to the Theology of the New Testament* (London: SCM, 1958), 77.

5. Stanley N. Gundry, *Love Them In* (Chicago: Moody, 1976), 46,115-16.

Moody said: "I used to think that Christ loved me more than God" (Ibid., 116).

6. Even Temple, by no means a liberal extremist, says by way of objection to any verdict of eternal condemnation:

>The scheme present certain administrative difficulties. It involves, in practice, the drawing of a sharp line between the awakened and the unawakened soul, and again between the pardonable and the unpardonable. . . . How can there be a Paradise for any while there is Hell, conceived as unending torment, for some? Each supposedly damned soul was born into the world as a mother's child, and Paradise cannot be Paradise for her if her child is in such a Hell. The scheme is unworkable in practice even by omniscience, and moreover it offends against the deepest Christian sentiments.

Temple goes on to affirm conditional immortality:"If the sinner so sinks himself in his sin as to become truly identified with it, God must destroy him also."

William Temple, *Nature, Man, and God* (London: Macmillan, 1934), 454,469.

Dispensational theology separates and multiplies the future judgments. It distinguishes the sheep and goat judgment of Matthew 25:31-46 from the great white throne judgment of Revelation 20:11-15. According to one dispensational version, the sheep and goat judgment refers to a judgment on Gentiles living on earth when Christ returns with His saints at the end of the great tribulation; the sheep are Gentiles saved after the pretribulation rapture of the church. The test of the judgment "is the treatment by individual Gentiles of those whom Christ calls 'my brethren,'" presumably faithful Israelites fearfully persecuted during the tribulation period. The great white throne judgment, on the other hand, is the judgment of the wicked at the end of the millennium.[7]

Restatement

In restating the doctrine of the last judgment, it is important to remember the parameters of the discussion. The focus is not primarily on temporal, divine judgments mediated through history. Nor is the first concern with the doctrines of heaven and hell, which are yet to be studied. The main features of a theology of the last judgment include such topics as the following:

- The certainty of the last judgment;

- The judge at the last judgment;

- The purpose of the last judgment;

- The basis for the last judgment;

- The time of the last judgment;

- The universality of the last judgment.

The Certainty of the Last Judgment

Robinson writes:

> For the first time for centuries we are living in a world where men have no idea what judgement means. Until recently the traditional picture of a day of judgement still bounded men's horizons. . . . But today we live in a world of justice without judgement. Our moral sense, if not our morality, is strong, and Christian and humanist alike, we draw up our charters of human rights. But judgement is an embarrassing theme. . . . We live in this twentieth century, in a world without judgement, a world where at the last frontier post you simply go out—and nothing happens. It is like coming to the customs

---

7. *The New Scofield Reference Bible* details seven judgments. See Matt. 15:32, note 2.

and finding there are none after all. And the suspicion that this is in fact the case spreads fast: for it is what we should all *like* to believe.[8]

Over against such modern skepticism, however, biblical writers never lose sight of the time when an all-powerful, sovereign, and righteous God will have the final say. They ground their certainty of the last judgment in several convictions:

- The sovereign righteousness of God;

- The universe as a moral order;

- The accountability of persons to God;

- The partial nature of the judgments of history;

- The ultimate triumph of God's redemptive purpose in Christ.

The last judgment is as sure as the truths on which it rests.[9] The modern mind is obsessed with present justice but scorns the final judgment, yet the final judgment stands for values which the modern mind often seeks to champion, values like the sanctity and worth of persons. Without a final judgment personal values cease to count.

The last judgment is also certain in that it is a definite event, even though it is a transcendent event that looms larger than history (Matt. 11:24; Acts 17:31). Just as the second coming and the resurrection are outward and visible and yet also inward and spiritual, so the last judgment is not only an invisible process within history but a direct encounter between the Savior-Judge and His accountable creatures. At the last frontier there *is* a customs to face! By the biblical standard, Dodd's idea of judgment as a merely impersonal, "inevitable process of cause and effect in a moral universe" is inadequate, despite its popularity in contemporary theology.[10]

---

8. J. A. T. Robinson, *On Being the Church in the World* (London: SCM, 1960), 135,137.

Robinson says that the traditional doctrine of judgment involves three main ideas, each of which he views as strange to the present age: the ideas that right will [win] out, that there will be a final separation between the sheep and the goats, and that we have a judge standing over us. Ibid., 136-37.

9. On the basis of such truths, Morris views the certainty of the last judgment as axiomatic. He says: "The final judgment is not something that must be argued for. It is something that may be argued from."

Leon Morris, *The Biblical Doctrine of Judgment* (Grand Rapids: Eerdmans, 1960), 55.

10. C. H. Dodd, *The Epistle of Paul to the Romans* (London: Hodder & Stoughton, 1932), 23.

Preiss finds it strange that the doctrine of the last judgment figures so little in the theology and preaching of the church today. He mentions the neglect of Barth, Cullmann, and Reinhold Niebuhr. He recognizes that a present judgment is implied in the events of history, but he insists that there is also the last judgment which relativizes our poor human judgments and puts them in their place; it is above all our great consolation: one day the men and things of this world will be allocated to their true position, a new earth will at last know the meaning of justice.

Theo Preiss, *Life in Christ*, trans. Harold Knight (Chicago: Allenson, 1954), 79.

The Judge at the Last Judgment

The judge at the last judgment is Christ Himself! Nothing else is so important for understanding the New Testament focus of last judgment. The ideal of justice at the last judgment contrasts sharply with non-biblical notions, both in what it affirms and in what it condemns.

One Islamic country punishes armed robbery by death, crucifixion, or amputation of hands and feet. Nineteen thieves lost limbs there during a recent year.[11] The New Testament teaches that the last judge will be Jesus Christ, and judgment will be based on a Christian view of judgment. This is the new element in the New Testament view. Given the biblical view of God as revealed in Christ, the fact that judgment belongs to God and not to humans is infinitely reassuring. Human judgments tyrannize and destroy, but God's judgments are altogether righteous (Rom. 2:1-11).

The New Testament leaves no question that the Father "has given all judgment to the Son" (John 5:22; Acts 17:31). Judgment is always God's (Rom. 14:10; Rev. 20:11), but the divine agent is Christ (Matt. 25:31; 2 Cor. 5:10; 2 Tim. 4:8). In the words of the Apostles' Creed, "Christ Jesus, His only Son, our Lord . . . will come to judge both living and dead."

Since Christ's purpose at His first coming was not to condemn the world but to save it (John 3:17), we are assured that the last judgment is a judgment of holy love.[12] It is a judgment in the hands of the Lamb slain, not one in the hands of a cosmic tyrant. This fact, however, in no way sentimentalizes the divine reckoning. The most damning, self-destructive force in the universe is *spurned love*. The impenitent cry out for the mountains and rocks to hide them from the wrath of the Lamb (Rev. 6:16).

That the judge is Christ is not only the most central feature of the last judgment, it is also its most solemn feature. Participation in the last judgment is exposure to the presence of Christ. This reassures believers (though they are ashamed that they have not loved Him more), but it is disconcerting for the impenitent. Studdert-Kennedy says, "There ain't no throne, and there ain't no books/ It's 'Im you've got to see."[13]

In conclusion, what is to be said of biblical references to believers' sharing with Christ in the task of judgment (Matt 19:28; Luke 22:28-30; 1 Cor. 6:2-3; Rev. 2:26-27; 3:21; 20:4)? This should not be overemphasized.

---

11. *The Christian Century,* August 29—September 5, 1984, 794.

12. Christ does not change roles from that of Savior at this first coming to that of Judge at His second coming. God in Christ does not change in this way (Heb. 13:8). The roles of Savior and Judge are not to be contrasted. Christ will be no less compassionate at the last judgment than He was throughout His life and ministry. He wept over the impenitent then (Matt. 23:37-38). We may well believe He will weep over the impenitent at the last judgment.

13. G. A. Studdert-Kennedy, as quoted without documentation, in: Stephen H. Travis, *The Jesus Hope* (Downers Grove, IL: InterVarsity, 1976), 63.

To follow Christ is neither to seek personal status nor to indulge in revenge. Summers explains:

> Nothing in any of [the passages just cited] promises actual ruling or judging on the part of Christians. By their loyalty to Christ they bring the witness which will be the basis of condemning those who have refused Christ. When all has been considered, the truth remains that God-in-Christ is the world's Redeemer, and God-in-Christ is the world's Judge. He and he only is the Judge.[14]

The Purpose of the Last Judgment

Two aspects of the purpose of the last judgment stand out in the biblical teaching: first, the last judgment manifests the character and the eternal destiny of every human,[15] and, second, it is the final vindication of the righteousness of God's redemptive purpose in Christ as it has been effected in history.

Manifesting character and destiny.—Since God already knows everything about His creatures, the purpose of the last judgment is not primarily to serve as a court of inquiry to sort out the facts. Rather its function is the manifestation of these facts openly. Although character and destiny are closely related, it will be well to discuss them separately.

To begin with the *manifestation of character*, at the last judgment nothing can remain hidden from God (Matt. 10:26-27; Rom. 2:15-16; 1 Tim. 5:24), not even the heart's innermost secrets (Matt. 6:46; Mark 4:22; 1 Cor. 4:5), including secrets of which the person himself may be momentarily unaware (Matt. 7:21-23; 25:37,42).

God is not impressed by outward appearances (Matt. 23:27-28). He is not deceived (Gal. 6:7). Nor are His judgments mere guesses. The evidence for them is written in a hundred ways, not the least of which are the recordings in the books which Scripture mentions (Rev. 20:12). Facades crumble. Excuses evaporate.

Yet nothing about this disclosure remotely suggests a medieval inquisition, with its malicious torturing of victims in order to force confessions of wrongdoing. Instead, what takes place is the manifestation of the consequences of human choices and actions, the full revealing of the person which each has chosen to become.[16]

---

14. Ray Summers, *The Life Beyond* (Nashville: Broadman, 1959), 163.

15. Biblical indications of a fall of angels and their subsequent judgment is a topic belonging to a discussion of angels.

16. Harris emphasizes two senses of judgment: "a judicial investigation that may lead to either a positive or a negative verdict; a negative verdict involving consignment to perdition." Murray J. Harris, *Raised Immortal* (Grand Rapids: Eerdmans, 1985), 158; cf. 180-81.

Instead of an emphasis on investigation and consignment, the stress on manifestation seeks to focus on the creature's freedom and responsibility, as well as on the righteousness and graciousness of the judge.

In addition to the disclosure of character, the last judgment also involves the *manifestation of eternal destiny.* Character issues in destiny. There is a way that leads to destruction and another way that leads to life. The last judgment witnesses to, rather than initiates, a division between those on the Judge's right and those on His left. To those on the right the Judge says, "Come, you who are blessed by my Father." To those on the left He says, "Depart from me, you who are cursed" (Matt. 25:34,41).

Essentially the difference between the saved and the condemned is between those who trust in Christ as Savior and Lord and those who reject Him (John 3:36). The issue is not simply who is good and who is bad, for all have sinned (Rom. 3:10,23). No one has any ground to plead personal merit. The saved are saved by grace, and the saving relation to Jesus Christ makes the difference.

Nothing is arbitrary, capricious, or heavy-handed about the disclosure of destiny. The fairness of the process is never in question, unless it is questioned by those who seek to justify themselves (Luke 18:9; Rom. 2:1-5). In the end, the condemned can only say that this is the way they themselves have chosen. Or, even more, they can only agree that, given the anti-God nature of sin, this is the way it has to be. God has done everything that almighty love can do to draw His creatures to the way of life (Matt. 23:37).

Vindicating the righteousness of God's redemptive purpose.—The second aspect of the purpose of the last judgment is the final vindication of the righteousness of God's redemptive purpose in Christ. God's judgments in history are limited, but at the last judgment God will vindicate the righteousness of His ways with humankind once for all. Not only individuals, but individuals as members of the human race and as members of particular societies and nations, will be judged. If judgment is to become final, the whole of history must be brought into perspective, not merely isolated parts of it. While for the present Christ's lordship remains partly hidden, at the last judgment He will triumph openly.

The fact of the last judgment reflects the biblical rejection of any concept of fallen history as its own redeemer. The day of judgment—the hour of the Redeemer's triumph—marks the moral and spiritual bankruptcy of a rebellious humanity that persists in its spurning God's grace.

In addition, the day of judgment also marks the reversal of earth's unrighteous judgments. History's injustices will finally be righted. The first will be last and the last will be first (Matt. 10:30; 20:16). Those who have exalted themselves will be abased, especially those who sought religious preeminence (Matt. 7:21-23; 21:31; Luke 18:9-14)), while those who have humbled themselves will be exalted (Matt. 23:12; Luke 2:52). The poor will hear good news; the captives will be released; the blind will see; and the oppressed will be freed (Luke 4:18). If bells ring for earth's armistices, emancipation proclamations, and independence days, and if all the world celebrates a moon landing or new olympic records—what will the second coming of Christ, the final resurrection, and the last judgment be like!

But why not now? If God is good and almighty, why is there not an immediate righting of earth's wrongs? Why is final justice delayed until the last judgment?

The Bible indicates that God has designed the present order as a time for moral discipline and probation. If every deed were immediately followed by its full consequences, whether of reward or punishment, discipline and probation would be eliminated. It is simply a fact of life that sacrifice of self in seeking first the kingdom of God nurtures moral discipline and spiritual growth. For the present, however, right often goes unrewarded and wrong often goes unpunished.[17]

In the last judgment God's judgments reach finality. As long as history continues, persons can change from Satan's side to God's side in the warfare between God and Satan. The present is the time of opportunity. Again and again, the biblical call to sinners is to repent while there is yet time. Paul says, "I tell you, now is the time of God's favor, now is the day of salvation" (2 Cor. 6:2). However the day is coming when God's invitation will be ended and the final verdict will be given. If God is sovereign, the conflict between right and wrong cannot go on indecisively forever. Denney says:

> It is not ethical to suppose that the moral condition of the world is that of an endless suspense, in which the good and the evil permanently balance each other, and contest with each other the right to inherit the earth. Such a dualistic conception is virtually atheistic, and the whole Bible could be read as a protest against it.[18]

The last judgment will fully vindicate the righteousness of God's judgments in the light of His redemptive purpose in Christ. The resurrection of Christ was a preliminary vindication of God's righteous purpose (Acts 4:10-12), but the last judgment will be its final vindication (Acts 7:31). God will be proved true though every person be false (Rom. 3:4). As Jesus

---

17. W. T. Conner, *The Gospel of Redemption* (Nashville: Broadman, 1945), 338-39.

See also the earlier discussion of the kingdom present as a continuing spiritual warfare, not a utopia.

18. James Denney, *Studies in Theology,* 2d ed. (London: Hodder & Stoughton, 1895), 240.

Mullins says: "We may say they that [the last] judgment is the finality demanded by the kingdom of God in all its aspects." He says that it is finality for the conscience, for history, and for the theistic view of the world. E. Y. Mullins, *The Christian Religion in Its Doctrinal Expression* (Nashville: The Sunday School Board, The Southern Baptist Convention, 1917), 481-83.

silenced His enemies at His first coming (Matt. 22:46), He will silence every rebellious mouth at the last judgment (Rom. 3:19), and every tongue will confess that Jesus Christ is Lord (Rom. 14:11; Phil. 2:11).

Since the crux of the last judgment for the modern mind is the severity of the final condemnation of the impenitent, it will be necessary to discuss this doctrine further when presenting the doctrine of hell.

The Basis for the Last Judgment

So far as those who are judged are concerned, the basis for the last judgment is each person's accountability to God for everything that person has ever thought, been a part of, or done. This accords with the purpose of the judgment as the manifestation of all that a person is, inwardly or outwardly. Without a revelation of God's will there is no accountability, and without accountability they will be no just judgment. The ultimate question is, what has each person done with his or her own God-given accountability?

The doctrine of general revelation teaches that everyone has some light from God, some knowledge of God and His will (Rom. 1:18-32). Gentiles show that the requirements of the law are written on their hearts (Rom. 2:14-16). Those who have more light are more accountable (Matt. 11:20-24; Luke 12:47-48). Those who do not respond positively to the light have, no basis for expecting that more light would change their attitude toward God (Luke 16:31). Some of the worst sinners have the most light (Matt. 23:27-28) and sinners have only themselves to blame for their sin (Rom. 3:9-20).

The accountability of persons before God underscores the relation between faith and works. James says, "Faith without deeds is dead. . . . I will show my faith by what I do" (Jas. 2:18). In this sense the final judgment is according to a faith that works (Matt. 16:27; Rom. 2:6; 2 Cor. 5:10; Rev. 20:12; 22:12). Everyone will be judged on the basis of all they have ever thought or done. God sees each person as a whole, as a collection of responses, attitudes, and actions.

Some may despair at the thought of accountability before God. In fact, anyone who cares at all about Christ Jesus cannot dismiss the thought lightly.[19] Still, it is important to remember that the Christ who judges is the same Christ who came to save. He who was once moved with compassion as He looked on the multitudes in deep spiritual need has not changed. While the spotlight of God's judgment is inescapable, it is also

---

19. Recognition of the depth of one's unworthiness can be a mark of a tender conscience (Luke 18:13; 1 Cor. 15:10; 1 Tim. 1:15). In this sense, those least concerned regarding their accountability before God could be the hardened sinners, not the perfect saints. Those who are the most saintly are the least likely to think they are! The saints know that they are sinners.

true that all of God's judgments are infinitely tempered with mercy! His judgments are just and true in every way.

The Time of the Last Judgment

The New Testament conjoins the occurrence of the last judgment with the return of Christ (Matt. 16:27; 25:31; John 5:28-29; Acts 17:31; Rom. 2:15-16; 1 Cor. 4:5; 1 Thess. 5:2-3; 2 Thess. 1:5-10; 2 Tim. 4:1-2; 2 Pet. 3:7,10). Only in Revelation 20:11-15, as interpreted by premillennialists, is a millennial interim interjected between the second coming and the last judgment. However, Ewert, a historical premillennialist, says:

> In the last book of the Bible, the millennial reign, which is inaugurated by the return of Christ (Rev. 19:11-12), precedes the final judgment (20:11-15). However, that does not alter the consistent teaching of the New Testament writers that the judgment of all humanity takes place at the return of Christ.[20]

Basically, as was noticed in discussing the time of the final resurrection, no conservative writer, who takes biblical authority seriously, questions that Christ's return is closely related to the last judgment.

Yet the New Testament also links judgment with the time of death for those who die in the interim between Christ's two advents (Heb. 9:27; Luke Luke16:22-24). Hoekema says:

> We conclude, then, that both the sufferings associated with Hades and the comforts associated with Abraham's bosom, as described in [Luke 16:19-31], occur in the intermediate state.[21]

Thus, the problem encountered in the discussion of the intermediate state recurs here, namely, the relation of resurrection and judgment to the state of those who die in the interim *before* the second coming.

Because history and time are real for God, the intermediate state is important for Christian doctrine. Death ushers the Christian into God's presence, and the character of each person is transparent to God. Since character determines destiny, persons are directly but provisionally rewarded and punished at death, even though the eternal destiny of each will be fully established only in the final judgment.

Biblical teaching about the solidarity of the human race also requires a distinction between judgment at the time of death and judgment at the time of the *parousia*. Since all persons are wrapped up in the bundle of life together, no individual will be fully judged in a general sense until his-

---

20. David Ewert, *And Then Comes the End* (Scottdale, PA: Herald, 1980), 124. Ewert's only explanation of his statement is that "we know little about the intermediate state of the righteous between death and resurrection, and even less about the intermediate state of the wicked. But we do know that when Christ appears he will judge the living and the dead (2 Tim. 4:1-2)." He might also have said that if we know little about the intermediate state, we know even less about a millennial interim following the *parousia*.

21. Anthony A. Hoekema, *The Bible and the Future* (Grand Rapids: Eerdmans, 1979), 101.

tory itself is ended and it becomes possible to tell the life story of every person completely. Yet, in the sense that when a person dies, the door of opportunity for salvation is closed, in this sense judgment is final at death. The inadequacy from a biblical perspective of notions of a second chance for salvation after death receives further notice in the discussion of the doctrine of hell.

The Universality of the Last Judgment

All persons will be judged (Matt. 25:32; Rom. 14:10; Heb. 9:27). No one escapes (Heb. 12:23). The living and the dead, the great and the small, the righteous and the wicked—all are included (Acts 10:42; 24:15; 2 Tim. 4:1; 1 Pet. 4:5; Rev. 20:12). Even angels will judged (1 Cor. 6:3; 2 Pet. 2:4; Jude 6).

Since God created persons as social beings and not merely as discrete individuals, He will judge us in the context of life's relationships. This is the corporate nature of the last judgment. Nations will be judged (Matt. 25:32), towns (Matt. 11:20-24), and even churches (cf. Rev. 2-3). Each person comes to the judgment as His neighbor's keeper.

Believers and unbelievers will be judged. Believers will be justified on the basis of faith in Christ alone (John 3:16; Rom. 3:28; 4:5), but some are more faithful than others in living out their faith in their daily lives and conduct. As we will see in discussing the doctrine of heaven, there are degrees of reward. Unbelievers will be condemned for their lack of faith in Christ (John 3:18) and will be held responsible for their use of the light they had.

The New Testament often warns that greater privilege involves greater responsibility. Judgments about works or the fruit of one's beliefs begin with the household of God (1 Pet. 4:17). Although believers face the last judgment in the full confidence that Christ will answer for them (1 John 4:17; Jude 24), they know that grace heightens rather than diminishes their religious and ethical accountability.

The doctrine of the last judgment points to the seriousness under God of the daily small deeds of ordinary people.[22] Thinking realistically about

---

22. Cox, writing on the theme of not leaving it to the snake, suggests that Adam and Eve did not take responsibility for deciding their fate but left it to the snake (Gen. 3:1-6).
He cites Adolf Eichmann of World War II infamy as a modern example:

> Adolf Eichmann is a figure from our history, not from a play. As he appeared in his trial in Jerusalem Eichmann is the perfect embodiment of the twentieth-century sinner: an insipid sad-sack guilty of crimes so monstrous they defy the imagination. Many people remarked during the Eichmann trial that he made them feel uneasy because he looked so ordinary, so much like us. He sat in his glass cell polishing his spectacles and officiously correcting the punctuation marks on transcripts of testimony. Seemingly incapable of Luciferean evil, this human cipher was the man who committed genocide simply by doing what he was told, keeping his nose clean, and seeing to it that the trains ran on time.

Harvey Cox, *On Not Leaving It to the Snake* (New York: Macmillan, 1967), xii.

the last judgment is to deepen our sense of accountability for life in the present. Instead of robbing the present of significance, the doctrines of the second coming, the resurrection, the judgment, and eternal destinies are meant to contribute to the transformation of careless unconcern into self-sacrificing commitment to Christ and to values that endure forever.

19 *Eternal Destinies: Hell and Heaven*

Each person is destined to eternal existence. Unredeemed sinners are destined to eternal punishment in hell, but those redeemed through faith in Jesus Christ are destined to eternal blessedness in heaven.

Both Scripture and Christian tradition recognize the distinction between heaven, the destiny of believers, and hell, the destiny of unbelievers.[1] This two-fold aspect of the subject raises the question as to

---

1. "Heaven and Hell: Who Will Go Where and Why?," Christianity Today Supplement, *Christianity Today*, May 27, 1991, 29-39.

331

which topic should be discussed first, heaven or hell? On the ground that God did not send His Son into the world to condemn the world but to save the world (John 3:17), it seems fitting to treat the doctrine of hell first, thus permitting the doctrine of heaven to have the final and preeminent word in Christian theology. Toon says:

> The primary and essential message of Jesus was that of the kingdom of heaven. . . . It can never be said that heaven and hell were given an equivalent emphasis and value in his preaching and teaching. . . . [Hell is] a secondary feature of his teaching, not a primary one.[2]

This manner of proceeding must not be permitted, however, to diminish a sense of the importance of the doctrine of hell. The doctrine of hell is important because the Bible witnesses to sin's intrusion into the human story as the supremely tragic dimension of history. Before the biblical account of history's beginnings has moved forward even three chapters, the record of the fall and of sin's entrance into God's good creation stains the pages of God's Word.

Hell

According to Genesis 3, the human tragedy is not primarily that there are natural calamities—physical exhaustion, the threat of hunger and deprivation, susceptibility to disease, aging, heat, cold, poisonous creatures, wild animals, lightning, fires, floods, famine, earthquakes, and volcanoes. The tragic dimension of history, according to the biblical reckoning, is sin—the rebellion of persons created in God's image, against a holy, righteous, and loving heavenly Father.

The real human problem is neither our ignorance nor our environment but ourselves. The human heart itself is all wrong. The problem, then, is spiritual, not merely physical. The tragedy is alienation from God, from others, from self, and even from the environment. Nurtured by our heinous rebellion against God are the ravaging, the loneliness, the emptiness, the atrophy, the self-destructiveness, and the lovelessness of sin. All of which is to say that we never understand the doctrine of hell if we deny the reality sin. Hell is hell because of sin.

Furthermore, the Bible never tries to camouflage the tragic dimension of history. Humans do. We have any number of euphemisms for sin and its consequences. Mary Baker Eddy's denial of the reality of sin and death is a familiar example. The biblical outlook, however, faces realistically the tragic aspect of sinful existence. How else can we explain the intensity of Jesus' repeated references to hell?

---

2. Peter Toon, *Heaven and Hell* (Nashville: Nelson, 1986), 3. Even if hell is, in a sense, a secondary feature of Jesus' teaching, at the same time it is an essential feature.

The often-cited objection that hell is inconsistent with happiness in heaven ignores, among other considerations, accountability for individual sin. Persons go to hell because they want to. It would seem that the redeemed in heaven can face such reality. God does not have to shield His saints from truth.

Biblical Resources

The discussion of the doctrine of hell is unavoidable in a biblically based theology. The issue regarding the subject is what the Bible says, not what people prefer to believe. That the idea of hell is offensive to modern minds resistant to scriptural authority is not the problem.

Apart from Daniel 12:2, the Old Testament contains no explicit reference to hell. *Sheol* is the place of the dead in general. Clear distinctions between the destinies of believers and nonbelievers, as well as between an intermediate and a final state, are lacking. Punishments for sin mentioned in the Old Testament are mainly punishments received in this life.

Following significant intertestamental developments, however, the New Testament references to hell are both explicit and frequent. The following terms reflect the varied vocabulary which the New Testament employs.

- *Hades* is the place of the dead in general (cf. the Old Testament *sheol*), but in Luke 16:23 it refers to the place of torment.

- *Gehenna* appears twelve times, eleven from the mouth of Jesus (e.g., Mark 9:43-47), always in the sense of eternal damnation.

- *Abussos*, the bottomless pit (Rev. 11:7).

- *Tartarus*, hell (2 Peter 2:4).

Add to these terms the following expressions: pits (dungeons) or chains of darkness (2 Peter 2:4); the fiery lake of burning sulphur (Rev. 21:8); unquenchable fire (Matt. 3:12); fiery furnace (Matt. 13:42); eternal fire prepared for the devil and his angels (Matt. 25:41); blackest darkness (Jude 13); outer darkness (Matt. 8:12); condemnation (Matt. 23:33); destruction (2 Thess. 1:9); second death (Rev. 20:11); weeping and gnashing of teeth (Matt. 25:30); a place where their worm does not die (Mark 9:46); self-exclusion from Christ's blessing (Matt. 7:23; 25:41); and exposure to God's fierce wrath (1 Thess. 1:10; Heb 10:27,31).[3]

Two comments regarding these New Testament references to hell are in order. First, no one speaks more explicitly about the reality of an eter-

---

3. See the articles on "Hell," "Eternal Punishment," "Hades," "Gehenna," "Annihilation," "Conditional Immortality," and "Universalism" in the *Evangelical Dictionary of Theology*; also David Ewert, *And Then Comes the End* (Scottdale, PA: Herald, 1980), 133-35.

nal hell than Jesus. This fact points up the irony of contemporary denials of hell that purport to respect the teaching of Jesus. Recent stress on social action as a corrective to the alleged otherworldliness of conservative theology, for instance, emphasizes Jesus' references to social action (e.g., Matt. 25:31-46) but carefully ignores the clarity with which the same passage sets forth His teaching about an eternal hell. William Barclay, who is said by his biographer to have "always loved, followed and obeyed Jesus," is quite convinced that Jesus' doctrine of an eternal hell is to be rejected.[4]

Second, a further comment concerns the pictorial aspect of the New Testament language describing hell. Here again, it is necessary to remember what was said in the introduction to the discussion of the kingdom consummated with reference to the nature of biblical prediction. Once we recognize that the only language available to the biblical writers to describe the awesome, beyond-this-life realities of heaven and hell was the language of present experience, it then becomes apparent that such language is inadequate to describe what is yet to be in the indescribable, transhistorical events of the consummation. The future involves not less but more than the pictorial descriptions of the New Testament suggest.

Historical Perspective

Although traditional theologians and the great creeds and confessions of Christendom speak clearly of the doctrine of eternal punishment, basic problems have persisted in treatments of the doctrine, problems such as the relation between God's love and His wrath. At times the church's proclamation has pictured a hateful God who delights to torture the damned. These presentations stress God's wrath and hell more than His love and heaven.[5] Even more serious than such imbalances, however, are the outright denials and perversions of the biblical doctrine of hell. Although these denials have circulated from the beginning of Christian history, they are commonplace in modern times. The three most familiar misconceptions are probation, conditional immortality or annihilation, and universalism. Such notions call for further comment.

---

4. For the statement of Barclay's biographer, see Clive L. Rawlins, *William Barclay* (Grand Rapids: Eerdmans, 1984), 392. For Barclay's universalism and his rejection of an eternal hell, see William Barclay, *A Spiritual Autobiography* (Grand Rapids: Eerdmans, 1975), 58-61.

5. Ewert cites teachings from Bede, Dante, and Edwards. He also quotes a hymn attributed to Isaac Watts: "What bliss will fill the ransomed souls,/ When they in glory dwell,/ To see the sinner as he rolls,/ In quenchless flames of hell." Ewert, *And Then Comes the End*, 136.

Marty says that much of our idea of hell "has come not from the Bible and theology but from *Faust* and cartoons, from folklore and popular cathedral art." Martin E. Marty, "Whatever Happened to Hell?," *The Lutheran*, April 2, 1986, 17.

Probation.—The theory of probation, which is not to be confused with the idea of purgatory, teaches that death is not final, and that unbelievers will have a further opportunity to repent and change the course of their lives after death. Probation is widely accepted in twentieth-century thought, even among theologians generally considered evangelical. P. T. Forsyth, who ignores the distinction between probation and purgatory, says: 'We threw away too much when we threw Purgatory clean out of doors. . . . There are more conversions on the other side than on this".[6] In a similar vein, Donald Bloesch writes:

> The metaphor that most nearly describes hell is not a concentration camp presided over by the devil, but a sanatorium for sick souls who are ministered to by Jesus Christ. . . . We do not preclude the possibility that some in hell might finally be translated into heaven. . . . Hell will not be seen as an evil, but as the place where those who reject Christ are still cared for by Christ—and not simply as Lord and Judge but as Savior and Healer.[7]

Despite the endorsement of influential theologians, ideas of a second chance in the life to come lack a basis in Scripture. According to the New Testament, today is the day of salvation (Heb. 4:7). After death comes judgment (Heb. 9:27), and judgment means separation between believers and unbelievers (Luke 16:19-31).

Conditional immortality or annihilation.—Conditional immortality or annihilation teaches the annihilation of unbelievers. This may occur immediately at death, or after a period of probation and continued rejection of God's mercy, or after suffering under God's wrath to the degree that each deserves.[8] Notice that annihilation is not necessarily an outright denial of hell, but of the fact that it is eternal.

---

6. P. T. Forsyth, *This Life and the Next* (London: Macmillan, 1918), 34. Forsyth qualifies his statement with the words, "if the crisis of death opens eyes [to a need for repentance] as I have said." But the qualification is only rhetorical. Forsyth affirms probation after death. He also advocates praying for the dead.

Forsyth's use of the term "purgatory" is quite misleading. In the Roman Catholic view, purgatory is for believers who are not yet perfect, not for unbelievers. Purgatory is discussed below in the section on heaven.

7. Donald G. Bloesch, *Essentials of Evangelical Theology,* vol. 2 (San Francisco: Harper, 1979), 225-26, 229.

For an affirmation of probation by a world Baptist leader, see F. Townley Lord, *Conquest of Death* (London: SCM, 1940). Lord says:

If we accept the Gospel portrait of God; if, that is, we think of Him as the loving Father eager to go to such great lengths for the redemption of His children, we are compelled to envisage a period of continued life in which the Divine grace and love can continue their redemptive work (Ibid., 143).

8. Walter A. Elwell, ed., *Evangelical Dictionary of Theology* (Grand Rapids: Baker, 1984), s.v. "Annihilation," by R. Nicole. Nicole recognizes that technically conditional immortality and annihilation can be distinguished. He list four types of annihilation theology.

Contrary to the idea of annihilation, the New Testament speaks of the resurrection and judgment of unbelievers (John 5:28-29; Rev. 20:11-15) and of a hell that is as eternal as heaven (Matt. 25:46). Furthermore, the Bible views immortality as a quality that God confers on persons by virtue of their creation in His image and of their relation to Him as accountable beings.

Universalism.—The third misconception regarding the future of unbelievers is universalism, the flat rejection of an eternal hell and the insistence that all of God's accountable creatures will ultimately be saved.[9] Some persons attempt to justify universalist ideas by appealing to Scripture passages such as Philippians 2:10, that "at the name of Jesus every knee should bow." Yet the Bible teaches that hell is eternal. Although persons today, with their relativistic mindset, find it difficult to conceptualize psychologically the lost person's persistence in unbelief even in hell, writers such as C. S. Lewis shed light on the power of habit to fix character in permanent rebellion against God's righteousness.[10]

The most serious weakness of universalism is its rejection of Scripture, but universalism should also be faulted because it refuses to recognize the stubbornness of sin in human experience.

In summary, the prevalence of probation, conditional immortality or annihilation, and universalism in contemporary theology raises the question as to why there has been a decline of belief in hell? According to Marty, some interpreters say belief in "eternal hell has declined because

---

Toon discusses the idea of conditional immortality according to Basil F. C. Atkinson, William Strawson, J. Arthur Baird, Stephen H. Travis, and John Wenham. Peter Toon, *Heaven and Hell*, 175-80.

LaSor, professor of Old Testament, Fuller Theological Seminary, suspends judgment regarding the eternal natue of hell: "In the absence of unanimity among scholars I would prefer to leave the question where, I believe, the Bible leaves it." William Sanford LaSor, *The Truth about Armageddon* (San Francisco: Harper & Row, 1982), 192.

With great hesitation and not wishing to dogmatize, Stott says: "I also believe that the ultimate annihilation of the wicked should at least be accepted as a legitimate, biblically founded alternative to their eternal conscious torment." David L. Edwards and John R. W. Stott, *Evangelical Essentials* (Downers Grove, IL: InterVarsity, 1988), 320.

Pinnock says: "Everlasting torment is intolerable from a moral point of view because it makes God into a bloodthirsty monster who maintains an everlasting Auschwitz for victims whom he does not even allow to die." Clark H. Pinnock, "The Destruction of the Impenitent," *Criswell Theological Review* 4 [Spring 1990]: 253

9. The tendency toward universalism is widespread today. See Toon, *Heaven and Hell*, chap. 9. Toon discusses the universalism of Friedrich Schleiermacher, J. H. Leckie, C. W. Emmet, J. A. T. Robinson, Emil Brunner, and Karl Barth. Also see "Universalism: Will Everyone Be Saved?" Christianity Today Supplement, *Christianity Today*, March 20, 1987, 31-45.

William Barclay's universalism was mentioned above in the section on biblical resources. For Macquarrie's, see John Macquarrie, *Principles of Christian Theology*, 2d ed. (New York: Scribner's, 1977), 367-68.

10. C. S. Lewis, *The Great Divorce* (New York: Macmillan, 1946).

temporal ones are sufficiently effective. . . . Who needs to be rescued from eternity when time prompts us to listen to God?" A list of today's hells, Marty suggests, includes nuclear destruction, a misused planet, hunger, warfare, separation, alienation, loneliness, and hatred.[11] We would be nearer the truth, however, if we spoke, not of the effectiveness of our temporal hells, but of their relativizing power. The secular mind is preoccupied with this-worldly issues, regarding the present world as the only world.

Marty himself, however, is reluctant to abandon the idea of hell altogether. When "the dark side of God" is abandoned, he asks, "how does one promote the sense of the holy, or justice?"[12] Bernstein has a similar concern:

> Our hells lack one crucial ingredient of the Biblical hell: justice. God's Hell contains only the wicked. . . . Our hells offer little recourse to the weak versus the mighty, to the exploited versus the exploiter. Hell was sought first [in the Bible] as a weapon against the tyrant. . . . That retributive side of Gehenna we have not reproduced. We have only feeble mechanisms to punish the creators of concentration camps or the instigators of large-scale suffering. Only when human society can justly punish evil will Hell be forgotten.[13]

It seems that the doctrine that God will one day judge the impenitent is not such an insignificant notion after all.

Restatement

We turn next to a restatement of the doctrine of an eternal hell, not out of a fiendish delight, but because of the teaching of Scripture, especially the teaching of Jesus. There is something about the fact that Jesus has spoken so plainly about hell that beckons us to take the idea seriously.

In attempting to restate the doctrine, however, it is important that we derive our views primarily from the Bible and not from the misrepresentations of Scripture that have marred traditional formulations. Since modern as well as ancient objections to the doctrine are directed more to inadequate interpretations of the biblical teaching than to the biblical teaching itself, the need for care in stating what the Bible says is all the greater.

The following restatement emphasizes that all persons deserve hell, that God takes no delight in punishing, that the nature of eternal punishment must be understood, and that hell is both final and eternal.

---

11. Marty, "Whatever Happened to Hell?," 17.
12. Ibid.
13. Alan Bernstein, "Thinking about Hell," *The Wilson Quarterly* 10 [Summer 1986]: 89.

All persons deserve hell.—Finnis says:

> No one who has thought seriously about ethics, and about his own character, will be inclined to shrug off the possibility that [hell] is the situation that he is heading for because he has already, implicitly, chosen it, or might tomorrow do so.[14]

Justification before God is by grace alone through faith in Jesus Christ. No one has the merit to answer to God on his own. Rather, all have sinned and have fallen short (Rom. 3:23). If each received his just dessert, apart from redemption in Christ every person would be helplessly, hopelessly, and eternally lost. There is none righteous, not even one (Rom. 3:10). No one without Christ lives up to the light received from God.

God takes no delight in punishing.—No one ever goes to hell primarily because God wishes it (2 Pet. 3:9). God desires that all persons be saved (1 Tim. 2:4). He is never merely vindictive but instead delights to bless. Christ, the Judge, is the good Shepherd who patiently and relentlessly seeks the lost sheep (Luke 15:3-7). His final word is still His first word, a word of earnest invitation: "Come" (Rev. 22:17).

What the doctrine of hell emphasizes is that God's holy love cannot merely overlook the injustices inflicted by sin and still remain love. Any love that condones sin, ignoring that sin destroys all that is highest and best for persons themselves, is not the love of God. God hates the person-destroying power of sin and seeks instead the well-being of persons. His wrath is the revulsion of His love to the anti-love nature of sin. In this respect, His wrath is the terrible wrath of the Lamb of God (Rev. 6:6).

God's highest will for His creatures is that they pursue what is best for themselves and for others. When they do less, God suffers for their failure more than they (Matt. 23:37). Hell is never God's arbitrary intention. Foreman suggests that the sign over hell's entrance must be: "Forever Out of Place."[15]

The nature of eternal punishment.—Several considerations are important with regard to the nature of eternal punishment.

First, hell is a place, not merely a state of mind. It is real, not imaginary.

Second, hell is not a medieval torture chamber where God is continually designing new ways to make the doomed more miserable.[16]

---

14. John Finnis, *Fundamentals of Ethics* (Washington, DC: Georgetown University, 1983), 152. Cited without documentation in Marty, "Whatever Happened to Hell?," 17.

15. Kenneth J. Foreman, "The Destiny of Man: One or Two?," *Review and Expositor* 51 [January 1954]: 21.

16. Pinnock's claim, cited above, that hell viewed as everlasting torment "makes God into a bloodthirsty monster who maintains an everlasting Auschwitz for victims whom he does not even allow to die" is a caricature. It seriously misrepresents the biblical understanding of hell.

Third, persons remain free in hell. The biblical notion with reference to the wrath of God is that persons bring God's disfavor on themselves by their rebellion, disobedience, and unbelief. Three times in Romans 1:18-32, Paul says with reference to God's wrath on the impenitent, therefore "God gave them over" to their own ways.

How else could it be in a moral universe where God's redemptive purpose is the nurture and growth of responsible persons? The sinner willfully chooses evil, and the wrath of God is God permitting persons the evil they choose. This is the judgment of God upon them. Persons are lost, not first of all because God rejects them, but because they reject God.

> Still, as of Old,
> Man by himself is priced.
> For thirty pieces Judas sold
> Himself, not Christ.[17]

The way to damnation leads past the cross of Christ. Persons are lost in spite of all that God does to win their trust and submission. Lewis says, "In the end there are only two kinds of people, those who say to God, 'Thy will be done,' and those to whom God says, 'Thy will be done.'"[18]

Fourth, hell is exposure to God's presence in judgment. Despite the prevalence of the notion that hell is exclusion from God's presence,[19] the biblical idea of hell is exposure to God's presence without Christ as mediator. Hell is not the absence of God but the spurning of His ever-present love and mercy. This is the essence of the idea of hell as torment. Nothing in all the world is so self-damning as spurned mercy and love.

Biblical references such as 2 Thessalonians 1:9 do not mean total exclusion from God's presence, which in the light of God's omnipresence would be a contradiction. These passages refer instead to exclusion from His mercy and blessing. In no way do they deny that if persons will not have His mercy, they must have His wrath. No one can ever completely escape His presence. Not even burial under a mountain of stone can hide unbelievers from the wrath of the Lamb (Rev. 6:15-17). If He is refused as Redeemer, He still must be faced as Judge. The sin which alienates persons from His mercy, exposes them to His wrath.

Fifth, there are degrees of punishment. Since some persons have a greater knowledge of God than others, there are corresponding differ-

---

17. Quoted by Leon Morris, *The Biblical Doctrine of Judgment* (Grand Rapids: Eerdmans, 1960), 52.

18. Lewis, *The Great Divorce*, 69.

19. For example, Travis says: "Hell, on the other hand, means to be excluded from God's presence." Stephen H. Travis, "The Problem of Judgment," *Themelios* 11 [January 1986]: 54.

ences in the degrees of accountability which persons have before God (Matt. 10:15; 11:20-24; 23:1-39; 25:26; Mark 12:40; Luke 10:12-16; 12:47-48; Heb. 10:29). God's judgments at the great white throne are based on what is written in the books, and judgment varies according to the individual's stewardship of his responsibility before God (Rev. 20:12).

This matter of degrees of punishment sheds light on the thorny problem of the destiny of those who have never heard the gospel of Jesus Christ. All persons have some knowledge of God (Rom. 1:18-32), and no one has lived up to light he has. Each, then, is already self-condemned to a hell of his or her own choosing.

Hell is both final and eternal.—At no point is biblical teaching about hell more seriously challenged today than at the point of hell's final and eternal nature. Here again we meet the problems, both of universalism with its denial of hell's finality, and of annihilation with its denial of hell's eternal nature.

First, hell's punishment is final. Over against universalist affirmations of a second chance beyond death, the New Testament warns that "Now," today, is the only time we can count on to establish a redeeming relation with God. Hebrews 9:27 views physical death as the terminus of opportunity. After death comes judgment. If, as universalists claim, it is biblical to believe that there is a further chance to repent after death, then the silence of Scripture regarding a clear affirmation of a matter so crucial is strange indeed.[20]

Furthermore, none of the biblical references to the last judgment suggests probation or tentativeness. Listen to the words of condemnation which Jesus Himself ascribes to the King at the sheep and goat judgment: "Depart from Me, accursed ones, into the eternal fire which has been prepared for the devil and his angels" (Matt. 25:41). Or recall again the story of the rich man and Lazarus and Jesus' insistence that a great and fixed chasm separates the doomed from the blessed (Luke 16:26). There is nothing in such references to suggest reversibility.

In affirmation of hell's finality, C. S. Lewis writes:

> I believe that if a million chances were likely to do good, they would be given. But a master often knows, when boys and parents do not, that it is really useless to send a boy in for a certain examination again. Finality must come some time, and it does not require a very robust faith to believe that omniscience knows when.[21]

---

20. Adeyemo says: "There is no hint of such an idea in the accepted canon of Scripture." Tokunboh Adeyemo, "Is Everyone Saved?," in *Eerdmans' Handbook to Christian Belief,* ed. Robin Keeley (Grand Rapids: Eerdmans, 1982), 419.

21. C. S. Lewis, *The Problem of Pain* (New York: Macmillan, 1947), 112.

Also in line with the finality of hell is the fact that character becomes fixed through habit formation. In the words of the familiar adage: "Sow a thought, reap an act; sow and act, reap a habit; sow a habit, reap a character; sow a character, reap a destiny."

The person yielding repeatedly to a self-destroying habit says, "It won't count this time." Yet each choice is counted! The body counts each decision, storing up information. If the choice is self-destructive, it works against the person when the next temptation comes. Sin enslaves, just as righteousness liberates. In this sense, the idea that nothing an individual does is ever forgotten is psychologically sound. Lewis expresses the matter graphically when he speaks of the grumbler who became a grumble![22]

Second, versus notions of conditional immortality or annihilation, hell's punishment is eternal. When Jesus said that the wicked will go away to eternal punishment but the righteous to eternal life (Matt. 25:46), He used the same word (*aionios*) for the endlessness of the punishment that He used for the endlessness of the life. He also taught that the fire of hell is unquenchable and that the worm does not die (Mark 9:43,48). God's wrath is said to abide (John 3:36). Over against the idea that destruction is annihilation, the Bible portrays it as eternal, not merely in its effect but in its duration (2 Thess. 1:7-9). Hell is forever (Jude 13; Rev. 14:10-11; 20:10).

After all of the objections to the idea of an eternal hell have been voiced, the doctrine stands in Scripture as a witness, among other things, to the fact that all roads do not lead to the same destination. There is a difference between the right and the wrong, between the true and the false, between the beautiful and the ugly. Evil does not eventually develop into good. Time, the deliverer from all problems in modern secular relativism, does not automatically heal all wrong. C. S. Lewis says, "If we insist on keeping Hell, we shall not see Heaven; if we accept Heaven we shall not be able to retain even the smallest and most intimate souvenirs of Hell."[23]

In conclusion, no Christian understanding of Jesus' teaching about hell is adequate if it fails to see that He addressed His sternest warnings of hell-fire to the scribes and Pharisees. These people were outwardly religious and moral, but they reflected little awareness of their sinfulness and need for God's forgiveness and help. They seemed to think of God as a heavenly bookkeeper who studiously keeps records of the number of good works over against the number of bad works (as they themselves

---

22. Lewis, *The Great Divorce*, 71.
23. Ibid., vi.

defined what is good and what is bad). This notion of earning one's way to heaven by good works is still prevalent. Guthrie, however, comments:

> To whom did Jesus address his gracious words of invitation and promise? To people who were obviously guilty—dishonest tax collectors, prostitutes, political and social outcasts rejected by respectable people. And to whom did he address his sternest warning of hell-fire and eternal misery? He almost never mentioned hell except when he spoke to the Scribes and Pharisees—the very moral, very religious, complacent, churchgoing people of his day.[24]

Jesus was once asked, "Lord, are only a few people going to be saved?" Forsyth paraphrases Christ's response as follows: "Few enough to make you afraid that you may not be there. See to your entry" (cf. Luke 13:23-30).[25]

Heaven

God is not finished with His creation! The majestic first words of Scripture, "In the beginning God created the heavens and the earth" (Gen. 1:1), anticipate the no-less-remarkable announcement that in the final consummation God will create the new heavens and the new earth (2 Pet. 3:13; Rev. 21:1). Paul says that God has made known to us the mystery of His will according to His good pleasure, which He purposed in Christ, to be put into effect when the times will have reached their fulfillment—to bring all things in heaven and on earth together under one head, Christ (Eph. 1:9-10, NIV).

But, how is life in heaven to be described? Just as views of God and of Christian spirituality vary widely from one Christian tradition to another, so views of heaven also differ. Before attempting a restatement of the doctrine, therefore, it will be helpful to outline the biblical resources and to indicate briefly the historical perspectives with reference to heaven.

Biblical Resources

Heaven is used in Scripture with different meanings. When Jesus refers to the birds of heaven (A.V., Matt. 6:26; 8:20), heaven specifies the air or the sky. More especially, however, Jesus referred to heaven as God's dwelling place, reflecting the close identification in biblical thought between God and heaven as His dwelling place. In the Synoptic Gospels (Matthew, Mark, and Luke), for instance, the kingdom of God and kingdom of heaven are interchangeable expressions (cf. Matt. 4:17 with Mark

---

24. Shirley C. Guthrie, Jr., *Christian Doctrine* (Atlanta: Knox, 1977), 398-99. See also Bloesch, *Essentials of Evangelical Theology,* 211-14.
25. P. T. Forsyth, *The Justification of God* (New York: Scribner's, 1917), 52.

1:15). Our discussion will take this second use of heaven as a reference to God's dwelling place as its point of departure. The doctrine of heaven says that God wills to have His people dwell with Him forever.

The Old Testament says little explicitly about heaven and hell as destinies of the saved and the lost. There are hints of the resurrection of the dead (Isa. 26:19; Dan. 12:2) and of a blessed destiny for the righteous in God's presence (Ps. 23:6). The psalmist can say to God that "Thy presence is fullness of joy; in Thy right hand there are pleasures forever" (Ps. 16:11), and that "afterward receive me to glory" (Ps. 73:24). There is also David's lament after the death of his son by Bathsheba: "Now that he has died; why should I fast? Can I bring him back again? I shall go to him, but he will not return to me" (2 Sam. 12:23). Yet the Old Testament does not develop these remarkable suggestions.

The New Testament uses various expressions to refer to God's dwelling place as the future home of believers.[26] Note three of these:

First, Jesus spoke of heaven as the Father's house (John 14:2). With this infinitely expressive term, He sought to comfort His distraught disciples after telling them that He must go away and that where He was going they could not follow. He insisted that He was not abandoning them; rather, He was leaving in order to prepare for them a future home, a home glorious beyond the power of words to describe. He said:

> In My Father's house are many dwelling places; if it were not so, I would have told you; I go to prepare a place for you. And if I go and prepare a place for you, I will come again, and receive you Myself; that where I am, there you may be also (John 14:2-3).

Such a destiny leaves nothing to be desired—no need unmet, no hope disappointed!

Second, heaven is the place where God's throne is (Matt. 5:34; 23:22; Acts 7:49; Heb. 1:8; 4:6; Rev. 4). It is where God is sovereign, where His will is freely and fully done (Matt. 6:10). Nor is a sharp distinction to be made between the Father's throne and the Son's throne. The New Testa-

---

26. No special effort is made in the present discussion either to distinguish sharply between the New Testament terms *hades*, paradise, the third heaven, heaven, or to determine the number of heavens.

Toon's insistence on a distinction between paradise and heaven and his conclusion that heaven was not in existence until Christ's ascension seem unduly dependent on medieval theology.

Similarly, discussions of the number of heavens appear fruitless, even though Paul refers to a third heaven (2 Cor. 12:2-4) and intertestamental sources refer to a seventh heaven. Since the Hebrew word for heaven (*shamayim*) is always plural, and since the plural idea is found in the New Testament, especially in the phrase repeated in Ephesians, "in heavenly realms" in Christ Jesus (1:3,20; 2:6; 3:10; 6:12), it is easier to say that heaven is spacious beyond our powers to conceive.

ment is clear about the Son's reign (Matt. 19:28; 25:31; Luke 1:32; Acts 2:30; Heb. 8:1; 12:2) and about the inseparable relation between the Father and the Son (John 14:9). Heaven is where Christ is exalted (Rev. 5), Lord of lords and King of kings (Rev. 17:14).

Third, heaven is the holy city, the New Jerusalem. In John's remarkable vision (Rev. 21:1—22:5) he uses rich and varied language to describe heaven. Heaven is:

- The new heaven and the new earth (21:1);

- The dwelling of God with men (21:3);

- The absence of tears, death, and pain (21:4);

- A gloriously spacious place, with gates opening in every direction and with multitudes pouring in from every nation, tribe, people, and language (21:12-13 and 7:9);

- Built on the foundation of the apostles and with a magnificence as indescribable as the radiance of rare and precious jewels (21:14-21);

- Where the river of the water of life flows (21:6; 22:1);

- Where the Lord God Almighty and the Lamb are the temple (21:22);

- Where there is no need of the sun, for its light is the glory of God and its lamp is the Lamb (21:23);

- Open to the kings of the earth, who bring into it their glory and honor (21:24);

- Where the gates never close, for no night is there and nothing impure ever enters (21:25-27);

- Where the tree of life grows for the healing of the nations (22:1-2);

- Where God's servants worship the Lamb, see His face, and wear His name on their foreheads (22:4);

- Where night is no more, and the saints reign forever and ever (22:5).

The reserves of meaning in these expressions are limitless. Only a person insensitive to the healing power of the Balm of Gilead and alien to the ecstasy inspired by the Name above every name could fail to be moved deeply by the grace and dignity of the Christian view of heaven.

Historical Perspective

Traditional orthodoxy, as reflected in the creeds and confessions of Christendom, as well as in the formulations of the theologians, has tended to think of heaven as a future, individual, and ethereal reality, neglecting important aspects of the biblical teaching.

Liberal theology, reacting against orthodoxy, goes to the opposite extreme, stressing earthly life but neglecting life after death. Often the only life beyond for the liberal is the possible survival in some vague sense of human personality.[27]

In addition to the problem of a lack of balance between the present and future aspects of the doctrine of heaven, two further inadequate historical notions require mention: purgatory and the beatific vision.

Purgatory.—Roman Catholic theology has given the idea of purgatory its most systematic development, though the notion has also been fairly constant in the theology of Eastern Orthodoxy. While the doctrine has no formal status in Anglican theology, some Anglican theologians during the nineteenth century linked the ideas of purgatory and the intermediate state.

In its Roman Catholic form, purgatory is the belief that those who have died in the grace of God must expiate their venial sins before they can be admitted to heaven and the beatific vision. The notion is based primarily on the apocryphal passage according to which Judas Maccabaeus "made propitiation for them that died that they might be released from their sin (2 Macc. 12:43-45)."[28] Matthew 12:32 and 1 Corinthians 3:10-15 are also cited, but these passages lend no real support to the idea. Purgatory must not be confused with hell. Hell is not probation or a second chance for unbelievers beyond death. Nor should purgatory be confused, as in the case of certain Anglican theologians, with the doctrine of an intermediate state.[29]

Protestant theology generally rejects the notion of purgatory and its related ideas such as atoning for sin through works of penance and prayers for the dead. Protestants more often view the state of believers after death in terms of justification by faith and endless, loving service to God in Christ.

---

27. DeWolf, as a "chastened," post-World War II liberal, speaks more readily of sin and redemption than older liberals, yet even he has little to say of heaven and hell. He refers to immortality but not explicitly to heaven. L. H. DeWolf, *A Theology of the Living Church,* 2d ed. (New York: Harper & Row, 1968), 286.

See also Carl E. Braaten, "The Kingdom of God and Life Everlasting," in *Christian Theology,* eds. Peter C. Hodgson and Robert H. King (Philadelphia: Fortress, 1982), 296-97.

28. F. L. Cross, ed., *The Oxford Dictionary of the Christian Church* (London: Oxford, 1957), 11,25-26.

29. Macquarrie, with his commitment to universalism, contends that purgatory is "indispensable to any reasonable understanding of Christian eschatology," and argues that "heaven, purgatory, and hell are ... [but] a kind of continuum through which the soul may move" on its way to its final destination. He makes a strong appeal for a doctrine of purgatory in Protestant theology. Macquarrie, *Principles of Christian Theology,* 367-68.

The beatific vision.—The beatific vision as described in older Roman Catholic treatments reflects the disciplines and rituals of monastic contemplation. The New Testament pictures of heaven, however, reflect the daily routines of ordinary people, not the ecclesiastical spritualtiy of monks, priests, and nuns.[30]

Restatement

Usually when the comment is made that heaven is a difficult doctrine, what the objector has in mind are sub-biblical views of heaven. Macquarrie, for example, objects that heaven easily becomes associated with egocentric longings, or with serving God for what one can get out of it. It would be difficult, however, to find such unworthy views of Christian service in the writings of responsible theologians. Even though some Christians sing "It Pays to Serve Jesus,"[31] it is unfair to assume that this can only mean serving Christ for selfish reward. Other perversions of the doctrine of heaven to which Macquarrie takes exception, such as static views of heaven's perfection, are also just as foreign to serious theological reflection.

In attempting to summarize a biblically based approach to the doctrine of heaven, the restatement which follows unfolds around the following emphases: the main idea of heaven; a present as well as a future reality; a place, not merely a state of mind; a resurrected, bodily existence; a corporate existence; a cosmic reality; degrees of reward; a place of activity; and a place of endless growth.

While the limitation of our knowledge concerning these themes easily intensifies the temptation to speculate unduly, the opposite danger is an unwarranted hesitancy to speak of them at all. An important guiding principle as we proceed is the biblical insistence that whatever else heaven is, it is a Christ-centered reality.[32] Again, the indispensable key to what God will do is what He has done.

The main idea of heaven.—The main idea in the biblical teaching about heaven is threefold: heaven is where God is, where Christ is exalted, and where God's redemptive purposes are perfectly fulfilled.

---

30. For a valuable resource for the study of widely varying ideas of spirituality, see Cheslyn Jones, Geoffrey Wainwright, and Edward Yarnold, SJ, eds., *The Study of Spirituality* (New York: Oxford, 1986).

31. Frank C. Huston (copyright 1937).

32. Bayly comments that his mother used to say that she did not find any particular attraction to golden streets in heaven. He said that he had no answer for her until he read a comment by F. B. Meyer, that in heaven all earth's values are turned upside down. "What do we count most valuable on earth?," he asked. "Gold. Men live for gold, kill for it. But in heaven gold is so plentiful that they pave the streets with it instead of macadam." Joseph Bayly, *Eternity*, October 1986, 32.

These are three aspects of one idea, the belief that heaven is the place of light and joy where the Redeemer is freely glorified forever by His creatures.

First, heaven is where God is. Heaven is the Father's house, God's dwelling, where God's throne is, and where His will is perfectly and gladly done.

Heaven as the place of God's throne is powerfully described in the vision of Revelation 4. The throne symbolizes God's sovereign control over all creation (v. 2). Around the throne are twenty-four thrones of twenty-four elders (v. 4) and four living creatures (v. 6), representing the glory of heaven's subjects. Day and night the living creatures never stop saying: "Holy, holy, holy is the Lord God, the Almighty, who was and who is and who is to come" (v. 8). Whereupon the twenty-four elders spontaneously prostrate themselves before the throne, lay their crowns at its feet, and say:

> Worthy art Thou, our Lord and our God,
> to receive glory and honor and power,
> for Thou didst create all things,
> and because of Thy will they existed
> and were created (v. 11).

The reason for their praise is not simply that it does God good or that it does them good, but that God is worthy. When today the redeemed, still living on this side of heaven, echo heaven's praise in their times of worship, their praise is a living witness to heaven's reality. Newport says: "When we cannot see the answer and yet praise, we are telling God that we trust Him, love Him, and dare leave the final and ultimate answer to him."[33]

Second, heaven is where Jesus Christ is exalted. This is the emphasis in Revelation 5, the heart of the throne-room vision that begins in Revelation 4. All heaven gapes in breathless suspense as a Lamb, once slain but now standing in the center of God's throne, takes the fast-closed scroll of human destiny, which no one in heaven, on earth, or under the earth could open, from Him who sat on the throne (vv. 6-7). Thereupon the four living creatures and the twenty-four elders fall down before Him and join in singing redemption's new song (vv. 8-10), as all heaven, thousands upon thousands, and ten thousand times ten thousand, break loose in adoration: "Worthy is the Lamb that was slain" (vv. 11-12). Finally, after all other creatures have joined in, the four living creatures say, "Amen," and the elders fall down and worship (vv. 13-14).

---

33. John P. Newport, *The Lion and the Lamb* (Nashville: Broadman, 1986), 173.

With matchless pageantry the vision explains that only the Lamb slain prevails to open the fast-closed scroll of human destiny and to lay bare God's redemptive purpose in history.

Since heaven is where Christ is enthroned, to be in heaven is to be "with Christ" in the fullest sense (Luke 23:43; 2 Cor. 5:8; Phil. 1:23).[34] Or, as the Book of Revelation says, the saints in glory "shall see His face" (Rev. 22:4). This is the fulfillment of Jesus' promise, "I will come again, and receive you to Myself; that where I am, there you may be also" (John 14:3; cf. 1 Thess. 4:17). It is also the realization of Paul's eager anticipation, when, over against the poor reflection we now have, he looks forward to the time when we will see "face to face" (1 Cor. 13:12).

This is the beatific vision in the best sense of the term, the best of heaven's gifts (Matt. 18:10; Heb. 12:14; 1 John 3:2,6). What more could Jesus promise the pure in heart than that they should see God (Matt. 5:8)?

Third, heaven is where God's redemptive purposes are perfectly fulfilled. In contrast to the present, passing order of things, which is marred by sin's intrusive pillaging, heaven is the place where God's purposes in Christ are forever consummated. When John sees the New Jerusalem coming down out of heaven from God, he hears a loud voice: "Behold, the tabernacle of God is among men, and He shall dwell among them and they shall be His people, and God Himself shall be among them" (Rev. 21:3). In other words, the new heavens and the new earth spell the end of all that now limits and hinders the doing of God's will, the righting of earth's tragic injustices, and the establishing of a perfect society.

John pictures the perfection of the New Jerusalem in three startling references to what is missing in the holy city (Rev. 21:22-27).[35] First, there is no temple (v. 22). Mounce explains, "There is no temple because the symbol has given way to reality. The temple is replaced by 'the Lord God Almighty and the lamb.'"[36] Carson says:

> Perhaps the most moving element in the description is what is missing: there is no temple in the New Jerusalem, "because the Lord God Almighty and the lamb are its temple" (21:22). Vastly outstripping the expectations of Judaism [with their focus on the old Jerusa-

---

34. Harris notes the use of different Greek prepositions in each of these verses, *meta, pros,* and *sun,* all of them together indicating a personal relation to Christ qualitatively superior to anything possible in the present Christian life. Murray J. Harris, "The New Testament View of Life after Death," *Themelios* 11 [January 1986]: 48. See also, Murray J. Harris, *Raised Immortal* (Grand Rapids: Eerdmans, 1985), 135-38.

35. In addition to the three items mentioned here, also missing in heaven according to Rev. 21:4 are tears, death, mourning, crying, and pain, and according to Rev. 7:16 hunger, thirst, and the sun beating down (remember the harshness of life in the Middle East dessert).

36. Robert H. Mounce, *The Book of Revelation* (Grand Rapids: Eerdmans, 1977), 383.

lem and the rebuilt temple], this stated omission signals the ultimate reconciliation.[37]

All else that we say about heaven is secondary to the sublime fact that the "Lord God Almighty and the Lamb are its temple."

Second, John says that there is no need for the sun or the moon, for the glory of God has illumined [the New Jerusalem] and its lamp is the Lamb. And the nations shall walk by its light . . . . And in the daytime its gates shall never be closed (vv. 23-25). By repeatedly associating glory and light with the presence of God and the Lamb, both in Revelation and in his Gospel, John images as does no other New Testament writer the majestic splendor which radiates from God and from the Lamb. And this despite the midnight gloom of persecution as a disciple of Christ which John knew so well.

Third, John says that "nothing impure will ever enter it" (v. 27; cf. Isa. 52:1). Earlier in the vision John saw unbelievers cast into the lake of fire (21:8) without access to the city.[38]

A present as well as a future reality.—Many object that concern with heaven undermines our sense of present ethical and social responsibility. The heavenly minded, it is charged, are so concerned with "pie in the sky by and by" that they lose interest improving the earth and neglect their present ethical and cultural responsibilities. Accordingly, the recognition of the importance of the doctrine of heaven must avoid preoccupation with the future to the neglect of the present.

An adequate emphasis on both the present and the future aspects of the kingdom takes note of the fact that the relation between them is marked by both continuity and discontinuity.

---

37. Walter A. Elwell, ed., *Evangelical Dictionary of Theology* (Grand Rapids: Baker, 1984), s.v. "Jerusalem, The New," by D. A. Carson.

Hunter says:

> To behold the God before whom angels veil their faces, the God who created us and, in Christ, redeemed us, who so loved his lost and wandering children that he came right down among us to show us what he is like and then died on a Cross to save us from our sins and make us heirs of life eternal, and, beholding him, to behold all things in him and in the light of his redemption, this truly were a well spent journey though seven deaths lay between.

A. M. Hunter, *Probing the New Testament* (Richmond: Knox, 1971), 156.

Guthrie, however, writing against the background of the anti-institutionalism of the 1960s, misses the point when he interprets the absence of the temple as the absence of the church! He writes regarding the "good news about the future extinction of the church." His emphasis stresses the discontinuity between earth and heaven to the neglect of the continuity. Guthrie, *Christian Doctrine*, 392.

38. Litton, surprisingly, entertains the possibility of a continuing conflict between the righteous and the wicked even in the eternal order. See the note which the editor added to deny any scriptural basis for such a notion. E. A. Litton, *Introduction to Dogmatic Theology*, ed. Philip E. Hughes (London: James Clarke, 1960), 605.

Concerning the *continuity between the present and the future* four comments are in order.

First, the continuity says that the present earth is God's good creation ("The earth is the Lord's, and all it contains," Ps. 24:1; 1 Cor. 10:26) and that the final consummation is the fulfillment of God's intentions for this earth.

Second, since Christ's purpose when He comes again is to transform this earth fully, the continuity between the present and the future says that believers are called now to await the coming consummation actively, not passively! They do this by engaging in actions on which heaven smiles, such as evangelizing the lost, building communities of the people of God, loving one another, feeding the hungry, and liberating the oppressed. In doing so they experience already something of the light of God's glory which is yet to be (1 John 2:8-10).[39]

Third, continuity says that what is done for Christ and His kingdom now counts for all eternity. Whale says, "It is illogical to tell men that they must do the will of God and accept his gospel of grace, if you also tell them that the obligation has no eternal significance, and that nothing ultimately depends on it."[40] Only in the light of eternity can we say that no sacrifice is ever too great in order to make this world a better place in which to live, and that no kingdom investment is ever in vain.

Fourth, continuity also means that heaven's occupations, such as corporate worship, are not for the future only, but for the present as well. If one does not enjoy praising and serving Christ now, death is not likely suddenly to change the situation.

Concerning the *discontinuity between the present and the future,* or the difference between life in heaven and life on earth, note the following three comments.

First, since the warfare between right and wrong continues until the return of Christ, there is no room in the Christian view of history for any naive triumphalism that expects the achievement of heaven on earth prior to the second coming. For the present, believers are pilgrims and strangers in an alien world. They are called to "go to [Jesus] outside the camp, bearing the disgrace that he bore. For here we do not have an enduring city" (Heb. 13:13-14). Mouw says:

> There is no clear biblical command to Christians to "transform culture" in any general way. It may be, of course, that what the Bible does tell us to do can be properly construed as a command to trans-

---

39. Richard J. Mouw, *When the Kings Come Marching In* (Grand Rapids: Eerdmans, 1983), 75-76.
40. J. S. Whale, *Christian Doctrine* (Cambridge: University, 1941), 186.

form our present culture. But . . . we must actively seek the City by suffering abuse outside the camp.[41]

Second, the discontinuity between the fleeting present and the abiding future should remind believers to seek first the kingdom (Matt. 6:33) and to store up treasure, not on the earth but in heaven (Matt. 6:20; 16:26; Luke 12:13-21).

Third, discontinuity means that present hardships are more bearable when we realize that the day is coming when sin, suffering, and death will all pass away and earth's injustices will be fully judged. The hope of heaven nurtures a change in outlook for those in trying circumstances. Instead of resigning to discouragement, the call is to conquer through heroic endurance. The problems are no less real but they appear in a different perspective. Waiting with no hope is one thing, but waiting with hope is quite another.[42]

A place, not merely a state of mind.—As surely as Christ was raised bodily and as surely as believers are to be raised bodily, heaven is a place, not just a state of mind. This emphasis in no way compromises the pre-eminence of the spiritual aspect of heaven. Heaven is where God is! But heaven is not just an idea. It exists. It is somewhere. It is a place where persons are primary, not the buildings and grounds.

Nor are believers embarrassed because they have not the slightest idea where heaven is located. They grant that biblical references to heaven as up or as above are not intended as travel directions for astronauts, and that phrases such as "he was carried away by angels" (Luke 16:22) are not reducible to instances of space travel. In the light of the unusual powers of Jesus' resurrection body, they recognize that there are dimensions to resurrection reality that are not exhausted by the measurement standards appropriate to physical geography.

A resurrected, bodily existence.—The resurrection body of Jesus is our best clue for understanding the nature of our resurrection bodies. The New Testament references to Jesus' resurrection body preserve the tension between a continuity of identity (cf. "this Jesus" in Acts 1:11) and a discontinuity in the particles making up the body, as was evident in the ability of the risen Jesus to appear and to disappear at will (Luke 24:15,31). The importance of personal continuity is not only the importance of believers recognizing one another in heaven, but also the indis-

41. Mouw, *When the Kings Come Marching In,* 76.
42. Yancey observes that black people in the ghetto often face death with more serenity than whites, even when they are materially less comfortable, because they are more likely to remember that this world is not their home, that they are only passing through. Philip Yancey, "Heaven Can't Wait," *Christianity Today,* September 7, 1984, 53.

Redeemed! Eschatological Redemption and the Kingdom of God

—352—

pensability for Christian thinking of the sanctity of each person as a unique individual.

Beyond these generalities, however, questions multiply more freely than answers. First, there is the question of a person's age. How old will persons be in heaven? On the basis of Ephesians 4:13 and the age of Jesus at the time of His crucifixion and resurrection, Aquinas, the medieval Roman Catholic theologian, believing that Jesus died at age thirty, suggested that the resurrection body of believers, regardless of a person's age at death, would have the development appropriate for a 30-year-old person.

Second, there is the question of memory. What will we remember in heaven? Some writers, contending that memory and blessedness are incompatible for believers in heaven, insist that the resurrection involves a blockage in one's memory of anything unpleasant in his or her earthly life. Remember, however, that we have already contended that the Christian idea of happiness is realistic and that God does not have to shield His people from any part of the truth.[43]

Third, there is the question regarding food. What will we eat in heaven? Will food of some kind be necessary to sustain the resurrection body? Grider appears to interpret Romans 14:17 as teaching that there is no eating and drinking in heaven,[44] but such an interpretation surely goes beyond what Paul actually says. Paul is merely indicating that spiritual concerns such as righteousness, peace, and joy in the Holy Spirit are more important for Christians than eating and drinking (cf. 1 Cor. 4:20, which is surely not a denial that persons will talk in heaven).

John, of course, speaks of the great wedding supper of the Lamb (Rev. 19:9) and of the tree of life in the New Jerusalem with its rich bounty of fruit (Rev. 22:2). Yet Paul says that flesh and blood cannot inherit the kingdom of God (1 Cor. 15:50); heavenly eating and earthly eating apparently have their differences. The body is sown a natural, perishable body; it is raised a spiritual, imperishable body (1 Cor. 15:54), discontinuous in some manner with the particular molecules that were laid in the grave. What kind of food is appropriate for the new, spiritual body!

Other writers press questions about the resurrection body even further. Along with immortality, incorruptibility, and indestructibility, Toon, for instance, speaks also of subtlety, agility, and clarity.[45] It is surely

---

43. See the earlier discussion of the doctrine of hell. For an insistence on a memory block, see Millard J. Erickson, *Christian Theology* (Grand Rapids: Baker, 1985), 12-33.

44. Walter A. Elwell, ed., *Evangelical Dictionary of Theology* (Grand Rapids: Baker, 1984), s.v. "Heaven," by J. K. Grider.

45. Referring to the marks of the resurrection body just mentioned, Toon says that "in essentials there is agreement among medieval, Protestant, and Roman Catholic theologians as to the 'marks' of the spiritualized (wholly amenable to the Spirit's action) and glorified (imbued and filled with the glory of Christ) resurrection bodies." Toon, *Heaven and Hell*, 142.

enough to affirm that in the new creation glorified human beings are marked for surprisingly heightened spiritual, mental, and bodily powers in their roles as Christ's servants. We can only wonder in what specific ways the transformation will be evidenced.

A corporate existence.—Biblical redemption is a togetherness with God and with others. Sin alienates and isolates, but redemption reconciles and unites! Love for God and for one another is the sum of the entire law (Matt. 22:37-40).

Key salvation words such as righteousness, peace, and joy (Rom. 14:17) are not only intensely personal and individual in meaning, but also have an inescapably corporate dimension. This is also true of other redemptive expressions:

• The kingdom of God• Choir of voices

• The Father's house• Marriage supper of the Lamb

• The New Jerusalem• The holy city

• New humanity• Bride of Christ

Even the term resurrection of the dead (Greek, *nekroi*, always plural in the resurrection context) has a corporate dimension.

What is the importance of this stress on the corporate nature of heaven? Why is it significant?

First, it speaks to something that only God can make possible. John saw the holy city coming down from God out of heaven (Rev. 21:2). The New Jerusalem is not first of all a human achievement but God's creation! As God's creation and gift it is new kind of community whose inhabitants are the spirits of righteous persons made perfect (Heb. 12:23). John sharply distinguishes those who dwell in the heavenly city (Rev. 21:5-7) from those in the lake of fire (Rev. 21:8; cf. Babylon, 17:4).

Second, corporateness is a reminder that just as there can be no consummation for the human individual apart from a consummation for humankind generally, so also there can be no consummation for the individual believer apart from a gathering together of the entire body of Christ. Over against rampant individualism in western culture, biblical thinking takes seriously both the individual and corporate dimensions.

Third, corporateness means that heaven is other people. For Sartre other people is hell, but in the biblical view persons as created in God's image are social beings, as well as discrete individuals. They discover themselves in self-fulfillment only as they relate constructively to others.[46]

---

46. Travis speaks of heaven as other people and refers to Sartre. Stephen Travis, *I Believe in the Second Coming of Jesus* (Grand Rapids: Eerdmans, 1982), 178.

Over against the loneliness which sin begets, heaven is the presence of loved ones, of old friends, and of delightful new acquaintances. It is throngs gathering for celebration as well as the peace of one's own quiet place.

Crossing every barrier and barricade of earth, heaven includes persons of every nation, tribe, people, and language (Rev. 5:9; 7:9). East sits down with West to feast with Abraham, Isaac, and Jacob (Matt. 8:11), evidencing the miracle of the one body of Christ, a wonder which only the presence of the Lord God Almighty and of the Lamb make possible (Rev. 21:22). Perhaps something like this is at least one aspect of the healing of the nations made possible by the leaves of the tree of life (Rev. 22:2).

Fourth, the corporate aspect of heaven is also a reminder that it is a city as well as a garden. Hunter says:

> At the end of the Christian road is a city—the City of God. In other words, the consummation of the Christian hope is supremely social. It is no "flight of the alone to the Alone" but life in the redeemed community of heaven.[47]

This is not the city as we know it now, with multiplied proliferations of evil to mar its every, often astonishing, achievement.[48] The heavenly city teems with life and excitement. It expresses the interdependence of persons, their need for one another, and the necessity for cooperation. It speaks to a great diversity of gifts and a wide variety of individual differences which are not possible in small and isolated groups. It witnesses to unbounded opportunity, activity, service, and growth.

A cosmic reality.—In John's vision of the New Jerusalem he "saw a new heaven and a new earth; for the first heaven and the first earth passed away" (Rev. 21:1). According to the Bible, God is to situate His

---

47. Hunter, *Probing the New Testament*, 155-56.

Newport emphasizes the continuity of identity with reference to the nations in the New Jerusalem. There is no "blurring of uniqueness or memory or relationships" but rather fulfillment of the ways in which each is different. He says that "the surprise is that the uniqueness does not isolate" but instead honors each nation and sets the nations free from old competitions and fears. There is no obliteration of legitimate differences as in Greek spiritualization which "really amounted to the absorption of the human spirit into the vague tapioca pudding of eternity." Newport, *The Lion and the Lamb*, 320-21.

See also Bernard Ramm, *Them He Glorified* (Grand Rapids: Eerdmans, 1963), 104-15.

48. Guthrie welcomes urbanization as a gift and sign of the possibilities of the kingdom of God. While he goes too far in suggesting that urbanization is an unmixed blessing, it is well to see with Houston that there is an element of "progression" in God's revelation of His purpose. Houston says:

In the new creation God does not preserve a primitive plan. He places the Adam in a garden, but He proceeds to place His new community in a city because He has not annulled human freedom. There is no return to a primitive lost age, there is progression into a new relationship of His love.

James M. Houston, *I Believe in the Creator* (Grand Rapids: Eerdmans, 1980), 250.

resurrected people in a new earth! What are we to make of this remarkable claim?

Asking whether the new earth is a renewal of the present creation or its complete annihilation followed by an entirely new act of creation *ex nihilo*, Gouvea says:

> Both [of these] views have ardent proponents, the Reformed tradition favoring renewal and the Lutheran tradition favoring re-creation. Both views seem to have adequate biblical support (e.g., for renewal, Rom. 8:18-21; Matt. 19:28; Acts 3:21; for re-creation, 2 Pet. 3:7-13).[49]

Stating the alternatives in this simple either-or fashion, however, will hardly do. Scripture makes it plain that the full truth of the matter involves, not just a choice between continuity or discontinuity, but the inclusion of aspects of both.

Four issues concerning the relation of the new earth to this earth are anticipated in these introductory remarks: the fact of continuity; the fact of discontinuity; the resulting problem of the extent of the continuity; and the significance of the new earth as a cosmic reality for the millennial issue. These topics provide the framework for the discussion which follows.

First, concerning the fact of continuity between the new earth and this earth, consider the clarity of the following Biblical claims. Jesus speaks of the renewal of all things when the Son of man returns to sit on His throne (Matt. 19:28). Peter is quoted in Acts as referring to a coming day when God will restore everything as He has promised (Acts 3:21). Paul is assured that the time of liberation of creation is in God's plan (Rom. 8:19-22). In fact, there is every argument for a continuity of identity between this earth and the new earth that there is for a continuity of identity between persons in this life and in the life to come.

Second, regarding the fact of the discontinuity between the new earth and this earth, the plain truth is that the new earth would not be new if there were no areas of discontinuity! The question is, how new is the new earth? In what ways is the new earth different from this earth?

According to Revelation 21, in the new earth there is no more sea (v. 1); no tears, death, mourning, crying or pain (v. 4); no thirst (v. 6); no temple (v. 22); no need for sun or moon (v. 23); no need to shut the gates of the city, no night (v. 25); and nothing impure (v. 27). Revelation 22 adds that there is no more curse (v. 3).

---

49. Walter A. Elwell, ed., *Evangelical Dictionary of Theology* (Grand Rapids: Baker, 1984), s.v. "New Heavens and New Earth," by F. Q. Gouvea.

In addition to these references, 2 Peter says that there will be a destruction by fire, as the elements of the old creation melt in the heat (2 Pet. 3:10-12).

Quite obviously, the biblical case for areas of discontinuity between the two earths is a strong one. The new creation is really new!

Third, in the light of both continuity and discontinuity, the real problem concerns the extent of the continuity between the new earth and this earth. Since the earth includes two dimensions, the natural order and human culture, the continuity problem relates to each of these realities. Will there be trees, mountains, and animals in heaven? And what of human culture? What is to happen to earth's vast artistic monuments and treasures? While questions pertaining to the natural order are inviting, the comments here are limited to the issue of human culture.

That there is cultural continuity between this world and the next is indicated by Revelation 21:24-27. Concerning the New Jerusalem, John says:

> And nations shall walk by its light, and the kings of the earth shall bring their glory into it. . . . And they shall bring the glory and the honor of the nations into it; and nothing unclean and no one who practices abomination and lying, shall ever come into it, but only those whose names are written in the Lamb's book of life.

What does John mean by "the nations . . . and the kings of the earth"? Who are they? The passage itself makes clear that the reference is to believers and not to the unbelieving nations and kings of the earth referred to elsewhere in the Book of Revelation (see 11:2,18; 18:3,23; 19:15), since only the redeemed have access to the city. Mounce says:

> Those who enter the city are not the wicked and defiant but those whose names have been written in the lamb's book of life. In the imagery of this paragraph the people with free access to the city are one with those who dwell within it.[50]

How else could it be in the light of the emphasis that "nothing impure" ever enters the New Jerusalem (v. 27).

Mouw addresses at length the questions raised by this passage. Claiming that the "filling" of the earth referred to in Genesis 1:28 includes human culture, he readily recognizes that "during the course of history sinful human beings have created a perverse 'filling' . . . contrary to the Creator's intentions." Yet, drawing from Isaiah 60:10-18 and the above passage from Revelation, he says:

---

50. Mounce, *The Book of Revelation,* 385.

But God still insists that the "filling" belongs to him. And he will reclaim it at the end time, in doing so transforming it into the kind of "filling" that he originally intended for his creation. . . . God's ownership over the "filling" must be vindicated at the end of history.

Mouw is careful to emphasize that taking the glory and honor of the nations into the New Jerusalem involves their transformation: "The 'filling' of the earth will be harnessed and remolded for the sake of God's glory."[51]

Evangelicals who stress the continuity between earth and heaven find in this passage from Revelation strong incentive for social and cultural involvement in the present. Travis says:

All the creative work of men and women which reflects the abundant creativity of God will be carried over into the transformed world. We can only guess at how this may be. But it tells us something of how God values the creative work of men and women— much of it produced out of suffering and at great personal cost. And it is another sign that the world to come is not a colorless, shadowy existence, but a totally fulfilling world, worthy of its Creator.[52]

On the other hand, interpreters who more readily recognize discontinuity as well as continuity tend, not only to be less triumphalist with reference to the Christian conquest of culture in the present, but also to be more cautious in their estimate of the immediate value of earth's culture for the New Jerusalem. Houston says:

The symbol of the New Jerusalem is the assurance that nothing has been wasted, nothing lost, even though in God's judgment much is

---

51. Richard J. Mouw, *When the Kings Come Marching In* (Grand Rapids: Eerdmans, 1983), 1617,75.

Mouw, by the way, has recently been named to replace David A. Hubbard (who is retiring) as president of Fuller Theological Seminary in 1993.

52. Travis, *I Believe in the Second Coming of Jesus*, 181.

Hoekema asks:

Is it too much to say that according to these verses, the unique contributions of each nation to the life of the present earth will enrich the life of the new earth? Shall we then perhaps inherit the best products of culture and art which this earth has produced?

Hoekema, *The Bible and the Future*, 286.

With reference to Isa. 60:4-5, in relation to the Old Testament background for Rev. 21:24-27, Mounce says: "The wealth of the nations comes back to Zion as her sons and daughters return from afar." Mounce, *The Book of Revelation*, 384. The New Testament vision of the New Jerusalem, however, is a vastly different expectation than the Old Testament prophetic hope for an earthly return of the Jews from exile.

This current stress, particularly by Reformed conservatives, on an incentive for increased social and cultural involvement has a very important bearing on the evangelism/social responsibility issue discussed earlier in relation to the doctrine of the kingdom present.

destroyed, purified and burned up. It is not dissolution, it is resolution. It is not abolition, it is recreation.[53]

Fourth, what is the significance of the new earth as a cosmic reality for the millennial question? Lawson can be regarded as speaking for historical premillennialists generally when he says that the millennial kingdom symbolizes the truth that this world is not destined to be cast as rubbish to the void. The earth, he continues, is to be saved and restored (Rom. 8:19-22) *during the millennium.*[54]

Is the hope for cosmic restoration limited to a millennial period after Christ's return and before the final consummation? The recent "endhistorical" emphasis of historical premillennialists, noted in the discussion of the millennial issue, finds the cosmic restoration emphasis in Revelation 21:1–22:5 as well as in Revelation 20:1-10. Hoekema contends that limiting the cosmic dimension of biblical hope to the millennial period is to diminish our hope. The new earth, he says is "not just for a thousand years, but forever."[55]

In the light of such considerations, some rationale other than cosmic transformation is needed to justify insistence on the millennial interim proposed by premillennialists.*Degrees of reward.*—Heaven is an ample place where all are blessed beyond measure (John 14:1-3; 2 Cor. 4:17). Yet Jesus exhorts His followers, "Lay up for yourselves treasures in heaven" (Matt. 6:20). Believers should serve faithfully (Matt. 25:21,23; Luke 19:17,19). Paul says that in the life to come, those who were less faithful and built with wood, hay, and straw will have less reward, while those who were more faithful and built with gold, silver, and costly stones reap more bountifully (1 Cor. 3:12-15).

---

53. Houston, *I Believe in the Creator,* 250. I take Houston to mean that the New Jerusalem is not the *total* dissolution or abolition of earth or of earth's culture.

In a recent article, Hoekema tends to go further regarding discontinuity than in his references just cited. He says:

> One [view of Rev. 21:24,26] holds that some of the actual cultural products of various ethnic groups will be found on the new earth: paintings by Rembrandt, sculptures by Michelangelo, music by Bach. This view, however, seems to be ruled out, since the Bible teaches that the first earth will then have passed away (Rev. 21:1), and that the earth and the works that are on it will be burned up (2 Pet. 3:10). A more likely interpretation is that in the life to come various types of people will retain their unique gifts. These gifts will develop and mature in a sinless way, and will be used to produce new cultural products to the everlasting glory of God's name.

Anthony A. Hoekema, "Heaven: Not Just an Eternal Day Off," *Christianity Today,* September 20, 1985, 19.

54. John Lawson, *An Evangelical Faith for Today* (Nashville: Abingdon, 1972), 89. See also his *Comprehensive Handbook of Christian Doctrine* (Englewood Cliff, NJ: Prentice-Hall, 1967), 253.

55. Hoekema, *The Bible and the Future,* 276.

Some writers readily affirm such variations in heaven's rewards. Morris, for instance, says:

> Here and now the man who gives himself wholeheartedly to the service of Christ knows more of the joy of the Lord than the halfhearted. We have no warrant from the New Testament for thinking that it will be otherwise in heaven.[56]

Shaw faults traditional Protestant theology, and particularly the Westminster Shorter Catechism, for denying degrees of reward and teaching that it will be equally well in heaven for all believers regardless of how they served Christ in this life. Citing Mark 10:40, where Jesus refers to places of honor on His right and on His left, Shaw says: "The places of honour are for those who have prepared and are preparing themselves for them by living lives of service and of self-forgetting sacrifice."[57]

Erickson, on the other hand, raises two objections to any variation in rewards. First, differences in rewards reduce the joy of heaven for those who receive the lesser rewards, since such differences would be a constant reminder of their unfaithfulness in the service of their Lord. Second, in the scriptural descriptions of life in heaven there is "no real difference" in the status of believers.[58]

The most common objection to degrees of reward, however, is not just to the idea of differences in reward, but to the idea of reward itself. Christian service, it is said, is never service rendered primarily for reward. This, of course, is true! Morris says:

> Selfishness is not less selfishness because it is directed towards spiritual rather than material ends. If we serve for reward then that in itself indicates that we have not begun to understand the Christian way, and that there awaits us only condemnation.[59]

---

56. Morris, *The Biblical Doctrine of Judgment*, 67.
In support of his position, Morris cites Hammond:
> Sin voluntarily permitted to remain in habitual operation in the life of the Christian cannot but cause his serious loss at the judgment seat. The Christian is never given any encouragement for antinomianism.

T. C. Hammond, *In Understanding Be Men* (London: InterVarsity, 1936), 199.

57. J. M. Shaw, *Christian Doctrine* (London: Lutterworth, 1953), 337. Shaw objects to "the traditional Protestant representation . . . that death for the believer means the entrance on a state of immediate perfection," and to Answer 37 in the *Westminster Shorter Catechism* that "the souls of believers are at their death made perfect in holiness, etc." Ibid., 331. His objection is to a formal, static interpretation of these notions.
Regarding the question as to how heaven can be both a place of perfection and a place of growth, see the discussion below of heaven as a place of endless growth.

58. Erickson, *Christian Theology*, 12-34.

59. Morris, *The Biblical Doctrine of Judgment*, 67.

In what sense, then, are any of the blessings of heaven legitimately called rewards? Macquarrie says, "Heaven is not a reward that gets added on to the life of faith, hope, and love, but is simply the end of that life, that is to say, the working out of the life that is oriented by these principles." He adds that the closeness to God which is the very essence of heaven is the furtherest thing imaginable from the satisfaction of an egocentric craving. He says it is the reward of having been delivered from any seeking for rewards and the only reward of such love is an increased capacity for it.[60]

Heaven's rewards, then, nurture self-forgetfulness. God's Word encourages the believer so to run the race as to win (1 Cor. 9:24) and to fight a good fight (2 Tim. 4:7) in order to encourage believers to strive to excel in kingdom service for the sheer joy it, not for self-acclaim or self-gain (Matt. 20:1-16). Furthermore, if those who serve Christ selflessly in this life already find greater satisfaction in Christian service than those who think only of themselves, on what basis could it automatically be different simply because of entering heaven?

Always, heaven's chief reward is God Himself (Matt. 5:8). God is not a means to our ends. The end of Christian service is not self-promotion. The service of God is itself the highest joy, and God's "well-done" is the supreme reward. "This is eternal life, that they may know Thee, the only true God, and Jesus Christ whom Thou hast sent" (John 17:3).

A place of activity.—Scripture pictures heaven as a place of active service. The view of life in heaven in terms of static perfection or of an endless holiday of doing nothing finds no basis in the Bible.

If heaven is a place of activity, how are we to understand biblical references to heaven as rest? For example, Revelation 14:13 states, "They may rest from their labor, for their deeds follow with them." Surely the rest of heaven is not the rest of glorified inactivity. Rather, it must be the rest of renewing, exhilarating, self-fulfilling, God-glorifying activity!

Notice the distinction in the verse just cited between labor and deeds. Labor carries with it the idea of wearisome toil, of exhaustion, while deeds suggest activities that are character-building and fruit-bearing. In heaven the redeemed end their labors, but their deeds go with them to unfold in an ever deepening expression.

Or what of the biblical emphasis that the main activity of heaven is worship (Rev. 4:8)? Without question, heaven is where Christ is exalted. Yet, as Van Engen sees, heaven's worship should be broadly interpreted. He says that it is "living joyfully and everlastingly in the immediate pres-

---

60. Macquarrie, *Principles of Christian Theology,* 365-66.

ence of God."[61] Grider says: "While there is to be on the part of the redeemed a continuous worship in heaven, it seems to be in the sense that all activities engaged in will be for the sole glory of God."[62]

Travis provides a valuable clue for the way in which the activities of heaven are to be pictured. Referring to the popular misunderstanding of heaven derived from images of golden harps and perpetual singing, he says:

> The biblical imagery, however, is broader and more varied. Most obvious is the image of the city, conveying ideas of community, relationship, vitality, action, creativity. And all the language about love is meaningless unless it involves active selfgiving to God and to others in relationship. This is both demanding and fulfilling, but not boring. A lover who is living at a distance from his fiancee and has to make do with letters and telephone calls does not speak of being bored at the prospect of spending unlimited time in her company.[63]

In a striking comment that seems to speak volumes of meaning, John says, concerning activity in heaven, that the redeemed "follow the Lamb wherever He goes" (Rev. 14:4; cf. 7:17). How following the Lamb, who is the Alpha and the Omega, the Savior, the Creator of the ends of the earth, and the King of kings, could possibly be conceived as boring eludes the committed Christian.[64]

A place of endless growth.—How can heaven be a place of perfection and yet at the same time a place of growth? Jesus' incarnate experience may suggest an answer. Jesus was sinless and perfect, yet He grew. Obviously perfection means different things in different contexts. Heaven, as a state of

---

61. Walter A. Elwell, ed., *Evangelical Dictionary of Theology* (Grand Rapids: Baker, 1984), s.v. "The Beatific Vision," by J. Van Engen.

62. Elwell, *Evangelical Dictionary of Theology*, s.v. "Heaven," by J. K. Grider.

Shaw insightfully cites C. Harris and H. B. Swete for the same emphasis. Shaw, *Christian Doctrine*, 334.

63. Travis, *I Believe in the Second Coming of Jesus*, 180.

Whatever the image used, whether city, throng at worship, garden, house, or some other, each picture suggests a wide variety of activities. God sustains and maintains no society automatically without the involvement of those who share its benefits. Even worship involves the learning of new songs (Rev. 14:3)!

64. Regarding the heavenly activity of Jesus, Harris says:

> Relief from toil does not amount to perpetual inactivity. There is no reason to think that Jesus is passively awaiting the End simply because he is "sitting" at God's right hand. On the contrary, he is permanently active, for he upholds the universe, exercises his reign over his church and kingdom, builds his church, affords support to those in temptation, advocates the cause of the repentant sinner, and engages in high-priestly intercession for his people. There is ceaseless work, but without exertion or failure.

Harris, "The New Testament View of Life after Death," 50. Although Harris is describing the activity of Christ in the interim between His two advents, the emphasis on heaven as a place of activity remains.

perfection for created beings, is not the absence of growth, but rather the removal of the hindrances to growth, especially the barrier of sin.

Some writers, however, find the idea of heaven as a place growth objectionable. Erickson, apparently reflecting the traditional Protestant view that believers are perfected in some static sense the moment they die, says that "we will not grow in heaven," and refers to glorified saints as possessing "a state of completion beyond which there can be no advance." His denial of growth is misleading, however, since he affirms that there is development in a qualified sense. He cites John Baillie, who speaks of "development *in* fruition" as opposed to "development *toward* fruition." If Erickson is willing to allow development in fruition, then it would seem that there is also growth, especially since the context of Erickson's quote from Baillie uses growth and development interchangeably.[65]

Why would any Christian question that heaven is a place of limitless possibilities and endless newness? If earthly life in Christ is new every step of the way, it will be infinitely more so in the life to come. Baillie says:

> A night at an inn is one thing and the journey accomplished is quite another. In the inn we sleep, but when the journey is accomplished, we are in a sense more active than ever. We are now enjoying something that is worth having for its own sake, whereas the journey was undertaken only for the sake of this to which it has led.[66]

This is where the Bible ends: "And I saw a new heaven and a new earth" (Rev. 21:1). This is also where the Apostles' Creed ends: "I believe in the life everlasting." Remember, however, that this is not what we usually mean when we speak of something ending. At the conclusion of the Narnia stories, Lewis observes that for himself and his readers "this is the end of all the stories." For the chief characters entering the new Narnia, however, "it was only the beginning of the real story. . . . Now at last they were beginning Chapter One of the Great Story, which no one on earth has read: which goes on forever, in which every chapter is better than the one before."[67]

---

65. Erickson, *Christian Theology*, 12-33. The Baillie reference is to John Baillie, *And the Life Everlasting* (London: Oxford, 1934), 234,cf.233.

Baillie's discussion focuses on heaven as fruition, not as merely straining after that which is good, but as completely possessing it in a sense. His claim is that such fruition is essentially an activity, not an endless "Long Vacation."

66. Baillie, *And the Life Everlasting*, 232. Baillie, it would seem, might better have said that the journey was undertaken "as a vital part of" instead of "only for the sake of" this to which it has led.

67. C. S. Lewis, *The Last Battle* (New York: Macmillan, 1956), 173-74.

"Now to Him who is able to keep you from stumbling, and to make you stand in the presence of His glory blameless with great joy, to the only God our Savior, through Jesus Christ our Lord, be glory, majesty, dominion and authority, before all time and now and forever. Amen" (Jude 24-25).

Glossary

Redemption. Redemption is God's primary biblical purpose, the central theme of the Bible, and the heart of evangelical theology. For fallen humankind it involves salvation from sin to new life in Christ. It has varied aspects, such as past, present, and future; individual and corporate; and cosmic.

Eschatology. Eschatology is the doctrine of last things. In the biblical view, last things relate to the outworking of God's redemptive purposes: through God's mighty redemptive acts (the biblical story of the formation of the people of God, centering in the incarnation, atoning death, resurrection, exaltation, and return of Jesus Christ), the eternal order (the last things) breaks into history and presses toward consummation.

Eschatological redemption. Redemption and eschatology are inseparable. As the inbreaking of the eternal into the temporal all redemption has an eschatological dimension.

The three stages of eschatological redemption.

First, Old Testament redemption is eschatological as the *promise* of Christ's coming kingdom (see "prophetic foreshortening" below).

Second, at Christ's first coming redemption is eschatological as the *initial* presence in history of Christ's promised kingdom, the first fruits of the last things, and the days of God's missionary patience (2 Pet. 3:9).

Third, at Christ's second coming, redemption is eschatological as the *consummation* of God's kingdom purpose in Christ. The consummation involves the second coming of Christ, the final resurrection, the last judgment, and eternal destinies of hell and heaven.

The last days. According to the New Testament, the last days represent the breaking into history in power at Christ's first coming of the promised kingdom of God (Acts 2:17 [cf. Joel 2-3]; Heb. 1:2). The last days are also the days just before the second coming of Christ (2 Tim. 3:1).

The two ages. According to the New Testament, these are the present evil age and the future glorious age ushered in at Christ's second coming (Matt. 12:32). Although discussions of the two ages often simply contrast them, the New Testament emphasis is on their present *overlapping*, that is, in Christ the age to come is already invading the present evil age (Rom. 12:2; Gal. 1:4; 2 Tim. 1:10; Heb. 6:5).

Prophetic foreshortening. Old Testament prophets, in their predictions of the coming great day of the Lord, did not clearly distinguish between Christ's *two* comings, thus failing to anticipate clearly the present missionary interim between the two comings, with the consequent delay of the final consummation.

D-Day/V-Day.D-Day/V-Day (decisive day/victory day) refers to the analogy for the significance of Christ's two comings drawn from the Normandy Landing of World War II. While with the Normandy Landing the decisive victory for the Allies in World War II was won, the war still raged on.

Similarly, while God's decisive redemptive victory has already been won with Christ's first coming, His final victory remains future.

The D-Day/V-Day analogy illustrates the *already/not yet* aspects of the coming of Christ's kingdom. It also explains why the present form of the kingdom is the form of God's kingdom as it exists *between the times*, that is, between Christ's two comings.

Kingdom present. The kingdom present represents the *already* aspect of the coming of Christ's kingdom. While the decisive victory over the powers of evil has already been won in Christ, and while God's people, as richly gifted with the Spirit and the Word, are boldly charged with the Great Commission (Matt. 28:18-20), yet the warfare between good and evil continues.

Subject Index

For the subjects treated see the table of contents, the outlines at the beginning of each of the five parts of the text, the outlines at the beginning of each chapter, and the outlines in the text at the beginning of each of the longer sections.

Name Index

Redeemed! Eschatological Redemption and the Kingdom of God

—368—

Redeemed! Eschatological Redemption and the Kingdom of God

—370—

Scripture Index

2 Corinthians